Praise for *The Bo[ok Thieves]*

"A chilling reminder of Hitler's twisted po[wer]"

"This history can still startle and surprise us . . . as researchers ask new questions and follow new leads, revelations are still possible. . . . Rydell's passion for the subject is undeniable. Serving as a courier, he manages to convey the emotional power of returning even a single book to a grateful descendant who has lost so much else."　　　　　—*Chicago Tribune*

"Reader-friendly and a riveting account, the book deserves a large reader ship."　　　　　—Jack Fischel, *Jewish Book Council*

"An erudite exploration of the systematic plundering of libraries and book collections by Nazi invaders. Looting books by mainly Jewish owners, collections, and libraries was an effective way of stealing Jewish memory and history, as this thorough work of research by Swedish journalist and editor Rydell attests. . . . An engrossing, haunting journey for bibliophiles and World War II historians."　　　　　—*Kirkus Reviews* (starred review)

"Fast-paced and well-written."　　　　　—*Haaretz*

"A fascinating and untold story about the greatest book theft in history."
—*Dagens Nyheter* (Sweden)

"Anders Rydell has written a compelling book about [the Nazis'] attempt to author a cultural history without any influence from the Reich's enemies. Rydell's book is a gripping read. . . . *The Book Thieves* is a personal, well-written, and greatly informative title . . . that fills a big gap in the field of research."　　　　　—*Svenska Dagbladet* (Sweden)

"Anders Rydell has written an equally harrowing and riveting book about the Nazis' plunder of Europe's libraries, a large-scale attack on its cultural heritage. . . . One can only praise the expert work Rydell has done, which has resulted in a book that can be read as an educative thriller."
—[...]

"Anders Rydell has written a fascinating cultural history account of the Germany that was transformed from the country of Goethe and Schiller, to that of Nuremberg, the Crystal Night, and the Holocaust."

—*Aftonbladet* (Sweden)

"An engaging work on the Nazis' book theft . . . Rydell's work is dedicated and constitutes a solid mapping of the quiet work being done in Berlin, Vilnius, Prague, Paris, and other cities. The author tells of the monstrosities committed in the best possible manner. He mixes his library visits and historical background with a consistently confident tone. It might appear cynical to talk about tone here, but Rydell's at times beautiful, at times matter of fact and restrained writing does wonders for the reader's engagement. Reality as it has been—and is today—does not have to be added to with emotionally loaded pointers."          —*Östgöta Correspondenten* (Sweden)

"One can only state that [Anders Rydell] has done it again. . . . The presentation has a depictive momentum and objective lucidity. *The Book Thieves* is a historical commentary of the highest quality. . . . The symbolism is as arresting as it is appropriate. This makes *The Book Thieves* into something much more than just a gripping tale of Europe's darkest years."

—*Sydsvenskan* (Sweden)

"Just like in Rydell's August Prize–nominated book *The Looters* from 2013, wherein the Nazis' great art thefts were uncovered, *The Book Thieves* opens the way for a multitude of fascinating perspectives and angles."

—Upsala Nya Tidning (Sweden)

"Dante had Virgil as his guide in the *Inferno*. Rydell guides the reader through the different circles of the hell on earth that the Nazis created."

—*Norrbottens-Kuriren* (Sweden)

"Rydell is an extremely effective popular history expert who solidly maps not only the book plundering, but also summarizes its long history."

—*Göteborgs-Posten* (Sweden)

PENGUIN BOOKS

# THE BOOK THIEVES

Anders Rydell is a journalist, an editor, and an author of nonfiction. As the head of culture at a major Swedish media group, Rydell directs the coverage of arts and culture in fourteen newspapers. His two books on the Nazis, *The Book Thieves* and *The Looters*, have been translated into sixteen languages. *The Book Thieves* is his first work published in English.

Henning Koch was born in Sweden but has spent most of his life in England, Spain, and Sardinia. He has translated the novels of Fredrik Backman and his translation of Tom Malmquist's *In Every Moment We Are Still Alive* was published in 2017. He has also written a short story collection, *Love Doesn't Work*, and a novel, *The Maggot People*.

# THE
# BOOK THIEVES

THE NAZI LOOTING
OF EUROPE'S LIBRARIES
AND THE RACE TO RETURN
A LITERARY INHERITANCE

*Anders Rydell*

*Translated by Henning Koch*

PENGUIN BOOKS

PENGUIN BOOKS

An imprint of Penguin Random House LLC
375 Hudson Street
New York, New York 10014
penguin.com

Originally published in Swedish as *Boktjuvarna* by Norstedts, Stockholm, 2015

First published in the United States of America by Viking Penguin,
an imprint of Penguin Random House LLC, 2017
Published in Penguin Books 2018

Photographs by Anders Rydell

ISBN 9780735221239 (paperback)

THE LIBRARY OF CONGRESS HAS CATALOGED THE HARDCOVER EDITION AS FOLLOWS:
Names: Rydell, Anders, 1982– author. | Koch, Henning, translator.
Title: The book thieves : the Nazi looting of Europe's libraries and the race to return
a literary inheritance / Anders Rydell ; translated by Henning Koch.
Other titles: Boktjuvarna. English
Description: New York, New York : Viking, [2017] |
Includes bibliographical references and index.
Identifiers: LCCN 2016044051 (print) | LCCN 2017018684 (e-book) |
ISBN 9780735221246 (e-book) | ISBN 9780735221222 (hardcover)
Subjects: LCSH: Book thefts—Europe—History—20th century. |
Libraries—Destruction and pillage—Europe—History—20th century. | Libraries and
national socialism. | World War, 1939–1945—Destruction and pillage—Europe. |
World War, 1939–1945—Confiscations and contributions—Europe.
Classification: LCC D810.L53 (e-book) | LCC D810.L53 .R94413 2017 (print) |
DDC 027.04—dc23
LC record available at https://lccn.loc.gov/2016044051

Printed in the United States of America
3  5  7  9  10  8  6  4

Set in Adobe Jenson Pro
Designed by Francesca Belanger

*To Alva, my love and inspiration*

# Contents

# Foreword

Last spring, I found myself sitting on a plane from Berlin to Birmingham with a small olive-green book in my rucksack. From time to time I opened the rucksack and the brown padded envelope in which the book was kept, just to reassure myself that it was still there. After more than seventy years it was going to be returned to its family, to a grandchild of the man who had once owned it. A man who had carefully glued his ex libris to a flyleaf and written his name on the title page: Richard Kobrak. At the end of 1944 he was deported with his wife to the gas chambers, on one of the last trains to Auschwitz. The little book in my rucksack is not especially valuable; in a secondhand bookshop in Berlin it would probably not cost much more than a few euros.

And yet, in the few days that I have been the guardian of the book, I have been plagued by what almost amounts to panic at the thought of its suddenly going missing. I have had anguished fantasies about forgetting my rucksack in a taxi, or having it stolen. The value of the book is not monetary, but emotional, and it is irreplaceable to those who grew up without their grandfather. The little olive-green book holds enormous value because it is the only remaining possession of Richard Kobrak. A book from a man's library. Tragically, it is only one of millions still waiting to be found. Millions of forgotten books from millions of lost lives. For more than half a century they have been ignored and rendered mute. Those who were aware of their origins often tried to erase the memory of their owners, tearing out any pages with labels, crossing out personal dedications and falsifying library catalogs, in which "gifts" from the Gestapo or the Nazi Party were substituted by mentions of anonymous donors.

But many have survived, perhaps because the plunder was far too widespread and there was no great desire to look into the history of these remnants.

The story of the Nazis' art thefts has been given great attention in the last few decades. In 2009 I began writing about it myself, basing my inquiries on a painting at Moderna Museet in Stockholm that was known to have disappeared during the Second World War—Emil Nolde's *Blumengarten (Utenwarf)*. Just like the olive-green book, it belonged to a German-Jewish family and was lost at the end of the 1930s. My initial subject later turned into the story of the Nazis' large-scale looting of art and the long, seventy-year battle to reclaim these works, my efforts eventually resulting in a book, published in 2013: *The Plunderers—How the Nazis Stole Europe's Art Treasures*.

As I immersed myself in the details of this theft driven equally by ideology and greed, I learned that not only art and antiquities were stolen, but also books. There was nothing curious about this in itself—the Nazi plundering organizations grabbed whatever they could.

The first thing I marveled at was the sheer scale of it, the fact that tens of millions of books disappeared in a plundering operation stretching from the Atlantic coast to the Black Sea. But something else also caught my attention, namely that the books seemed much more important on an ideological level. The art was distributed mainly among the Nazi leadership, not least Adolf Hitler and Hermann Göring themselves. This art was intended to show, legitimize, and impart honor on the new world the Nazis intended to build on the ruins of Europe. A more beautiful, cleaner world, as they saw it.

But the books served another purpose. They were stolen not for honor and not only out of greed either—but rather for even more disturbing reasons. Libraries and archives all over Europe were plundered by the most important ideologues of the Third Reich, by organizations led by the head of the SS, Heinrich Himmler, or the party's chief ideologue, Alfred Rosenberg. The greatest book theft in history was orchestrated and implemented during the war. The targets of this plunder were the ideological enemies of the movement—Jews, Communists, Freemasons, Catholics, regime critics, Slavs, and so on. This story is not widely known today, and its crimes are still largely unsolved. I decided to follow the trail of the looters, on a journey measuring thousands of miles through Europe. I did this partly to try to understand but also to find out what remains—and what was lost. I went from the scattered émigré libraries in Paris, to the lost, ancient Jewish library in Rome, its origins reaching back to the very beginning of our epoch. And then, from hunting for the secrets of the Freemasons in The Hague to the search for fragments of an eradicated civilization in Thessaloniki. Or from the Sephardic libraries of Amsterdam to the Yiddish libraries of Vilnius. There were traces everywhere, though oftentimes very few: places where people and their books were dispersed and in many cases destroyed.

This is to a very great extent a story of dispersal—about the thousands of libraries forever scattered during the Second World War. Millions of individual books, once forming a part of collections, are still on shelves all over Europe. But they have lost their context. Fragments of once fantastic libraries built up over generations and forming the cultural, linguistic, and identity-defining heart of communities, families, and individuals. Libraries that were irreplaceable in their own right—a reflection of the people and societies that once created and nurtured them.

But this is also a book about the people who waged a war to defend their literary inheritance, putting their own lives in the balance and sometimes losing them as a result. These people were well aware that the theft of their literary culture was a way of robbing them of their history, their humanity, and, in the final analysis, any possibility of remembrance. These were people who desperately tried to hide their manuscripts, buried their diaries, and held on to their one, most beloved book on their last journey to Auschwitz. We owe thanks to these people for our ability to recall the terrible things that took place—both those who lost their lives and those who survived and have since then described their experiences in order to inform the world. They added words to what was intended to remain unspoken. We are living in a time when the last Holocaust survivors will soon be passing away. We can only hope that what they have given us will be enough for us to continue remembering. When I wrote this book I realized that these memories are central, they were the very reason for the book plundering. Robbing people of words and narrative is a way of imprisoning them.

Books are rarely unique in the same way as works of art, but they have a value that so many more people can understand. In our time, the book has retained a symbolic value that is almost spiritual. Discarding books is still considered sacrilegious. The burning of books is one of the strongest symbolic actions there is, correlating with cultural destruction. While mainly identified with the Nazi book pyres of 1933, the symbolic destruction of literature is as old as the book itself.

The strong relationship between humans and books relates to the role of the written word in the dissemination of knowledge, feeling, and experience over thousands of years. Gradually the written word replaced the oral tradition. We could preserve more and look further back in time. We could satisfy our never quite satisfied hunger for more. The ability to read and write, until quite recently the preserve of a few, was therefore associated with magical abilities. Whoever had mastery of such knowledge could commune with our ancestors—and possessed knowledge, authority, and power. Our simultaneously emotional and spiritual relationship to the book is about how the book "speaks to us." It is a medium connecting us to other people both living and dead.

American slaves, long prevented from learning to read, referred to the Bible—used by the white slave owners as a means of justifying their captivity—as "The Talking Book." An important part of their liberation came about when they appropriated the Bible and used it against their oppressors. The book was an instrument of both repression and liberation. Even today, the interpretation of holy writings lies at the very core of global conflicts. The book does not only transfer knowledge and emotions—it is a source of power.

This is often something that has been obscured by the smoke of the infamous book burnings in Germany in 1933—when works of authors loathed by the regime were thrown into the flames. The image of Nazis as anti-intellectual, cultural vandals has been persistent, possibly to some degree because it is easy to comprehend, and possibly because we would like to see literature and the written word as fundamentally good.

But even the Nazis realized that if there was something that gave more power than merely destroying the word, it was owning and controlling it. There was a power in books. Words could act as weapons, resounding long after the rumbling of artillery had stopped. They are weapons not only as propaganda, but also in the form of memories. Whoever owns the word has the power to not only interpret it, but also to write history.

# [ 1 ]

## A FIRE THAT CONSUMES THE WORLD
### *Berlin*

*Where books are burned, in the end people will be burned too.*
—Heinrich Heine, 1820

These words are engraved on a rusty red metal plate sunk into the cobblestones of Bebelplatz in Berlin. Berlin's summer tourists wander past the square, situated between Brandenburger Tor and Museumsinsel, on their way to see one of the city's more grandiose sights. The location still holds symbolic tension. In one corner of the square stands an elderly woman with tousled white hair. She has wrapped herself in a big Israeli flag—the Star of David across her back. Another war has broken out in Gaza. Some thirty people have gathered to demonstrate against the anti-Semitic sentiments that, seventy years after the Second World War, are once more reawakening in Europe.

On the other side of the broad, fashionable thoroughfare of Unter den Linden, trestle tables have been put out in front of the gates of Humboldt University. For a few euros one can buy well-thumbed copies of books by Thomas Mann, Kurt Tucholsky, and Stefan Zweig—all authors whose works were thrown into the fire here in May 1933. In front of the tables is a row of cobblestone-size metal plates. Each plate bears a name: Max Bayer, Marion Beutler, Alice Victoria Berta, all of whom once studied at the university. After each name is a date, with a place-name that needs no further explanation: "Mauthausen 1941," "Auschwitz 1942," "Theresienstadt 1945."

Heinrich Heine's words, actually a line of dialogue from the play *Almansor*, have since the Second World War been seen as an insightful prophecy of what came to pass here, and the catastrophe that would follow. On May 10, 1933, in Bebelplatz, which at that time was known as Opernplatz, history's most famous ceremony of book burning was staged—an event that has remained a powerful symbol of totalitarian oppression, cultural barbarism, and the merciless ideological war waged by the Nazis. The flames of the book-burning pyre have also come to symbolize the intimate connection between cultural destruction and the Holocaust.

Earlier that same spring, the Nazis had assumed power in Germany using another fire—the Reichstag fire in February 1933—as a pretext. The Nazis claimed it was the work of Communists and that Germany was threatened by a "Bolshevik plot," and set in motion the first extensive wave of terror, arresting Communists, Social Democrats, Jews, and others in political opposition. These accusations were fueled by the Nazi Party newspaper, the *Völkischer Beobachter*, which had been stirring and agitating for years against Jewish, Bolshevik, pacifist, and cosmopolitan literature, setting the stage for the Nazis' ascendance.

The Nazis had been sabotaging cultural events since before 1933—everything from "displeasing" film screenings to exhibitions of so-called degenerate art came under attack. In October 1930, Thomas Mann, who had won the Nobel Prize the previous year, attacked the prevailing mood in an open reading held at the Beethoven Hall in Berlin.[1] Joseph Goebbels, tipped off about what was in the offing, had sent twenty Brownshirts from the party's SA storm troops to the reading, all in black tie to blend in with the audience, a group that included some right-wing intellectuals. Mann's speech was met with applause from some sections of the audience, and heckling from the saboteurs. Eventually the atmosphere grew so inflamed that Mann was forced to leave the premises by the back entrance.

Threats were even more widespread. The Mann family and writers such as Arnold Zweig and Theodor Plievier had been receiving a constant stream of threatening telephone calls and letters. The homes of writers were vandalized with graffiti. And selected writers were subjected to individual monitoring by SA patrols that waited outside their houses and followed them wherever they went.

Lists of objectionable literature were produced. In August 1932, the *Völkischer Beobachter* published a blacklist of writers who should be banned once the party assumed power.[2] Early that same year, a declaration had been published in the same newspaper, supported by the signatures of forty-two German professors, demanding that German literature should be protected against "cultural Bolshevism." In the winter of 1933, when the Nazis took power, the focus attack against objectionable literature shifted away from the street and into the machinery of state. In February 1933, President Paul von Hindenburg signed a law "for the protection of people and state," which imposed restrictions on printed publications—further amendments in the spring of the same year imposed more controls on freedom of expression. The first casualties were Communist and Social Democrat newspapers and publishers. Hermann Göring was charged with leading the battle against so-called dirty literature: Marxist, Jewish, and pornographic books.

It was this attack on literature that led up to the book burnings in May—but in fact the initiative did not come from the Nazi Party, but rather from the Deutsche Studentenschaft—an umbrella organization of German student federations. Several of these student federations had more or less openly been supporting the Nazis since the 1920s. It was not the first time in the interwar period that German right-wing conservative students had made book pyres. In 1922 hundreds of students gathered at the Tempelhof airfield in Berlin to burn "dirty literature," and in 1920 students in Hamburg burned a copy of the Treaty of Versailles, the terms of surrender that Germany had been forced to sign after the First World War.

The Nazi Party's attack on literature fed into attacks already being carried out by groups of conservative, right-wing students. For these student groups, book burnings were a German tradition of defiance and resistance going back to the days of Martin Luther and the Reformation. In April 1933 the Deutsche Studentenschaft announced an action against "un-German literature," casting Adolf Hitler as a new Luther. To evoke the Ninety-five Theses with which Luther began the Reformation, the student federation published its own "theses" in the *Völkischer Beobachter*—twelve theses "Wider den undeutschen Geist!" (Against the un-German Spirit).

The students argued that language held the true soul of a people and that German literature for this reason had to be "purified" and liberated from foreign influence. They stated that the Jew was the worst enemy of the German language: "A Jew can only think in a Jewish way. If he writes in German he is lying. The German who writes in German but thinks in an un-German way is a traitor."[3] The students demanded that all "Jewish literature" should be published in Hebrew and "the un-German spirit eradicated from public libraries." German universities, according to the students, should be "strongholds for the traditions of the German people."

Their proclamation was the beginning of a national action to clean out "un-German" literature. Student associations subordinated to Deutsche Studentenschaft at German universities and formed "war committees" to organize coordinated book burnings all over Germany. The book burnings were to be manifested as celebratory events, and the committees were exhorted to market their events, sign up speakers, collect wood for the fires, and seek support from other student federations and their local Nazi leadership. Those who opposed this work, especially teachers, were threatened. The war committees also put up posters with slogans such as "Today the writers, tomorrow the professors."[4]

But the primary task of the war committees was to collect "unclean" literature for burning. Students were ordered to begin the cleanup in their own private libraries, later expanding to public libraries and local bookshops, many of whom cooperated willingly. In the spring of 1933 a more general blacklist of books and authors also began to be compiled. Wolfgang Herrmann, a librarian who had involved himself with right-wing extremist student groups as early as the 1920s, had been working for several years on a list of literature "worthy of being burned." The first draft only listed 12 names, but this was soon expanded to 131 writers, subdivided into various categories. They included Communists, ranging from Trotsky and Lenin to Bertolt Brecht; pacifists like Erich Maria Remarque; Jewish intellectuals like Walter Benjamin; and many other literary and intellectual figures who had gained prominence during the Weimar Republic.

Quite apart from critics of nationalism, historians were also blacklisted when their perspective on history did not coincide with that of the Nazis, particularly in books on subjects including the First World War, the Soviet Union, and the Weimar Republic. There were also some thinkers whose global view was utterly rejected by the Nazis, such as Sigmund Freud and Albert Einstein. Both were attacked on the basis of advancing "Jewish science."

In addition to "cleaning" their own libraries, the students asked public libraries and local bookshops to make a contribution by giving up their own holdings of "dirty literature." In many instances, university registrars and teachers collaborated with the students to clean out the school libraries.

But the war committees also applied more violent methods, aided by local police and storm troopers from the SA, to get their hands on books. A few days before the book burnings, in early May, the students attacked lending libraries and Communist book dealers. The former were especially hated by conservative forces and were described by Wolfgang Herrmann as "literary brothels" spreading dirty, Jewish, decadent literature among decent, ordinary people. Libraries had become extremely popular since the First World War. On account of the economic depression and inflation in Germany during the interwar years, fewer and fewer Germans could afford to buy their own books. Traditional libraries could not provide for the great demand for books, which led to more than fifteen thousand small lending libraries being set up. These libraries provided a low-cost book-lending service, and bought large volumes of the best sellers of the time such as the works of Thomas Mann. These "people's libraries" were easy victims for the students, while the SA troops also raided private libraries. One much-publicized raid was carried out against an apartment building in Berlin owned by Schutzverband deutscher Schriftsteller, an organization working to protect German writers actively opposing censorship and other forms of state intervention in literature. Some five hundred of the association's members living in the building had their apartments searched and vandalized. Suspicious books were confiscated or destroyed on the scene, and writers caught with "socialist" literature were detained.

The most notorious raid was carried out a matter of days before the book burnings, when about a hundred students attacked Institut für

Sexualwissenschaft (Institute of Sexual Studies), situated in Tiergarten in Berlin. The institute, founded by the medical doctors Magnus Hirschfeld and Arthur Kronfeld, conducted groundbreaking research into sexuality and also worked to promote the rights of women, homosexuals, and transsexuals. For three hours the students went berserk in the building, pouring paint over carpets, breaking windows, covering the walls in graffiti, and destroying paintings, porcelain, and other household goods. They took away books, the institute's archive, and a large collection of photographs along with a bust of the founder Magnus Hirschfeld.[5]

Already in 1932, many Jews and Communists, who could see where the political winds were blowing, had begun to clear out their private libraries and destroy photographs, address books, letters, and diaries. The Communists had sent out warnings to their members that if they were carrying "dangerous" documents they had to be prepared to swallow them. In this way there were also thousands of lesser book pyres, where people set fire to their own libraries in stoves, fireplaces, and backyards. They would soon find out that it was easier said than done: burning books is a time-consuming activity. Instead, many people chose to dump their libraries in forests, rivers, or abandoned streets—others posted them anonymously to nonexistent addresses.[6]

After 1933, a large number of German authors chose exile, of their own accord or under duress. Apart from Thomas Mann, they included his brother Heinrich Mann, Bertolt Brecht, Alfred Döblin, Anna Seghers, Erich Maria Remarque, and hundreds of others. By 1939 some two thousand writers and poets had felt compelled to leave Nazi Germany and Austria. Many of them would never return. But a large number also chose to stay. Some writers who were not expressly political went into what has later been referred to as "interior exile." They stayed in their German sphere, or "Heimat," but made the decision not to publish. Alternatively, they released books that were accepted by the board of censors: children's books, poetry, and historical novels. Others were prevented from publishing their works, because membership in the National Chamber of Literature, a division of Joseph Goebbels's

Ministry of Public Education and Propaganda, was required before one could be published.

But there was also another group of writers that joined ranks with the regime. In October 1933 a series of German newspapers published a proclamation signed by eighty-eight German writers and poets under the headline *Gelöbnis treuester Gefolgschaft,* a sort of oath of allegiance. The proclamation was in direct support of Germany's recent decision to leave the League of Nations. Among the signatories were authors such as Walter Bloem, Hanns Johst, and Agnes Miegel, now mainly forgotten, as their rise and fall is so intimately associated with the regime to which they swore their loyalty.

At the time, great rewards lay in store for authors who embraced National Socialism. Positions previously closed to them in Germany's most respected literary academies, foundations, and associations began to open. They also laid claim to new groups of readers, once the regime assumed control of the nation's foremost book clubs. In 1933 the Nazi-run book club Buchergilde Gutenberg had 25,000 members, whereas a few years later its membership had increased to 330,000. By relying on book clubs like this, the regime was able to efficiently distribute everything from Goethe and Schiller to nationalist, conservative, and Nazi writers to millions of readers.

The propaganda ministry instigated a literary and political drive that has never been equaled in German history—and probably not in modern history either. The ministry awarded more than fifty literary prizes annually.

Over the course of the 1930s, Goebbels's propaganda ministry took complete control of the German book industry, including some 2,500 publishers and 16,000 book dealers and secondhand bookshops.[7] One of the first measures was to weed out "Jewish influence" in the world of books by gradually excluding Jews from academies, literary associations, writers' professional bodies, publishers, book dealers, and printers. Jewish publishers, printers, and book dealers were "Aryanized"—transferred to Aryan owners. Some of these Jewish publishing houses were among the largest in the industry. For instance, Julius Springer was the world's largest publisher in the field of scientific publishing. It was a step-by-step process that continued throughout the 1930s. Initially the takeovers of Jewish companies and the exclusion of Jews were cautiously handled, to avoid companies losing value or the disruption of international relations. Jewish owners were simply persuaded to sell, and if they refused, the regime resorted to varying degrees of coercion, harassment, and threats. The Aryanization of publishers raised enormous sums of money for the party, the state, and individual businessmen, and after 1936, the practice was legally formalized in the Nuremberg Laws.

Although the Nazi Party had forced many of the country's most lauded writers into exile by as early as 1933, it would take considerably longer to get rid of their books. The process was gradual—for example, new editions of Thomas Mann's works continued going into print until his citizenship was revoked in 1936. Getting German publishers to kick out their authors and preventing new print runs was one thing, but controlling the secondhand market was quite a different matter—not to speak of what was already on the shelves in German homes. In practice, it was an impossible task to get rid of these books entirely, and most blacklisted writers continued to be available throughout the war—even if it was under the counter. The most effective tool available to the regime was self-censorship, meaning that people cleaned up their own collections.

Another method was to offer the German people new literature. During the 1930s, some twenty thousand new titles were published every year. Books viewed by the propaganda ministry as "educationally beneficial to the people" were pumped out in large, sponsored editions. Books that had only reached limited numbers of readers until then were suddenly in mass circulation. In 1933 alone, Adolf Hitler's *Mein Kampf* had a print run of 850,000 copies.[8] When it was first published in 1925, it had sold 9,000 copies. Hitler's biggest customer was the German state, which bought over six million books. The Nazi Party's own publisher, Franz Eher, which in addition to *Mein Kampf* also produced Alfred Rosenberg's *Der Mythus des 20 Jahrhunderts* (The Myth of the Twentieth Century), would eventually grow into one of the party's most successful companies.

Classic German literature was given a prominent role in the Third

Reich, featuring writers such as Rainer Maria Rilke and Johann Wolf-gang von Goethe. One genre that lay a good deal closer to Nazi ideology was prose and poetry emphasizing and praising the Aryan race. This would occasionally be presented in an understated way, but frequently by means of vile caricatures of Jews, Slavs, Roma, black people, and Asians. These stories often accentuated the direct connections between race and personal traits, in other words that Jews were "unreliable," "greedy," and "devious" by nature. The greatest success was Hans Grimm's *Volk ohne Raum* (People Without Room). In this novel, Grimm proposed that the Germans lost the First World War because they had "too little space to live in." Germany would never be able to achieve its full potential without more land in Europe and the colonies. The book sold almost half a million copies in Nazi Germany, and the title was used by the regime as a slogan.

◆ ◆ ◆

At 11 p.m. on May 10, 1933, Berlin students marched toward Opernplatz in a torch-lit procession, holding aloft a bust of the founder of the Institute for Sexual Studies, Magnus Hirschfeld, like the severed head of a deposed king. Later the bust was thrown into the fire with books from the institute. On the same night, book fires were lit in ninety different places in Germany. Deutsche Studentenschaft had made detailed plans for how the fires should be organized and coordinated. They were held in central, public locations, and in many cities powerful spotlights had been acquired to heighten the effect. The pyres had often been built up days in advance and decorated with photographs of Lenin and flags of the Weimar Republic.

In some places the blacklisted books were brought into the squares on manure carts drawn by oxen—as if on their way to execution. In other places, books were nailed to pillories. Students wearing ceremonial faculty uniforms and the badges of their regional student federations marched with uniformed vanguards of Hitlerjugend (Hitler Youth), SA, SS, and Stahlhelm, the latter a free paramilitary group. Military music was played and songs sung, such as the Nazi battle song "Kampflied der Nationalsozialisten." While books were ritually thrown into the fires, nine prepared "fire oaths" were sworn, in which the names of some of the condemned writers and the charges against them were specified.

Students, teachers, principals, and local Nazi leaders gave speeches to the assemblies, and this attracted large crowds. In Berlin it is believed that as many as forty thousand people were gathered in Opernplatz, and in other cities there were reports of crowds of up to fifteen thousand people.[9] Even greater numbers were reached via the radio, which broadcast live from the events in Berlin—where Joseph Goebbels made an address to the crowd. A camera team was there to capture it all, the film later shown in cinemas around Germany.

Goebbels, who had recently set up his propaganda ministry, had secretly encouraged the students' initiative, although it would be a while yet before Wolfgang Herrmann's blacklist became a part of official cultural policy. There were also varying ideas within the Nazi movement about the sort of literary policy that ought to be pursued. Certain wings in the party were concerned about strong international condemnation of the book burnings. There was also a justified fear in the new regime that it could lose control of the extensive right-wing revolutionary fervor sweeping across Germany in the spring of 1933. Even Goebbels waited until the last possible moment before publicly giving his support to the arrangements.

The book burnings were above all ritual dramas rather than in any real sense a full "cleansing" of Germany's libraries and bookshelves. Goebbels was well aware of the symbolic importance of the book pyres, from both a historical and a political perspective, as fevered baptismal ceremonies for a reborn Germany. Purification through fire was an ancient ritual that appealed to the new regime. Goebbels emphasized this in his speech to the crowds in Berlin, proclaiming that "here, the intellectual foundations of the November Republic sink to the ground, but from the debris a new spirit will rise triumphantly like the Phoenix."[10]

Books continued to be burned all around Germany well into the summer. In certain cities, such as Hamburg and Heidelberg, there were several book burnings. But contemporary opinion diverged on the importance of the burning of books. Many German intellectuals, such as Heinrich Böll and Hans Mayer, toned down the events—which they viewed as nothing more than student antics, even if very unpleasant ones. They believed that the book burnings were expressions of revolutionary spring fever, and in time the new regime would "grow out of" such things.

Sigmund Freud's laconic comment on the book burnings was "Just our books? In the olden days they would have burned us with them." Others were considerably more shocked about the sheer speed at which the political realities had shifted. The writer Stefan Zweig later described in his memoirs how it had "seemed quite beyond the limits of what was conceivable, even to people of foresight."[11]

Even on an international level there were different opinions about the importance of the book burnings. Some quarters dismissed them as "ludicrous," "meaningless," and "infantile." Others, including Helen Keller, *Newsweek* magazine, and the writer Ludwig Lewisohn, saw them as a barbaric attack on ideas themselves.[12,13] The most emphatic reaction of all came from the American Jewish Congress, based in New York, which regarded the book burnings as an expression of the regime's anti-Semitism and persecution of German Jews. Demonstrations were held in several cities in the United States, and in New York some 100,000 people marched on May 10, 1933—one of the largest demonstrations ever seen in the city.

The visual power of the book burnings and their media penetration were already pronounced in their own time, yet because of the symbolic connection with the Holocaust, they would acquire even more potency in the postwar period. Although it was neither the first nor the last time in history that books have been burned, the book burnings in Germany would eventually become the most striking metaphor of all for censorship and oppression—and a continued moral warning whenever books are burned. In the United States, a parallel was later drawn in the 1950s as a protest against Senator Joseph McCarthy's anti-Communist crusade, when "subversive" books were removed from many American libraries.

The book burnings established the reputation of the Nazi regime as "cultural barbarians." The burnings became an image of the intellectual destruction that would follow in the 1930s and 1940s, when Nazism took control of an entire people's linguistic, cultural, and creative outlets. But they were also an indication of how the Nazis' genocides against their enemies were not only physical but also cultural.

Yet at the same time, the smoke of the book pyres and their cultural repercussions have hidden something else. The way in which posterity interpreted the book burnings has not been so very distinct from that of the Nazis themselves, who regarded them as ritual games and propaganda spectacles. The image of burning books has been altogether too tempting, too effective, and too symbolic not to be used and applied in the writing of history. But the burning of books became so powerful a metaphor for cultural annihilation that it overshadowed another more unpleasant narrative, namely how the Nazis did a great deal more than simply destroy books—they were also driven by a fanatical obsession to collect them.

While the embers of Germany's book fires slowly cooled, a plan was beginning to form in the intellectual and ideological circles of the Nazi Party. This plan was not intent on intellectual, cultural, and literary annihilation, but in fact had other, far more alarming intentions. All in all, only a few tens of thousands of books were burned in May 1933. But the raids organized by the party confiscated and plundered far more books, often in secret. After the students had vandalized the Institut für Sexualwissenschaft in Berlin, the SA impounded most of the institute's library—in excess of ten thousand books. However, they were not taken to Opernplatz but rather to the SA headquarters.

The Nazis were not going to destroy their enemies by eradicating the literary and cultural inheritance of Communists, Social Democrats, liberals, homosexuals, Jews, Roma, and Slavs. Nazis were not, properly speaking, the sort of "cultural barbarians" they were purported to be, nor were they anti-intellectual. They intended instead to create a new sort of intellectual being, one who did not base himself on values such as liberalism and humanism but rather on his nation and race.

The Nazis did not disapprove of professors, researchers, writers, and librarians; they wanted to recruit them to form an army of intellectual and ideological warriors who, with their pens, theses, and books, would wage war against the enemies of Germany and National Socialism.

Inaugurated in Munich in 1936, the Forschungsabteilung Judenfrage (Research Department for the Jewish Question) was an institute aiming to legitimize the regime's anti-Jewish policies. It was a branch of Nazi historian Walter Frank's Reichsinstitut für die Geschichte des neuen Deutschland (National Institute for the History of New Germany).[14] The institute aimed to justify Germany's desire to lay claim to the world, laying low her enemies with "science" and building the intellectual foundations on which the Third Reich would rest for a thousand years. Just as the Roman Empire, the prototype on which National Socialism based itself, was not only armies and architects but also historians and poets, the Thousand-Year Reich would be built not only with blood and stone but also with words.

In this war, books would not be so much a casualty as a weapon. The Nazis wanted to defeat their enemies not only on the battlefield but also in thought. This victory would endure long after the grave, after the genocides and the Holocaust. Not only to wipe out, but also to justify their actions. It was not by destroying the literary and cultural heritage of their enemies that the Nazis intended to prevail—rather, by stealing, owning, and twisting it, and by turning their libraries and archives, their history, inheritance, and memory against themselves. To capture the right to write their history. It was a concept that set in motion the most extensive book theft in the history of the world.

# 2

# GHOSTS AT BERLINER STADTBIBLIOTHEK

*Berlin*

I am led down a long, deserted corridor, the walls of which are painted a sun-bleached hue of mustard yellow. Here and there are pictures with thin frames, soulless prints commonly seen in hospitals or low-grade civil service offices. The corridor leads into a room that seems to lack any kind of purpose, apart from connecting with more mustard-yellow corridors that lead off in various directions. There is something labyrinthine and unplanned about the building, like a medieval town center. This can be explained. Berlin's central library, Zentral- und Landesbibliothek, situated just a short walk from Bebelplatz, is built on the ruins of Berliner Stadtbibliothek, its predecessor. The imposing building, on the island in the middle of the river Spree, was hit by bombs during the war and to all intents and purposes utterly destroyed. After the war, the library, which lay in the Soviet zone, was rebuilt from within the ruins. Today it is a somewhat schizophrenic building, with its grandiose neoclassical facade and sparse GDR interiors, contrasting with other, modernized areas.

Sebastian Finsterwalder stops by one of the many gray-painted doors we have passed and fishes out a key. Sebastian, a researcher at the library, is in his thirties, with untidy shoulder-length hair, a studded belt, shoes with neon-yellow soles, and leather gloves with cut-off fingertips. He looks like someone who has just stepped out of one of the nightclubs of Kreutzberg. Sebastian smiles at me as he opens the door and theatrically inhales the smell of an abandoned library: dusty air, dried leather, and faded yellow paper. The room is absolutely pullulating with books, densely packed rows of shelves with worn book spines. As we walk down one of the aisles, I have to turn myself sideways to be able to make my way between the books, which press against my stomach.

"It's actually been organized now. When we came here the first time there were books in piles everywhere. All over the floor, in any old order. For decades, people had just thrown them into this room. There were forty thousand books in here. It took months to go through them," he tells me, showing me a shelf in which every book is marked with a white paper flap and a number.

"These are some of the books we suspect have been plundered," says Sebastian, holding out his arm toward the shelf, which stretches some twenty yards to the other end of the room.

No one today knows exactly how many plundered books there are in the Zentral- und Landesbibliothek in Berlin. Sebastian Finsterwalder shows me room after room, all crammed with books in the same way. There are stolen books in every corner of the enormous building—the largest public library in Germany. Most have not yet been separated from the general collection, which holds in excess of three million volumes. And several tens of thousands have not yet been found.

Nothing on the surface sets these books apart from any others. They include fairy tales; novels; poetry collections; books about fungi, aircraft, and engineering; songbooks; dictionaries; and religious writings. In order to understand that there is something different about these books one must open them and look inside. Often the first few pages give them away.

There one may find a red or black stamp in ink. Or a prettily illustrated ex libris, a bookplate glued in at some point by the owner of the book. Often this is an indication of the book's being a part of a larger collection. Sometimes one also finds a dedication, a signature, or good-luck wishes—as in a German edition of *In Darkest Africa* by the British explorer Henry M. Stanley, where this dedication has been beautifully written in longhand:

> *To my beloved Rudi, on his thirteenth birthday,*
> *From Mum.*
> *25.10.1930.*

According to Sebastian, the book probably belonged to Rudi Joelsohn, born in 1917 in Berlin. On August 15, 1942, he was deported to Riga, where three days later he was murdered. [1]

If one looks carefully at the flyleaf, one can also make out a cryptic but revealing letter, entered in pencil: *J*. An abbreviation that gives the book away and reveals the fate of the owner: *Judenbücher* (Jews' books).

Sebastian leads me into his office, where we meet an elderly man who looks like a member of an old German punk band. He defies the stifling July heat with a thick fleece top and a knitted hat. His name is Detlef Bockenkamm, and he is a librarian and a specialist in the library's historical collections. He was also the first person to start digging in the library's unpalatable past. Now there is a small but dedicated team of researchers trying to establish some clarity and clear up certain aspects of the library's complicated background. Together, they have tracked down and manually examined tens of thousands of books in the collection. Along one wall of the office some of the fruits of their labor are kept. On a veneer bookshelf the books lie in piles, and by each pile hangs a paper flap with a name written on it: Richard Kobrak, Arno Nadel, Ferdinand Nussbaum, Adele Reifenberg, and many more. These are the books whose owners Bockenkamm and Finsterwalder have managed to identify.

One name I do recognize, at the bottom of a pile of five volumes: Annæus Schjødt was a Norwegian lawyer and resistance fighter who fled to Sweden in 1942. After the war it was Schjødt who led the prosecution of Vidkun Quisling and secured his death sentence. Bockenkamm and Finsterwalder have not yet found any documents to explain how and when these books were plundered. But in some rudimentary way they were able to guess. The books must have been stolen from Schjødt's home after his escape, either by the Gestapo or some other Nazi organization, and then shipped to Germany. They were then almost certainly part of a larger collection found in Schjødt's home. In Berlin the collection was broken up, and a couple of these books were donated or sold to Berliner Stadtbibliothek. The plunder of Schjødt's books was not at all out of the ordinary. On these shelves are books from every corner of Europe—wherever the Nazis were active and busy with their plunder.

Compared with the looting of art, these stolen books have attracted a good deal less attention. Only in recent years has the question begun

*On shelves in the Zentral- und Landesbibliothek in Berlin, the plundered books are waiting to be identified. Finding their owners' descendants today is often a time-consuming and complicated process.*

to stir some public interest in Germany. Zentral- und Landesbibliothek in Berlin, thanks to Detlef Bockenkamm, was one of the first libraries to look into the problem. In the early 2000s he was working on a thesis about the large collection of bookplates that had been found in the library. The owners' plates had been cut out of the library's collection, often when the books were deaccessioned. Bockenkamm found hundreds of bookplates with Jewish names and motifs, which made him wonder how these books had actually ended up in the library. He had also started finding some books whose provenance, to say the least, was remarkable.

In 2002 he recovered some seventy-five books bearing the stamp "Karl-Marx-Haus Trier," a museum founded by the German Social Democratic Party, which had already been banned in 1933, and whose members were imprisoned, murdered, or forced into exile. Bockenkamm realized that these books had probably been plundered from the party. He started looking for more books with a suspicious provenance. They were everywhere in the collection. Bockenkamm's first estimate of plundered books in the library was an astounding 100,000, although later this would prove to be a rather modest approximation.

Bockenkamm also made the unpleasant discovery that his predecessors had not been unaware of the books' origins. Quite the opposite: They had actually tried to hide and erase this history. In many books the flyleaves had been cut out. Others bore the marks of the owners' labels having been torn out or scraped off by librarians. Books had also been cataloged with forged origins—or as "unowned" copies.

"I tried to talk about it with an old librarian still in decent shape and willing to talk. He admitted certain things, but not everything. He took most of the secrets with him into the grave," says Bockenkamm. He puts a big ledger with a cover of ribbed gray paper on the table. On the cover is a little white label with the inscription "1944–1945 Jagor."

The ledger, which Detlef Bockenkamm found in 2005, was the most important and revealing evidence to date of the library's efforts to cover up the story. It contained about two thousand book titles, cataloged in the collection in the last two years of the war. The name Jagor was a reference to Fedor Jagor, the German ethnologist and explorer, who lived in the latter half of the nineteenth century. The books had therefore been marked with a *J*. But this was incorrect, as these books had never belonged to Fedor Jagor. The letter *J* did not denote Jagor but rather *Judenbücher*. Registered as number 899 in the ledger is Rudi Joelsohn's copy of *In Darkest Africa*.

The two thousand books proved to be part of a much bigger collection of plundered books acquired by the library during the war. Despite the fact that detailed documentation about the management of the library during the war years has been lost, some of the correspondence concerning the collection has survived. In 1943, the library bought about forty thousand books from Städtische Pfandleihanstalt, Berlin's pawnbroker, to which enormous numbers of books had been brought after being confiscated from homes in Berlin belonging to deported Jews. The most valuable books had been claimed by Einsatzstab Reichsleiter Rosenberg (ERR), the SS, and other Nazi organizations. The remains were brought to the pawnbroker to be sold. The library, which contacted Berlin's municipal office, at first demanded the book collections of "resettled Jews" at no charge. This was denied, as the books belonged to the Third Reich and money raised by their sale would be used to "solve the Jewish question," a phrase that in 1943 could only mean one thing. Confiscated Jewish property, like a sort of self-financing project, was used to pay for deportations, concentration camps, and mass murder. Ultimately, the library was made to pay 45,000 reichsmarks for the books.

The last book in the ledger was cataloged on April 20, 1945. On that same day the Red Army instigated a terrible artillery bombardment on Berlin's city center, at the same time as several other armies started pushing into the city. It was the beginning of the final attack on Berlin as well as a message to Adolf Hitler, who was celebrating his fifty-sixth birthday on this day in the Chancellery.

Berlin lay in ruins, in other words, as did the Berliner Stadtbibliothek.

"It's extraordinary to think that there was still a librarian sitting here in the cellar, cataloging plundered books," says Sebastian Finsterwalder.

But in fact the process did not come to an end after Armistice Day.

Registration of books purchased in 1943, which have survived the bombardment, continues in the postwar years as if nothing has happened. The only difference is that now the books are no longer labeled as *Judenbücher* but with a G, as in *Geschenk* (gifts).

Bockenkamm found out that the cataloging of books bought from the pawnbroker in 1943 continued into the 1990s. And when Bockenkamm and Finsterwalder a few years ago started looking through the library's storerooms they found thousands of books from this collection that had not yet been cataloged. But these were not the only stolen books to more or less unobtrusively fill the library shelves.

The library had lost masses of books on account of the war, with some having been destroyed in the bombings. A large part of the collection had been evacuated to Poland and Czechoslovakia toward the end of the war, where much of it remained and some was plundered by the Red Army. The collection needed to be rebuilt, and certainly there were plenty of abandoned books in a Berlin that had been reduced to rubble. After the war, libraries had their books confiscated if they belonged to party members, public authorities, research institutes, and other organizations in the Third Reich.

Even books that were regarded as "unowned," for instance, when found in buildings that had been bombed, were collected. The books were supposed to be commandeered and sorted by Bergungsstelle für wissenschaftliche Bibliotheken (Rescue Organization for Scientific Libraries), which was housed in a building on the other side of the street from the Berliner Stadtbibliothek. The organization labeled the books with a number, depending on the place in which they were picked up, before they were redistributed among various libraries in the city.

On Bergungsstelle's list there were 209 pickup points, but Finsterwalder, with the researcher Peter Prölls, who is an expert in the area, has managed to establish that books were actually only picked up at about 130 locations.

"In certain districts there were no books left; they had been ruined, evacuated, or plundered," says Finsterwalder.

On one of the walls in his office is an old map of Berlin from 1937.

Finsterwalder has marked the various pickup points using flags of various colors: green for places where books were taken, red for places where none were taken, and blue for places where he does not as yet know what happened. Finsterwalder is working with Prölls on a study of Bergungsstelle, an organization whose work remains largely unknown. By means of historical detective work they are trying to find out how the plundered books were distributed. Ultimately, Berliner Stadtbibliothek was to become the most significant recipient of these "rescued" books.

"One of the reasons we acquired so many of these books was that the director of Bergungsstelle and the head of the library were good friends. They were both Communists and had been imprisoned during the war, so there was a bit of cronyism going on."

Where the books actually came from does not seem to have been an issue worthy of consideration at the time, despite many of them having been confiscated from some of the most criminal organizations of the Third Reich. Books labeled "13" came from Joseph Goebbels's propaganda ministry, while books labeled "7" came from Hermann Göring's air force ministry.[2] Books marked "4" came from the private library of the architect and armaments minister, Albert Speer, while books marked "5" came from the home of the German writer Walter Bloem. Bloem, one of Germany's most popular writers in the early 1900s, had been an enthusiastic supporter of Adolf Hitler and even published a eulogy to the Führer.

Also on Bergungsstelle's list were some of the organizations that were involved in plundering books in occupied Europe. Books labeled "25" were from Alfred Rosenberg's extensive Reichsministerium für die besetzten Ostgebiete (National Ministry for the Occupied Eastern Territories), which was the ministry for civic governance in the Baltic countries and the Soviet Union.

Alfred Rosenberg also used this ministry to build influence for his organization, ERR, which set up a number of local offices in the east to plunder libraries and archives. The organization had several depots in Berlin, but only a fraction of the millions of books it stole were still in Berlin at the end of the war, most having been evacuated to what is now Poland.

Many of the pickup points listed by Bergungsstelle as possible book depots proved to have already been plundered, in many cases by the trophy brigades of the Red Army, which confiscated books from all over Germany.

After the war, the director of Bergungsstelle, Günther Elsner, paid a visit to the abandoned Chancellery for the Occupied Eastern Territories, where in the cellars he found two hundred large wooden crates of books. When staff members went back about a week later to pick up the books, the boxes had been forced open and most of the books had been taken.

One of the most extensive depots of plundered books to end up at Bergungsstelle carried the number 15, which meant that it came from Rosenberg's foremost competitor in the hunt for Europe's libraries. Or, to be more precise, the enormous library of plundered books built up at RSHA, SS-Reichssicherheitshauptamt, in Berlin. This was the German national board of security, which coordinated the police and intelligence services of the Third Reich, both those of the state and of the Nazi Party. The RSHA, controlled by Heinrich Himmler, was Nazi Germany's notorious terror organization. At its peak, it had sixty thousand employees conducting surveillance and monitoring the nation's enemies through a number of subordinate departments such as the Gestapo and the SD (Security Service).

One of these was Section VII, the Department for Ideological Research and Evaluation, which ran an in-depth mapping activity of the enemies of the state. Section VII built up a library in a building confiscated from one of Berlin's biggest Freemasons' lodges on Eisenacher Strasse, and filled this with books stolen from all over Europe. The project grew so ambitious that other buildings also had to be acquired. It is estimated that upward of three million books were sent to Berlin.[3] After the war some five hundred thousand of these books were found at Eisenacher Strasse. Most of the library had been evacuated in the last years of the war, and other stock had been destroyed by aerial bombardment. Some of what was found was returned to the countries from which the books had been taken, but an unknown number of volumes were also distributed among Berlin's libraries.

Sebastian Finsterwalder holds up one of the latter, showing me the flyleaf on which the number 15 has been written in pencil. It is a light blue, somewhat tatty biography of the Dutch philosopher Baruch Spinoza, from 1790. The owner's ex libris can also be seen inside, with an image of a little pixie sitting on a book. It once belonged to the German-Jewish author and journalist Ernst Feder, who was active in the intellectual circles of the Weimar Republic. After the Nazis assumed power, Feder first fled to Paris and then, after the outbreak of war, to Brazil, where he eventually moved in the circles around Stefan Zweig in Rio de Janeiro. The reason this particular book ended up in the RSHA library probably had more to do with the subject than the owner: Spinoza was a Jewish philosopher. The purpose of the RSHA's library was to collect books, publications, and archives that could assist the SS and the SD in studying the nation's enemies in depth: Jews, Bolsheviks, Freemasons, Catholics, Poles, homosexuals, Roma, Jehovah's Witnesses, and other minority groups.

Because Bergungsstelle labeled the books with a number, depending on their point of origin, Detlef Bockenkamm and Sebastian Finsterwalder have been able to track down thousands of them. But the library also acquired tens of thousands of books from other sources after the war, and in these cases it has not been possible to trace provenance. Right up to 2002, when Bockenkamm first noted the presence of the plundered books, libraries bought collections without investigating their origins.

Bockenkamm's and Finsterwalder's efforts to locate the plundered books in the collection of the Zentral- und Landesbibliothek has been a Sisyphean labor both in an administrative sense and in terms of the sheer amount of research required, where a single book can take weeks of detective work. The library obtained collections from many different sources before, during, and after the war—and in all of these there could be plundered books.

Berliner Stadtbibliothek rarely obtained any complete collections but rather the remains of thousands of different libraries. For this reason, the librarians have to laboriously track down books from thousands of individual victims. Even if they manage to establish that a book has been plundered, it is not always possible to ascertain how it came to the library, who plundered it, and who owned it. So far they have found 203 books from the RSHA's library, but only 127 of these have any sort of mark inside enabling the identification of previous owners.

Furthermore, they are fighting a retroactive battle against their former colleagues, who for decades have been rubbing out, tearing off, or falsifying the provenance of these books—all to make them blend into the collection. However, neither Finsterwalder nor Bockenkamm are giving up easily, and they have managed to identify previous owners by studying fragments of torn-off book labels and comparing their color and size with intact book labels in other books.

In 2010, Zentral- und Landesbibliothek began a systematic investigation into its collection. With their colleagues, Bockenkamm and Finsterwalder have manually examined some 100,000 volumes. According to Bockenkamm's present estimate, there could be more than a quarter of a million plundered volumes in the library.

The most difficult part of the work is not finding the plundered books but tracking down their owners or descendants. Only about a third of the plundered books found by Bockenkamm and Finsterwalder have any kind of bookplates, signatures, or stamps that make it possible to establish previous owners. It is even more difficult to find surviving victims or their descendants to try to return the books.

At first they tried to trace the owners in every instance. While in certain cases they succeeded, in the end it proved too time-consuming a task. Instead, in 2012, they launched a searchable database into which plundered books could be entered with information and images of signatures and owners' labels.

"We're trying to make the descendants come to us instead. The database is searchable on Google, so a lot of people involved in genealogical research find us. It's working; we are returning books every month," says Finsterwalder.

The database currently contains fifteen thousand books, and new titles are being added all the time. It will take years before all the books are registered.

Sebastian Finsterwalder shows me a ledger listing about two thousand stolen books cataloged during the war. The books were marked with the letter J, an abbreviation for Judenbücher.

Yet resources are scarce. The project is being supported by the city of Berlin and Arbeitsstelle für Provenienzforschung, a federal organization that finances research into provenance. However, funds are allotted to the project for a few years at a time.

"A couple of years is really just enough to start understanding how to tackle the work. We have to build everything from scratch because there's no one who knows how to do this. Libraries have rarely had any interest in the provenance of books, only their contents, and book labels or signatures have not been registered," says Finsterwalder.

He reports that the level of interest in dealing with book plundering, both in local authorities and libraries, is still insignificant, and most libraries and institutions in Germany tend to ignore the question.

"There is neither the political will nor the resources to really do something about this. Of the thousands of libraries we have in Germany only about twenty or so have actively checked their collections. There is no collaboration; all the libraries conduct their own research. People are more interested in art, because it's so valuable," says Finsterwalder gloomily.

The books that ended up in Berliner Stadtbibliothek's collection are, with a few exceptions, not worth very much in a financial sense. They are normal books once owned by normal people: novels, children's books, songbooks—books that can be bought in a secondhand bookshop for a few euros. But they often have great personal value when they are returned to people.

Between 2009 and 2014 in the region of 500 books were returned, a mere drop in the ocean when one considers that there may be 250,000 plundered books in the library.

"We really want to give these books back. But there are only a few of us working with this. As things stand, we have found fifteen thousand volumes with a 'suspicious' background, and three thousand that have definitely been plundered. It would take us decades to find every descendant, if there even are any," says Bockenkamm, while he puts some unusually beautiful bookplates on his desk. Quite clearly, he has a deep attachment to these plates. He knows each one of them. It was through these images that he first started revealing the library's past. He shows me an ex libris depicting an angel fighting two snakes with a pair of javelins. Another shows a lion walking upright, with its tongue out, and a third is of a woman armed with a goose quill, mounted on a winged horse. Most of these marks are further decorated with the Star of David and have Jewish names on them, such as Hirsch, Bachenheimer, and Meyer. They are highly personal works of art, many illustrative of events in their owners' lives, often also their relationship to reading, culture, and literature. But they are also full of symbolism from a lost world, and from lost lives—no one can interpret their meaning anymore. It is a world of books and readers that was crushed and dispersed.

"Even worse, it's impossible to finish this work. It's impossible! But we have to do what we can," he says.

Many of the plundered books have no identifiable owners' marks. What will happen to these books is something Bockenkamm and Finsterwalder do not know. Maybe one day they will be possible to identify, but the likelihood of it is small.

"These books are like ghosts in the library. We know they are stolen, but from whom?" says Finsterwalder, with a resigned shrug of the shoulders.

Although it has only been possible to return a small part of the total, Bockenkamm feels that every individual volume returned is a meaningful act. In a couple of instances, they have managed to return books to actual Holocaust survivors. One of them was Walter Lachman, a German-Jewish Berliner who was only a teenager when he was deported with his grandmother in 1942 to a concentration camp in Latvia. His grandmother was murdered, while Lachman was moved to the Bergen-Belsen concentration camp, where he was held at the same time as Anne Frank. Frank died, probably of typhoid, just one month before the camp was liberated by British forces in April 1945. Lachman managed to survive even though he was also seriously ill with typhoid fever. After the war he emigrated to the United States.[4] Sixty-seven years later he was called up by a friend who had read an article in the German magazine *Der Spiegel* about the plundered books at the Zentral- und Landesbibliothek. One of the books the magazine had chosen to quote from was one of Lachman's childhood books—a book of fairy tales for Jewish children, which had been given to him by his teacher.[5]

"He couldn't go himself. But his daughter came all the way from California to pick up the book. He had nothing left of his childhood apart from a couple of photographs and a hat he wore in the concentration camp. According to his daughter, her father had never really spoken about the past, but this changed once he got the book back. It brought him out of himself and he started telling his story. Now he is giving talks in schools, to children," says Sebastian Finsterwalder, who feels that this is just one example of why this work is so important.

"These books are keepers of memories. They are not worth much in a financial sense, but they can be priceless to the people and the families who once owned and then lost them. In some cases, when we handed them back it was the first time that children or grandchildren were confronted with their parents or grandparents' stories. It's a very emotive process," Finsterwalder continues.

"When I started looking into the history of these books and went onto the Internet to search for the names I found written inside them, the search results kept indicating Auschwitz. Every time the trail led to Auschwitz. We can't give people their lives back, but maybe we can give them something else. A book, and maybe a memory," says Detlef Bockenkamm as he looks down at the bookplates spread across his desk.

◆   ◆   ◆

I look up at the dark blue Ishtar Gate from Babylon, reaching up to the ceiling. But I don't have time to admire the golden oxen, because the elderly brown-haired woman who is leading the way quickly passes through. She has seen it many times. A few hundred yards from the Zentral- und Landesbibliothek lie the offices of the Arbeitsstelle für Provenienzforschung, housed in one of the wings of the Pergamon Museum—a federal authority charged with helping and financing museums, libraries, archives, and other institutions in their efforts to look into provenance issues from the Nazi era.

I am brought to Uwe Hartmann, an art historian and the head of the office. Hartmann is a tall, middle-aged man with an angular face, short-cropped gray hair, and half-rimmed glasses. He started working on provenance questions relating to plundered art during the 1990s, and he has headed the federal authority since it was set up in 2008. In 2013 he was also put in charge of the team whose task was to identify plundered works in the notorious art collection of some fourteen hundred works that had recently been found in Munich with Cornelius Gurlitt, the son of an art dealer who had worked for the Nazis.

Hartmann has rolled up his sleeves. It is stuffy in the office despite several windows being wide open. Arbeitsstelle für Provenienzforschung has helped finance the work in progress in the Zentral- und Landesbibliothek.

"We have known for some time that we had these books in our collections. We have been able to see for ourselves the stamps, the signatures, and the ex libris. There has been talk of 'guilt in the cellars.' But nothing was done about it," says Hartmann.

Zentral- und Landesbibliothek is far from an isolated case; it was not even one of the libraries that took an active part in the plundering that went on in Germany. The library received neither the most nor the most valuable books in the Third Reich. Certain other libraries, particularly those with a more academic outlook, were prioritized by the Nazis to a far greater extent. Unlike public libraries like Berliner Stadtbibliothek, university and research libraries that were closed to the general public could also take in plundered "forbidden" literature.

One such library that played a very active part in the plundering was the reputable Preussische Staatsbibliothek, now known as Staatsbibliothek zu Berlin—Germany's largest library, with a lineage going back to the 1600s. Its collections include the original manuscript of Beethoven's Symphony no. 9, the lion's share of Johann Sebastian Bach's notes, and the world's oldest illuminated biblical text, from AD 400. In the war years, Preussische Staatsbibliothek was able to get its hands on considerably more valuable books than the Berliner Stadtbibliothek. The history of the library was brought to light when a student, Karsten Sydow, in his master's thesis of 2006, revealed that there could be in the region of 20,000 stolen books in the historical collection.[6] After conducting its own research, the library has been able to verify that some 5,500 books have, beyond any doubt, been plundered.[7] More books would certainly have been found, had it not been for the fact that the Red Army, in turn, plundered the library. Two million books in the library's collection are estimated to have been taken to the Soviet Union, including most of the Jewish and Hebraic books and manuscripts.[8]

Preussische Staatsbibliothek also played an important role as a distribution channel for plundered books in the Third Reich. There was an obvious distribution policy for the thousands of libraries and archives that were plundered in Germany and the occupied territories. The most important collections, which were considered significant for the ideological work, were shared between Heinrich Himmler's RSHA and Alfred Rosenberg's ERR. These two organizations were often direct rivals when it came to the most valuable collections.

In addition to these, there was a series of other Nazi organizations, institutes, and government departments, all of which competed to get their hands on plundered books and build up their own libraries. Tiered behind them were the nation's libraries, universities, and other institutions.

After the Nazis seized power, the Preussische Staatsbibliothek was assigned with distributing books that had been stolen from German Jews, Socialists, Communists, and Freemasons. Later in the war, the library continued doing the same with books that had been taken in France, Poland, the Soviet Union, and other occupied areas.

Preussische Staatsbibliothek distributed books to over thirty German university libraries.[9] But German libraries also acquired books in other ways. Often, regional libraries were given a piece of the cake when the Gestapo and local party chapters raided forbidden organizations. Books were donated to local town libraries as "a gift from the Party." It was not unusual for local librarians to be well aware of the better collections in their area, which were worth getting their hands on. However, books were also purchased, as in the case of the Berliner Stadtbibliothek, from the city's pawnbroker or at "Jewish auctions," where fleeing Jews had no choice but to sell their belongings for a fraction of their true value.

"The extent to which books were moved around in this way is difficult to estimate, because the books have been dispersed and integrated into so many different German collections. For instance, in the 1960s the GDR [German Democratic Republic] sold large numbers of books to West Germany for economic reasons, in order to get hold of D-marks. These were then handed out to newly formed universities in the West. Today in these collections it is possible to find many books that were stolen from Jews, Communists, and Freemasons," explains Uwe Hartmann.

"Several of the large libraries in Germany have begun to examine their collections to a certain degree. But we have eight thousand smaller libraries and only one of these has applied for funding from us to examine its inventory. There is an enormous amount of work ahead of us."

Most German libraries have not so far shown either the interest or the will to start looking for plundered books in their collections. When an expert on stolen property sent out forms to six hundred libraries, only 10 percent chose to reply.[10] Quite apart from a general reluctance to confront the issue, there is also the problem of limited resources that tends to put a stop to any progress. Nor is there in Germany any law that obliges institutions to go through their collections, although it has been proposed that one should be drafted. The work is voluntary.

Initially, Hartmann's institution had an annual budget of one million euros to distribute, which was increased to two million euros in 2012. This money, however, has to be shared among all cultural institutes, and most of the money goes to museums. Up to 2013, the institution had financed 129 projects, of which 90 were museums and only 26 were libraries. Nor does the institution offer full financing but rather offers to share the costs, which results in many smaller libraries taking the position that they cannot afford to get involved.

"Unfortunately the media interest is much greater for plundered art than for books. A recovered masterpiece, perhaps with a value of millions, generates newspaper headlines, whereas a single book could not ever hope to do so, even in highly emotive and moving cases."

Uwe Hartmann points to another problem with books.

"Art often has a provenance. Old works can be found in exhibition catalogs, auction registers, or they are referred to by art critics. They can be traced. The same can rarely be said for books. If there aren't any stamps in them, it becomes difficult. Books are rarely unique, after all. An enormous amount of work is required."

The number of plundered books hiding in German libraries today cannot be estimated by anyone.

"It's a very difficult question to answer. Thousands of German libraries have not even gone through their collections as yet. It's a case of millions of books that have to be manually checked."

It is also not easy to determine how many libraries were plundered. Thousands of the libraries that were sacked were never reestablished and their books never returned. There is also a lack of registers or catalogs that can tell us how extensive these collections were, or what they held. For instance, before the Nazis seized power in Germany there were thousands of "people's libraries" in the country, set up by labor unions, Socialist organizations, and the German Social Democrats. In all, there were more than one million books in these libraries. Most were never returned.

Millions of books were plundered from German Masonic orders, who were forced to disband after the Nazis took power. By 1936, the SS had built up a collection of 500,000 to 600,000 books from German Masonic orders alone.[11] These were destined to end up in the national security council's library, when the various security organs in the country were gathered under the executive control of the RSHA at the end of the 1930s.

Yet even this plunder was on a modest scale when compared with the ravages of the Nazis in Europe as a whole. In France alone, ERR confiscated the collections of 723 libraries, containing over 1.7 million books. Of these, tens of thousands were antique and medieval manuscripts, incunabula, and other valuable books and writings.[12]

In Poland, probably the country that was hit hardest, it is estimated that 90 percent of the collections belonging to schools and public libraries were lost. In addition, 80 percent of the country's private and special-ized libraries disappeared. More or less the entire collection of the Pol-ish national library, consisting of some 700,000 volumes, was scattered. According to one estimate, 15 million of Poland's 22.5 million books were lost, but it is unclear what proportion of these were plundered, lost, or destroyed during the war.

The extent of the plunder in the Soviet Union is more difficult to quantify. According to most available calculations the losses are almost astronomical. According to one suggestion from UNESCO, as many as 100 million books may have been destroyed or looted in what was then the Soviet Union.[13]

Far from all the plundered books ended up in German collections after the war. Most of the enormous book collections that the Nazis collected through plundering were themselves subject to plunder, dis-persal, and disappearance. Above all the victorious powers helped themselves. The Library of Congress in Washington sent over a special delegation to Germany that shipped home more than one million books.[14] The Red Army ended up confiscating more than ten million books. No one knows how many books were destroyed by bombing raids. The centrally located city libraries were easily combustible victims of Allied fire-bomb raids. In total, Germany is believed to have lost between a third and a half of all of its book collections, as a consequence of fires, bombing, and plunder.

Yet, in spite of all these losses, large numbers of plundered books remained in German libraries. Many, as in the case of Zentral- und Landesbibliothek, plugged the gaps in their collections with books from various Nazi organizations. The German historian Götz Aly es-timated in 2008 that there were at least one million plundered books in Germany libraries.[15] It was a conservative estimate, and probably the actual figure is much higher. Just as in the case of the Zentral- und Landesbibliothek, the numbers tend to swell once a library starts pur-posefully going through its collections. When I ask Uwe Hartmann how long it will take to go through the German book collections, he answers with a smile.

"When I lecture before students, I usually tell them that this is something that will be ongoing throughout their lives. It will go on for many, many decades ahead. The next generation that takes over at libraries and in museums will also have no choice but to deal with this. These objects bear a history that we cannot ignore."

# 3

# GOETHE'S OAK

## *Weimar*

*The monster was forced onto its knees in agony. Die, you beast, you symbol of the German Reich. And Goethe? To us, Goethe did not exist anymore, Himmler had exterminated him.*

— Diary of Prisoner 4935

A thick fog envelops the lush woodland like an opaque membrane. It is difficult to see more than ten yards ahead. I follow the cracked asphalt. At the blurred edges of the fog I see others, carefully advancing. Their voices whisper. Then I can make out the gates of the camp, with their brown wooden tower, reminiscent of an old village church. The iron gates are emblazoned with the words *Jedem das Seine*, a German version of the Latin motto *Suum cuique*, which, in English derivation, means more or less "to each his own." It is an idiomatic expression with deep roots in German culture, appearing in the writings of Martin Luther and other German Reformation thinkers. It is also the title of a cantata by Johann Sebastian Bach, first performed in 1715 only some four miles from the spot where I am standing, in the culturally significant German city of Weimar. The expression can be interpreted in a variety of ways, but on the gates of the concentration camp of Buchenwald there can be little doubt about the message it conveys: All shall get what they deserve. I have traveled a few hours south of Berlin to the green German heartland of Thüringen. Just inside the gates lies the crematorium, a gray concrete building dominated by a roughly constructed brick chimney. Here many of the tens of thousands of people who died were incinerated.

Buchenwald, one of Germany's largest concentration camps, is situated on the hill of Ettersberg, in the middle of a lovely deciduous forest known for its beech trees and ancient oaks. Elie Wiesel, the author and

Nobel Prize winner, who was deported here as a sixteen-year-old, said of the place when he visited it long afterward: "If these trees could talk."[1] According to Wiesel, there was a special irony in the contrast between Ettersberg's enchanting woodlands and the nightmares that were played out here between 1937 and 1945. Wiesel was not the only future Nobel Prize winner to be kept here as a captive. Another inmate was the Hungarian writer Imre Kertész, who has described this period in *The Man Without a Destiny*. Many other authors, poets, artists, musicians, architects, academics, and intellectuals were here. More than 230,000 prisoners from all over occupied Europe were sent to Buchenwald: the political and intellectual enemies of Nazidom, Jews, homosexuals, Poles, Roma, the mentally ill, the lesser abled, Freemasons, Catholics, criminals, and prisoners of war. Fifty-six thousand of them were murdered. Especially cruel methods of torture and execution were applied by the camp guard and SS-Hauptscharführer, Martin Sommer. He now goes by the name of "the Hangman of Buchenwald," because, in the woods to the north of the barracks, he used to string up the prisoners in the trees by their hands tied across their backs. This method of torture, known as strappado, had also been used during the Inquisition.

The weight of the body often leads to the arms being wrenched out of the shoulder sockets. At the same time, it is said, Sommer and his guards walked among the trees, striking the helpless prisoners' faces, legs, and genitals with wooden cudgels. "The torture drove some of the prisoners to the edge of madness. Many of them asked the SS men to shoot them so they would not have to endure the agony," the survivor Willy Apel testified.[2] The tormented cries and moans that were heard resulted in the place being named "The Singing Forest."

One of the trees in the Ettersberg forest would take on a particular significance. I walk from the crematorium and follow rows of gaping concrete foundations—the remains of the prisoners' barracks. On the left lies the camp block that once housed Allied war prisoners, homosexuals, Jehovah's Witnesses, and army deserters. Almost down by the large brick building, which also included the disinfection unit, I see it between two barracks: a stout gray-green tree stump, its roots still firmly gripping the ground. The inscription on a rough-hewn stone slab reads "*Goethe-Eiche*" (Goethe's oak).

When the woods in Ettersberg were cleared in 1937 to make space for the concentration camp, the SS guards left one of the oaks standing. There was a rumor that Goethe himself used to sit under this thick, mighty oak. It was not the only oak in Thüringen to be associated with the national poet, but this particular oak was destined to be charged with a very particular symbolism of the camp, its guards, and its prisoners. Goethe, who lived most of his life in Weimar, used to make excursions on horseback to Ettersberg, a popular place for romantic day trips in the 1700s. Goethe told his friend and biographer Johann Peter Eckermann that in this wood he felt "great-hearted and free."

When Buchenwald was constructed, the SS initially had the intention of naming the camp "K.L. Ettersberg." This, however, was met with howls of protest from the bourgeoisie of Weimar, because of Ettersberg's well-established connotations with Goethe and Weimar classicism. It was not considered an appropriate name for a concentration camp. For this reason, Heinrich Himmler decided to give the camp a made-up name: Buchenwald (the beech forest).[3]

According to one local tradition, it was at this exact tree that Goethe wrote the Walpurgis Night passage in *Faust*, when Mephistopheles takes Faust to Brocken Mountain for the witches' nocturnal Sabbath. Also, according to hearsay, he had sat under this tree while he wrote "The Wanderer's Night Song," which he sent in a letter in 1776 to his friend and lover Charlotte von Stein, with a dedication from "the slopes of Ettersberg":

> Thou that from the heavens art,
> Every pain and sorrow stillest,
> And the doubly wretched heart
> Doubly with refreshment fillest,
> I am weary with contending!
> Why this rapture and unrest?
> Peace descending
> Come ah, come into my breast!

(Translation by Henry Wadworth Longfellow)

Maybe the two lovers had even once sat together under the tree? But there was another myth intricately bound to this tree: that this oak in some mystical way was connected to the destiny of Germany. As long as this tree lived, Germany would endure. But if it fell, on the other hand, the German nation would fade.

In fact, the oak eventually took on two entirely different symbolic realities, one for the SS guards who had decided that the oak had to be preserved, and another for the prisoners of the camp. For the SS, the oak was a link to a great Germanic cultural tradition, of which they felt they were the true inheritors. The SS corps that guarded the camp participated actively in the cultural life of Weimar. At the National Theater, of which Goethe had once been the director, some of the best seats were reserved for the "Death's Head" Regiment of the SS. The ensemble also made visits to Buchenwald, where it performed for the guards. On one occasion the romantic operetta *The Land of Smiles* was performed—ironically enough it had been written by one of the inmates of the camp, the Austrian librettist Fritz Löhner-Beda. He was later sent to Auschwitz, where he was beaten to death by a guard.

For many of the camp prisoners, this oak, in the middle of this infernal world, took on a representation of dreams, fantasies, and hopes that were still keeping them alive. For prisoners who were rooted in German culture, the tree symbolized another, brighter, and more enlightened land than the one that kept them incarcerated. The German author and poet Ernst Wiechert described in his depiction of camp life, *Der Totenwald* (The Forest of Death), how the tree gave consolation to his alter ego, Johannes:

Dusk was already falling when Johannes yet again left the gap between the barracks where they spent their hour of leisure in the evenings. It only took him a minute of walking, and then he was standing under the oak, whose shadow was said to have fallen once on Goethe and Charlotte von Stein. It grew in one of the camp lanes, and here was the only spot from where one had an unimpeded view of the land below. The moon had risen now over the tree-covered hills, and the last sounds of the camp ebbed into silence.

For a while he looked out over the darkening sky, so alone, as if he were the last human on earth, and he tried to recall all the verses he knew from the one who had perhaps stood here a hundred and fifty years ago. None of his greatness had been lost, and even if he had been chained to a galley at the age of fifty, nothing would have been lost. "Noble, helpful, and good . . ." No, not even this had gone under, as long as there was still one human being who repeated it to himself, and tried to preserve it till his last hour had come.[4]


For Wiechert, Goethe personified the true German cultural tradition, like a beautifully illuminated path, although the people had lost their way and strayed into darker parts of the forest. Many survivors from the camp described the oak. The French artist and resistance fighter Léon Delarbre often sat under the oak, sketching its network of branches.

Not everyone shared Wiechert's perspective. Rather, they viewed the oak as a symbol of the inherent evil of Germanic culture, of oppression and cruelty. These prisoners kept alive the myth of the oak being tied to the fate of Germany. And it gave them hope. The oak in the camp started slowly withering and dying. The leaves failed to rejuvenate after one winter, and the bark fell off until the trunk stood white, dry, and naked. But the tree was still standing, until one day in August 1944, when Allied bombers carried out a raid on the factories adjoining the concentration camp. One of the bombs hit the laundry, which caught fire. Before long the flames had spread to the vulnerable oak tree. A Polish prisoner known to us only by his camp identification number, 4935, described the event as follows:

I could hear the crackling of the fire and see the sparks flying: the burning branches of the oak fell down and rolled across the tar paper on the roofs. I felt the smell of smoke. The prisoners formed a long human chain, and passed buckets of water from the well to the fire. They saved the laundry but not the oak. In their faces one could see a secret joy emerging, a silent triumph: Now we knew that the prophecy would come true. Before our very eyes, as smoke mixed with fantasy, this was not a tree but a many-armed monster, writhing in the flames. We could see how its arms fell off and the trunk grew smaller as if collapsing unto itself. The monster was forced onto its knees in agony. Die, you beast, you symbol of the German Reich. And Goethe? To us, Goethe did not exist anymore, Himmler had exterminated him.[5]

◆ ◆ ◆

In front of the National Theater in Weimar stand Goethe and Schiller, with their eyes fixed on infinity. Goethe's hand rests on his friend's shoulder, while Schiller reaches across to accept the laurel garland that Goethe holds out to him. Ernst Rietschel's statue from 1857 is typical of its time, and would eventually, in the mid-1800s, be used as a model for many other statues erected all over the country of the two literary giants. Statues of Goethe and Schiller were a direct expression of the strong nationalist sentiments whipped up all over Germany, at a time when Weimar became a cult.

At the edge of the city core lies the Park an der Ilm, a park with little footpaths through wooded areas growing so densely that the paths are turned into green tunnels. One leads to an open meadow, another to a garden folly, one to a fountain gushing out of a boulder, another to a cave or a picturesque ruin. The park is a romantic fantasy. It has not changed very much since the end of the 1700s, when it was established, inspired by English gardens. Overlooking open fields lies the poet's white garden house, where he lived during his first years in Weimar. By this time Goethe had already achieved fame all over Europe with his debut novel, *The Sorrows of Young Werther*—whose passionate, overwhelmingly emotional prose gave rise to enormous consternation in a century much occupied with reason, rationality, and Enlightenment thinking. This romantic idea of devotion to beauty, worship of nature, and poetry has become an important aspect of German self-perception. Yet at the same time it seems to hold a dark spot within itself. How could the inheritors of this culture, within a few generations, be hanging, torturing, and murdering people in the very same woods where Goethe once sat writing poetry? The image of it, on the one hand filled with radiance, and on the other with darkness, has sometimes been referred to as the "Weimar-Buchenwald dichotomy." These two aspects form a microcosm of the German dilemma, the Janus face of Germany. The paradox is amply illustrated by the divergent perspectives on Goethe's oak in Buchenwald.

Some have wished to see these two sides of German culture as wholly separate, in order not to besmirch the radiance of the classicist's era. This has been the predominant approach in Weimar for most of the postwar period. Others maintain that this is a historical simplification, even a falsification, for the plain reason that these two sides are interlinked by cultural, philosophical, and literary roots. Not directly related, perhaps, yet National Socialism grew and mercilessly exploited some of these ideas, which sprang from the same root: German nationalism and the rejection of Enlightenment ideals.

High German romanticism was strongly resistant to the emotional paucity of the Enlightenment era. Of particular importance were the ideas that took form at the university in Jena, about twelve miles east of Weimar, during the first half of the nineteenth century, when thinkers such as Friedrich Hegel, Johann Gottlieb Fichte, and Friedrich von Schelling, as a counterreaction to the Enlightenment, began to formulate the thinking that is known today as German idealism. They left behind a voluminous inheritance of ideas easily mined for inspiration by twentieth-century National Socialists—the most influential of these being the emphasis on Germany's uniqueness, in the form of spiritual elevation. Of even greater influence was the philosopher and historian Johann Gottfried Herder, one of the great thinkers that Goethe had brought to Weimar, who some have suggested may even have been the poet's prototype for Faust. Herder's idea of the unique people's soul and his strong emphasis on patriotism would prove decisively important in the emergence of German nationalism. Herder's goal was above all to distance German culture from the strong French influence of that time—European culture in the 1700s had been dominated by France. Johann Gottlieb Fichte, another philosopher often referred to as the father of German nationalism, felt that the German people were possessed of unique characteristics, and that for this reason Germans should "create and lead a new era in human history."[6] Already with Fichte there was a fully articulated anti-Semitism: he took the view that it would damage the German nation if Jews were given equal citizen's rights—as they had elsewhere across Europe, in a process of political development that had spread since the French Revolution. In France, Jews had been given citizen's rights, which had been the beginning of the Jewish emancipation in which European Jews increasingly chose to break their isolation in the ghettos and assimilate linguistically and culturally with European society.

The goal of an emergent German nationalism in the first half of the nineteenth century was above all the creation of a linguistically and culturally homogenous Germany. The nationalist sentiments culminated in 1848, when a wave of revolutionary fervor swept across Europe. In Germany there was an uprising of liberals, intellectuals, students, and workers against the old, autocratic, and repressive elites in the German ministates, but it was put down by the conservative principalities.

It was during the aftermath of this revolution and the political gloom following in its wake that Ernst Rietschel's statue of Goethe and Schiller was erected before the National Theater in Weimar.

"After the wars of liberation in German lands had brought neither political freedom nor national unity, the citizenry began to seek in cultural pursuits a substitute for what they still lacked. For example, they erected monuments to intellectual giants, usually at the most conspicuous location in the city, an honor that until then had been reserved for princes and military men," writes the German art historian Paul Zanker.[7]

Until the mid-1800s it had been unusual to raise costly monuments to artists, but after the revolution, statues of Goethe and Schiller would adorn every other town, as an expression of a literary, nationalistic movement. According to Zanker, these statues of authors and poets were regarded as representatives of ideal Germans, moral paragons depicted in contemporary dress—not naked, untouchable Greek divinities, but citizens. A cult was created around these monuments, inspiring the publication of newspapers, illustrated books, and plush volumes of the authors' collected works. It was during this period of activity, writes Zanker, that the Germans began to regard themselves as "a people of poets and thinkers." Yet, Zanker continues, these monuments were not supposed to inveigle the people to new revolutions and protests—rather the opposite. The bourgeoisie raised these statues to promote citizenly virtues: order, obedience, and loyalty to one's superiors. That the great Weimar writers had been in service at the Weimar court was considered an ideal worthy of emulation.

Goethe, the national poet, who came to personify these ideals, was destined to be transformed in the late 1800s into the moral role model of the new German nation. Everything that did not conform to this image of Goethe was hidden at the bottom of the archive and even destroyed. Letters of admiration, sent by Goethe to Napoleon, were burned. Goethe had openly spoken in favor of both cosmopolitanism and internationalism, yet his ideas were reinterpreted after his death as strictly nationalist—not least after the German dukedom was formed in 1871. The same distortions also afflicted philosophers such as Hegel, Fichte, and Herder, whose ideas were misapplied, overemphasized, or even falsified in order to confer legitimacy on nationalism.

Goethe's criticism of the political sphere was later used by right-wing nationalists as a cudgel against the formation of political parties and democracy.[8] Meanwhile, the Left regarded Goethe as a proponent of liberalism and parliamentarianism. The battle for Goethe's soul was set to continue into the next century. The strong inner tensions between the light and the dark side of Weimar, and the place and stage for this conflagration was a symbolic one: the National Theater behind Rietschel's statue of Goethe and Schiller.

◆ ◆ ◆

On February 6, 1919, a congress opened at the National Theater in Weimar. More than four hundred delegates from some ten political parties took their seats before the stage that had once belonged to Goethe and Schiller. They had gathered there to save Germany. The dukedom, hardly fifty years old, which until quite recently had appeared strong and even invincible, was in dissolution. The German nation, forged by Bismarck with "blood and iron," was imploding like a house of cards. In order to save Germany, they had gone back to their roots and convened in Weimar.

Almost one year earlier, on March 21, the German army had instigated the *Kaiserschlacht* (Kaiser's Battle), a massive attack along extensive stretches of the western front, in an attempt to break the stalemate. In fact, the show of strength was a desperate last-ditch attempt to win the war. When the Allies counterattacked in the summer, the German lines teetered on the verge of complete collapse. In late October 1918, naval personnel in Kiel mutinied, and within a matter of days the November Revolution had spread across the whole of Germany. The war was over. But the uprising went on, with terrible political chaos as rival groups clashed and millions of disillusioned German troops returned from the front. German Communists formed Soviets, based on the Russian precedent, and they even managed to seize power in Bavaria in the spring of 1919. But the German Social Democrats put up resistance, as did the Freikorps (free corps), paramilitary groups formed by decommissioned soldiers and officers, who brought back with them a brutal, inhuman culture of violence nurtured in the trenches.

The shadow of these events hung over the delegates as they gathered in February 1919 in Weimar, on the initiative of the German Social Democrats whose ambition was to form a parliamentary democracy. After the abdication of the kaiser, the party led by Friedrich Ebert had formed a provisional government. Ebert, a moderate and pragmatic politician, had had no choice but to form an alliance with nationalists and reactionary groups of free corps, in order to isolate the radical left. It had been Ebert's idea to relocate the constitutional representatives to provincial Weimar, where a new constitution would be drawn up for the establishment of what would later become known as the Weimar Republic.

The choice of Weimar was both an act of symbolism and realpolitik. The risk of a coup against Ebert's government was profoundly likely in Berlin, where the so-called January Uprising had broken out. The free corps had put down the remaining resistance in both Berlin and Munich with astonishing brutality: hundreds of people were murdered in summary executions, with the Communists unable to resist the battle-hardened frontline troops. And so, although the dawning German democracy was cast in blood, Friedrich Ebert had the intention of washing it clean with the help of Goethe. Ebert's choice of Weimar as the birthplace of German democracy was thus an attempt to gain legitimacy for the new democracy by associating it with the elevated ideals of Weimar classicism.

But the choice of Weimar as a capital was not only classical nostalgia but also the mark of a new brand of culture, which would eventually define the new republic. The modern movement, most articulately portrayed in German expressionism, would permeate and revitalize literature, art, music, theater, architecture, and design in the Weimar Republic. In all areas, a new generation broke away from the ossified conventions of the past. Yet Weimar culture became a point of focus for an incandescent struggle between German's two irreconcilable aspects—modernism, cosmopolitanism, and democracy on the one hand, and the beauty cult, violence, and fascism on the other. In literature, a new kind of experimental prose emerged, in which empty, bourgeois ideals, patriarchal family structures, and repressed feeling became standard themes. The new movement could release its pent-up energy without restraint, finding essential oxygen for its growth in the existential vacuum left behind by the war. "This is more than just a war that has been lost. A world has ended. We have to find a radical solution to our problems," wrote the German architect Walter Gropius, founder of the Bauhaus school.[9,10]

Yet, even though the old world seemed to be down for the count, it was never defeated. The modern movement had immediately divided Weimar and Germany into two entities. Modernism was met with animosity from the old Wilhelmian elite: the aristocracy, the reactionary bourgeoisie, and the universities, which regarded themselves as the guardians of tradition. The new movement was seen as depraved and immoral—and there were some that felt physically sick at what they saw, heard, and read.

The reactionary backlash began to mobilize. Resistance to the Weimar Republic, its democratic ideals, culture, and modernism, was destined to be of a violent nature, from conservatives, nationalists, and right-wing extremists.

Unlike the Communists and democrats, the German Right had been holding out for a true conservative revolution. This was a reaction to modernism, which, in their eyes, was stampeding into the arena of life, in the process creating a soulless mass society, robbed of all magic.[11] The counterwave rejected the materialism, rationalism, and capitalism of the time—which hollowed out human relations and idealism. The new world eroded the aristocratic and romantic values that were considered higher than any other: honor, beauty, and culture. As a movement it had already started growing before the war. Many had put their faith in a conservative rebirth as a consequence of the Great War. Only the war could alter the course of the ongoing collapse, submitting the nation to a necessary purification rite, and forcing the people to raise themselves above materialism to a higher spiritual level. To these conservative revolutionaries the First World War was not about territory, natural resources, or trade hegemony, it was actually a spiritual war in which French civilization was pitted against German culture. In other words, a war between French Enlightenment and German romanticism.

One of those who took this view, and who spoke in favor of a conservative revolution, was Thomas Mann, who long remained skeptical and even hostile to democratic development, which, he felt, was alien to the German people. Mann romanticized the war and felt that the violent life in the trenches brought out the best in the human beings who were there. According to Mann, the war would finally induce "the masses" to sacrifice themselves for a higher purpose and, in so doing, turn themselves into a "people": "The War is the effective cure for the rationalistic destruction of our national culture," continued Mann, who was dreaming of an authoritarian nationalistic state in which power and culture were integrated—a "Third Reich," as he prophetically decided to call it. Such ideas do not pass away with the war or its horrors and the unimaginable losses suffered by Germany—far from it, the resistance was rather dependent on such ideals to mobilize its rejection, and during the democratic "decadence" of the Weimar Republic, these were the very concepts that formed the world picture of the extreme right. Conservative intellectuals like Thomas Mann had a slightly different point of departure, but their fiery nationalism, their concern for feudal ideas and the romanticism of war as a higher spiritual struggle nonetheless contributed to legitimizing National Socialism and its even more radical view of reality.

Literary resistance to modernism took form in a genre of its own, known as free corps literature. Free corps groups, which had been formed by returning soldiers, were destined to go on throughout the 1920s and fill the spiritual vacuum created as a result of the German army being limited by the terms of the Treaty of Versailles to 100,000 men. The free corps were out of sync with the new order of the Weimar Republic, in which the old military virtues of honor, obedience, and brotherhood were ridiculed and spat upon. Their sacrifices at the front now seemed largely meaningless. It was in free corps groups that the so-called Legend of the Dagger Thrust (*Dolchstosslegende*) was cultivated, this being the view that Germany had not been defeated on the western front but rather on the home front—where Social Democrats, Socialists, and Jews had stabbed the nation in the back. Widely established in German society, the theory eventually became the main political question asked by the newly formed Nazi Party.

Free corps literature, emerging in the 1920s, was a genre of books often sold in kiosks or similar pulp outlets, in which war, violence, and manliness were idealized. It achieved broad success in the interwar years, and certain books even reached a larger, mass audience. The books vented the feelings of bitterness, disgust, and hatred experienced by many Germans after the war, but also a longing for something deeper—a world that had been lost.

The archetypal action in these stories centers on a young man of bourgeois background and his journey of self-development. Confused by the shallow materialism and spiritual poverty of contemporary life in the cities on "the home front," the young man seeks a deeper meaning. It is in the presence of death, at the front, that he "wakes up" and reaches an insight into the actual meaning of life, this being that he must accept his fate and sacrifice himself for his fatherland, his friends, and his blood. The lessons learned at the front form an existential, almost religious, experience. This is also the source of the Dagger Thrust: the uninformed masses in the city drive the dagger into the backs of the honorable soldiers, whose return from the front becomes an experience filled with humiliation and disgust. Here, the veterans meet all the revolting aspects of the emerging modern movement: democratization, the advance of workers, experimental culture, sexual liberation, and women's emancipation. The combat ideal of free corps literature—the repressed sexuality, the romanticization of violent acts, and the feelings of revulsion at the modern world—were in most cases closely allied to, and incorporated into, the Nazi ideology of violence.

But there were also those who presented another perspective. In *All Quiet on the Western Front*, Erich Maria Remarque examined the ideals of frontline combat and laid bare the emptiness and dishonesty of "honorable" sacrifices. He also depicted the close friendships that were created by the constant proximity of death, but there was no heroism, and the friends were seen meeting a coincidental and meaningless fate. Remarque, who was also a veteran, delivered a blow to the very heart of combat-inspired romanticism. For this reason, when it was published in 1928, the book gave rise to vehement response from reactionaries and the far right—and was therefore one of the first to fall victim to the book burnings in 1933.

Between the wars, there was also an emergent genre of more explicitly racist, anti-Semitic novels, some of which reached mass audiences. Literature became a mass medium for spreading and establishing the Fascist concept of the world. The Germans were a book-reading people, and they kept not only Thomas Mann's *Buddenbrooks* on the bedside table, but also novels that are no longer widely known, such as Hans Grimm's *Volk ohne Raum* and Karl Aloys Schenzinger's *Der Hitlerjunge Quex*.

Until the assumption of power by the Nazis, contemporary modernist and expressionist ideas coexisted with the free corps writings that glamorized violence, as well as anti-Semitic and racist novels. The bound-up tension between violence and progressive ideas was constantly present in the literature and cultural life of the Weimar Republic. On the one hand there were left-leaning, liberal writers and poets such as Heinrich Mann, Kurt Tucholsky, and Bertolt Brecht, and, on the other, right-wing extremists and nationalistic writers such as Emil Strauss, Hans Carossa, and Hanns Johst.[12] Yet there were also writers that ended up somewhere in the middle.

The most difficult position was that occupied by bourgeois, conservative intellectuals like Thomas Mann, who were worried by democratic developments while also revolted by vulgarities of the Nazis. In 1922, after the brutal murder of the German foreign minister Walter Rathenau, Mann saw no other option but to redefine his stance, which he did in a much-publicized speech in Berlin: *Von deutscher Republik* (The German Republic). In his lecture he publicly rejected the imperial ambitions of Wilhelmian Germany and spoke instead in favor of the Weimar Republic. Mann proclaimed that he had now come to see that democracy was, in fact, more "German" than he had previously thought. It was a conversion driven by his feelings of guilt at having in some way played a part in promoting the political violence.[13] But there was probably also a measure of fear of the "demon," which the violence, the war, and the military defeat had conjured, and which now took its first tottering steps as a radical, Fascist party in Munich.

Old, hierarchical Germany with its militaristic, imperial, and nationalistic ideals had been reincarnated as a new political movement radicalized by the war and nurtured by the Legend of the Dagger Thrust. In turn, the free corps had found a new conduit for displays of violence on behalf of the growing National Socialist Party.

The movement was destined to make its first gains on the very stage of the birth of the Weimar Republic. The Nazi Party re-formed in 1925, having been outlawed after its failed Beer Hall Putsch a few years earlier. Only four years later the Nationalsozialistische Deutsche Arbeiterpartei (National Socialist German Workers' Party, or NSDAP) had its first major election gain in Germany, when the party was included in the coalition that took charge of Thüringen. The Nazis, led by the state minister for internal affairs and education, Wilhelm Frick, instigated a fierce attack on Weimar's cultural life by the introduction of an extreme, institutionally racist cultural program developed by Alfred Rosenberg and his circle. His organization, Kampfbund für deutsche Kultur (Militant League for German Culture), was set up in 1928 and sought to amalgamate the country's abundant radical right-wing cultural organizations to clear out Jewish and other "alien" influences from German culture. In a matter of a few years, Weimar changed from a free zone for modernist experimentation to a cult site for Nazism. Thüringen became the test map and a model state for the radical race politics that were soon to be rolled out across Germany as a whole.[14]

The film dramatization of *All Quiet on the Western Front* was prohibited in the state, and the Castle Museum in Weimar was cleared of works by Wassily Kandinsky, Franz Marc, and Paul Klee. Composers such as Stravinsky were blacklisted, as was "black" music, including jazz.

Just as previously the state had attracted progressive artists, Thüringen would now begin to draw intelligentsia of a darker ilk. Wilhelm Frick promoted the eugenicist Hans F. K. Günther to professor of race biology at the university in Jena. Günther, who went by the nickname of Race-Günther or the Race Pope, was regarded at this time as the preeminent world authority on race research. Günther's theories would to a large degree form the basis for Nazi race politics. Another race theorist, the architect and culture critic Paul Schultze-Naumburg, was appointed the head of the Art College in Weimar, which had replaced Gropius's Bauhaus school. Schultze-Naumburg, who among other works had written the book *Kunst und Rasse* (Art and Race), felt that real art could only be created by racially pure artists. Frick's right-hand man, the hard-boiled Nazi and literary expert, Hans Severus Ziegler, was brought in as the political expert for culture, art, and theater. A few years later he became the president of the Schiller Association and the creative director of the National Theater in Weimar.

An extensive program was also set in motion to "Nazify" Johann Wolfgang von Goethe, which required a great deal of dexterity and work. Although nationalists had already during the 1800s begun to twist the image of Goethe, he was still known as a humanist and an internationalist—values to which the founders of the Weimar Republic had paid allegiance. Goethe was also enveloped in a range of "uncomfortable" connections, not least of which was the suggestion that he had been a "friend of the Jews," and even certain rumors that Goethe himself had had Jewish blood. Further still, the Goethe Association and several of the institutions in Weimar with links to the national poet were "infiltrated" by Jews. For instance, Professor Julius Wahle, the previous director of the Goethe and Schiller Archive, was a Jew.

Fortunately, the then head of the archive, Hans Wahl, was willing to take on the task of "laundering" Goethe and preparing a place of honor for him in the National Socialist pantheon. A few years earlier, Wahl had taken part in the establishment of the Weimar chapter of the Militant League for German Culture.

Wahl was prepared to go the extra mile to save the honor of Weimar's great son. As the vice chairman of the Goethe Association, he ensured that non-Aryans were forbidden from becoming new members, and he asserted that the association was "the most anti-Jewish of all literary associations in Germany."[15] In actual fact the literary association did not kick out its Jewish members until the end of the 1930s. The association tried, using its journal, to scour away Goethe's humanist "aura" by publishing texts on how the poet had predicted the rise of the Third Reich. Hans Wahl suggested that Goethe had been both an anti-Semite and an opponent of Freemasonry, which was a clear lie— the poet had even been a Freemason himself. Wahl made threats to silence any researchers who suggested that Goethe had been a "friend of the Jews." The chairman of the association, Julius Petersen, took the process one step further when he likened Goethe to Hitler—both were "great" statesmen and artists. When Thomas Mann arrived in the city in 1932 to take part in the centenary of the poet's death, he noted with distaste: "Weimar is a center of Hitlerism."[16]

The crowning glory of Wahl's act of mutilation was the new Goethe Museum, the financing of which was personally ensured by Adolf Hitler. The museum opened in 1935, in a building adjoining Goethe's home. At the entrance, Wahl placed a bust of Adolf Hitler, with a plaque giving fulsome thanks to their patron. On the wall, a "family tree" of Goethe was put up, as a way of pointing to the poet's pure Aryan lineage.

Today, every trace of the museum's patron has been tidied away. The bust has been removed, as has the family tree. But there is still a medallion of Adolf Hitler somewhere in the mortar of one of the cornerstones.

✦   ✦   ✦

"Everything started with the fire," says Michael Knoche as he gazes out the window. The room at the top of the house, known as the Green Castle, has a beautiful view toward the Park an der Ilm. Lush July greenery almost presses in through the window, which is wide open. Knoche, a modest-looking man in a gray checkered suit, is the director of one of the most famous libraries in Germany: the Duchess Anna Amalia Library. In 1761, Duchess Anna Amalia of Braunschweig-Wolfenbüttel had her sixteenth-century castle converted into a library for the collections of the court. The library, furnished in rococo style, is on the list of UNESCO's World Heritage sites. Today it is a part of the Klassik Stiftung Weimar, a foundation that oversees the running of Weimar's cultural institutions.

"When I came to Weimar in the early 1990s I did not believe there was a problem here with plundered objects. I had some contacts with Jewish organizations in connection with this matter, but I said to them, 'There are no problems with it here.' That was the general view. But the fire changed that," says Knoche.

One night in September 2004 a spark shot out from a damaged electrical cable and caught in the dry roof beams. The upper floor of the renowned white rococo library, with tens of thousands of tinder-dry volumes, caught fire. The same went for the oil paintings, portraits of five centuries of royalty in the German Empire. Fifty thousand volumes were lost in the flames, many of them irreplaceable first editions from the 1500s. The Anna Amalia Library, where Goethe worked, housed Germany's largest collection of editions of Shakespeare and *Faust*. Thousands of books were also damaged by smoke, heat, and water.

"Some of what was lost is irreplaceable; other losses will take decades to replace," says Knoche, who is nonetheless relieved that he managed to save the library's Gutenberg Bible from the flames.

The library has been rebuilt, but tens of thousands of books are still being kept frozen while awaiting extremely time-consuming resto-ration work. The fire not only decimated a part of Germany's cultural inheritance—in fact, the flames also exposed a much less edifying part of the library's history.

"After the fire we started going through every book in the library. We had to form an overall idea of what had been lost. We scrutinized the old journals to check when and how the books had been acquired. The journals did not expressly suggest anything 'illegal' had taken place, but there were other signs that raised our suspicions about the books not having come into the collection in a proper manner, if you could put it like that . . . There were stamps, correspondence, and other things that indicated something of that nature."

The library's investigation showed that more than 35,000 books had been added to the collection between 1933 and 1945, the prove-nance of which was "suspicious." This new information has forced the Anna Amalia Library and Klassik Stiftung Weimar to completely re-assess its own history and the role of the library during the war. Hans Wahl has long been regarded as the savior of Weimar, and he is still a controversial figure in the history of the town—so controversial that recently a whole research conference was held to look into his record.

After the war, Hans Wahl managed to convince the Soviet authori-ties of his innocence, in spite of having been a member of the Nazi Party and his repeated assertions of an aggressive anti-Semitism. Wahl not only managed to retain his old job in the new regime, in 1945 he was even promoted to vice chairman of a newly formed cultural body for the democratic rebuilding of Germany, the first task of which was to rid German culture of Fascist influence.[17] In 1946 he was also made the head of the Nietzsche Archive in Weimar.

Wahl's apologists have suggested that he played a double game dur-ing the Nazi era in order to save the cultural inheritance of Weimar. Deep inside, they go on, he was a democrat who steered the town through its most difficult period, in the process making the political compromises that he believed were necessary. After the war Wahl main-tained that his purpose all along had been to "keep Goethe's face clean through this period."[18] On the other hand, the image of Wahl as an "involuntary Nazi" has become increasingly difficult to defend. Five years before the Nazis assumed power in Germany he had already been involved in the formation of the Weimar chapter of Alfred Rosenberg's Militant League for German Culture.

New information about the Anna Amalia collection in recent years has further weakened the defense of Wahl. His ability to get off so lightly, not to say wholly without blemish, after the war, is partially explained by the interest of the new regime in gaining legitimacy, much as the Weimar Republic and the Third Reich, by making use of Goethe. Yet again the substance of Goethe was going to be cast in a new form. Wahl, who a decade earlier had transformed Goethe into an anti-Semite, would now help conjure the poet into a Socialist hero.

Hans Wahl died of a heart attack in the Goethe year of 1949. In recognition of his custodianship of Goethe's spiritual legacy, Wahl was given a state funeral and laid to rest beside Schiller and Goethe at the Historische Friedhof in Weimar. In his honor, the street leading to the Goethe and Schiller Archive on the other side of the Park an der Ilm was named after him, and to this day bears his name.

"He is still a person who's much talked about in Weimar. For some people he's a hero, and for others . . . Well, he's not a person to be seen in those terms. The truth is that the Communists needed people like Wahl. They needed Weimar. The Red Army trophy brigades stole art and culture all over Germany, but they left the town untouched. As if Weimar were a holy place," Knoche tells me.

Today, three experts on provenance investigation are going through the entire Klassik Stiftung Weimar and the millions of books, documents, letters, works of art, and other objects that the foundation holds in trust. I take the elevator down from Knoche's office on the upper floor. It descends past the entrance lobby, under the cellars, and even farther down. Under the castle, the institutes, the library, the beer halls, and the slanted, cobbled lanes, long straight catacombs extend outward in an underground network. It is quite beautiful, with the reflections of the lamps on the polished floors. The greater part of the collection, nowadays, is kept in this subterranean complex—in controlled conditions in terms of light, air, and temperature.

Two of the foundation's provenance researchers, Rüdiger Haufe and Heike Krokowski, show me to a shelf along the wall of a very long corridor. Here they have collected their "finds."

No less than the librarians in the Stadtbibliothek in Berlin, Hans Wahl accepted the unique opportunity presented to him of expanding the collection. Haufe and Krokowski take some books from the shelf and show me the beautiful nameplates of Jewish families who once lived here in Weimar. Some of the books were "gifts" from the Gestapo or the party. Others came from the central sorting station of the Preussische Staatsbibliothek in Berlin. A few larger batches were purchased from unscrupulous book dealers who had made good business out of fleeing Jews, from Vienna among other places.

But Hans Wahl also kept his eye on particular collections—more specifically, those belonging to the Jewish businessman Arthur Goldschmidt, who had made his fortune manufacturing animal feed. However, Goldschmidt's real passion lay elsewhere, namely in the collection of books. At the time of the Nazis' assumption of power he had a library comprising about forty thousand books. The jewel of this library was a unique, and well-known, collection of some two thousand antique almanacs from 1600 to the 1800s. Goldschmidt had been fascinated by the proliferation in this era of illustrated almanacs on various themes, everything from ballets and carnivals to insects and agriculture.[19] The almanacs were often aimed at certain groups, and referenced important festivals or the dates of flowering of certain plants. Literary almanacs were also issued, featuring poets and authors. Not unexpectedly, Goethe, finding himself interested in the format, had published a few almanacs of his own, of which Goldschmidt had managed to acquire first editions. In 1932 Goldschmidt published a bibliography on the subject, entitled *Goethe im Almanach*, a publication that Wahl took note of. It just so happened that the Goethe and Schiller Archive in Weimar lacked these precise almanacs in its own collection. A few years later Wahl got his chance when Arthur Goldschmidt's company was confiscated by the state. For the sake of his own survival, Goldschmidt was forced to sell his collection to the Goethe and Schiller Archive. Goldschmidt himself estimated that the value of the collection was at least 50,000 reichsmarks. Wahl notified him that the archive could not pay more than one reichsmark per almanac. Goldschmidt ought to be willing to "make a sacrifice" to see his collection brought into the renowned archive, Wahl argued.[20] Like so many other Jews in 1930s Germany, Goldschmidt did not find himself in a decent bargaining position. It was impossible to get such a well-known collection out of Germany, and the family's assets had started running dry. Goldschmidt had no option but to accept Wahl's offer. Wahl, in an internal report, was able to confirm with satisfaction that the whole thing "had been an unusually advantageous affair, resulting in a very desirable addition to the archive's poor collection of almanacs." He also mentioned how the archive had managed to purchase the collection at such a modest price: "for the obvious reason that Herr Goldschmidt was a Jew."[21] Toward the end of the 1930s, the family managed to leave Nazi Germany and flee to South America, where Goldschmidt died, impoverished, in Bolivia.

After the war, the almanacs were moved from the Goethe and Schiller Archive to the Anna Amalia Library.[22] The provenance for these valuable almanacs was only indicated by a cryptic A, to denote the owner's first name. Only in 2006, once the library had begun its investigation, did suspicions arise that something was amiss.

"With the help of the London office of the Commission for Looted Art in Europe we managed to trace the descendants, who came here to look at the collection," Rüdiger Haufe says.

After negotiations the two parties agreed that the collection should remain in Weimar, but that the foundation would compensate the family for the actual value—which eventually led to the library paying 100,000 euros for the collection.

The Goldschmidt case is the most valuable restitution to date from a German library. But in spite of almost ten years of investigations at the Anna Amalia Library, a lot of work still remains to be done. The library has managed to give back a small number of stolen books, but

1914–1918
ARTHVR
GOLD/CHMIDT.

The collector Arthur Goldschmidt's ex libris, an illustration of his own experience as a German frontline soldier in the First World War. Among other items, the Duchess Anna Amalia Library in Weimar acquired his valuable collection of literary almanacs.

many more are still hiding in the catacombs under Weimar. "By 2018 we plan to have completed our run-through of the years from 1933 to 1945. But then there will be all the books still to look at that came into the collection after the war, all the way up to the present day. Quite honestly I don't know how much time it will take, but quite clearly it will go on for at least another decade. Sometimes people speak of this as a process that will take an entire generation," Michael Knoche tells me before I leave his office.

Down underground, Rüdiger Haufe and Heike Krokowski carry on taking books from a shelf and placing them on a table in front of me. As in so many other German libraries I am about to visit, they want to separate these books from the rest, also in a physical sense, as if they were contaminated. To cut them away from the main body of the library and keep them in isolation on a shelf, at a safe distance from the rest of the collection, avoiding the risk of contagion. Hundreds of books from hundreds of collections.

Haufe shows me a book that they recently found, from Arthur Goldschmidt's library. On the inside is his ex libris depicting a soldier, sitting under a tree, reading. The bookmark is dated 1914–1918. The illustration is of Goldschmidt himself, who fought for Germany in the First World War. Maybe it is a memory of the consolation that books gave him in the wartime trenches, a possibility to escape for a moment in dreams. Every book carries a story of theft, blackmail, and a tragic fate. At best, it may be a story of flight, of bailing out on a life—but at worst a story of people who have left no trace behind except for these books. I ask the two men what they will do with the books that are left behind, unable to find a way home. Haufe and Krokowski look at each other; the thought seems never to have occurred to them. They shrug, as if to say, Don't know. Maybe they'll just stay where they are, then.

# 4

# HIMMLER'S LIBRARY

## *Munich*

At first sight, the yellow colossus on Ludwigstrasse in Munich looks like an ominous fortress, with bare facades and small, slit windows. The massive brick building, which houses the Bayerische Staatsbibliothek, extends across a whole block. The historian Stephan Kellner, a man with stubbly black hair and a gold ring in one ear, meets me by the entrance.

"This is the easiest way," he says, leading me out of the fortress. We go around the building, crossing the unkempt park behind the library. At the far end of it is a little house, half-overgrown with ivy. On the other side of the house one can make out the English Garden, where in 1937 Adolf Hitler inaugurated his museum, Haus der Deutschen Kunst. For the past ten years, in this little house behind the Bayerische Staatsbibliothek, Kellner and his colleagues have been examining the library's enormous collection, focusing on thefts from the period of the Third Reich. The library, whose collection numbers some ten million volumes, is built on the royal library of Bavaria and, even as early as the 1500s, was already considered the finest library north of the Alps. Its historical collection is one of the most renowned in the world, with one of the largest collection of books printed before 1500, so-called incunabula. But like so many other German libraries, the Bayerische Staatsbibliothek also carries a heavy burden of pilfered stock.

"This is not a hobby for me, it's a sort of obligation. It's about my family history; my grandfather was a Jew. He lived here but he was forced to emigrate to Colombia. That's why I feel a personal duty to work with this," Kellner says, showing me into a room where books have been neatly laid out on a large table.

Prior to this visit, I sent Kellner a wish list, because, in fact, the Bayerische Staatsbibliothek is the owner of a unique collection—some of the first books that the Nazis ever stole. Given that the library existed in the very town where National Socialism was born, a town that from 1936 was led by Rudolf Buttmann, the Nazi who carried the fourth membership card issued by the party, the Bayerische Staatsbibliothek had particularly good opportunities for taking part in the plundering. Some of the first collections that came here in the 1930s belonged to the foremost Jewish families in Munich. Also here were books from religious groups, Freemasons' orders, and other groups under Nazi assault.

"Few complete libraries ended up here. The librarians mainly picked out the rarest books, first editions from the 1700s or copies of works that the library did not have," Kellner tells me.

Books from the private collection of Thomas Mann, among others, ended up in the library. These were stolen from his house, which lay within walking distance along the river Isar, on the other side of the English Garden. While Thomas Mann was off on a lecture tour abroad in the spring of 1933, he received news of a wave of arrests of intellectuals in Germany. His family advised him not to come back, and Mann settled temporarily on the French Riviera. Six months later, Mann's house on Poschinger Strasse was confiscated.[1]

After the end of the war, the US Army handed over a motley collection of some thirty thousand books to the Bayerische Staatsbibliothek. Some of them have been arranged with their flyleaves open, on the table in front of me, and this is the first time I have seen certain stamps that are difficult to misunderstand. On the flyleaf of a book entitled *Polnische Juden* (Polish Jews) I find black-stamped text: "Reichsinstitut für die Geschichte des neuen Deutschland" (National Institute for the History of New Germany, headed by the historian Walter Frank). This text runs around the Nazi state crest, an open-winged eagle with its talons gripping a wreath decorated with swastikas. In the book *Das Deutsche Volksgesicht* (The Face of the German People) there is another stamp of the German eagle, this one larger and oval and ringed by the words "Ordensburg Sonthofen Bibliothek," which was one of the elite schools of the Nazi Party. It is a photographic book, with black-and-white head shots of weather-beaten, grim-faced Germans, many of them

A book bearing the stamp of the Bayerische Politische Polizei,
led by Heinrich Himmler from 1933. The secret police in Bayern
was used as a model for the terror machine that Himmler
built up during the 1930s.

in profile with their noses clearly outlined. The last stamp I see in one
of the books on display is much simpler—a blue rectangle with the text
"Politische Bücherei. Bayerische Politische Polizei" (Political Library.
Bayern Political Police).

The books on the table are individual fragments, early shards of the
ambition that would eventually lead to the most extensive theft of
books in the world. Maybe one can see these books as archaeological
remains of this plan, which extended from research institutes and elite
schools to the ideological warfare of secret police organs. One might
describe them as "early shards" because these stamps represent some of
the earliest attempts by the regime to establish an ideological program
of knowledge acquisition, which proposed to not only study its enemies
but also build a new, ideologically based culture of research and education in the Third Reich.

As time passed, these fragmentary efforts grew and were replaced
by ever larger and more ambitious projects, as the Third Reich began to
enjoy rapid success. The common feature of this vision was a frenzied
obsession with the collection and ownership of knowledge. The books
on the table are remnants, components of a series of new libraries that
the Nazi regime had begun to build up in the early 1930s.

How this collection of books from entirely separate organizations
was brought together and how it ended up in the Bayerische Staatsbibliothek is somewhat of a mystery to this day, according to Stephan
Kellner. The books were most likely confiscated by the Western Allies
from an extensive number of institutions, public authorities, and organizations in the Third Reich. Many of the books were taken to the
United States, while others were handed over to German libraries in
order to rebuild collections that had been destroyed during the war.

"We see so many stamps in this collection from different organizations within the Third Reich. There were constant conflicts and rivalries
over these books. Building up a library of one's own became a sort of
status indicator in the Nazi movement. Book collecting was a mania.
The foundation of this lay in the idea of totalitarian ideology, the desire
to control every aspect of citizens' lives. The same totalitarian thinking

also applied to the sciences, where there was an attempt to redefine every area. Everything had to be National Socialist. Everything, everywhere. They didn't only strive to replace old structures and systems with their own, they wanted to create entirely new ones too. It wasn't enough to 'Nazify' a traditional university. They had to found a new school, in a new building, with a new name, and teach a new ideology," Stephan Kellner tells me, before going on to the significance of *Mein Kampf* in German society. "This urge to replace everything, to do everything from scratch, had some quasi-religious aspects. Couples that had wedded earlier would receive a Bible as a gift, but now they got a copy of *Mein Kampf*. That's an example of how far they were prepared to go."

The rubber-stamped books are a clear expression of this totalitarian urge. The stamp of the Bayerische Politische Polizei (BPP) on an anthropological study of child care among indigenous people caught my eye, suggesting that the security police had wider ambitions than merely studying Communists and politically subversive groups. In fact, this political police entity would constitute an early building block for that organ within the Third Reich that would take the totalitarian philosophy furthest of all: the Schutzstaffel, abbreviated as the SS.

The Bayerische Politische Polizei was originally a part of the Weimar Republic's decentralized police system, in which the states had their own independent departments of secret police. This police system would change radically in the Third Reich. When the Nazis assumed power in 1933, the BPP in Munich found itself with a new chief: a thirty-three-year-old agronomist by the name of Heinrich Himmler.

Himmler had grown up in a conservative and strict Catholic family in Munich. He was regarded by his school friends as an introspective, socially uncomfortable person suffering from poor health, including stomach problems that continued to plague him throughout his life. In spite of this he tried to pursue a career in the military. To his great disappointment, he never had time to get to the front before the Armistice, and he opted instead for a course in agronomy at the Technical University in Munich.

Himmler admired the free corps, which had crushed the Communists in Munich. He began taking an interest in the far-right outlook, defined by anti-Semitism, militarism, and nationalism, while also developing a deep interest in religion, occultism, and German mythology. He joined the NSDAP in 1923, on the recommendation of Ernst Röhm, with whom he had become acquainted in the city's far-right circles. Röhm was a decorated war hero and the cofounder and leader of the party's paramilitary offshoot, known as the SA.

Himmler was thrown right into the ferment after the failed Beer Hall Putsch. He managed to avoid prison, and he rose quickly through the ranks in the vacuum that arose while the party was banned and its leaders had either fled or been imprisoned. When the NSDAP was reformed in 1925, Himmler became a member of the SS, a small elite bodyguard within the SA whose main purpose was to protect Adolf Hitler from threats—including those from within the movement. Initially, this small organization consisted only of a dozen or so men. Himmler was no foot soldier, but he proved to have a noteworthy talent for bureaucracy, organization, and planning. He already seemed to have had a clear vision for the SS. In 1927, he told Adolf Hitler his plans for developing the SS into a racially pure elite force, a loyal military group, and an ideological spearhead organization personally answerable to Hitler.[2] Hitler saw Himmler's plans as a way of balancing the power of the SA, which had grown in an almost uncontrollable manner during the Weimar Republic.

With Hitler's support, Himmler rose quickly within the SS, and in 1929, he was made Reichsführer-SS, the head of the entire organization. At that stage the SS scarcely had 300 members. By the end of 1933, it had more than 200,000 members.[3]

Unlike the SA, which principally recruited members of the working class, Himmler opted for well-educated middle-class men. He viewed the SS as a racial and intellectual elite. In order to be admitted as a member, one had to be able to demonstrate an unimpeachable Aryan family tree going back to 1750. An educational background in law, for instance, often took precedence. Attributes such as ruthlessness, fanaticism, loyalty, and brutality were also important.

The SS was permeated by Himmler's personal interest in history, mythology, and racial dogma. The formation of the SS was inspired by historical elite groups such as the samurai, the Teutonic order of knights, and the Jesuits. The SS would be an Aryan warrior class in which the SS man embodied a new human being, a "superhuman." In 1931 Himmler started building the intelligence wing within the SS: Sicherheitsdienst des Reichsführers-SS—usually abbreviated as SD.

After the transfer of power in 1933, the process of fusing the old intelligence machine of the Weimar Republic with the party's own network began. In time the SS was given virtually unlimited power to expand and infiltrate the fabric of German society. Himmler soon controlled all of the police forces in Germany.[4]

The sizable expansion of the SS in the first few years of the 1930s put it on an inevitable collision course with its parent organization, the SA, which by 1933 had grown into Germany's largest military force, with over 3 million members. Adolf Hitler, suspecting that Ernst Röhm was planning a coup to overthrow him, secretly gave Himmler the job of preempting the SA. In the last few days of June 1934 the SS struck against the leadership of the SA, displaying the efficiency and brutality that would become the hallmark of the organization. Some two hundred people in the top echelons of the SA's leadership were arrested or murdered in what became known as the Night of the Long Knives.

The secret police at state level changed its name to Gestapo, which was also the name of a secret police department in Berlin set up by Hermann Göring. By this time, the SD had already moved its head office from Munich to the capital. In connection with this move an inventory of confiscated literature was taken, which indicated that the collection had already grown to more than 200,000 books.[5]

◆ ◆ ◆

In 1936 a new kind of library began to take form in the new Berlin head office of the SD. Ever since the Nazis took power, the secret police in the federal states and the SD had been watching various sectors of the book market. Everything from literary criticism, libraries, book publishing, and the importation of books to the arrest and harassment of authors, book dealers, editors, and publishers was under scrutiny. Hundreds of thousands of books had been seized from enemies of the regime. On the other hand, there was no coherent plan about what to do with all this literature. Some of the books were donated to libraries, others were collected by the various organizations in a more or less structured manner. However, in 1936 the SD officially set up a research library for politically undesirable literature in Berlin and a number of librarians were employed to start cataloging the collection.[6] At the same time an order went out from Himmler to all departments of the secret police in Germany. They were ordered to go through their inventories of confiscated literature and immediately send such materials to a new Zentralbibliothek für das gesamte politisch unerwünschte Schrifttum, a library of literature about "political undesirables." The library was soon expanded in terms of its content to all kinds of literature with some connection to the "enemies of the Reich"—for instance, authors who in one way or another had been opponents of the Nazi ideology. According to one witness, by May 1936 the library had already grown to between 500,000 and 600,000 volumes.[7]

After 1936, the inflow of literature increased enormously as a consequence of the general intensification of persecution against the Reich's "internal enemies." In mid-1937, the SD stepped up its attacks on churches and congregations. The regime lashed out at what it regarded as "political activity" within the church. Some felt that the church was working against Nazi ideology and should therefore be banned, but Adolf Hitler was not prepared to go that far. The persecution hit hardest against Catholics, evangelical groups, and clergymen who opposed the regime. And after the annexation of Austria in March 1938, the SS led a nationwide sweep of political and ideological enemies. Einsatzkommando Österreich, a special commando group from the SD, confiscated libraries and archives from organizations, government departments, parties, institutions, and private individuals. In May the organization sent a trainload to Berlin of some 130 tons of impounded books and archive materials.

At the end of 1938, there was a wave of new additions to the collection from another dramatic event—Kristallnacht. In a pogrom across the country in November 1938, more than a thousand synagogues were torched, and over twenty thousand Jews arrested and sent to concentration camps.[8] This also gave rise to a new wave of book burnings across Nazi Germany, this time of Jewish religious literature. In hundreds of towns, synagogue libraries were plundered by Nazis and local residents, who dragged out Torah scrolls, the Talmud, and prayer books into the streets, tore them apart, stomped on them, and burned them. Just as in 1933, the destruction of literature had a ritual, festive atmosphere that frequently attracted thousands of onlookers and participants. In the little town of Baden, Nazis marched up and down the streets with Torah scrolls before they finally flung them into the fire. In Vienna's Jewish quarter, writings and religious artifacts from a number of synagogues were collected into a large pile and then burned. In Hessen, Torah scrolls were rolled out in the streets, while children from the Hitlerjugend cycled over the holy texts. And in the little town of Herford in western Germany, children used them to make confetti for a folk festival. In other places, the Jewish texts were allegedly used as toilet paper, or for games, where children played soccer with them. In Frankfurt, Jews were forced to tear up and burn Torah scrolls and other religious writings.[9]

But despite the extensive destruction, many of the collections were saved by an unexpected hand. Just as in 1933, when the most important parts of the library and archive of the Institut für Sexualwissenschaft were saved from the flames by the SA, some of the most important Jewish collections escaped the general plunder of Kristallnacht. By a secret order, a number of especially valuable archives and libraries were removed.[10] More than 300,000 books from seventy different Jewish congregations, including the Israelitische Kultusgemeinde in Vienna and the Jewish Theological Seminary of Breslau, were confiscated and taken to Berlin.

In 1939, there was an extensive reorganization of the proliferating security apparatus of the regime, which led to the establishment of the Reich Main Security Office: Reichssicherheitshauptamt (RSHA), a superorganization in which police and intelligence entities such as the

Gestapo, the SD, and Kriminalpolizei were arrayed to fight the enemies of the state. The library that the SD had begun to build in Berlin
now ended up in the new department Amt II (second office) of the
RSHA, tasked with investigating political enemies. Franz Six, an
SS-Brigadeführer, was chosen to head the section. As the chief of Amt
II, Six presented the purpose of the section's library as follows: "In order to understand the spiritual weapons of our ideological enemies, it is
necessary to go deeply into the writings that they have produced."[11]
However, this research library would soon move to an entirely different
section of the RSHA, which Franz Six was put in charge of. Office
seven, Section VII, was a more specifically dedicated research division
devoted to "ideological research and evaluation."[12]

Only when the war broke out did the RSHA get its big opportunity
to plunder books. By the end of 1939 the first spoils arrived, six railroad cars of Jewish literature from Poland. These books had been taken
from just one library belonging to the Great Synagogue of Warsaw.
Thousands of libraries would eventually be plundered in Poland
alone.[13] Section VII's activity became so extensive that it had to be
housed in two confiscated Freemasons' lodges on Eisenacher Strasse
and Emser Strasse in Berlin. The library of Section VII ended up consisting of a series of departments focusing on a variety of enemies. The
most extensive of these was the department of Jewish literature. There
was also another department of syndicalist, anarchist, Communist,
and Bolshevik literature, as well as a department of pacifist and Christian literature, and those of various sects and minorities.

By and large, the library of Section VII would reflect the subjects in
which Himmler himself took an interest, covering much more ground
than merely "enemies of the state"—it was a reflection of the worldview
of Himmler and the SS. The most curious inclusions in the RSHA's
library were the sections devoted to occultism. The relationship of the
SS to occultism has commonly been exploited in popular culture, in
often sensationalist documentaries and books. Yet the occult inclusions in the RSHA library testify to the great seriousness of the subject
in the SS. An "occult library" had already been in the making within

the SD before the RSHA came into being. This was used as the foundation for a library devoted to the subject: the Zentralbibliothek der okkulten Weltliteratur.[14] It included, among other things, a section called Sonderauftrag H, focusing on the magical arts and incantations. There was a collection of books on occult science, *Geheimwissenschaftlichen*, and other works on theosophy, sects, and astrology. Much of this literature can be traced back to plundered German Freemasons' orders. Another section, Sonderauftrag C, was on pseudo-religious subjects and also contained a large collection of pornography and literature on sexology. Yet the SS did not limit itself to stealing books on behalf of Section VII—paradoxically enough, it also stole human beings. Several Jewish scholars and intellectuals were kidnapped and taken to the RSHA's book depots in Berlin, where they were made to work in libraries, sometimes on elucidating texts written in Hebrew and Yiddish for the SS.

The library or, more correctly, the libraries of the RSHA's Section VII were a very tangible manifestation of the SS and Himmler's extensive totalitarian ambitions. The research in progress at the RSHA was not only about improving their awareness of their enemies in order to be able to overcome them more effectively—but also the injection of knowledge into the SS's ideological and intellectual development. The SS was waging war against what it regarded as Jewish intellectualism, modernism, humanism, democracy, the Enlightenment, Christian values, and cosmopolitanism. But this war was not only fought by means of arrests, executions, and concentration camps. It is certainly no coincidence that Heinrich Himmler saw his organization as a National Socialist equivalent to the Jesuit order, which, after the spread of Protestantism in the 1500s, functioned as the spearhead of the Catholic Counter-Reformation. According to Himmler's view of the world, the SS would in the same way form a bastion against the enemies of Nazi ideology. The danger of taking a one-sided perspective on the Nazis' relationship to knowledge is that it risks obscuring something even more dangerous: The desire of totalitarian ideology to rule not only over people but also their thoughts. There is a tendency to view the Nazis as unhinged destroyers of knowledge. It is also true that many libraries and archives were lost while under the control of the regime, either through systematic destruction or indirectly as a consequence of war. Despite this, a question that needs to be asked in the shadow of Himmler's library is the following: What is more frightening, a totalitarian regime's destruction of knowledge or its hankering for it?

# 5

# A WARRIOR AGAINST JERUSALEM

## *Chiemsee*

*The holy hour for Germans will be at hand when the symbol of their reawakening—the flag with the swastika—has become the only true confession of faith in the Reich.*

—Alfred Rosenberg

With a soft, swaying shudder the ferry leaves its berth in the harbor below the village of Prien. I have taken a seat at the far end of the stern, on the sundeck, so I can get a good view. The deck has quickly filled with retirees in neon-colored clothes and school-age adolescents sitting on top of each other, vying to get a place in the sun. Hundreds of small white dinghies on the lake are doing their best to catch the faint breeze. I have traveled southeast on the train from Munich for an hour, to where the agricultural landscape begins to be replaced by rolling foothills and then gradually by valleys and mountains—the Bavarian heartland, with its half-timbered houses, green hills, and snowcapped Alps. Halfway between Munich and Berchtesgaden, where Adolf Hitler had his mountain retreat, Berghof, lies Lake Chiemsee. A large, clear blue lake fed by meltwater from the Alps, it is sometimes known as the Bavarian Sea. Stephan Kellner from the Bayerische Staatsbibliothek pointed out on my map the place I have come to visit, a place on the opposite side of Chiemsee.

We have not yet left the bay surrounding Prien, but the view is already striking. At the south end of the lake lies that part of the Alps known as the Chiemgauer Alpen, whose peaks reach more than a mile into the sky. Beyond them lies Austria. After a short crossing the ferry docks at Herreninsel, the largest island in Chiemsee. The retirees and students disembark and walk ashore on a long, skeletal jetty to make their way to the island's noteworthy spot, Herrenchiemsee.

The palace was erected at the end of the 1800s by the psychologically unstable King Ludvig II of Bavaria as a more or less identical copy of Louis XIV's Versailles, though of lesser dimensions. Ludvig II died before the palace was completed, and the work was immediately abandoned because of the fantastical sums the king had already spent on it. For my own part, I have come to see another lunatic's project by the Chiemsee, which also never came to fruition—a building of which not a single stone was ever laid. This is probably the reason for my remaining on the ferry on my own while the disembarking elderly ladies, slowly but filled with anticipation, wander off toward Herrenchiemsee, immersed in their guidebooks' descriptions of the Hall of Mirrors and the world's largest chandelier in Meissen porcelain.

After the ferry has rounded Herreninsel, the vista opens up, and I can see across to the lake's far shore. At the same time, I also have a view of the site of this invisible monument, between the village of Chieming in the south and Seebruck by the north shore of the lake, where a promontory juts out. The spot for Alfred Rosenberg's university project, Hohe Schule der NSDAP, was carefully chosen. The motorway undulates along Chiemsee's southern shore and the Chiemgau foothills, a connection of the eastern and western regions of south Germany. Construction of the road was begun in 1934 as a part of the extensive motorway system, the Reichsautobahn, that would connect all of Germany by asphalt.

After the annexation of Austria in 1938, the motorway began to be extended to Vienna, as a way of binding together the sister kingdom. For all who traveled south on this road, the building would have been visible as soon as the Chiemsee came into view. Despite the university never having been built, it is still possible to envisage how it would have looked to a contemporary. The architect's drawings and photographs of the model are preserved in the Library of Congress in Washington.[1] Rosenberg commissioned Hermann Giesler—along with Albert Speer, Nazi Germany's most renowned architect—to design the building. The drawings and models indicate that it would have been a monumental complex, with several interconnected buildings. What immediately stands out is the entrance to the main building, where a tower almost like a high-rise block rises four times higher than the wings. The upper-most part of the tower is formed as a classical temple. It is an example of the dominant architectural style of the Third Reich, a new classicism conveyed in monumental, almost brutal proportions. The buildings were intended to impress and intimidate the observer into submission.

"Hohe Schule shall one day be a center for National Socialist and ideological research and thinking," Adolf Hitler declared.[2]

Although the building was never constructed, another aspect of the Hohe Schule project was certainly implemented. After all, the school on the eastern shore of Chiemsee was merely the architectural manifestation, the physical shell of an ideological research project that had been set in motion long before.

Alfred Rosenberg would turn out to be Heinrich Himmler's foremost competitor in terms of ideological production, research, and education. The two men slugged it out in an intense battle for Europe's libraries and archives. Their two respective organizations ran extensive plundering operations during the war, with special commando units and local offices established from the Atlantic coast in the west to Volgograd in the east, from Spitzbergen in the north to Greece and Italy in the south. Just as the activities in RSHA's Section VII were influenced by the disposition of their chief and his view of the world, the various research and library projects under the auspices of Rosenberg's organization, Amt Rosenberg, would also prove to be a reflection of his. Himmler and Rosenberg competed to be the primary ideological fountainheads of the movement, but their ideas and outlook were different to a certain degree. While Himmler was drawn to mythological and even occult-inspired ideas, Rosenberg had a fanatical obsession with what he regarded as the Jewish global conspiracy. When it came to ideological production, Rosenberg's ambitions were comparatively more serious and ambitious.

Hohe Schule was a grandiose attempt to lay down the foundations of an entirely new kind of science and a new sort of scientist. The National Socialist view of science would encompass and permeate all the disciplines—and be constructed on the understanding that there was a unique and race-specific "German science."

But possibly Alfred Rosenberg's most important project was his attempt to give National Socialist ideology a philosophical framework that might lend the movement a certain amount of recognition both in Germany and internationally.[3] When the Nazis came to power in 1933, they did not possess a movement with a fully evolved ideological approach; the National Socialist movement included a diverse collection of varying and often contradictory opinions and groups, from conservative nationalists to fanatical race ideologists. There were veins of socialism and, in the Nazi union movement, syndicalist tendencies. The party leadership included both regressive nostalgics and others with a comparatively modern outlook on the world that, to a certain extent, also included an acceptance of artistic modernism.

On their way to power, the Nazi Party had absorbed a series of other far-right movements and organizations. Large numbers of its membership had earlier been members of other radical right-wing parties, only to abandon these when the NSDAP became the dominant force. Different forces and groups within the movement were constantly trying to pull the party in various political directions. Apart from a few hardened positions, National Socialism was undeveloped and therefore malleable. Throughout the period of the Third Reich there were political differences in the party, but these grew less significant with the passage of time, and the overall tolerance for diversity diminished. The immutable core that held together this untidy political movement was basically Adolf Hitler himself and the principle of leadership that had taken form with the Führer. It was the so-called Führer Principle—blind and absolute obedience to the leader—that was the most important pillar of the ideology.

The principle in question was based on a conception of Germans, without a charismatic leader, as merely an ungovernable and shapeless mass; only once they were firmly subordinated to the Führer were they transformed into a unified people with a goal and a direction to get there. According to this idea, the leader gained his legitimacy as the embodiment of the inner will of the people, their spirit and their soul. Democracy, on the other hand, was guided by popular will and was nothing but a corrupt rule of the mob, like a herd of sheep without a shepherd.

Without the leadership principle the movement would have been fragmented by internal rifts and, most likely, would never even have united in the first place. Factions, organizations, and leaders within the party were constantly fighting, the conflicts ranging from questions of how to define a Jew to discussions on German expressionism. In the final analysis it was usually Adolf Hitler, not a clear-cut ideology, who settled the disputes.

As the central figure of the leadership cult, Hitler was turned into an ideological prophet, yet he was by no means always clear in his views. Often he preferred to keep out of ideological battles and even encouraged a measure of controlled rivalry in the movement as a way of playing off the factions against each other.

After coming to power in 1933, the party had to convert its political visions into practical politics. Another challenge was the enormous inflow of new members to the party, the widespread fear being that the political machine would be flooded with opportunists and infiltrators. There was an almost paranoiac conception that such people would dilute "the true vision." Ideological untidiness was therefore viewed in the early 1930s as a growing problem. Robert Ley, the Reichsorganisationsleiter—head of the national organization of the Nazi Party—had already turned to Alfred Rosenberg, complaining about the "serious fragmentation in the movement relating to how the world should be seen."[4] Adolf Hitler also recognized the problem of ideological "fragmentation." How could the party cement its position of power and handle an inflow of members counted in the hundreds of thousands, without losing its ideological soul? For this reason, in 1934 he put Alfred Rosenberg in charge of the party's spiritual and ideological development and education. Rosenberg's official title was Beauftragter des Führers für die gesamte geistige und weltanschauliche Erziehung der NSDAP, or the Führer's Representative for All Spiritual and Ideological Research in the NSDAP. An organization was set up in the same year in Berlin, by the name of Dienststelle Rosenberg (Section Rosenberg); however, Amt Rosenberg would later be used as an umbrella name for the various projects, titles, and organizations of Alfred Rosenberg for the party.

What had most of all consolidated Rosenberg's position as the chief ideologue was his philosophical work, *The Myth of the Twentieth Century*, published in 1930. He had also gathered around him a network of researchers, ideologues, race experts, and philosophers, often far more gifted than he was—their purpose to help build up, establish, and safeguard the ideological legacy of National Socialism.

Rosenberg's position as an ideologue was based on his status as one of the movement's "old warhorses" that had survived, both literally and in a political sense. Rosenberg's survival was partly due to his loyalty to Hitler, but also to the fact that he never posed any real threat to the latter's standing in the party. Rosenberg was not engaged in realpolitik, he was actually more of a fanatical idealist: "It was Rosenberg's tragedy that he really believed in National Socialism," wrote the German historian Joachim Fest.[5]

◆　◆　◆

In February 1917, Alfred Rosenberg, then twenty-four years old, was living in an apartment block about an hour outside Moscow. A few years earlier he had begun studying architecture at the Technical University in Reval, now known as Tallinn. When in 1915 the Russian front had started threatening Estonia, the university with its students and teachers had quickly been evacuated to the interior of the Russian imperial nation. In 1917 Alfred Rosenberg was getting close to graduating, and he spent his days reading Goethe, Dostoyevsky, Balzac, and Indian philosophy. The serious and introspective scholar seems to have been utterly unaware of the social tensions in imperial Russia, and the violent revolutionary wave that was about to break over the country. "At the end of February came news about strikes and bread riots, and then one day it happened—the revolution."[6]

At first, Rosenberg was enthused by the atmosphere; he even went into Moscow and joined the hundreds of thousands of people that thronged the streets in a general state of "hysterical joy." He describes in his memoirs his sense of relief at the "corrupt" tsarist regime having fallen at last. But once the joyful celebrations were replaced by anarchy, disintegration, and Bolsheviks, his feelings began to be replaced by something else.[7] One day in the summer of 1917, the year of the revolution, while he was sitting in his room studying, an unknown man came in and put a book on his table. Written in Russian, which Rosenberg spoke fluently, the book proved to be the proceedings of a secret Jewish conference allegedly held in 1897: *The Protocols of the Elders of Zion*. For Rosenberg, this document was to have pivotal importance. As far as he was concerned, it showed the real background to the fall of the tsar. The revolution was not instigated by German workers and the peasants rising up against the oppressive tsar, but was in fact part of a global conspiracy that had been planned by the Jews.

In the 1800s there had been waves of pogroms directed at the large Jewish population of imperial Russia. The tsarist regime had publicly condemned the attacks on Jews, while secretly both supporting and encouraging them, as a desperate political measure of using anti-Semitism to unify a multicultural and ethnically diverse empire on the verge of breaking up. By directing the hatred against the Jews, there was the hope that the real problems could be hidden. The instigators of the pogroms tended to be anti-Semitic, nationalist groups that regarded Jews as "revolutionary" elements.

The Russian extreme right began at an early stage to exploit "Jewish revolutionaries" in its propaganda, and this left a highly influential legacy for National Socialism. By the turn of the century, the notorious tsarist secret service, Okhrana, had produced a document that was widely distributed in Germany between the wars, the very same document that ended up in young Rosenberg's hands in 1917. *The Protocols of the Elders of Zion* purported to show the minutes of a secret conference held at the end of the 1800s, in which a group of influential Jews, known as the Elders of Zion, swore an oath to take command of the world. By infiltration and corruption, the Jews would enlist the help of others, including capitalists, liberals, Freemasons, and Communists, to control the world while remaining out of sight.

For Rosenberg, reading the document was a decisive moment in his life. He was himself a part of the ruling minority that perceived itself as threatened by the revolution. He had grown up in Reval and was a

Baltic German, the German minority that had dominated this region since the Middle Ages through the Teutonic order of knights and the Hanseatic League. The cities were controlled by a German bourgeoisie, while the countryside was dominated by German landed gentry, which had for many years controlled a largely feudal class of Baltic and Slavic peasants. The Baltic Germans regarded themselves as custodians of a higher culture than that of their neighbors. As so often happens with émigré communities, the image of the home country was both cherished and romanticized, a concept known as *Heimat*. For Alfred Rosenberg, Germany was a dream, a fantasy, a society of idealized people steeped in the spirit of Schiller and Goethe. Weimar classicism was at the very core of Baltic German identity.

Rosenberg's growing up in multi-ethnic tsarist Russia would play a decisive role in his subsequent thinking. The concept of the superiority of Aryans, the Jewish-Bolshevik conspiracy, and the given right of Germans to expand eastward were all products of his background. Later, in *The Myth of the Twentieth Century*, he would argue that Russia had everything to thank its Aryan invaders for: Vikings, the Hanseatic League, and Baltic Germans. Without their presence in history, Russia would have fragmented into chaos and anarchy just as it did after the revolution of 1917.[8]

*The Protocols of the Elders of Zion* would confirm the ideas and misconceptions with which the young Baltic German was already encumbered. As a devoted adherent of high Germanic culture, he had already read one of the most influential works of that time—which he would later even attempt to transcribe into a National Socialist version— Houston Stewart Chamberlain's *Die Grundlagen des neunzehnten Jahrhunderts* (The Foundations of the Nineteenth Century).

Chamberlain, a British cultural philosopher, had been seduced by German culture in his youth while studying in Geneva. He settled in Bayreuth and married Eva von Bülow-Wagner, Wagner's stepdaughter. In his magnum opus, published in two volumes around the turn of the nineteenth century and running to a length of some fourteen hundred pages, Chamberlain tried to build a bridging argument that united German cultural idealism with the Aryan racial myth. For reference, he relied on the most important race ideologist of the 1800s, the French count and diplomat Arthur de Gobineau and his historical-philosophical work, *Essai sur l'inégalité des races humaines* (Essay on the Inequality of the Human Races). Gobineau attempted, much as Carl von Linnaeus had done in the botanical kingdom, to divide humanity into various races. He believed that it was not economics that functioned as the prime mover of history—rather it was the racial struggle.[9]

According to Gobineau, the different races were irreconcilable, and the greatest threat to Western society was interbreeding between races—the noble blood of Aryans being diluted with that of people of lower standing. As he saw it, the calls in the 1800s for social reform, democracy, and equality were signs that this fall was imminent. Humanity would henceforth be thrown into a more bestial state of being, incapable of refined culture. Gobineau's apocalyptic vision of the rapidly approaching fall of man made a deep impression on Chamberlain. In his own work, a half century later, he would fix upon the Jews as the cause of this disintegration, a view that had already been proposed by his father-in-law in the pamphlet *Judaism in Music*, in which Wagner suggested that the Jews, by infiltrating Western culture, had started to break down the true culture rooted in the people.[10] In *The Foundations of the Nineteenth Century*, Houston Stewart Chamberlain attempted a fusion of Gobineau's race theory with Wagner's anti-Semitism, while taking the ideas one step further. In Chamberlain's universe the Germans and Jews were opposing poles, fighting a historical battle between good and evil. The tall, blond, and blue-eyed Germans were inherently infused with ideals such as duty, freedom, and faithfulness. The Jews represented the opposite of this, especially in their drive to destroy what was pure and beautiful.

Alfred Rosenberg came to regard himself as the inheritor of Chamberlain's ideas. He was also able to offer more tangible solutions to the "Jewish question." According to his own version of events, he had begun his work on *The Myth of the Twentieth Century* as early as the summer of 1916, when he rented a house with his young wife, Hilda, in Skhodnya, outside Moscow.[11]

Like many other Baltic Germans, Rosenberg hoped that the German

army would liberate Estonia from the Bolsheviks, a wish that was fulfilled in February 1918. However, the hopes of the Baltic Germans to
be united with their *Heimat* were dashed no sooner than they had presented themselves, when the German Empire imploded in November
1918. That same month Alfred Rosenberg made the decision to abandon his home country and go back to what he regarded as his spiritual
fatherland.[12] Before leaving at the end of November, he held his first
public speech in Reval's city hall on the subject that would come to define him as a politician: the Jewish question and the connection between the Jews and Marxism.

Like many other Baltic emigrants, Rosenberg settled in Munich,
where several of his friends already lived. Munich's extreme-right circles proved a good breeding ground for Rosenberg's Jewish-Bolshevik
conspiracy theory. Rosenberg, who wanted to write about his Russian
experiences, soon came into contact with Dietrich Eckart, a playwright, journalist, and something of a key figure in extreme-right circles
in Munich. According to Rosenberg, his first words to Eckart were
"Are you in need of a warrior against Jerusalem?"[13]

Soon Rosenberg joined Eckart's obscure political party, the NSDAP—
he was one of its first members. It was also in Eckart's home that he met, for
the first time, a thirty-year-old ex-corporal by the name of Adolf Hitler. According to Rosenberg, they spoke of how Bolshevism had the same degen-
erative effect on the nation as Christianity had once had on the Roman
Empire. Neither of the men ever openly admitted to being at all influenced
by the other, and throughout their friendship the two ideologues found it
difficult to exchange any sort of positive recognition.

Long afterward, Hitler commented that Rosenberg was a Baltic
German with a "terribly elaborate" way of thinking, while on the other
hand Rosenberg could never bring himself to praise *Mein Kampf*.[14] Yet
Hitler did make an indirect admission of Rosenberg's role as one of the
main architects of Nazi ideology when in 1937 he made him the winner
of the newly established *Deutscher Nationalpreis für Kunst und Wissenschaft* (German National Prize for Art and Science). This was an attempt by Nazi Germany to replace the Nobel Prize. Hitler had decreed

that Germans could not accept any Nobel honors after the Peace Prize was awarded in 1935 to Carl von Ossietzky, who was in a German concentration camp. Rosenberg was awarded the new prize "because he helped establish and consolidate the National Socialist global perspective both scientifically and intuitively."[15]

The actual influence of Rosenberg on ideological development has been the subject of an ongoing debate among historians since the Second World War. His importance as a figure in the regime has been perceived in a variety of ways, depending on trends in historical research. After the war he was viewed as the demonic brain behind the whole ideology. Later, during the 1960s, his role was diminished when the historical perspective in general pulled back from personality-based descriptions in order to seek out structural and social mechanisms. In the 2000s, Rosenberg has once more come into the spotlight, not least as a consequence of German historian Ernst Piper, whose extensive thesis and biography, *Alfred Rosenberg: Hitler's Chief Ideologue*, suggests that Rosenberg had decisive importance by spreading anti-Semitic propaganda, transforming conspiracy theories into "truths," and establishing ideas in relation to the Jewish-Bolshevik conspiracy in Germany. For these reasons, Piper feels that there are good reasons to designate him as the chief ideologue, which has often been questioned by other historians.

Historians have long held that Hitler was already a convinced anti-Semite and anti-Marxist when he went to Munich—something that seems ripe for reevaluation in modern research. Since the 1990s, more and more historians have pointed to Munich's spiritual and revolutionary climate; that this had a transformative effect on Hitler and made him into a fanatical anti-Semite. This, for instance, is the claim that the historian Volker Ullrich makes in his major publication from 2013, *Adolf Hitler: Die Jahres des Aufstiegs* (Adolf Hitler: The Years of Ascension). Based on such a perspective, the more worldly Rosenberg must have been highly influential.[16]

It was very likely either Rosenberg or Eckart who gave Hitler *The Protocols of the Elders of Zion*. The document was as decisive for Hitler as, a few years earlier, it had been for Rosenberg. Not long afterward, Hitler held his first speech on the Jewish-Bolshevik conspiracy in one of the city's beer halls.

The idea of a conspiracy had quite an explosive power at this time. The revolution in Russia and the international revolutionary workers' movement were regarded by many more than right-wing extremists as a threat; in fact, the revolution set the ground shaking under the feet of the bourgeoisie. By designating the revolutionary movement a Jewish conspiracy, as opposed to an expression of the working classes demanding social and economic change, the Nazis gained a legitimacy that went far beyond their narrow circles.

Adolf Hitler eventually made Rosenberg the editor in chief of the party newspaper, the *Völkischer Beobachter*, a position he would hold until 1937.

Rosenberg, who had found his life's mission, threw himself into Munich's far-right circles with fanatical productivity. During the 1920s there was a veritable stream of essays, anthologies, and books penned by Rosenberg, most of which were a variation on a single theme: Jews. Among these was *Die Protokolle der Weisen von Zion und die jüdische Weltpolitik*, an edition of *The Protocols of the Elders of Zion* with his commentary. It was not the first German-language edition, but Rosenberg's book sold very well and was reprinted three times in one year. Two years later, Adolf Hitler used the text as a foundation for his anti-Semitic attacks in *Mein Kampf*. The original document had already been exposed as a forgery, which Hitler dismissed as Jewish propaganda: "It is absolutely irrelevant from what Jew's lips these revelations come; the most important thing is that they reveal, with horrifying certainty, the essential nature of the Jewish people."[17] Joseph Goebbels, who for his own part was convinced of the counterfeit nature of the *Protocols*, expressed in his diaries a more pragmatic approach, which would become commonplace in the movement, that he believed in "the innate but not factually based truth of the *Protocols*."[18]

In 1930 came the book that more than any other would cement Alfred Rosenberg's position as the chief Nazi ideologue: *The Myth of the Twentieth Century*. Rosenberg, just as Houston Stewart Chamberlain had tried to do a few decades earlier, wanted to create a philosophy of his own time. But he was also attempting to solve a problem.

National Socialism lacked a real philosophical foundation. The Nazis did not in any real sense have a Karl Marx or a "sacred text" on which to base themselves. Admittedly *Mein Kampf* had been accorded almost biblical status in Nazi Germany, but unlike Marx and Engels, Hitler had not created a fundamental or timeless philosophical system that could still be applied fifty or a hundred years after his death. Hitler liked to speak of the Thousand-Year Reich, but in *Mein Kampf* he was mainly busy with day-to-day business: the Weimar Republic, Jews, the Versailles Treaty, Bolsheviks, and expansion to the east. These were political challenges that could be resolved in his own lifetime. But what would happen after that? Rosenberg wanted to fill this vacuum.

*The Myth of the Twentieth Century* did not have the same political firepower as *Mein Kampf*; it was both elaborate, puffed up in its use of language, and in many ways just as "terribly elaborate" as Hitler had described its author. Its cornerstone was almost banal in its simplicity: the eternal battle between good (Aryans) and evil (Jews). This battle ran like a defining red line through Western history. On this point Rosenberg did not part ways greatly from Chamberlain; the only operative difference was that Rosenberg would make the racial myth politically useful.

It was not so much the foundations of a new philosophy that Rosenberg wanted to lay down; it was rather a new religion. The solemn language of the book, almost like something out of the Old Testament, was a deliberate device. Rosenberg wanted to evoke a prophecy, a race theory based on a mystical framework, writing, "Today a new religion stirs and wakes—the myth of blood; the belief in the defense of blood is the same as defending man's divine nature." According to Rosenberg, "Nordic blood" had begun to be victorious at long last, and it would replace "the old sacraments."[19]

Like Chamberlain, Rosenberg felt that the races had inherited attributes, and the love of freedom, honor, creativity, and a true sense of consciousness could only exist in the "Nordic races." The foremost of these was "the heroic will." It was by recourse to this idea that the new

German would be formed, a heroic man tied to his earth through blood—ready to sacrifice himself in a heroic death. Between the two racial extremes, Aryans and Jews, Rosenberg went on to make subdivisions of other peoples such as Arabs, Chinese, Mongols, black people, and Indians, in each case scrutinizing their moral characteristics and creative achievements. Admittedly the Arabs had created the lovely arabesque, but "this is not true architecture, merely handicraft."[20] In cases where "Nordic attributes" appeared in other races, it was because of imitation or interbreeding with Nordic blood. Jews, on the other hand, lacked all capacity to form a higher culture "because Jewishness, as a totality, lacks a soul from which higher virtues can spring."[21]

The blood myth was not an individualistic belief, because Aryan blood was connected to a higher collective "racial soul." This was the soul that tied all Aryans together: "The racially interconnected soul is the measure of all our ideas, our will, and our actions." To Rosenberg, individualism was as damaging as universalism. "A human being in his own right is nothing; he only acquires a personality once he is integrated in sense and soul with thousands of others of his race." Rosenberg further claimed that the history of philosophy had omitted any consideration of this blood myth because it could not be expressed within a rational system. It was not possible to understand the "racial soul" in a rational, logical way, because "race is untouchable—it is an inner voice, a feeling, a will. Germans have to awaken and listen to the voice of their blood." Rosenberg ended his book with a prophecy about when this would happen: "The holy hour for Germans will be at hand when the symbol of their reawakening—the flag with the swastika— has become the only true confession of faith in the Reich."[22]

◆  ◆  ◆

About a month after Rosenberg had been assigned to lead the party's "spiritual and ideological development and education" in 1934, he held a speech at the Kroll Opera House in Berlin, where the German parliament had moved after the fire in the Reichstag. The country's gauleiters, local Nazi Party leaders from all over Germany, had gathered to hear him. From the podium Rosenberg said, "If we were just satisfied with having power over the state, the National Socialist movement would not have achieved its goal. The political revolution in the state has admittedly been completed, but forging the senses of the intellectual and spiritual human being has only just begun."[23] This was the goal that he had formulated in *The Myth of the Twentieth Century*, which would now be implemented: "It is the great task of our century: on the basis of this new myth of life to create a new human being."[24]

The foremost tool for this spiritual transformation would be the educational system of the Third Reich. Propaganda could affect people, but education could change them at their very foundations. The Nazification of the traditional school system on all levels, from kindergarten to university, was implemented in steps after 1933. The Nazis would come to view the school system as a significant part of the ideological rearmament of the Third Reich, but it was regarded as a long-term goal—a transformation that would shape generations to come.

Some of the first measures were highly predictable. One was to "cleanse" the school system of "Jewish influence," targeting both teachers and pupils. Already on April 25, 1933, a law was introduced to limit the number of Jewish pupils at public schools. Much of this cleansing took place organically by the rejection of Jewish applicants to schools and the firing of Jewish teachers without any explanation. At the universities, Jewish professors were attacked by pro-Nazi student federations, which demanded their resignations. Those who hung on to their jobs faced discrimination and humiliation. Among other things the Berlin student federation demanded that all "Jewish" research should be published only in Hebrew, this being a way of simultaneously banning Jews from the German language while exposing their alleged infiltration.[25] Even teachers that were liberally disposed became targets of this intellectual pogrom. Not only were Jews and freethinkers excluded from the school system, the Nazis also opposed women having access to higher education, which, it was believed, might lead to demands for equality. In the Nazi worldview, the role of women was mainly about producing children for the new "master race."

In 1936, Jewish teachers were banned by law from teaching at public schools, and in 1938 all Jews were barred from the universities—even as students. Nazis and pro-Nazi ideologues were given prominent positions at the most important universities. Many of these were a part of Alfred Rosenberg's circle, including Ernst Krieck and Alfred Baeumler, two of the most important Nazi pedagogues in the Third Reich who were also charged with devising the foundations of the new German school system. The regime gained particular legitimacy from the famous philosopher Martin Heidegger, who in 1933 joined the NSDAP and was made rector of the university in Freiburg.

One of the first large-scale reforms was the centralization of the school system, which, like most things in Germany, had previously been very much decentralized. This was a necessary measure in order to make the education system serve Nazi dogma. Germany had never and would never again be so unified as under the Third Reich—a result of the regime's totalitarian efforts to create "a people."

When the Nazis came to power, the German school and university system was considered the best in the world. No other school system had produced more Nobel Prize winners. By 1933 Germany had won thirty-three Nobel Prizes, while the United States had won only eight. The university in Göttingen, under the prefecture of Niels Bohr, was regarded as the world's leading center of theoretical physics. The problem for the Nazis, however, was that a disproportionately large number of Nobel Prizes had been given to German Jews, such as Albert Einstein, Gustav Hertz, and Paul Heyse.

Just as Chamberlain and Rosenberg had categorized people according to their inherited or racial abilities in art, architecture, and even their general personalities, every race also had its own unique "physics" and "science." The German physician and Nazi, Philipp Lenard, who had won the Nobel Prize in 1905, developed these theories in a four-volume work during the 1930s. Lenard proposed the existence of something he described as "Japanese physics," "Arab physics," "black physics," "English physics," and then "Aryan physics"—the latter the only true one. The most damaging of all was "Jewish physics": "The Jew wants to create contradiction everywhere and dissolve existing relations so absolutely that the poor naïve German cannot find any sense in it at all."[26] Similarly to the cultural sphere, there was a concept that science had fallen into disrepair and created a "fragmented reality," as Education Minister Bernhard Rust put it, this being the work of the corrosive Jews.[27] In other words, relativity theory was too confusing to fit into the totalitarian worldview of the Nazis, who were quite determined to make the fragmented world whole again. Not unexpectedly, Rosenberg was an admirer and protector of Lenard. One positive result of these twisted ideas was the slowing down of Nazi atomic research. Ironically enough, research largely carried out in German universities by Jewish scientists such as Albert Einstein, Niels Bohr, and Robert Oppenheimer ended up giving the United States the first atomic bomb.

Despite the internationally acknowledged excellence of the German school system, Nazification met little internal resistance. One of the reasons for this was the strong Nazi support among teachers and student bodies. As many as a third of all teachers are believed to have backed the Nazis when they came to power, far more than other professions. Teachers had long been viewed by the Nazis as a key group in society, and already in 1929 they had formed an alternative association: the Nationalsozialistische Lehrerbund (National Socialist Teachers League, NSLB), the purpose of which was to prod the teaching body in the appropriate ideological direction. After 1933, the NSLB was the only association of teachers in the Third Reich.

The NSLB became an important tool in the top-to-bottom process that would follow, in the transformation of the philosophical and pedagogical fundamentals of the school system, as well as its values. Schoolbooks were rewritten, subjects were switched, and, above all, brains were indoctrinated.

Just as in the army, teachers were made to swear an oath of allegiance to the Führer. The NSLB, appropriately enough led by a former free corps soldier, Hans Schemm, set up Schulungslager, indoctrination camps where teachers were sent for "retraining." By 1937 there were more than forty such camps. According to one British observer, the most important ideological source materials used there were *Mein Kampf* and writings by Alfred Rosenberg. New subjects were introduced into the school curriculum, such as "racial hygiene." The goal, as Rosenberg put it, was that Nazi ideology should permeate every aspect of the curriculum from history to mathematics.

The teachers effectively became "Führers" in their own classrooms, and many actually chose to go to school in their party uniforms. Under the Nazis, the classroom became a microcosm of the totalitarian state. There was always a portrait of Adolf Hitler, and the school day began and ended with the Hitler salute—in certain cases also the beginning of each lesson. Education in the Third Reich would not only be defined by a school system where the teachers kept their students under surveillance, but also where the students scrutinized their teachers. Teachers expressing "un-German" opinions could be reported by their students to the Hitlerjugend or the Gestapo.

Over the course of the 1930s, while Alfred Rosenberg did not personally lead the reformation of the research and education establishment, he certainly hovered over the entire process like an ideological spirit. Rosenberg had a handbook written, *Ideological Theses*, which briefly described the main foundations of the National Socialist view of the world. The book was intended to form a basic manual for the entire German school system. Education minister Bernhard Rust ensured that every school library in the country had a copy of *The Myth of the Twentieth Century*.[28] The Nazification of the existing school system was never completed in the period of the Third Reich, but one should look at the reforms as embryonic of the totalitarian utopia envisaged by Nazis such as Rosenberg. The new human could only fully come forth among those who were wholly untainted by yesterday's degeneration: in other words, the children.

To form the generation that would lead the Third Reich into the future, the traditional school system was not enough. In order to create a fundamentally new human being, a new kind of school would be required. For this reason, in the 1930s the foundations were laid down for a number of elite schools: NS-Ordensburg and the Adolf Hitler schools. The first Adolf Hitler school was inaugurated on April 20, 1937, on the Führer's birthday. To be accepted by the schools the pupils had to show leadership qualities as well as submit to rigorous racial and medical examination. The teachers of the twelve existing Adolf Hitler schools were usually drawn from the SS, the SA, the Gestapo, or other areas of the Nazi terror machine.

The young boys who underwent this education were later prepared for entry to one of the four Ordensburg schools, which admitted party acolytes between twenty-five and thirty years old; the chosen students were subjected to hard ideological and military training. The training included regular trials of the students' courage, with activities such as parachute jumps, but there were also internships in the machinery of the party. Just as in the SS, a mixture of ruthlessness and intellect was encouraged. "To us, the battle of Leuthen is as much a test of character as *Faust* or Beethoven's Eroica," Alfred Rosenberg proclaimed.[29]

The third and final stage after Adolf Hitler school and Ordensburg would be the Alfred Rosenberg Hohe Schule der NSDAP.[30] The idea was that these young graduates would form the future leadership of the Third Reich. Their schooling would forge them into an ideological "fraternity"—or a Nazi order of knights, if one should wish to put it like that. It was considered necessary to create a "ruling class," and this was how the ideology would be preserved and safeguarded for the Thousand-Year Reich. At the same time these schools were a way of controlling the legacy of the existing leadership.

As some Nazis pointed out, there was a clear problem whenever one attempted to fuse physical and intellectual abilities—after all, the latter so often got the upper hand. Few in the contemporary ruling class were prime physical specimens—Himmler's chin was hardly equal to those displayed by his SS staff. The leadership's racial purity was highly dubious, and often a well-kept secret. When all was said and done, the Nazi elite was a fairly sickly bunch. Göring was corpulent and a morphine user. Goebbels had a clubfoot, and Hitler suffered from chronic stomach complaints and probably, toward the end of his life, Parkinson's disease. The Nazi leadership was less "a brotherhood bound by common oaths" than a pack of wolves ready to launch into one another whenever the chance presented itself. Adolf Hitler had created a Darwinist leadership culture that actually worked surprisingly well in a totalitarian system like the Third Reich, a system where a mixture of cunning, scheming, terror, flattery, disloyalty, bureaucratic skill, and ruthlessness was what took one to the top, as opposed to muscle power or purity of blood. Lost in their Aryan utopia of the new human being, they were incapable of seeing that the way to power in Nazi Germany was anything but heroic.

◆　◆　◆

Rosenberg's greatest hour did not present itself until the end of the 1930s. In the early years, Amt Rosenberg was an organization only in name, with a modest office near Tiergarten and a small number of employees. But slowly and successively, Rosenberg managed to take over more and more areas of responsibility. As the head of ideology he had the possibility of interfering in a whole range of departments. Wherever he saw operations slipping up in their observance of ideological discipline, he was there with his pointer. The fact that he was still the editor in chief of the *Völkischer Beobachter*, which he was more than willing to exploit in his ideological battles, made it difficult for other Nazi leaders to entirely ignore this pretentious Baltic German.

Amt Rosenberg functioned as a think tank, conducting ideological surveillance, lobbying, and research. There were departments for ecclesiastical issues, the visual arts, music, education, theater, literature, ancient history, Jews, and Freemasons. A special department started in 1934 for scientific questions was overseen by Alfred Baeumler, who set out the foundations of an entirely new sort of scientist. "Science is not a product of superficial intellect, but rather a creation that has arisen in the depths of the heroic intellect," said Alfred Baeumler in one of his lectures.[31] According to Baeumler, both logic and reason had played out their roles in science, which could only now be driven onward by this heroic intellect. In fact, it was the same old "heroism" that had chimed with Alfred Rosenberg and the free corps writers.

Heroic science was political in its innermost being, which Baeumler illustrated by comparing the new scientist with the old. The traditional type, referred to as "the theoretical man," was characterized by passivity, pure consciousness, and absolute contemplation. The new, "political man," on the other hand, stood out because of his dynamism, direction, and participation. As Baeumler saw it, the scientist should not limit himself to the objective examination of the world; he should actively seek to form it. What he was describing here was a new type of scientist, a willing instrument of the regime—absolutely crucial for giving an aura of scientific legitimacy to the plethora of National Socialist myths, lies, and conspiracy theories.[32]

Rosenberg's high school and research project, Hohe Schule der NSDAP, was given Adolf Hitler's approval in 1937. The embryo for this school had been growing in Amt Rosenberg over a number of years. Plans for a high school were mentioned in the organization's correspondence in 1935. Just as the education of the leaders of the future could not be left to the traditional school system, the future of science had to be similarly nurtured. Hermann Giesler's drawing and model of the new school was shown to Adolf Hitler, who personally examined and approved it. It is also Hitler who decided that it should be built on the eastern shore of Chiemsee. Hohe Schule der NSDAP, like all the other Nazi elite schools, was to be under direct party control.

From a broader perspective, the Hohe Schule would above all serve the purpose that had been Alfred Rosenberg's life's work: the creation of philosophical and scientific cornerstones for National Socialism. Rosenberg felt that he had identified the weak point of the movement. Even if the Nazi Party had devoted itself to breeding a new ruling class that would later take over power, this was far from a guaranteed future for the movement. Rosenberg was painfully aware that ultimately it was the Führer Principle, not National Socialism in its own right, that held the Third Reich together. Adolf Hitler would not be able to lead the movement forever, as Rosenberg pointed out in a speech as early as 1934. Therefore, he said, it was "our will that the National Socialist movement should lay down the structures that will preserve this state for hundreds of years ahead."[33]

People evolve, change, and die, but ideas are immortal. In the end, it was only a strong ideological foundation that could guarantee the continuance of the Thousand-Year Reich. The Nazis had to create structures

that were ideologically strong enough to survive the passage of time—
and above all the death of the Führer. Alfred Rosenberg's vision was that
Hohe Schule der NSDAP, described as "National Socialism's foremost
center for research, education, and teaching," would function as a cornerstone of this ideological cathedral.

# 6

# CONSOLATION FOR THE TRIBULATIONS OF ISRAEL

## *Amsterdam*

Wout Visser carefully places a small brown box on the table and opens the lid, then takes out a light brown, leather-bound book with worn edges.

The cover, decorated in a printed pattern of foliage within a rectangular shape, reveals little about its contents. It looks like a small and not especially rare book from the turn of the last century, something that could fairly easily be found in a secondhand bookshop—apart from the distinguishing feature of an almost half-inch hole near the top left corner of the book. There's a cavity of a fingertip's width where the leather has given way. Carefully I open the book; I notice that the hole has not only penetrated the cover but continued through the flyleaf, where it has consumed the name of the author—the Portuguese-Jewish writer Samuel Usque. Holding the book against the light admitted by the high windows, I see that the hole has cut all the way to the last page of the book, the pressure making the paper dented and cracked. The twisted bullet has made a coppery tint; wedged on its side, the slug has remained in this exact position for the last seventy years.

"This book was stolen along with the rest of the library and brought to Germany by the Nazis. We actually believe the bullet was discharged in Germany," says Wout Visser, a man in his forties, with suspenders to hold up his trousers and the vague hint of a goatee. He is a librarian and researcher in the special collections section of the Amsterdam University Library, housed in a three-story brick building by the beautiful Singel canal. We are sitting in the reading room of one of the university's best-known collections, the Bibliotheca Rosenthaliana, to which "the book with the bullet," as Visser describes it, belongs.

The book has taken on an almost mythical status in the Rosenthaliana collection, giving rise to a number of theories as to who really shot at the book. A forensic examination of the bullet has only deepened the mystery, for it was not fired from a German rifle but actually from an English-manufactured submachine gun. It has even been possible to trace where this is likely to have taken place, twelve miles or so north of Frankfurt in the little town of Hungen.

Only a few hours before my visit to Rosenthaliana I arrived at Amsterdam Centraal station, after a seven-hour train journey from Munich via Frankfurt and Cologne. What struck me on the way here was the ease of crossing the border between Germany and the Netherlands. There are no natural boundaries here, such as the forested and mountainous Ardennes and Alps to the south. By comparison, the Flemish lowlands are as flat as a motorway, a fact of which Hitler and his generals were highly aware. The Netherlands had declared itself neutral when the war broke out in 1939. The country had managed to keep out of the First World War, when the German army chose to pass through Belgium. As the Germans saw it, with hindsight, this had been a serious military and strategic error, because the German army was held up longer than had been expected by a ferocious Belgian defense. Hitler had no intention of repeating the mistake. The Netherlands lay on the Wehrmacht's route to Paris, and this was what sealed the country's fate in May 1940, as well as that of Rosenthaliana and many more of Amsterdam's renowned libraries.

The city's libraries upheld a unique culture, formed by the religious, intellectual, and economic freedoms that had been the very hallmarks of the sea-trading city since the Middle Ages. Calvinists, Baptists, Quakers, Huguenots, as well as intellectuals and freethinkers, had found their way to the free city by the river Amstel. Two groups of refugees in particular had put their mark on the city and its libraries: Ashkenazi Jews who had fled pogroms in the East, and Sephardic Jews forced out of the Iberian Peninsula. In the 1500s, Amsterdam was one of the few places in Western Europe where Jews could live in relative freedom, which had resulted in the city being named Jeruzalem van het Westen (Jerusalem of the West).

The immigrants were to play an important role in the emergence of

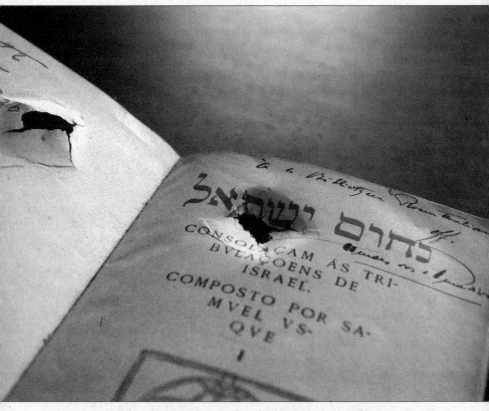

*Samuel Usque's* Consolation for the Tribulations of Israel, *the mysterious bullet-damaged book at the Bibliotheca Rosenthaliana in Amsterdam. The bullet is believed to have been fired in Germany, where the plundered library was taken.*

Holland as an international power during the 1600s. The city's commercial life was of especial importance, and the foundation of its power. Amsterdam became the birthplace of an economic revolution. The world's first multinational company, the Dutch East India Company, came into being here, as well as the beginnings of the world's first modern stock exchange and one of the world's first national banks.

Thanks to these new institutions, the Netherlands in the 1600s was dominant in world trade and especially the spice trade with Asia. The rapid rise of the Sephardic Jews in international trade was facilitated by their already established trading network with the Spanish-speaking Americas, and before long also with Asia. But it was also a consequence of a guild system that barred entry to newcomers. This led to many of the Sephardic Jews devoting themselves to the new economy, which before long proved considerably more profitable.[1] Some of the largest fortunes in the city were built up by these immigrants, and as a direct consequence of this, also some of its foremost libraries.

Amsterdam's freedoms not only served minorities, they also helped printers. Freedom and trade transformed the Netherlands into Europe's intellectual center in the 1600s, a hub for the dissemination of new, exciting, and dangerous ideas made possible by the printing press. Freethinkers, writers, philosophers, and religious minorities found their way to the city, where they could publish what in other parts of Europe would have led to excommunication and persecution. From Amsterdam, their works could be printed and then shipped all over the Continent with the help of the world's largest merchant fleet.

The Dutch government's tolerance had less to do with idealism than sheer economics. Few were concerned about what was being printed, as long as someone was willing to pay, and the sale of ideas was very good business for the trading empire. And in addition to freethinkers, Amsterdam's printers also served totalitarian rulers and religious fanatics. Peter the Great of Russia gave one printer in Amsterdam a fifteen-year monopoly on the printing of all Russian literature. Like many other monarchs in Europe, he feared the dangerous printers, and wanted to keep them at a safe distance from Russia. In the 1600s Amsterdam became known as "Europe's publisher."[2]

Amsterdam also became a center for Jewish literature during the 1600s, when Menasseh ben Israel became the first Jew to establish a Hebrew printing press in the Netherlands, his parents having fled the Inquisition in Portugal. Menasseh was much more than a printer; he was a writer, a rabbi, and a diplomat with an international network of contacts. It was Menasseh who personally convinced Oliver Cromwell to let the Jews return to England in the 1650s—from where they had been expelled at the end of the 1200s. He was also the teacher of the philosopher Baruch Spinoza and a friend of Rembrandt van Rijn. Menasseh ben Israel's press and other presses supplied Jewish minorities all over Europe with cheap books.[3]

"We have a more or less complete collection of the books printed by Menasseh ben Israel in the 1600s. I think there's just a handful of them missing. But we also have books from a number of Amsterdam's other Jewish printers. No other library in the world owns a collection like this," says Visser, gesturing at the bookcases that surround us in the reading room of Rosenthaliana. On the shelves are a representative selection of the collection with a focus on history, religion, and philosophy. But what can be seen here is only a fraction of the library, which comprises some 100,000 books, as well as thousands of Jewish journals, pamphlets, manuscripts, and archive material. The oldest of them are manuscripts about Jewish festivals, religious events, and legends from the 1200s. Among the rarities are the first book ever printed in Istanbul, an incunabulum from 1493: *Arbaab Turim* by Rabbi Jakob Ben Asher, a work on fourteenth-century Jewish law printed by Sephardic Jews who had been expelled in 1492 and settled in the Ottoman Empire. Prints up to the year 1500 are considered incunabula, because after this time the printing was done with loose letters. Many of these books often only existed in a single copy or at most a few copies. It is believed that in the region of 150 editions of books in Hebrew were printed before 1500, of which 34 can be found at Rosenthaliana. The collection also includes handwritten copies from the 1400s of the Arab philosopher Averroes's commentary on the scientific writings of Aristotle.[4]

Despite the collection today being very much slanted to the history of the Jews in the Netherlands, the library originally hails from Germany.

"Its origin is with Leeser Rosenthal in the mid-1800s. He was a Polish-born rabbi working in Hannover for the rich families of the city, which gave him the opportunity of building up his collection at this time. He collected books on the history of the German Jews, religious writings, and the Jewish Enlightenment," Visser tells me.

The Jewish Enlightenment, or Haskalah, was an intellectual movement among Jews that had been inspired by the French Enlightenment. The founding figure was the German Jewish figure Moses Mendelssohn, who attempted a synthesis of Jewish religiosity with the philosophical rationalism of the time. The movement encouraged Jews to break with their cultural isolation and assimilate into European societies by learning new languages and adopting new professions in science and art.

Rosenthal's collection ended up in the Netherlands after his death in 1868, because his son moved to Amsterdam.

"When Rosenthal died, his family tried to sell the collection, but no one wanted to buy it. It was offered to the German chancellor Otto von Bismarck, to be housed in the Kaiserliche und Königliche Bibliothek in Berlin. But he declined," says Visser.

Rosenthal's collection was considered at this time to be one of the finest Jewish private collections in Germany. The library consisted of six thousand volumes and a collection of manuscripts. In 1880 the family decided that they would donate the collection to Amsterdam's university. The family also offered to pay for a librarian, which they continued to do until the outbreak of the First World War, when they ruined themselves after some investments in the Hungarian railroad network.

The collection grew quickly after being established in Amsterdam, where it was complemented with literature on the Netherlands' Jews. By the time of the Second World War the library had multiplied many times over. "Some of Amsterdam's private Jewish collectors hid their books in Rosenthaliana in the hope that they could be saved there. We think some of their books are still here, but we can't find them," says Visser, who a few years ago was asked to track down the missing collections.

The library's chief librarian, Herman de la Fontaine Verwey, who had good contacts with Amsterdam's collectors, was responsible for this clandestine storage of books.

"Fontaine Verwey wrote about one case when a collector 'donated' his library. If he returned he would have his collection back, otherwise it would accrue to the library. This was just one case. But we have never been able to find these contracts, I believe they were destroyed after the war, when there was an assumption that the owners would never come back."

Of Amsterdam's Jewish population of eighty thousand people, only about a fifth survived the Holocaust.

"After the war, Fontaine Verwey was highly secretive about this matter; it was never clarified how many of these books were left in the collection. I have to admit that I have failed in my investigations. He took his secret with him into the grave, and it is now part of the dark history of this library," says Visser.

Visser opens Rosenthaliana's ledger from 1940. After the Nazi invasion of the Netherlands in May, new books continued to be cataloged for another six months. On November 18, 1940, someone made an entry for *Hebrew Education in Palestine* by Eliezer Rieger, one of the founders of the Hebrew University in Jerusalem. The book was bought for 2.65 guldens. It is the last entry, and after it there is nothing but empty lines. No new books were cataloged in the following six years. On that day, the reading room of Bibliotheca Rosenthaliana was closed by the SD. Jews working for the library, the majority of the employees, were immediately fired without notice. One of them was the library's curator, Louis Hirschel, who wrote dejectedly in a letter to a friend, "This has meant a temporary end to the outstanding history of Rosenthaliana."[5]

◆ ◆ ◆

A few hundred yards from the Bibliotheca Rosenthaliana, by the Keizersgracht canal, stands a three-story white stone house. Judging by the black-and-white photographs from the 1930s that I have found, the house has not changed in any significant respect. Today it holds an institute for media and art. Keizersgracht 264 is neither the oldest nor the most beautiful house along the canal, but it is sitting on a most remarkable story.

During the 1930s this house was the epicenter for one of the most important rescue operations in the history of archives and historical research. Paradoxically, within a few years the same house was being used as one of the hubs of the greatest-ever thieving operation of archive materials and books.

In June 1940, just a few weeks after the capitulation of the Netherlands, staff from the SD came to Keizersgracht to seal off the white house. The decision was not made by coincidence. The building was the home of the Internationaal Instituut voor Sociale Geschiedenis (IISG)—the International Institute of Social History. It was founded in 1935 by Nicolaas Wilhelmus Posthumus, the country's first professor of economic history at the Nederlandsche Handelshogeschool. The purpose of the institute was to collect, or rather to save, archive material from left-wing movements such as trade unions and Socialist parties, but also from important private collections.

Today, IISG is situated in Amsterdam's east harbor, in a modern office building that, from a distance, looks as if it is made of recycled cardboard. At the entrance I meet Huub Sanders, a researcher at the institute. He explains that it was his involvement in the left-wing student movement of the 1970s that first got him involved with the institute. "I got interested in why the Karl Marx Archive was in Amsterdam," says Sanders with a smile. It's a question that goes back to the formation of the institute in the 1930s and its passionate founder Nicolaas Wilhelmus Posthumus. "Posthumus was a man who always looked for primary sources in economic and social history. He started collecting materials relating to the field of economics as early as before the First World War."

It was very much expected that the institute would be the first victim of the Nazis' plundering operation in Holland. Posthumus had founded the institute as a direct answer to advancing fascism in Europe. A torrent of refugees from the Soviet Union, Germany, and Italy had come to Western Europe over the course of the 1930s. With them, they brought valuable documents, archives, and books. Posthumus's vision was, through the creation of the institute, to establish a safe harbor for archives belonging to the Socialists, trade unions, and workers' movements that were being mercilessly hunted both by Fascists and Bolsheviks.

"Posthumus was the right person for the job. He was himself a Socialist. And he had an international network both in political and academic circles. His motivation was that he wanted to save the historical inheritance of the workers' movement," says Sanders while we go into an industrial elevator, which descends into the innards of the ISG. Here, on thousands of feet of dark gray shelving, is the world's biggest archive of social history: in all, it encompasses four thousand separate archives, from Amnesty International, Greenpeace, and the European Trade Union Confederation among others. There are also millions of journals and magazines here. On a shelf, wrapped in brown paper, lie piles of the Swedish journal *Arbetaren* (The Worker) from 1932.

A unique and valuable part of the great archive is what Posthumus, with a small group of coworkers, managed to acquire in a matter of a few years at the end of the 1930s. Sanders shows me to a shelf covered by a light-excluding blind, which he sweeps aside with a dramatic gesture. The documents are lined up on the shelf behind a sheet of glass.

"This is the manuscript of *The Communist Manifesto*," says Sanders, pointing at some bleached papers with tightly written lines of slightly forward-slanted handwriting. Caught off guard, I ask if this is really "the only one."

"I suppose there can only be one," says Sanders, laughing.

The papers, covered in emendations and additions, are close to illegible. But I can make out Karl Marx's signature. Also in evidence are some pages in longhand from *Das Kapital*, a protocol from the First International in 1864, and documents by Leon Trotsky.

The Karl Marx and Friedrich Engels Archive consists of more than five shelf-yards of materials, notes, manuscripts, and extensive correspondence between the two men. The archive was put together by the Social Democratic Party in Germany, and smuggled out of Nazi Germany along with the party archive in 1933. The German Social Democrats, whose assets had been confiscated in Germany, were in financial need, and had no other choice but to sell the archive. The most eager prospective buyer was the Marx-Engels-Lenin Institute in Moscow, in other words Joseph Stalin. Archives that could be traced back to the founder of the ideology were being frenetically collected there.

"They were prepared to pay the most. But thank goodness the party realized it would have been shameful selling it to Stalin. Instead, Posthumus managed to buy it," says Sanders.

Documents from the First International were acquired from the party, along with the archive of the Social Democrats themselves. Posthumus's work to save the Socialists' historical legacy in Europe had been a phenomenal success. From Spain, the archive of the anarcho-syndicalist movement had been taken out of Spain before Catalonia fell to Franco's troops. A number of Socialist archives had also been saved from the Nazis after the annexation of Austria. The private collections were every bit as impressive—the institute had secured the archives of anarchists Mikhail Bakunin and Max Nettlau. Further, important archives from the Russian Revolution had been acquired, belonging to the Socialist Revolutionary Party and the Mensheviks.

Posthumus had also opened branches of the institute in Paris and Oxford. The Paris office had been given an important collection of Leon Trotsky's papers, donated by his son Lev Sedov. In 1936 it became evident that the threat did not only come from the Right, when agents of Stalin's feared security service, the GRU, broke into the Paris office on rue Michelet and stole many of the most important Trotsky documents. But this theft was on a rather modest scale when compared with what lay in store. It had not escaped the regime's attention that the institute had snitched valuable archives right under the nose of Nazi Germany. "In German reports, the institute is described as 'an intellectual center for the Marxist struggle against fascism.' That was why it was considered so important to get their hands on the institute's collections," says Sanders.

For the Nazis, the Marx and Engels Archive was the Holy Grail. As both a Jew and the father of Communism, Marx was considered one of the brains behind the Zionist world conspiracy. Posthumus's institute was also included in this conspiracy, and after its closure a report stated

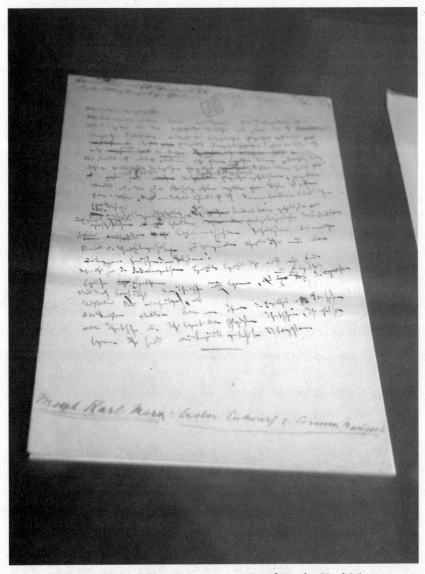

*The first draft of* The Communist Manifesto *by Karl Marx
and Friedrich Engels. The Marx and Engels Archive in Amsterdam was
hunted by the Nazis, but there was time to bring it to safety in England.*

that the invasion of the Netherlands had prevented the emergence of "a powerful, global organization."[6]

Nicolaas Wilhelmus Posthumus's mission of saving the historical records of the European workers' movement came to a tragic and abrupt close in the summer of 1940, when the white house on Keizersgracht 264 was sealed off. Posthumus did not only have his archive stolen from him, he was also relieved of his professorial post. Instead, Alfred Rosenberg's newly formed organization, Einsatzstab Reichsleiter Rosenberg (ERR), moved into the house, which now became the head office of Rosenberg's plundering operations in the Netherlands. Reichsleiter (national leader) was a reference to the rank held by Rosenberg in the Nazi Party, the second-highest rank in the NSDAP. The national leaders formed the top echelon of the party and were only answerable directly to Adolf Hitler.

The ERR was set up in June 1940 as a direct consequence of the successful war on the western front. The outbreak of war had temporarily halted the building plans for the Hohe Schule der NSDAP near Chiemsee. But the preparatory work for the establishment of the school continued, and would even intensify as the hostilities escalated.

Amt Rosenberg's ideological activities, which had previously focused mainly on domestic matters, now grew into an international operation. Until 1939 the Nazis had devoted themselves to fighting their internal enemies, such as German Jews, Socialists, Communists, liberals, Freemasons, and Catholics. This ideological war was now to fan out across Europe in the wake of the Wehrmacht's victorious armies.

The Nazis waged their war on two levels: first, by conventional means, with their armies pitched against others in military conflict, and second, by war against the ideological opposition. The latter was not a conflict that took place on the battlefield; it was rather a silent war of disappearances, terror, torture, murder, and deportation, whose frontline soldiers were the Gestapo, the SD, and other parts of the regime's terror machine. It was a war in which the intention was not to vanquish but to liquidate. On the eastern front, initially in Poland but later also in the Soviet Union, the conventional and ideological wars were fully integrated for the first time, with terrible consequences.

The ideological war was not only waged through the use of terror, for it was also a struggle of thoughts, memories, and ideas, a battle to defend and legitimize the National Socialist vision of the world. In this war, so to speak, the ERR mobilized the academic foot soldiers. The organization was destined never to get involved in the bloody, brutal acts, which were handled by the SS. The ERR only stepped in once these had been concluded. When the organization was formed in the summer of 1940, Alfred Rosenberg had already penciled in a dozen or so academic areas of interest for the Hohe Schule. For him, the Hohe Schule complex by the Chiemsee was merely the architectural manifestation of a project with far loftier ambitions. Hohe Schule stretched out its tentacles like an octopus over the Third Reich, by means of a series of external research institutes located in cities throughout the nation, acting as separate entities under the umbrella of the Hohe Schule. At least ten separate institutes were planned, each with a specific research area:

Munich: The Institute of Indo-European History
Stuttgart: The Institute of Biology and Racial Studies
Halle: The Institute of Religious Studies
Kiel: The Institute of Germanic Research
Hamburg: The Institute of Ideological Colonial Research
Münster and Graz: The Institute of German Folklore
Prague: The Institute of Eastern Studies
Römhild: The Institute of Celtic Studies
Strasbourg: The Institute for the Study of Germanicism and
     Gallicanism
Frankfurt: The Institute for Research on the Jewish Question

The last-mentioned Institut zur Erforschung der Judenfrage, the most extensive of all, was the only one to officially open during the war. Rosenberg opened the institute in Frankfurt in March 1941 with a conference on the Jewish question. The task before the ERR was to secure archives and libraries in occupied territories for later use in the institutes. But there were also plans for an ambitious library at the Hohe Schule: Zentralbibliothek der Hohen Schule. In 1939, Rosenberg had selected Walter Grothe as the director and chief librarian charged with putting together a collection. Grothe was a philologist who had earlier worked at the Rothschildsche Bibliothek in Frankfurt, founded by the Frankfurt branch of the Rothschild family at the end of the 1800s.

He had joined the party in 1931 and, among other things, had worked as a so-called *Parteiredner*, a public speaker who had received rhetorical training from the NSDAP. In a document from October 1941, Grothe provided a description of the purpose of the Zentralbibliothek der Hohen Schule: "The goal is to create the first great scientific National Socialist library, an entirely new sort of library."[7] In January 1940, Adolf Hitler gave his instructions on how the work on the Hohe Schule should proceed during the war:

"Its [Hohe Schule's] construction will take place after the war. But in order to facilitate the preparatory work, I order Reich leader Alfred Rosenberg to initiate this preparatory work—particularly so that the research and work of creating a library can go on. Any departments within state or party that are affected by this, should give him every possible support in this endeavor."

Six months later Rosenberg was mandated to carry out the following operations in occupied territories: First, to impound and confiscate valuable cultural artifacts considered as "ownerless Jewish property." Second, to search public libraries and archives for material of value to Germany. And finally, to seek out and confiscate materials belonging to churches and Masonic orders.[8]

In the summer of 1940, ERR in Paris set up a head office for the occupied western territories under the name Amt Westen. In the same year an operational network was set up in Western Europe with a number of local working groups tasked with making raids, sorting, and confiscating materials—known as Hauptarbeitsgruppen. Each group was responsible for its own geographical area: France, Belgium, and the Netherlands. Under these groups, a number of specialized units were intent on various kinds of materials. Sonderstab Bildende Kunst focused on art, while other departments were sectioned off for music, churches, archaeology, and ancient history. Sonderstab Musik, which plundered instruments, sheet music, and music literature, stole in the region of eight thousand pianos in France alone.[9] The first department set up under the ERR was Sonderstab Bibliothek der Hohen Schule—this library group was led by Walter Grothe, head of the Zentralbibliothek der Hohen Schule, and Wilhelm Grau, head of Rosenberg's Frankfurt institute.[10] ERR would be responsible for the plunder of over one thousand large libraries in Western Europe.

At Keizersgracht in Amsterdam, the ERR established a sizable operation with a few dozen employees—led by the tough SS-Sturmbannführer, Alfred Schmidt-Stähler, who proudly signed his initials in SS-inspired runic letters. The fact that SS men were also working within Amt Rosenberg is yet one more complicated detail in the power structure of the Third Reich. SS men were found in all areas of the Nazi state and party machinery, although loyalty was predominantly owed to whoever paid their salaries.

Later in the autumn of 1940, ERR was given responsibility for the plundering of art in France, which would turn out to be the organization's most extensive operation during the war years. However, art theft would be a sideshow as far as Alfred Rosenberg was concerned. Most of the artworks confiscated by the ERR were sold, reserved for Adolf Hitler's Führermuseum in Linz, or passed to Hermann Göring's private collection at Carinhall. Hitler distributed the lucrative art hauls among various organizations. One reason that this task often, but not always, fell to the ERR was that Rosenberg did not have any plans or particular interest in trying to keep the art.

But it was an entirely different matter when it came to books, archives, and documents, over which the ERR and Rosenberg engaged in ferocious bureaucratic battles with a long line of competitors, chief among them the SS and the RSHA's Section VII. It was a showdown between two competing library projects, playing itself out using all available methods of the internal warfare continuously being waged within the movement: subterfuge, lies, flattery, alliances, and horse trading. But very often in the competition between organizations and leaders in the Third Reich, it was also a question of dynamism—in other words, who got there first. The SS, with its enormous military and police strength, had an obvious advantage. Rosenberg's organization lacked any troops of its own; however, he alleviated this imbalance by means of a number of strategic alliances, most importantly with Hermann Göring. It was certainly a curious alliance, because Göring was probably the least ideological person in the top echelons of the Nazi leadership, but it did serve their common interest. Rosenberg got the soldiers he needed and transportation from the Luftwaffe, and Göring got as much art as he could pack into his private train.

The enormous scale and intensity of the Nazi plundering operation has to be understood from this perspective—the force of it was fed by the ferocious inner life of the Third Reich. But in order for this competition not to swerve into pure anarchy, it also had to be reined in by rules and regulations. For this reason, an unholy alliance was forged between the SS and Amt Rosenberg. Himmler would get the libraries and archives that were useful for "intelligence purposes"—in other words, material helpful to the SD and the Gestapo in their fight against the enemies of the nation. Rosenberg would get the libraries and archives that had a value in ideological research. In simplified terms this could be seen as a subdivision between "historical" and "contemporary" material. In reality things were never quite so simple.

One of the first battles, a bitter and protracted fight, was fought over IISG's valuable archive on Keizersgracht 264. Reinhard Heydrich tried to secure the archive for the RSHA, while Arthur Seyss-Inquart, Reichskommissar for the Netherlands, wanted to keep it in Amsterdam. Robert Ley, leader of the Nazi union movement, took the view that his organization was the proper owner of this Socialist legacy.[11] The ERR won the fight for the archive, which really fell within the jurisdiction of the RSHA, because Hitler finally gave his backing to Rosenberg—and because the ERR had physically taken possession of the archive. The ERR was also the first to get inside the institute's Paris office, which housed some of the most important collections belonging to Russian émigrés. The office was raided just three days after the fall of Paris. Yet in spite of having preempted the competition, the ERR lost the bureaucratic struggle for control of this archive, which was handed over to the SS.

After the ERR had made a rough assessment of the IISG's archive and library, it confirmed that this would be its biggest seizure in the Netherlands. In the library of the institute alone there were more than 100,000 books, and the archive held at least another 180 shelf-yards of materials. It took until 1943 for the ERR to pack everything into nine hundred large crates, dispatched to Germany by train and cargo ship. Yet the ERR had not found an essential part of the archive: the Karl Marx and Friedrich Engels documents.

"After the Munich Accord in 1938 when the Western powers gave Hitler Czechoslovakia, Posthumus became convinced that war was inevitable, and for this reason he had the Marx and Engels archive shipped to the institute's branch in Oxford. One has to say he was extremely prescient," says Huub Sanders, sitting in his office.

Staff at the IISG had also had time to destroy the most compromising material, such as correspondence with political prisoners from Germany. Posthumus was questioned by the SS, but because he was not politically active, and was for this reason viewed as an academic, he managed to get himself released. The loss of the IISG did not stop Nicolaas Wilhelmus Posthumus from immediately starting another collection.

"Incredibly enough he managed to set up a new institute that began collecting material about the war while it was still ongoing. It was in his nature to always keep collecting, irrespective of the circumstances. This institute was formally established three days after the liberation of the Netherlands in May 1945, and today is known as Instituut voor Oorlogs-, Holocaust- en Genocidestudies. However, when Posthumus went back to Keizersgracht 264 after the liberation of the Netherlands, there was not a great deal left. Everything had been stolen; it was utterly empty. The Nazis had even taken the furniture."

◆　◆　◆

Not far from the Rembrandt Museum lies the Portuguese Synagogue, a large brick building from the end of the 1600s. The synagogue, which has been described as one of the most beautiful in the world, is a monument to the presence of Sephardic Jews in Amsterdam. Outside, I meet

Frits J. Hoogewoud, a man in his seventies, who throws his arms into the air like a conductor when he speaks. Hoogewoud, now retired, was previously the chief librarian of Bibliotheca Rosenthaliana. He has made it his life's task to map out the city's Jewish libraries and their changing fortunes during the war.

The synagogue is surrounded by a low brick building, which functions almost as a perimeter wall. I follow Hoogewoud to one of the houses outside the synagogue where Ets Haim, the renowned library, is kept—which is what I came here to see. The world's oldest Jewish library still in use, it has been the cultural and intellectual heart of the city's Sephardic community since the 1600s.

"The library is almost four hundred years old. It was started as a school for Jews who had fled Spain and Portugal," says Hoogewoud. The light is dim in the three large rooms of the library, which are lined with golden-brown, wine-red, and cobalt-blue books from floor to ceiling. Through two octagonal openings one catches a glimpse of the upper floor of the library, reached via a beautiful wooden spiral staircase.

"The library is absolutely unique, this building was erected specifically for the library, and it was constructed to let in natural light. It was dangerous to have naked flames in a library, of course," says Hoogewoud, and points up at the skylights.

What really makes Ets Haim unique is that it reflects the existential crisis faced by many of the Sephardic Jews once they came to Amsterdam. "Many of the Sephardic Jews had converted to Christianity. And then suddenly they came to a place where they once again had the opportunity of practicing their original religion. It was not an easy thing. They had to rediscover their identities, and they did it by reading, writing, and engaging in debate. Who are we really? Is the Jewish faith truer than Christianity? This library is the product of that search," Hoogewoud explains as we take a seat in the library's reading room.

Sephardic identity had been formed during one of history's veritable ages of gold. The Spanish and Portuguese Jews brought with them to their new homes a unique educational culture—which, for many years, was the finest in Europe.

The Iberian Peninsula, named Al-Andalus by the Arabs, had been conquered by the Muslims of North Africa in the early 700s. This was the beginning of an almost five-hundred-year epoch of Islamic high culture, excelling in areas such as art, astronomy, philosophy, literature, and poetry—owing a great deal to an invention that had spread from the East. The Chinese had invented papermaking as early as the Han dynasty in 200 BC, but it was the Muslims who brought it to Europe.[12] The spread of paper facilitated the Muslim translation movement, in which works of the classical era spanning a variety of disciplines were copied and translated into Arabic. The caliphate, which financed much of the work, sent out learned people all over the world to collect manuscripts. The center of this movement was the House of Wisdom in Baghdad—the Muslim world's correlative to the library in Alexandria—where hundreds of thousands of texts from Roman, Greek, Chinese, Persian, and Indian literature were translated, copied, and commented on. Much of this translation was done by Syrian Christians and Jews, who were proficient in Greek, Latin, and Arabic.

Córdoba became another center of this movement. The competition between the Umayyad dynasty of the Iberian Peninsula and the Abbasid dynasty, which ruled in Baghdad, was not only military but also cultural. In the tenth century, Córdoba held one of the world's largest libraries—the Umayyad library is believed to have contained some 400,000 volumes. There was nothing comparable in Christian Europe, and it would be another few hundred years before the use of paper became widespread.

Al-Andalus was also a golden age of Jewish culture. Just as in Baghdad, many of the translators were Jewish students and scholars. Under their Muslim rulers, Jewish communities enjoyed a high level of autonomy, and Jewish intellectuals devoted themselves to philosophy, medicine, mathematics, poetry, and religious studies. The reason for the existence of such large numbers of Jewish intellectuals, translators, and scholars in the Muslim world was the unique Jewish scholastic culture, which, even then, was in excess of a thousand years old, founded on an intellectual, religious, and philosophical discourse on how one should interpret and live in accordance with the Torah.

Many learned Jews in Al-Andalus held high positions at the court.

Yet, even though they enjoyed greater freedoms here than in Christian Europe, they did not entirely escape persecution. When the political stability that had been a mark of Al-Andalus began to crumble after AD 1000, there was increasing insecurity also for the Sephardic Jews. A terrible awakening came when the Jewish population in Granada was massacred in 1066, in a Muslim pogrom. The great catastrophe took place after the last Muslim stronghold in Granada fell to Christian Spaniards in 1492. The Christian conquerors gave three choices to the city's Jewish population: convert to Catholicism, and thereby earn permission to stay, or be exiled from Spain. The third option, if they chose neither to convert nor to emigrate, was death. Most decided to emigrate east and form new settlements in Venice, Belgrade, and Thessaloniki. Others moved to the west, including those Portuguese Jews who were later expelled from Portugal.[13]

But thousands of Sephardic Jews decided to convert so that they could stay. Despite their concession, Marranos—or *conversos* as they were often called—were never accepted. The Inquisition in the 1500s mercilessly hounded the Marranos, thousands of whom fell victim to torture and burning. Ultimately most Marranos had no choice but to emigrate, only to find that in exile even more humiliation and isolation awaited them, as they were often rejected by Jewish communities.

Many of these doubly condemned people decided to settle in the Netherlands, where they were treated with more understanding than in many other places. They are the subject of the book with the bullet hole at the Bibliotheca Rosenthaliana. Samuel Usque was a Portuguese Marrano Jew, and the book, *Consolaçam às Tribulaçoens de Israel*, which in translation means "Consolation for the Tribulations of Israel," was a religious self-help book for Marrano Jews, written in 1553. It tells the story of the long suffering of the Jewish people, and the consolation to be found in studying the Torah and the prophets. Usque argues that Marranos can only ever be liberated from their torments by openly returning to and embracing the Jewish faith. Most of the Jews who went to Amsterdam did precisely that, but they also kept certain aspects of their unique culture.

"What the Sephardic Jews brought here was the cultural melding that had taken place in Spain between the Jewish, Arab, Christian, and even classical culture. One can see the influences in the beautiful illustrations in the manuscripts here. Amazingly profuse floral patterns, inspired by Muslim art. They were very much formed by the culture they had come from. Clearly they did not only want to move on, but also remember the land they had lost," says Heide Warncke, a librarian at Ets Haim, who joins us in the reading room.

The library was founded in 1616 and today contains some thirty thousand books and over six hundred manuscripts, the oldest of which dates back to 1282. The collection covers a broad spectrum of subjects: poetry, grammar, calligraphy, philosophy, mysticism, and religion. "The library reflects the development of the Sephardic community in Amsterdam over a period of four hundred years. Here you can follow the spiritual, religious, and cultural changes that society went through," Hoogewoud tells me.

The Sephardic Jews who had been Marranos would form their own community and cultural identity in the larger Jewish society. They were always in a minority, even within the broader Jewish population. But after several centuries had passed, as had happened during the expulsions from Spain in 1492, the persecution also reached the "Jerusalem of the West."

"In actual fact, at first after the occupation began in 1940, not very much happened. Life went on as before. Also, cultural activities carried on, people wrote books, organized seminars, and put on plays. It is difficult for us to understand it, now that we have the benefits of hindsight. But they were so used to the freedom and tolerance they had been living under that they just couldn't conceive of it being withdrawn one day," says Warncke.

"It happened gradually. Step by step the Jewish population was separated from others, just as the Nazis had done in Germany," Hoogewoud interjects.

The ERR was not in a hurry to impound the Jewish libraries. Only in August 1941 was an operation launched with a focus on the most important Jewish collections. For the first year, it had mainly been concerned with political opponents such as the IISG, the church, and Freemasons' orders. It was no surprise that the Jewish collections should come into the spotlight in 1941, as this was the moment when policy hardened toward the Jewish population. From the beginning of the year, Dutch Jews were forced to register, and by February the first deportations to Buchenwald were in motion. In August, the SD sealed off a number of Jewish libraries, including Ets Haim and Rosenthaliana, whose reading rooms had already been closed to the general public. Bet Hamidrash, a valuable library belonging to Amsterdam's Ashkenazi Jews, was also closed. The libraries were not available to anyone except SS and ERR staff members. What they had not realized was that some of the most valuable books had already been hidden.

Six months earlier the Portuguese congregation had picked out its most valuable artworks, which had been sent to the Rijksmuseum's bunker under the sand dunes by the coast. They also had five crates packed with books and manuscripts from Ets Haim, including eight Hebrew incunabula, sixty manuscripts from the 1600s and 1700s, and over 150 printed illustrations. The crates were placed in a vault of the bank Kas-Associate on Spuistraat in Amsterdam.[14] The reason for these precautions was not the risk of plunder, which was probably not considered likely at this time, but rather the fear that the library might be damaged or destroyed in a bombing raid.

Fontaine Verwey's rescue operation at Rosenthaliana was more conscious of the precarious situation. The library's former curator, Louis Hirschel, had put together a secret list of the most valuable writings that had to be saved. Together the two men made their way into the sealed-off building and smuggled out, among other things, some sixty manuscripts, twenty or so incunabula, and a drawing by Spinoza from the 1600s, all of which were hidden in the cellars.[15] They also hid the library's catalog so that the ERR would not be able to check what was missing.

The ERR was extremely keen to get its hands on Ets Haim and Rosenthaliana, and this can be discerned in a weekly report sent from the group's headquarters in the Netherlands, in the same month that the libraries were sealed off:

> It is possible that previously unknown sources can be discovered here from the Cromwell era, both from the so-called glorious revolution of 1668, and the alliance between England and the Netherlands. In particular, new conclusions may emerge on Cromwell's relations with the Jews—and maybe even Jewish influence on the creation of the British secret service.[16]

The report demonstrates just how ideologically motivated the ERR's work was. The libraries and the archives were not stolen primarily because they were "Jewish property" but rather because it was believed that they might provide materials backing up the theory of Jewish world conspiracy. There was a highly particular background to the Nazis' interest in Jewish-British relations. Hitler and Rosenberg were both admirers of the British Empire, and found it fascinating that a small minority could run India, whose population numbered hundreds of millions. Rosenberg tried until the very end to make Nazi Germany form an anti-Bolshevik pact with Great Britain. Even Hitler was pursuing the same train of thought. The war with Great Britain, and the country's stubborn refusal to make peace, was partly blamed on "Jewish influence." That Cromwell, as a result of Menasseh ben Israel's diplomacy, had allowed Jews to return to England was viewed as evidence of such Jewish influence.

"It was a very ridiculous way of looking at it. That it was the British-Jewish connection that was the real enemy. But I think it's important for us to understand that this was really how they thought about things. This was how the Nazis legitimized what they did. In the final analysis, they wanted to prove that Nazism was right, that this was the logic of what they were doing," Hoogewoud explains.

In 1942, both Ets Haim and Rosenthaliana were visited by one Johannes Pohl, whom Alfred Rosenberg the year before had appointed as head of the Jewish section of the Institut zur Erforschung der Judenfrage in Frankfurt. Pohl had previously been a Catholic priest, but he had converted to National Socialism. At the end of the 1920s he had been a promising biblical scholar whose doctoral thesis had been a study of the prophet Ezekiel. In the early 1930s he had spent several years in Jerusalem, studying biblical archaeology.

When Pohl returned to Germany in 1934, he gave up the priesthood in order to marry and at the same time began publishing articles in anti-Semitic journals such as *Der Stürmer*. Oddly enough, he had never previously during his years of research expressed any anti-Semitic ideas, which would seem to suggest that he was either an opportunist or had cultivated a personal anti-Semitism, which he only dared articulate once the Nazis had come to power. Pohl issued special warnings about the dangers of the Talmud, on which he also wrote an anti-Semitic book.[17]

Pohl was an advocate of *Judenforschung ohne Juden*—Jewish research without Jews—which drew him to Rosenberg's circle and also the institute in Frankfurt, where he later became the organization's foremost book plunderer.

After Pohl's inspection in 1942, it was decided that both Ets Haim and Rosenthaliana should be taken to the Frankfurt institute. In the autumn of 1941 the ERR and the RSHA also started raiding Jewish private collectors in the Netherlands. One of the better-known libraries to be taken was that of Isaac Leo Seeligmann, the son of the historian, bibliographer, and Zionist Sigmund Seeligmann, who had died in 1940. Isaac Leo Seeligmann had inherited one of the finest Jewish private libraries in Europe. Himself a biblical scholar and teacher of Jewish history, he had followed in his father's footsteps and built up an impressive collection of his own. Together, the two libraries contained between 20,000 and 25,000 books.[18] The RSHA took charge of Seeligmann's collection, most likely for the reason that his father had been a well-known Zionist. Another valuable Jewish book collection confiscated by the ERR belonged to Paul May, the banker, who committed suicide with his wife by taking cyanide on the same day that the Netherlands capitulated to Nazi Germany.

In 1942, the ERR commenced operation M-Aktion (Möbel [Furniture] Action) along with the Zentralstelle für jüdische Auswanderung (Central Office for Jewish Emigration), which handled the deportation of the Dutch Jews to concentration camps. As part of the operation, homes belonging to deported Jews were plundered to provide German soldiers and settlers in the East with household goods.

Alfred Schmidt-Stähler writes in a report that the organization made 29,000 successful raids in the Netherlands.[19] In most cases the homes were comprehensively cleared of all furnishings and goods, which were loaded on trains or ships and sent to Germany or Eastern Europe. The operation also cleaned out the literary inheritance of Holland's Jews, down to the tiniest bookcases or scattered volumes on bedside tables. It is estimated that the ERR seized between 700,000 and 800,000 books. Some of these were distributed to schools in the Netherlands or handed over to local Nazis.[20] Others were sold or shipped to Germany.

It took until the middle of 1943 before the ERR finally packed up Ets Haim. Worse still, it found the list of documents that had been moved to the bank vault, a list that the staff had forgotten to hide. The congregation's secretary was frog-marched to the bank, accompanied by personnel from the ERR and the SD, where most of the books and manuscripts were confiscated. In August the contents of the library, 170 crates, were loaded on a train to Frankfurt.

It would take another year before Rosenthaliana left Amsterdam, as the library had become the subject of yet another dispute. The collection belonged to Amsterdam's university and was therefore public, and not Jewish, property. Even Amsterdam's pro-German mayor stepped in to save the collection and keep it in the Netherlands. While the war of words raged, Herman de la Fontaine Verwey seized the opportunity to smuggle out the documents that had earlier been hidden in the cellar. In the autumn of 1943 the university began evacuating other valuable collections to bunkers under the sand dunes by Zandvoort, outside Haarlem. By secreting the Rosenthaliana manuscripts among these collections Fontaine Verwey managed to bring them to safety.[21] Despite the protests, no one could stop the ERR from getting its hands on Rosenthaliana. "The law of property has no meaning when it is a matter of Jewish objects" was Alfred

Rosenberg's final answer to Amsterdam's mayor. In June 1944 the library was packed into 143 crates and loaded on a train eastward.

The mass deportations of Dutch Jews began in the middle of 1942. Most were sent to the transit camp of Westerbork. Almost every Tuesday until September 1944 a freight train departed to the east. Sixty-eight trains, carrying 54,930 persons, went to Auschwitz-Birkenau. Nineteen trains, with 34,313 people, went to Sobibór. Most of the deportees were murdered on arrival.[22] Other trains, with far fewer passengers on board, were bound for the concentration camps of Bergen-Belsen and Theresienstadt. In two years, three-quarters of the Jewish population in the Netherlands was exterminated. Of the Sephardic Jews, only about eight hundred would survive.

Rosenthaliana's curator Louis Hirschel and Isaac Leo Seeligmann were among the deportees; both were sent with their families to Westerbork. According to a colleague who visited Hirschel in the barrack where he was interned, he was working right until the end on a bibliography that would be the foundation of a book on the history of the Netherlands Jews: "In the dark barrack, surrounded by wretchedness and misery, he wrote his extensive bibliography, without any access to other literature, on small scraps of paper."[23] Hirschel was deported with his wife and four children to Poland. His wife died in Sobibór in November 1943. Hirschel survived until March 1944; he was most likely selected for slave labor, which extended his life by a few months.[24] Isaac Leo Seeligmann was "lucky"—his name was on a list of "selected" Jews to be sent to the Nazi "model camp," Theresienstadt. By a remarkable coincidence, Seeligmann was reunited with his library before the war was over.

# 7

# THE HUNT FOR THE
# SECRETS OF THE FREEMASONS

## *The Hague*

In order to understand alchemy you have to ask yourself the question, What is gold? Is it the metal you are after or something else? Alchemy is about the search for one of life's great secrets, namely the secret of eternal life."

Jac Piepenbrock gives me a watchful look, as if to assure himself that I am keeping up, while he explains the innermost essence of alchemy. I am not sure that I do, but in spite of this I nod by way of an answer.

"But what actually is the meaning of eternal life? Is it life here on earth, or the soul's ascent into eternal light? Alchemy is the search for life's deepest meaning," Piepenbrock continues. He is a short man, a Freemason with fine silky white hair. In his arms he holds a book of such large dimensions that two people are required to turn its pages. While Piepenbrock opens the eight-inch-thick volume, his colleague Theo Walter carefully turns the yellow, almost brown pages. Every page or two is richly illustrated with curious, frightening woodcuts. Snakes writhing around humans. A field in which the ground is covered in skeletons surrounded by swarms of birds. Dragons devouring one another. A mob with clubs and lances, striking a prostrate man. Doves armed with bows and arrows. Stars, angels, planets, and signs that I have never seen before. The book, *Bibliotheca chemica curiosa*, is an anthology from 1702 of alchemical literature, compiled by the medical doctor Jean-Jacques Manget. The magical book is in stark contrast to the room in which we find ourselves—an oxygen-depleted, cramped little hole without windows. The glum gray metal shelves, which Walter and Piepenbrock roll back and forth, give you the impression that you have found your way into an archive of forgotten auditors' reports. But if you can see beyond these meager surroundings, the room holds one of Europe's rarest collections of books on Freemasonry, alchemy, magic, the mysteries of antiquity, cathedral builders, and Knights Templar.

The Freemasons' lodge of Grootoosten der Nederlanden, which traces its history back to 1756, has its principal seat behind an anonymous dark green door in the center of The Hague. A few decades back, like so many other Freemasonry orders in Europe, it began to open up its once-so-secretive activities. The lodge now houses a cultural center, Cultureel Masonniek Centrum, with a reading room and a museum about Freemasonry. The order owns a collection of more than 25,000 valuable artifacts associated with Freemasonry: antique regalia, art objects, drawings, and etchings. But the lodge's most famous collection is the Bibliotheca Klossiana—one of the world's oldest Freemasons' libraries. The collection has its origins with the German doctor, historian, and Freemason Georg Kloss, who built up the collection in the early 1800s. "Kloss was a frenetic collector of books and manuscripts on Freemasonry and other subjects of interest to the lodges. He managed to build up the best collection on the subject in Europe," says Piepenbrock, who is the keeper of the library. After Kloss's death the library was bought by Prince Frederick of the Netherlands, who donated the collection to the order of which he was the grand master. The Kloss collection consisted of seven thousand books and two thousand manuscripts.

In addition to that library there was an extensive archive on the 250-year history of the order, and materials from some eighty discontinued Dutch Masonic orders. Today the collection fills some eight hundred yards of shelves. "Kloss collected books and manuscripts in order to look for the origins of Freemasonry. How the rituals were first created, when they were first written down, how they evolved, and which were the true rituals of Freemasonry," says Theo Walter, who is the librarian of the order.

Freemasonry was a subject that greatly interested the Nazis, but despite this, the Third Reich's assault on Freemasonry is a chapter that has rarely been examined. After the Nazis seized power in Germany, the German Masonic orders were some of the first organizations to come under attack, but at the same time the persecution of Freemasons, with a few exceptions, was not as systematic or brutal as that pitted against Jews and political opponents. The Nazis' opposition to the orders was rather an attack on the spirit of Freemasonry, which was considered an ideological rather than a racial problem of the kind presented by Jews, Roma, and Slavs. In other words, the Nazis sought to do away with Freemasonry as a phenomenon, but only to a lesser degree with the actual Freemasons themselves.

Hermann Göring proclaimed at an early stage that "there is no place in National Socialist Germany for Masonic orders."[1] At first the regime tried in a variety of ways to get the lodges to disband or give up Freemasonry in order to pursue other things. People who were, or had been, members of Masonic orders were denied membership in the Nazi Party. Freemasons were also subjected to harassment and boycotts, and were often fired if they worked in the public sphere. However, many were later able to restart their careers.

Masonic activity in Germany at the time was extensive, with upward of eighty thousand Freemasons. Many of them were or had been high-status individuals in German society. Some of the larger orders tried as early as 1933 to adapt by taking names such as the National Christian Order of Frederick the Great or the German Christian Friendly Order.[2] In order to be able to continue with their activities, the regime required the orders to stop using the word *Freemasons*, break off all international ties, exclude members of non-Aryan origins, open up their secret activities, and stop using rituals that could be linked to the Old Testament.

In 1935, Freemasons' orders were entirely banned and labeled "enemies of the state." With this, Germany's Masonic organizations were disbanded and their property confiscated. Heinrich Himmler, who was hugely interested in the orders, saw to it that the SD and the Gestapo impounded the Masonic libraries and archives. These later formed the foundations of the occult collection at the RSHA Section VII.[3]

Also in the 1930s, a number of campaigns were held to denigrate Freemasonry, by the conversion of some confiscated Masonic lodges into museums where exhibitions were held. One example was the notorious *Entartete Kunst* in 1937, when the Nazis arranged an exhibition of modern "degenerate" art. "The shaming exhibition" was a concept to which the Nazis returned time and time again in their propaganda. In addition to "shaming exhibitions" about art, similar events were organized on the themes of jazz and Jewish culture. The exhibition *Sowjet-Paradies*, in 1942, achieved particular popularity, presenting items that had been brought back after the invasion of the Soviet Union. The exhibition, inside a large pavilionlike marquee, covered an area of nine thousand square yards. Its purpose was to highlight the poverty and misery in Russia under the Bolsheviks. According to reports, some 1.3 million Germans visited the exhibition.[4] The "shaming exhibitions" were not only supposed to pour scorn and humiliation on their subjects, but were also preventive measures. In the exhibitions on Freemasonry there was a desire to reveal the secrets of the orders by letting the German people step into the rooms of these mysterious fellowships, the idea being to show how the orders were secretly devoting themselves to perverse, un-German, and Jewish rituals, which presented a real threat to Germany. Particular emphasis was given to ritual objects such as human skulls, bones, Hebrew texts, and other "Oriental" objects. There was a sensationalist focus on the secret blood rituals that the Masons supposedly practiced. The largest of these museums, opened in a confiscated lodge in Chemnitz, are reported to have had a million German visitors.

Masonic orders had never, in fact, presented any sort of political threat to the National Socialists. Most of the orders were wholly apolitical. But in the apocalyptic worldview of the Nazis, the Freemasons were performing a special function in the Jewish world conspiracy. The secret societies had been conspiring for centuries to overthrow Germany.

When the party newspaper, the *Völkischer Beobachter*, reported in 1935 on the disbanding of the Masonic orders, an astonishing accusation was kicked into the ring: the Freemasons had started the First World War. According to the newspaper, Freemasons had planned the 1914 murder in Sarajevo of the successor to the Austro-Hungarian throne, Franz Ferdinand.[5] Thereafter, Freemasons had conspired to force Germany into the war, and Freemasons had ensured Germany's defeat.

Such conspiracy theories flourished in far-right circles in Germany during the interwar years. The German general Erich Ludendorff, who had played a decisive part in the last few years of the First World War, was one of the most outspoken critics of Freemasonry. In the last year of the war, Ludendorff was the most powerful man in Germany, both planning and commanding the German offensive on the western front in 1918, when the country depleted its last reserves of strength in this final attack. The failure of the offensive, and the Allied counteroffensive, not only led to the collapse of the German lines but also to the psychological breakdown of Ludendorff himself. When Ludendorff failed to broker a truce in the autumn of 1918, the German emperor relieved him of his command.

The revolution broke out in Germany in November of that same year. Ludendorff fled to Sweden with the help of a forged passport, and he waited out the revolution on the country estate of the Swedish landowner and equestrian, Ragnar Olson, in Hässleholm. Broken down, embittered, exiled, and disappointed with the humiliating Versailles Treaty, Ludendorff wrote his memoir of the war. Published in 1919, it became one of the sources of the Legend of the Dagger Thrust, which took on such decisive importance in the fortunes of the National Socialists. Ludendorff, unable to shoulder his own failings in the events that had taken place, argued that it was Social Democrats, Socialists, and Freemasons on the home front that had caused the defeat. Without this "dagger thrust" in the army's back, Germany would have been victorious.

Ludendorff's descent into the murky gloom of conspiracy theories did not end with his memoir. Gradually he was drawn into the right-wing radical circles of Munich and the NSDAP. During the Beer Hall Putsch in 1923 when the Nazis tried to take power, Ludendorff marched alongside Adolf Hitler to topple the government. Unlike Hitler, he escaped a prison sentence.

During the 1920s, Ludendorff began to view the Freemasons as the root of a global conspiracy. In 1927 he published the book *Eradication of Freemasonry Through Uncovering of Its Secrets,* in which he further developed his conspiracy theories. Although Ludendorff was billed as the sole author of the work, he actually cowrote it with his wife, Mathilde, who if possible was an even more fanatical opponent of Freemasonry. Later she would publish her own pamphlet, *Mozart's Life and Violent Death,* in which she alleged that the composer was murdered by his Masonic brothers because of his breach of the order's vow of silence. She also claimed that Freemasons were responsible for the deaths of Martin Luther and Friedrich Schiller.[6]

The Ludendorffs were convinced that the Freemasons had supernatural powers and thereby posed a threat to the whole German nation and its people. They also believed they had found evidence of Freemasons, through their international networks, leaking German military secrets to the nation's enemies during the war.[7] In his memoirs, Erich Ludendorff postulated that the Masonic orders were controlled by Great Britain.

*Eradication of Freemasonry Through Uncovering of Its Secrets* also had another, not entirely unexpected figure emerging from the wings: the Jew. The entire Masonic movement was, in fact, created and controlled by Jews. According to the Ludendorffs, the secrecy of the lodges was a way of hiding this Jewish influence. The Masonic orders were what the Ludendorffs referred to as a *künstlicher Jude,* an "artificial Jew." Their suggestion was that while the Masons were not officially Jewish, nonetheless the lodges acted as agents of Jewish interests. The couple also believed that the Jews had entered into a secret pact with the Jesuits to jointly take control of the world economy.[8]

The book did not garner the sort of critical acclaim that Ludendorff had been hoping for. Most newspapers dismissed his ideas as verging on the eccentric and even slightly pitiful. The Bremer *Tageblatt* made comments insinuating that the old general had become "psychologically unstable."[9]

Yet, there was a good deal more receptiveness to his ideas in rightwing circles, where the conspiracy theory in question was already well established. The concept of a Jewish Masonic conspiracy was almost as

The Freemasons at the Bibliotheca Klossiana in The Hague show me
a book from their renowned collection—the illustrated work
Bibliotheca chemica curiosa.

venerable as the lodges themselves. According to popular myth, Freemasonry was first established among the guilds formed by freelancing cathedral builders in the medieval era. Whether this was really how Freemasons' orders were first established has not been firmly proved, but this was the mythology on which the Masonic movement was based. The lodges first took form in the early 1700s, when the scientific revolution and the Enlightenment led to a new interest in existential questions, mysticism, and spirituality—as well as various kinds of societies. It was still perilous to question the authority of the church openly. During the 1600s and the 1700s, therefore, a myriad of religious, spiritual, and philosophical societies were set up, in which people could discuss and share such potentially dangerous ideas behind closed doors.

The Grand Lodge of England was established in 1717, and is usually considered the first great lodge of Freemasons. From England, Freemasonry spread to France, and afterward fanned out across the Continent. Masonic orders sought to convey theoretical and spiritual knowledge through philosophical and religious inquiry. A resurgent interest at the time in the occult, magic, and séances also influenced the various orders. But the orders were not mere spiritual conversation clubs, they were in large part segregated associations for the social elite, from which women and people of lower social backgrounds were excluded.

The secrecy, the rites, the esoteric elements, and the many prominent members created from the very beginning a plethora of widespread rumors and conspiracy theories. The first official condemnation came from Pope Clement XII at the end of the 1730s, when he spoke disapprovingly of Freemasonry as a practice in opposition to the Catholic faith. Initially, criticism was largely on religious grounds; however, after the French Revolution a political dimension emerged. In the general hunt for scapegoats to blame for the political turmoil, Freemasons and the Bavarian Illuminati were framed as the conspirators and initiators. As the 1800s progressed there was an added element of criticism from (liberal) nationalists. As many of the orders were part of international networks, the phenomenon was regarded by nationalists as a threat to national cohesion.

The alleged link between Freemasonry and the Jews was particularly odd since many of the orders, especially those with a Christian focus, did not admit Jews as members.[10] In the more humanist orders Jews were only allowed membership from the 1850s. Of the eighty thousand Freemasons believed to have existed in Germany in 1933, only some three thousand are estimated to have had a Jewish background.[11]

In far-right and conservative circles an idea was cultivated in the 1800s, to the effect that the Jews were infiltrating and manipulating the ideology of the Freemasons for their own purposes. That many orders were supportive of Enlightenment ideals such as equality and positive belief in the future was considered to serve "Jewish interests" by clearing a way for Jewish emancipation. Freemasons and Jews were believed to have conspired to overthrow both church and monarchy in order to achieve equal rights for Jews.

Around the turn of the century, Freemasons had a role in every conspiracy worth its salt. In France the Freemasons were purportedly involved in the Dreyfus affair, in which the French-Jewish artillery officer Alfred Dreyfus was found guilty of espionage—on the basis of falsified evidence. In Russia, the Freemasons had a role in *The Protocols of the Elders of Zion* as an instrument for the Jews to take over the world. In England, Freemasons were accused of having links with Jack the Ripper.

A book written by the Austrian politician Friedrich Wichtl in 1919 achieved particular standing: *The Freemasons of the World—World Revolution—the World Republic. An Investigation into the Origins of the First World War and Its End.*[12] It was Wichtl who coined the expression "artificial Jew" and presented evidence that the heir to the Austro-Hungarian throne was murdered in 1914 by the machinations of a group of Freemasons and Jews.

The Ludendorffs and Wichtl would find a receptive supporter in Alfred Rosenberg, who had himself published a book on the subject in 1922: *The Crimes of the Freemasons, Jews, Jesuits, and German Christianity*. In *The Myth of the Twentieth Century* he accused the Freemasons of spreading "tolerant and humane principles, such as how a Jew or a Turk has the same rights as a Christian," which was, in Rosenberg's universe of racial myth, a horrific thought. It was the Freemasons, he alleged, who "led the democratic revolutions in the 1800s." It was this very humanism, as espoused by Freemasons, that had caused the democratic, racial, and moral decline in which "every Jew, negro, or mulatto can become a citizen with the same rights in a European nation."[13]

Heinrich Himmler was convinced that blood rituals were being used in Masonic lodges. The manner of it was described more closely in a report filed by the Bavarian political police, the BPP: "The candidate cuts himself in the thumb and drips the blood into a chalice. Wine is then mixed in, and then blood from the other brothers (from when they first carried out the ritual). Then the candidate drinks the liquid, and absorbs the blood from all Freemasons, including Jews. With this the triumph of the Jew is complete."[14]

At the same time there was within the SS a curious fascination with Freemasonry. Himmler regarded the orders not only as enemies of the state but also as sources of knowledge and inspiration. It was therefore no secret that a large part of the literature seized from German Masonic orders in the 1930s ended up in the library of the RSHA. The rituals, secrets, and symbolism of the Freemasons were of great interest to Himmler, who wished to re-create his own not entirely dissimilar rituals and orders within the SS.

The Nazis were not the first to ban Freemasonry in the 1900s. Most emerging totalitarian regimes in the interwar years also attacked it. In Italy, Mussolini accused the Masons of being enemies of fascism and subsequently banned them, as did the Soviet Union and Spain under Franco. In Nazi Germany, Reinhard Heydrich set up a special division within the RSHA for Freemasons. One of the individuals recruited to register German Freemasons was Adolf Eichmann. How many German Freemasons fell victim to Nazi persecution is difficult to estimate, as many members were also detained and sent to concentration camps on account of other political activities.

Freemasonry was an important component of the propaganda leveled against exterior enemies no less than interior ones. That both Winston Churchill and Franklin Roosevelt were Freemasons was often mentioned in German propaganda. When the German field marshal Friedrich Paulus capitulated at Stalingrad, contrary to Hitler's orders, he was smeared in German propaganda as "a Freemason of the very highest rank."[15] Yet the Nazis did not mention quite as stridently that Goethe, Mozart, and Frederick the Great had all been Freemasons.[16]

✦ ✦ ✦

In the summer of 1940, the ERR in Amsterdam mapped out the network of Freemasons' lodges in the Netherlands. In their completed list there were thirty-one Freemasons' lodges and ten lodges belonging to Droit Humain, a mixed-gender order of Freemasons. There were also thirty-five local Odd Fellows and fifteen Rotary clubs. In early September, the ERR launched a series of coordinated raids, with Grootoosten in The Hague as the most important target. Quite apart from its famous library, this Masonic lodge was an umbrella organization for a long list of regional lodges with a membership in excess of four thousand. "On the fourth of September 1940 all the members were summoned to the lodge, and they were also told to bring all their regalia from home. Those who refused had their homes searched," Piepenbrock tells me. The members were registered, and thereafter the lodges were disbanded. Most of the members were released, but the grand master of Grootoosten, Hermannus van Tongeren, was arrested and sent to Sachsenhausen concentration camp, where he died.

The property of the orders was wholly confiscated, including buildings, regalia, and libraries. As in Germany, Freemasons' lodges often ended up being used as offices, warehouses, or coordination centers for various Nazi organizations.[17]

Another theme exported from Germany was the concept of the "shaming exhibition," used here as an attempt by the occupiers to win over the citizens in the territories to their struggle against Jews, Freemasons, and Bolsheviks. In Paris, an anti-Freemasonry exhibition opened in June 1940, and Brussels put on a similar show one year later.

In France, the ERR started preparing the plunder of the Masonic lodges earlier than in the Netherlands. Even while the military operation was still going on, Alfred Rosenberg had sent personnel to France to carry out reconnaissance for the imminent confiscations. On June 18, 1940, one of the emissaries, Professor Georg Ebert, reported that he had occupied France's largest lodge of Freemasons, Grand Orient of France, on rue Cadet in Paris.[18]

In France and Belgium, the orders were plundered as thoroughly as in the Netherlands. In Denmark, Norway, Poland, Austria, Greece, and the Balkans, orders were also raided and cleared.

There were bitter skirmishes between the ERR and the RSHA for the right to acquire the libraries and archives of the Freemasons. The RSHA was often given precedence, which forced the ERR to hand over much of the already confiscated Masonic literature. It was considered important from a security perspective to be able to map out the Freemasons' international networks by having access to their membership registries, correspondence, and other materials. But it was also clear that the "occult literature" that had been the property of the orders was of great interest to the SS. The RSHA had already built up a considerable collection, plundered from the German Masonic orders—prior to the Nazi accession to power they had held the world's second-largest membership.[19] The seizure of books and archive materials from the German lodges had been enormous, and most ended up in the library on the enemies of the Reich, housed in Section VII of the RSHA in Berlin.

Already in the German collections the RSHA had found plenty of material that could underpin the conspiratorial fantasies and occult interest of the SS. One such archive was the Schwedenkiste (Swedish chest) from the Masonic lodge Ernst zum Kompass in Gotha. This was a collection of documents and letters that the Illuminati order had held at the end of the 1700s. The secret order, surrounded by myths, had been founded by the German philosopher Adam Weishaupt. Its purpose had been to reach consensus on the fundamental values of the Enlightenment among intellectuals and decision makers, and in this way encourage rational social reforms in a progressive spirit. Weishaupt's organization recruited assiduously within this target group, and regarded the Illuminati order as an institution for the development of an elite in which a loyal cadre group would coordinate its high ideals for the betterment of humanity.

The order was banned by the Bavarian state in 1785 and several of its members imprisoned. And yet, despite the brief life of the order, the Illuminati were soon surrounded by a proliferation of conspiracy theories, with one popular assertion that the order lived on in secret.

John Robison, the Scottish philosopher and conspiracy theorist, accused the Illuminati in his book *Proofs of a Conspiracy* (1797) of having infiltrated Masonic groups on the Continent and starting the French Revolution. In 1780, the Illuminati had instigated a collaboration with Freemasons, which was regarded as evidence of the order having continued its subversive activities under the guise of the Masonic orders. Schwedenkiste consisted of documents hailing back to the time when the Illuminati were still active, including information identifying the members. Duke Ernst II of Sachsen-Gotha-Altenburg, a member of the order, regarded the contents to be of such sensitivity that he had them sent to his contacts in Sweden. In Stockholm the Illuminati archive would be protected from publication, which was guaranteed by the Swedish royal family. One of those listed as a member of the Illuminati was none other than Johann Wolfgang von Goethe. Schwedenkiste would remain in Sweden until 1883, when the collection was sent back to Germany and ended up with the Masonic lodge Ernst zum Kompass, where the Gestapo found it in the 1930s.

There were few Freemasons' libraries on the Continent that could measure up to Bibliotheca Klossiana in terms of breadth and depth; it was one of the most important in the world for those who wanted to look into the origins of Freemasonry. The library also contained materials that were studied by the Freemasons, such as books on natural history, biology, philosophy, and the history of various cultures and their beginnings—books from the 1600s and 1700s on indigenous people and their rites and religions. Alongside these were classical Greek tragedies. The library was absolutely crucial to the activities of the Freemasons. It was through such materials that they could attain new knowledge about themselves. "It was a way to catharsis," says Theo Walter, the Klossiana librarian.

Apart from books on magic, theosophy, astrology, alchemy, rites, music, song, and symbolism, Klossiana also has one of the world's most substantial collections of anti-Freemasonry literature. But the library's value lies not only in written literature but also in a rich stock of illustrations, etchings, and drawings that demonstrate how to conduct the secret rituals.

Among Klossiana's rarities are five of the oldest editions of the Scotsman James Anderson's *The Constitutions of the Free-Masons* from the early 1700s, the work that forms the basis of the British Masonic system. Another even more mythologized document found in the collection is the *Charter van Keulen* (Cologne Charter), which is said to date back to 1535. The document, written in Latin, demonstrates that there was already widespread Masonic activity during the 1500s. According to the myth in circulation, the document was found in a dormant lodge in Amsterdam in the mid-1600s, hidden in a chest locked with three locks, behind three separate seals. It was widely discussed in Masonic circles during the 1800s. Kloss, who first chanced upon the document, was one of those who could reveal that this was very likely a case of forgery.

Also of interest to the Nazis was the large archive of materials from defunct orders, held by Grootoosten der Nederlanden, many of these having had connections with the East India Company. In the archive of the lodge was something of at least comparable value, namely a card index of every individual who had been a member of a Masonic order in the Netherlands since the 1700s.[20]

After the raids in 1940, the ERR's Netherlands section was able to report on the significant success of the action. Hundreds of thousands of books and other materials had been confiscated.[21] Also included with these were art and ritual artifacts, including the golden hammer of the grand master, which had been found at Grootoosten's lodge. The ERR estimated the golden hammer's value at 3,000 reichsmarks.

There was no doubt about what was regarded as the foremost trophy: "In order to calculate the value of the Bibliotheca Klossiana, which contains many rare works, one must bear in mind that in 1939 Grootoosten was offered five million dollars for the library by Freemasons in the USA," the ERR writes in a report.[22] But not only the financial value was emphasized; in fact, the impounded books were said to be of "extraordinary scientific value": "One can state without any hesitation that the library of Hohe Schules, without enormous labor, will now offer a quite remarkable amount of treasures that will give the library a leading position in questions touching upon Jews and Freemasons."[23] But the ERR did not merely make do with the library itself: "Also, steel shelving units sufficient for about 30,000 books were removed from the building."

# 8

# LENIN WORKED HERE

*Paris*

Jean-Claude Kuperminc runs his fingers over the book titles, reading them quietly to himself as he moves slowly between the rows of bookshelves until he finds what he is looking for. He pulls out a beige-white cloth-bound book. The ceiling light, with its buttery yellow glow, makes it difficult to read the title. Kuperminc opens the thick blackout curtains that cover the wall toward the inner courtyard and then holds up the book spine to the sunlight. The title is *Weltgeschichte des jüdischen Volkes* (World History of the Jewish People) by the Russian-Jewish historian and activist Simon Dubnov, murdered in Riga by the SS in 1941. At the bottom of the spine, a small label is glued on, bearing the text "B. z. Erf. d. Jud. Frankfurt a. Main." On one of the flyleaves is a blue rubber stamp with the same text, except unabbreviated: "Bibliothek zur Erforschung der Judenfrage Frankfurt a. Main." It is the first time I have seen a stamp from Rosenberg's Frankfurt institute. Even the catalog number from the institute's library is preserved: "42/1941," in a quick but entirely legible scrawl, written with a sharpened pencil.

When Kuperminc puts the book back, I see other labels from the institute on book spines along the shelf. Some look almost new, while others are in varying degrees of disintegration. Many of these books have stayed here, almost untouched, since the Second World War.

"We have thousands of books here marked with Nazi stamps," Kuperminc tells me in his halting English, with a heavy French accent.

From the Freemasons in The Hague I have taken a fast train south to Paris. Here in the French capital, the ERR and the RSHA would initiate the most extensive plundering operation in Western Europe. The center of ERR's art plundering operation was the commandeered museum Jeu de Paume, in central Paris, where tens of thousands of works of art were brought, sorted, cataloged, and dispatched to Germany. Some of the most audacious of all thefts of libraries and archives took place here in France. One of the victims was the Alliance Israélite Universelle, at 45 rue la Bruyère in Paris, south of Montmartre, where I meet Jean-Claude Kuperminc, head of the organization's library and archive. A short man with thinning hair, about fifty, he has spent years researching the whereabouts of the library during the war years.

The Alliance Israélite Universelle was established partly as a result of the so-called Damascus affair—a pogrom triggered in 1849 by the rumor that Jews were behind the ritual murder of a monk in Damascus. The city's synagogue was attacked by a mob, and a number of Jews were imprisoned and submitted to sadistic torture, including having their teeth pulled. The events were noted on the international stage, and a Jewish delegation was sent to negotiate.

"It was an important event, because it was the first time that Jews took international action to help other Jews in the Middle East. It was on the basis of this that the idea for the Alliance emerged. The reason for it was that one wanted to protect and strengthen the rights of Jewish minorities everywhere. The founders were all children of the French Revolution. They belonged to the first and second generations of Jews that had been allowed to become proper citizens of France, with equal rights. The organization was set up to disseminate these ideals," explains Kuperminc.

The Alliance assisted Jews fleeing the pogroms in tsarist Russia and helped them resettle in France and the United States. But its most important work was the establishment of an international school system for Jewish children. By the turn of the twentieth century it was running about a hundred schools in North Africa, the Middle East, and Eastern Europe, with a total of 24,000 pupils. The education was largely based on the Enlightenment ideals of the founders: French culture, language, and civilization. However, the Alliance very clearly distanced itself from the emerging Zionist movement, which campaigned for the creation of a Jewish state in Palestine.

"Alliance was working for the integration of Jews in their own countries. In France we spoke of *régénération*—the rebuilding of identity based on modern Western culture alongside Jewish knowledge and culture," Kuperminc explains. As part of the strong pedagogical ambition a library was set up. "They wanted to gather knowledge about all the different Jewish cultures that existed in the world. But also about Jewish history. Some of the most valuable manuscripts of the collection, from Cairo, are Jewish writings from the 800s. Others go back to the Jewish philosopher Maimonides in the 1100s. But above all the library is known for its modern-day collections of books, journals, pamphlets, and newspapers. It includes an almost complete collection of books and writings published on the Jewish question in Germany from 1700 and up to the 1900s, including anti-Semitic publications, and the organization also collected writings on the notorious Dreyfus affair in the 1890s.

"In the 1930s it was one of the most important Jewish libraries in Europe, maybe the most important anywhere. Everything published that touched upon Jewish themes, both studies and subjects, was bought and collected."

To house the growing collection, a library was built toward the end of the 1930s in rue la Bruyère. The library in which we stand is an eight-story, functionalist tower, located in the inner courtyard of a palatial Parisian building. The low ceilings and the narrow, almost claustrophobic, stairs leading from floor to floor are reminiscent of a multistory parking garage for books. The building was ready in 1937, and before long it held the Alliance library of some fifty thousand books and the extensive archive and collection of journals.

But the tenure of the new library would not be a long one. The shelves would soon be filled with books of an entirely different kind, by the occupying German power.

Baron Kurt von Behr, enlisted to lead the ERR's operations in Western Europe via the office of Amt Westen, arrived in Paris with the German army in June 1940. The administrative office was at first set up in the Hôtel Commodore, but was later moved to a residential house on avenue d'Iéna, which had been confiscated from the Gunzburgs, a Jewish banking family.[1]

Von Behr, an aristocrat who learned French as a prisoner of war during the First World War, was almost a caricature of a Prussian nobleman—according to witnesses he often wore a corset, highly polished boots, and a monocle.[2]

The Alliance Israélite Universelle had already taken precautions to save the collection, but like many other libraries, organizations, and collectors, it misjudged where the real threat lay. The Alliance had built a bunker in the cellar to protect the most valuable parts of the collection from bomb attacks. However, it could not save it from looters. In a last desperate measure, just before the fall of Paris in June 1940, manuscripts and archive materials were loaded on a truck that tried to make it to Bordeaux. It never arrived.

"No one really knows what happened to the truck, but judging by the details we've managed to obtain, it seems that German troops caught up with the vehicle."

When in the summer of 1940 the ERR secured the office at 45 rue la Bruyère, it found the greater part of France's most important Jewish collection still intact on the shelves. As with the IISG in Amsterdam, the ERR also commandeered the organization's premises. Already by August 1940 the library at rue la Bruyère had been packed into crates ready for shipment to Germany. Most of the library was sent to the Institut zur Erforschung der Judenfrage in Frankfurt. The empty shelves in the Alliance Israélite Universelle's library were soon filled with other plundered collections, as the ERR began using it as a book depository.

By September 1940, after seven weeks of plundering, Alfred Rosenberg was able to state with some satisfaction in a report that a significant amount of booty had fallen into their hands in Paris. Among other items, the ERR had confiscated a number of valuable libraries belonging to members of the French Rothschild family.[3] An even more valuable seizure was made at the Rothschilds' renowned Paris bank, de Rothschild Frères, which, for more than a hundred years, had been one of the world's biggest banks. The enormous archive of the bank apparently filled more than 760 crates. This, from a Nazi perspective, was priceless material for "research" into the networks of Jewish world capitalism. In addition to the Rothschilds', libraries were taken from prominent Jewish intellectuals such as Léon Blum, Georges Mandel, Louise Weiss, and Ida Rubinstein. Several of these libraries had great historical and cultural value, containing first editions with personal dedications from Marcel Proust, Salvador Dalí, André Gide, André Malraux, Paul Valéry, and Wanda Landowska.[4]

Ten thousand books were stolen from the rabbinical school, Ecole Rabbinique, in Paris, including a very valuable collection of Talmuds, while four thousand books were plundered from the Fédération des Sociétés Juives. Synagogues and Jewish book dealers were also plundered—for instance, the book dealership Librairie Lipschutz had its entire stock of twenty thousand books stolen.

Only a handful of collections gave the looters the slip; for instance, the little Yiddish library Bibliothèque Medem, founded by Jewish immigrants from Eastern Europe. The Gestapo did not manage to find the cellar where the books had been hidden. But it was scant consolation, as the library only amounted to some three thousand volumes.[5]

The plunder in France was enormous; estimates suggest that the ERR stole 723 larger libraries containing more than 1.7 million books.[6] This would be dramatically stepped up once the ERR instigated its M-Aktion in France and plundered the homes of Jews who had fled or been deported. In Paris alone, 29,000 apartments were comprehensively cleared, and everything packed onto trains and sent to the East.[7]

There was something extraordinarily malevolent about this systematic sweeping out and expurgating of the existence of Jewish people in Europe. All personal belongings that were left—such as letters, photo albums, and notes—were confiscated, scattered, burned, or pulped in paper mills. After the homes had been emptied, new owners moved in. It was as if the Jewish people who had lived there—their lives, memories, and thoughts—had never even existed.

How many private libraries and books were seized by M-Aktion is unclear, but it must have run into millions. The operation was on such a scale that three processing stations had to be set up, manned by slave workers, to sort, mend, and load the confiscated property. One of them,

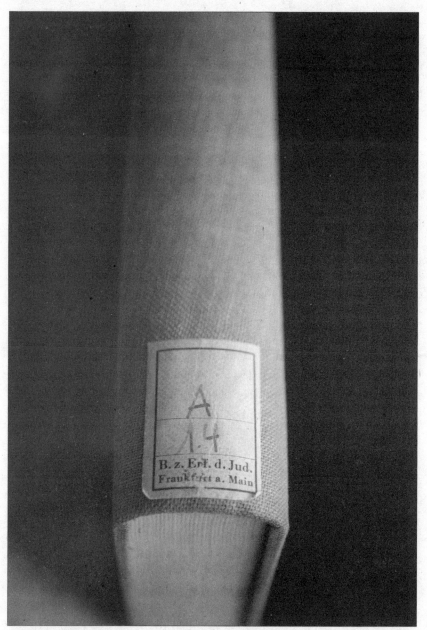

A book from the library of the Alliance Israélite Universelle in Paris, with the label from Alfred Rosenberg's Institute for Research on the Jewish Question still on the spine. The library was plundered during the war and taken to Frankfurt to be included in the institute's collection.

in a warehouse in the Thirteenth Arrondissement in Paris, was called Lager Austerlitz by the Germans. The prisoners chose instead to refer to it as "Galeries Austerlitz," an ironic allusion to the luxurious department store, Galeries Lafayette.[8] The work of handling the confiscated property continued right up to the moment when the troops of the Western Allies were drawing close to Paris in August 1944.

A literary cleaning-out of a different order was carried out in Alsace-Lorraine, which had been annexed by Nazi Germany. Here the Nazis seized all French literature in an attempt to "Germanize" the area and wipe out the French culture and language.[9]

Although the ERR confiscated the lion's share of the pickings in France, the RSHA did not come away with nothing. Many of the libraries and archives from more politically active Jewish organizations were later handed over to the RSHA, including certain parts of the archive of the Alliance. By the time the Institut zur Erforschung der Judenfrage formally opened and a conference was held on March 26, 1941, many of the Paris libraries had already arrived in Frankfurt.

In his inaugural speech, Alfred Rosenberg boasted that the institute possessed the world's finest Jewish library: "This library, a part of the Institute for Research into the Jewish Question, which opens today, already contains a large number of documents that are significant in Jewish history, and for Europe's political development. This is now the largest library in the world devoted to Judaism. In the coming years this collection will be expanded in a most purposeful manner."[10]

Any books that bear the stamp of Alliance Israélite Universelle belong to the comparatively small number that had time to be cataloged. The inflow of plundered collections was far greater than the staff could ever cope with. By 1943, half a million books had arrived in Frankfurt.[11]

The historian Philip Friedman argued that it was important for the Nazis to plunder Jewish libraries and institutions active within higher education, research, or other intellectual activity. The plunder would thereby serve a dual cause, partly depriving the Jewish population of its cultural base and learning, and partly enriching Nazi ideological research. From this perspective, the Alliance Israélite Universelle was a prime target.

+  +  +

The taxi driver stops abruptly and points down a side street. I hesitate. This does not seem like a street where one might find a renowned library. The traffic exhaust–stained balconies are cracked and seem ready to collapse at any moment. I have taken the address from a letter, and I am now on the other side of the city, in the southern part of the Latin Quarter. The buildings in the street remind one of a housing project but at the same time there is something rounded and Jugendstil-like about the architecture. Later I find out that the houses were built after the war, to provide homeless Parisians with a roof over their heads.

The house number, which I have jotted down on a scrap of paper, leads me to an apartment block with an anonymous-looking entrance where a couple of walkers have been left. After spending a few moments looking through the long list of names I have been given, I find, between the Missoux and Chauvell families, a little lopsided label with the text "Bibliothèque Russe Tourguéniev." I have seen this name before, in the ERR's reports from Paris, but I was unsure of this library's continued existence until I found a long essay on its tragic and fascinating fate, written by the historian Patricia Kennedy Grimsted.

In the apartment on the first floor I meet Hélène Kaplan, an elderly woman with raven-black hair and bright red lips, who walks with the aid of a crutch. Kaplan is the librarian and head of the association that runs the library.

It takes a moment for my eyes to get accustomed to the gloom; only a few sparse rays of sunlight penetrate the small, covered windows in the library. The apartment is absolutely crammed with books, from floor to ceiling. Between the bookcases are yellow-faded busts of Russian authors, old suitcases, trash bags, and dilapidated reading lamps. In a corner lies a Russian rag doll and a model of an Orthodox church, carved in wood. Hundreds of books that have no space on the shelves lie piled up on the floor or on tables sagging under the weight.

"We have a special floor, you know, books are very heavy," says Kaplan, striking her crutch several times into the rug.

Bibliothèque Russe Tourguéniev belongs to a special category of libraries that fell victim to the plunder during the war: the émigré libraries. For hundreds of years Paris had been a city that attracted political and intellectual refugees: artists, authors, and others who had found their way to the city, looking for a place to exercise free thought and expression. Anarchists, Communists, dissidents, stateless aristocrats, monarchs, and dictators have all at various times made Paris their home.

In the 1800s the city took in a wave of political immigrants from the east. Some of the earliest settlers were Poles, forced to escape Poland after the November 1830 uprising in Warsaw, an attempt to reestablish a free Polish state, which had not existed since 1795. One of those who settled in Paris was the Polish prince and statesman Adam Czartoryski. During the Napoleonic era he had been the foreign minister in tsarist Russia, but in 1830 he joined the rebellion and was chosen as the first president of Poland. After the uprising was crushed in 1831, more than six thousand officers, politicians, and intellectuals fled or were forced to leave Poland, in what is known there as the great migration. Czartoryski's residence at the Hôtel Lambert by the Seine was to become a center for the Polish émigré community and the opposition that yearned to create an independent Poland once more. In 1838, the Bibliothèque Polonaise was founded and soon became the epicenter of a colorful French-Polish cultural scene, including personalities like Frédéric Chopin, George Sand, Zygmunt Krasiński, and the romantic Polish poet Adam Mickiewicz. The library became the largest autonomous Polish cultural institution outside Poland, and an important symbol for the Polish struggle for independence.

The Poles were not the only group of exiles that had come from tsarist Russia. A wave of political and intellectual refugees from Russia would also settle in Paris during the 1800s. As early as 1825, after the Decembrist revolt, a large group of Russian writers had been exiled by the tsar. Even greater numbers emigrated when the political upheavals intensified at the end of the decade. The strict censorship imposed by the tsarist regime led to the creation of an independent literary scene and publishing environment in Paris.[12] Before long the focus of this activity centered on the Bibliothèque Russe Tourguéniev. The library was founded in 1875 by the Russian revolutionary German Lopatin with the assistance of his compatriot, the author Ivan Turgenev, who at this time was living in Paris.

"German did not merely want to create a library, but a meeting place for the revolutionary youth. It was a Russian library, but it was entirely autonomous of the Russian state. The library has preserved this outlook right up to the present day," Hélène Kaplan tells me as she leads me into the little reading room. One of the long walls is entirely bare, apart from a bust of Turgenev.

Lopatin was one of the first Russian revolutionaries to be influenced by Karl Marx and Friedrich Engels. Earlier, he had been imprisoned by the tsarist regime and sent into exile to Stavropol in Siberia. From there he managed to escape, get to France, and join the First International.

The library's basic collection was supplied by Turgenev, who donated some of his own books; the author also organized a literary matinee in Paris to collect donations of money and books. The library, which was given its current name after the death of Turgenev in 1883, organized readings, concerts, exhibitions, and revolutionary Christmas parties.

"It became one of the biggest Russian libraries in Europe. There were Russian libraries in other cities, but they did not survive. This is the largest and oldest of these libraries still in existence. It is something quite unique, because it was never given any financial support from Russia, and only grew because of support from various Russian exile groups—often by people donating books or working as volunteers at the library."

The library and the revolutionary sphere around it would be a nursery for several generations of Russian revolutionaries. One revolutionary who worked at the library before the First World War was a Russian named Vladimir Ilyich Ulyanov, later known as Lenin. After the failed revolution in Russia in 1905, the Bolsheviks had decided to move their activities to Paris. Lenin, who hated the city and referred to it as "a dirty hole," arrived in Paris under protest in 1908.[13]

The Turgenev Library became an important meeting place for Paris-based Bolsheviks in exile. So important, in fact, that in 1910 Lenin personally ensured the transfer of the library and archive of the Russian Social Democratic Party to the Turgenev Library.

"No single political group was dominant at the library; the entire spectrum of colors was represented: Bolsheviks, Mensheviks, social revolutionaries, and anarchists. They were political opponents, but here in the library they could meet and have debates. The library rose above their ideological differences; here it was Russian culture that held the center ground," Kaplan tells me.

The Russian Revolution had a negative impact on the Turgenev Library, when Paris was emptied of its revolutionaries, who hurried off to join the uprising. Yet these Russian exiles were soon replaced by a new and considerably larger exiled Russian community after the revolution, when tens of thousands of Russians descended on the capital. The most prominent of these were the Belorussian immigrants, the White émigrés of diverse and colorful backgrounds, including aristocrats, bourgeoisie, nationalists, reactionaries, intellectuals, military staff, and priests. They were united only in their opposition to the Communists. But there were also socialists here, many of them the same exiled Russians as before—Socialists, Communists, and Social Democrats, who had joined the revolution only to be forced into exile once the Bolsheviks had seized power.

One of them was Hélène Kaplan's father, Venedikt Mjakotin. "My father was a Russian historian and socialist, one of the people who had started the revolution before the Bolsheviks took over. He refused to join the Bolsheviks. But he was lucky; after the civil war Lenin allowed a small convoy of intellectuals, people who had been important to the revolution, to leave Russia. It was no more than two hundred people and it only happened once," says Kaplan, who was born in Prague, where Mjakotin and his wife sought refuge. "Obviously he was almost totally deleted from the history of the Soviet regime."

During the interwar years, a new circle of exiled Russian intellectuals congregated around the Turgenev Library, many of them authors, journalists, and artists, all fallen from grace in the Soviet Union. This was the heyday of the library—the time when Paris became the capital of the Russian community in exile. The circle around the Turgenev Library included writers such as Mikhail Osorgin, Mark Aldanov, and Ivan Bunin (the chairman of the foundation that ran the library), who in 1933 became the first Russian writer to win the Nobel Prize in Literature.

With this new wave of émigrés the collection grew exponentially. At the turn of the century there were about 3,500 books in the library. By 1925 it had increased to 50,000 books, and ten years later the collection had doubled in size. Before long, the Turgenev Library was considered one of the absolutely leading Russian libraries. As the library's renown spread, it also gained support. In the 1930s, the city of Paris offered the library the possibility of moving out of its modest premises on rue du Val-de-Grâce into the palatial Hôtel Colbert on rue de la Bûcherie.[14]

"Here you could find all the books that had been banned in Russia. It became known as the great library for émigré literature," Kaplan explains.

In addition to Russian émigré literature, the library had first editions of Voltaire, François de La Rochefoucauld, and the Russian author Nikolay Karamzin—and also historically valuable works such as *Sudebnik*, Tsar Ivan IV's lawbook from 1550 with commentary by the historian and statesman Vasily Tatishchev. The collection included personal archives and documents belonging to exiled Russian writers and books with annotations and signatures by, among others, Bunin and Lenin. In the interwar years another émigré library took form in Paris: the Symon Petljura Library. Symon Petljura was a Ukrainian journalist, writer, and politician who in 1917 had been involved in the formation of a short-lived Ukrainian popular republic. It had been an attempt to free the Ukraine from the shadow of Russia and the revolution. But the Petljura republic left a notorious legacy of the bloodiest persecution of Jews until the Holocaust. During the brief existence of the Ukrainian popular republic, tens of thousands of Jews are believed to have been murdered in more than thirteen hundred pogroms.[15] When the Red Army occupied the Ukraine, Petljura was forced to flee, and in 1924 he settled in the Latin Quarter in Paris, from which he led the Ukrainian National Republic (UNR) in exile. With Bibliothèque Russe Tourguéniev and Bibliothèque Polonaise as models of what he wanted to achieve, Petljura planned to start a Ukrainian public library. However, the library project had not even started in earnest before Petljura was murdered by another émigré, the Russian-Jewish poet, Sholom Schwartzbard.[16]

After the murder, a library was founded in his honor, and the Bibliothèque Ukrainienne Symon Petljura opened in 1929. The library, in an apartment on rue de La Tour d'Auvergne, built up an important archive of documents from the Ukrainian government and its leader, as well as Petljura's private library. By the time the war broke out in 1939 the collection numbered some 15,000 volumes, compared with the 100,000 volumes of the Turgenev Library and the 136,000 volumes of the Polish library.

The émigré libraries played an extraordinarily important role for these minority communities. They became the literary homes for people who had lost their language and culture. Not only did they uphold lost cultures, to an even greater extent they were meeting places in which linguistic and national identities could live on and continue to evolve. In this sense they were absolutely crucial. At the same time they operated as a sort of resistance movement. For the Poles, the Bibliothèque Polonaise was a way of salvaging Polish culture, which was being subjected to strong pressure from Germanization and Russification processes—specifically, persecution, victimization, and a downgrading of the language and culture in Polish-speaking areas.

These libraries also symbolized an alternative version of written history. They pointed to the other Russia, the other Poland, and preserved the stories that would otherwise have been lost. In the exile libraries, Russian, Polish, and Ukrainian literature could keep evolving and be read, debated, and criticized. For the poets, authors, and journalists that had not only lost their home countries but also their readers, this was especially important. Yet a catastrophe lay in wait for Paris's flourishing émigré communities, and it would come from an enemy that did not

merely intend to stifle and censor Russian, Polish, and Ukrainian culture but raze them to the ground and utterly extinguish them.

✦ ✦ ✦

Early one autumn day in 1940, the Russian exile author Nina Berberova
rode her bicycle into the center of Paris from the small house where she
was living, in the countryside on the outskirts of Paris. She had emigrated in 1922 with the poet and critic Vladislav Chodasevitj. In Paris
they had socialized with an impoverished but prominent circle of young
exile writers such as Vladimir Nabokov and Marina Tsvetajeva. Nina
Berberova had herself debuted while she was living in exile, and she
would later become known for her short stories, which depicted the lives
of Russian immigrants in Paris during the interwar years.

She often made these bicycle excursions to buy milk, potatoes, and
books. A month or so earlier she had taken out a book by the philosopher Arthur Schopenhauer, in a Russian translation, from the Turgenev Library, or as it was known among the émigrés, "Turgenevka." It
was her intention to return the book that day.

"Hôtel Colbert lies in a little street near Notre-Dame. The clock was
not even showing ten in the morning when I walked in. The whole courtyard was filled with rough wooden crates, long as coffins—three dozen
of them standing or lying on the ground. They were empty. I tapped on
the window of the concierge, who knew me, and asked if I could keep the
book until four o'clock. She gave me an irascible look: 'They're here.'

"I immediately went up the stairs. The doors were wide open. There
were two crates on the landing and two more inside the hall. Quickly,
efficiently, with rhythmic movements, the books were being packed. I
was shocked. But in spite of this I asked in my bad German what was
going on, although it was abundantly clear. I got the polite answer that
the books were being sent away. Where? Why? No one answered."[17]

Nina Berberova cycled at once to the home of Vasily Maklakov, an
old Russian politician, democrat, and diplomat. Maklakov had been the
country's ambassador in Paris in 1917 when the Bolsheviks took power.
He had occupied the Russian embassy for seven years before France felt

compelled to recognize the Soviet Union and throw Maklakov out of the embassy.

Conferring among themselves and with the historian Dimitri Odinets, the head of the library committee, they agreed that the only way to save the library was to make an appeal to their second-worst enemy: Stalin. Odinets hurried off to the Soviet embassy to try to put a stop to the looting. At the embassy they showed him first into one room, then another. He asked if he could see the principal secretary, or the first consul, or if possible the ambassador in person. He spoke to one person, then another, then a third—without any of them even introducing themselves. Over and over again he explained the reason for his visit: to try to save the Russian library.

"It was founded by Turgenev," he explained, "the author of *Fathers and Sons* and *Rudin*, while he was living in Paris." But their eyes remained blank. He went on: "It was important to act quickly, before the books were removed. . . ." The embassy staff just shrugged their shoulders: "What's the importance of this to us? Dramatic writings by migrants!"

"All of a sudden," Odinets told me, "I had an idea. I explained that Lenin had once worked in this library. That there were books here with his annotations in the margins, and other books that he had donated to the library. Even his chair was still here!" Never before, he admitted, had his imagination worked so hard. "People started running about around me and getting worked up. They called in other people. I had to repeat what I just said about Lenin."

He rounded off his story: "They showed me through a new set of doors. They continued opening and closing them. Someone promised me that he would intervene, but I could not quite believe him. That a telephone call could make a difference! That night I stayed yet again with my friends in Boulogne. The next day when I arrived at Hôtel Colbert it was all over. The chests were gone, the doors had been shut and sealed. The largest Russian exile library had ceased to exist."[18]

Nina Berberova kept her Schopenhauer. Another émigré, the historian Nikolai Knorring, also witnessed the plunder. Judging by the

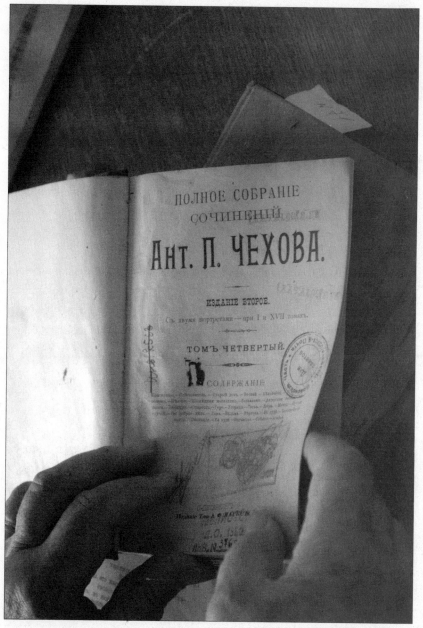

Librarian Hélène Kaplan displays one of the few books from the Russian Turgenev Library that have been returned. The unique émigré library, where among others Lenin worked, was plundered and scattered during the Second World War.

numbers on the crates, he estimated that nine hundred crates of books and archive materials were taken away. Other sources, however, have indicated a smaller number."[19] According to Knorring, the ERR also stole paintings, busts, and portraits. A few items slipped through its fingers; among other things the librarian Marija Kotljarevskaja managed to save some correspondence between the anarchist Peter Kropotkin and the philosopher Pavel Bakunin.

Hélène Kaplan opens one of the library's prewar catalogs on the table. These were also not picked up by the Nazis, and in fact they were found a few years ago in an old cardboard box in the cellar of the Hôtel Colbert. The catalogs testify to the breadth of the collection before the war, with an abundance not only of literary books but everything from geography to economics and law.

A similar story to the one that Berberova described was also played out at the Bibliothèque Polonaise, which was only a short walk from the Hôtel Colbert, in a house from the 1600s on the Île Saint-Louis, in the middle of the Seine. The library, which had recently celebrated its centenary, had 136,000 books in its collection, with an additional 12,000 drawings, 1,000 manuscripts, 2,800 antique maps, 1,700 Polish coins and medallions, and a rich archive of photographs.[20] It was a priceless collection, representing a free Polish culture, and it had been laboriously collected over a full century of exile.

The collection also included the Pelplin Bible, a Bible printed by Gutenberg, which had been saved after the assault on Poland in 1939. The Gutenberg Bible is the literary equivalent of Leonardo da Vinci's paintings. The Bibles, in two volumes, were printed by Gutenberg in the middle of the 1400s, and are considered the first significant edition of printed books in Europe. There are only twenty known complete copies. No Gutenberg Bible has been put on sale since the 1970s, but the current market value is estimated to be in excess of $35 million. The so-called Pelplin Bible was famous for having a unique mark, which is believed to have been caused by the printer dropping a section of type. The Pelplin Bible was inlaid with gold and bound in red kid leather. It was also one of only nine Gutenberg Bibles still to have its original binding from the 1400s.[21] When the war broke out in 1939, the Bible was in a library in Pelplin, a small town in an area of western Poland that would be brutally Germanized and integrated into the Third Reich. The Nazis viewed the Gutenberg Bibles as German national treasures, which absolutely had to be returned to the Reich. For this reason, the Pelplin edition, Poland's one and only Gutenberg Bible, was a coveted prize. Father Antoni Liedtke at the seminary in Pelplin was painfully aware of this, and he had the local saddle maker construct a leather case with hidden compartments, in which he hid the two volumes whose combined weight was close to ninety pounds. In October 1939, while Poland was capitulating, the Bible was being smuggled onto a cargo ship loaded with grain, bound for France and the Bibliothèque Polonaise. The consignment also included some valuable books that had been saved from the National Library in Warsaw.[22]

After receiving reports from Poland, the staff at the Bibliothèque Polonaise was aware of what to expect if the country fell. When Amiens in northern France was taken by German forces in May 1940, the Bible was evacuated once again. In early June, a truck loaded with a selection of Poland's literary inheritance, including the Pelplin Bible, traveled south. The books left on a small Polish steamer, which slipped its moorings only a few hours before the Germans attacked the town. The ship also managed to cross the English Channel, which was full of German submarines. Finally, the Bible was in safe hands.[23]

However, the collection at the Bibliothèque Polonaise was much too large to be saved in its entirety. The most important items were evacuated: drawings, maps, and original manuscripts by Adam Mickiewicz were hidden in various French libraries. Despite such efforts, the lion's share of the library remained in the building on the Île Saint-Louis, which was searched by German security police two days after the fall of Paris.[24]

Two months later, on August 25, staff arrived from the Paris office of the ERR. According to the head of the library, the historian Franciszek Pułaski, who witnessed the events, the work was overseen by three men from Rosenberg's office and about forty French workers, who packed the collection into crates like those Berberova had seen at the Turgenev Library. The contents of each crate were carefully noted down, and in all, 780 crates were filled, of which 766 contained books, newspapers, and other printed materials.[25]

In October 1940 the library was transported to La Chapelle in northern Paris and loaded onto a train bound for Germany. This time, the ERR also had to share the booty with another organization, known as the Publikationsstelle Berlin-Dahlem, a department of the Prussian state archive devoted to what was known as Eastern research.[26] As a subject it had existed before 1933; however, its purpose now was to promote German expansion to the east. Most of the Polish library was taken to the Publikationsstelle Berlin-Dahlem.

The Bibliothèque Ukrainienne Symon Petljura was also visited by the plunderers. In January 1941 the library on rue de La Tour d'Auvergne was cleared in a matter of three days of its books and archive materials, which were packed and sent to the sorting center in rue la Bruyère— once the head office of the Alliance Israélite Universelle.

The intention at first had been to send the Petljura library to the RSHA in Berlin, but after an assessment of the collection, it was concluded that it lacked relevance for the intelligence services. The books were handed over to the ERR. Alfred Rosenberg would find a place for the collection in a new library that had taken form in Berlin under his leadership—the Ostbücherei, a research library under Amt Rosenberg that would aggregate any material relating to Bolshevism and Russia and Eastern Europe in general. The Turgenev Library was eventually added as well. These émigré libraries from the "West" would make up the foundations of a collection that after the invasion of the Soviet Union started to grow exponentially.[27]

The historian Patricia Kennedy Grimsted argues that the Nazi attacks on the émigré libraries in Paris were an aspect of the preparations for the invasion of the Soviet Union, which was already under way in 1940 under a cloak of great secrecy. The libraries were considered to be possible sources of valuable intelligence for the coming war.[28]

✦ ✦ ✦

Hélène Kaplan rises, takes her crutch, and walks up to a gray metal cupboard with frosted glass doors, which she opens. She reaches in and runs the tips of her fingers over the spines of the books inside. What immediately strikes me is just how tattered the books are. Some of the spines have split. The binding has loosened and the threads stick out. Some of the books are in such bad condition that they seem to be held together only by their place on the shelf. They are neither old nor valuable, but they have had hard lives—émigrés, some having arrived with refugees from Russia before the war, only to go back east at a later stage. More than sixty years later they have come home to Paris.

As for Hélène Kaplan, she came to Paris in the third wave of Russian immigrants, after the Second World War, when her family left an Eastern Europe that was just about to be trapped behind the Iron Curtain. Not until the end of the 1980s, after perestroika, was she able to revisit her homeland. By that time, she was already involved in the Turgenev Library; then, after retiring fifteen years ago, she became its protector.

"After the war there was nothing left. Everything had been stolen, and for that reason we weren't allowed to keep Hôtel Colbert. I mean, there were no books to preserve. But then, slowly, we started rebuilding the collection, and at the end of the 1950s we were able to open the library in this apartment, which we were given by the city," Kaplan tells me.

The Turgenev Library was never able to rebuild the collection into anything comparable to what it had before the war. Yet the library, as soon as it had been reinstated, took on its role as a freestanding, oppositional literary scene in relation to its home country. During the Cold War, Russian literature by authors blacklisted in the Soviet Union once again began to be collected. Today the library has no ties with Russia and survives on a small annual grant from the city.

"It's enough for the rent and a few books. But this has always been an impoverished library. People have always worked here without getting paid for it. It's part of the culture. I think we can survive as we go into the future. We have already survived most things," says Kaplan in her Russian-accented French, and smiles at me.

She goes back to the gray metal cupboard. The worn books on the shelves don't look like much, but they hold a special value for Kaplan. These few books, 112 to be precise, are the only volumes from the original Bibliothèque Russe Tourguéniev to be returned out of the 100,000 that disappeared. She pulls out a pale gray book that was once black and opens the flyleaf. I can't read the title in the Cyrillic script, but the stamp of the library is in French, with its old address on rue du Val-de-Grâce.

"There was a rumor that the Germans took this library so they could give it to Stalin—as a gift of friendship. That was while Germany and the Soviet Union were allies. But it never happened like that. Alfred Rosenberg was very interested in this library. After all, he spoke Russian and had studied in Moscow. So they took it."

# 9

# THE LOST LIBRARY

*Rome*

The air is cool in the Centro Bibliografico. I follow the librarian, Gisèle Lèvy, a cheerful woman with a large mop of curly hair, down the stairs and into a room with white-painted concrete walls. Even before I step into the room, I pick up that distinctive smell of old library: dried leather, vellum, ink. On the shelves are sturdy volumes in dark brown leather, which rather reminds me of twisting, ancient tree trunks. Then, wedged between them, yellowing bands of parchment, like old silver birches. Some of the books seem to be in a century-long process of disintegration—bindings slowly coming away from the spines, thread poking out like dry ligaments; leather, split and crumbling in layers. Each book documents a unique decay. Volumes that were printed at the same time have parted ways. Some are pining away; others are aging more daintily.

The Centro Bibliografico is in a house from the 1700s on the west bank of the Tiber in Rome, not far from the Ponte Sisto. It is a cultural center belonging to the Unione delle Comunità Ebraiche Italiane (Union of Italian Jewish Communities). In order to get inside I have to make my way through locked doors that function more or less like security gates. It is not an unfamiliar experience. Every Jewish center, synagogue, library, and museum that I have visited on this trip has had similar security systems in place: surveillance cameras, sluice gates, suspicious glances, and questions. The security routines are sometimes a little like those at airports, with metal detectors, X-ray scanning machines, checking of bags, and sometimes frisking. Jewish institutions in Europe have become fortresses. The insight gives one an unpleasant sense of historical continuity. On the other side of the Tiber, not far from here, lies Rome's Jewish ghetto, established in the 1500s. A small area of no more than seven acres, it was surrounded by high walls, inside of which lived Rome's Jewish population. The inhabitants were given leave to move outside the ghetto by day, but they had to go back before dark fell, when the ghetto gates were locked. This continued every night for over three hundred years, until liberation at the end of the 1800s. Down in the cellar at the Centro Bibliografico, Gisèle Lèvy searches the shelves for a book.

"Here it is," she says.

She does not lift out one of the impressively large tomes, just a little vellum book about the same size as the palm of her hand. Carefully she opens it, with a slight splintering sound. An entire section is missing in the middle, as if something has taken a big bite out of it. "It's probably a mouse that's been feasting on it. Mice have always liked books. Whenever I go to old libraries I usually see mice scampering off. And then I scamper off too," Lèvy says, laughing.

"It's a Tanakh, a Jewish Bible, printed in Amsterdam in 1680. We don't know so very much about this book, apart from the fact that it belonged to a family called Finzi, who lived in Florence," says Lèvy, showing me the inside cover where someone has written "Finzi" and "Firenze" in ink.

The little mouse-eaten book is somewhat of a mystery. It came back to Rome about ten years ago after it had turned up in the little town of Hungen, outside Frankfurt. After the war the book ended up with the only Jewish survivor in Hungen, Jeremias Oppenheim. The book was handed over to an Italian delegate at a conference on plundered property in Hannover in 2005. It is unclear how it ended up with Oppenheim.

"You can see the stamp here," says Lévy , and shows me a small, ornate stamp, faded and yellow, across the spine of the book, with the Italian text "Biblioteca del Collegio Rabbinico Italiano."

The Jewish congregation keeps its written, literary legacy at the Centro Bibliografico. The most valuable part of the collection hails from the Biblioteca del Collegio Rabbinico Italiano, a library belonging to a rabbinical school founded in 1829.[1] The school, one of the oldest rabbinical schools in Italy, is still active, although there are not so many students anymore.

*A small, mouse-eaten Tanakh, a Jewish Bible, which came back to Rome in the early 2000s. The library of the priceless Biblioteca della Comunità Israelitica is still missing without a trace, in spite of repeated attempts to track down the collection.*

"I can count them on my fingers. They attend normal schools in the daytime, and then they come here afterward, or sometimes at the weekends."

The Collegio Rabbinico's library consists of a large collection of Jewish works from the 1500s and on. It includes many books from renowned Jewish-Italian printers such as Soncino, De Gara, Bragadin, Bomberg, and Vendramin. But there are also Jewish books here from other presses in Jewish cultural centers such as Amsterdam, Frankfurt, Thessaloniki, and Vilnius. The rabbis of the Collegio Rabbinico Italiano traveled all over Europe to purchase books for the collection. Lèvy shows me a shelf with the Talmud in a sturdy ten-volume set. Age has given a marbled patina to the light brown leather. "It's an extremely rare edition from Basel, printed in 1580," she tells me.

The Centro Bibliografico's historical collection consists of 8,500 volumes. Some are from minor Jewish congregations around Italy; these disappeared when Italy was unified in the 1800s and Jews were given the freedom to move to cities such as Venice, Florence, or Rome. Lèvy shows me several shelves of books of this kind, from places like Pisa, Sienna, and Pitigliano, a small town in Tuscany that was once known as Little Jerusalem on account of its flourishing Jewish community.

The collection at the Centro Bibliografico tells the story of the Italian Jews. It is a story not only expressed on the bound page—but also one that has left exterior traces.

Gisèle Lèvy pulls out a bulky leather-bound volume from a shelf and opens the front flyleaf, which is absolutely covered with words, sentences, symbols, and squiggles in ink. Mere jottings, but nonetheless beautiful—layers upon layers of words and signs.

"They did not have very much paper in the olden days, so they used books for note-taking. Some of these names were the people who owned the book. But it also functioned as a diary. Here it says, 'My son was married last week.' And here it says"—Lèvy points at another scrawl—"'On this day my grandson had his brit milah.'"[2]

The book, from 1745, contains notes from several generations of a family of Sephardic Jews from Pisa.

"The book was printed in Amsterdam; it was common for Sephardic Jews in Italy to purchase their books from there."

In the early 1900s, the Biblioteca del Collegio Rabbinico Italiano was housed on the upper floor of the large synagogue on Lungotevere de' Cenci, on the other side of the Tiber, a building that stands out in the cityscape because of its Babylonian-Syrian architecture. It was constructed at the end of the 1800s in memory of the ghetto, as a symbol of the new-won freedom of the Roman Jews. Yet there was also another library in the synagogue, which was both older and more valuable than that of the Collegio Rabbinico—a library that was lost without a trace during the war, belonging to the Jewish congregation in Rome: the Biblioteca della Comunità Israelitica. The collection contained the literary, religious, and cultural legacy of the oldest Jewish congregation in Europe. Among other things, the collection included manuscripts about Jewish intellectual and religious life in medieval Rome—also a large collection of incunabula, including rare works brought by Sephardic Jews from Spain.[3]

It was a library that bore the cultural hallmarks of the Roman Jews. Unlike most of the world's Jews, the latter did not have their origins with either the Sephardic Jews or the Ashkenazi Jews of Central and Eastern Europe. The first Jews reputedly arrived in Rome as early as 161 BC, sent by Judas Maccabeus, the leader of the Maccabean Revolt, who was seeking the support of Rome against the Seleucid Empire. A Jewish community with several synagogues was established in Rome well before the birth of Christ.

Later, when Rome's imperial ambitions reached into the eastern Mediterranean, Judea was conquered and brought into the fold of the empire. In the centuries that followed, the Jewish population rose up on a number of occasions—with catastrophic consequences. Rome responded to rebellions mercilessly and with pathological brutality.

Many of those who were not killed in the wars were enslaved. Others chose to leave war-torn Judea to settle in other parts of the empire, or emigrate to the east into Persia. Before long the Jews who had chosen to stay in Judea were in the minority. Jerusalem, from which all Jews were forbidden, was replaced by the pagan Roman city of Aelia Capitolina. In Jewish history, the expulsion of Jews is regarded as the beginning of two thousand years of the Jewish Diaspora. However, in academic research the Diaspora is regarded as a considerably longer and more complicated process. Judea's strategic position between Europe, Asia, and Africa has meant that the region, for thousands of years, has endured invading armies of Egyptians, Assyrians, Babylonians, Persians, Greeks, Romans, Arabs, and Turks. The migration and dispersal of the inhabitants of this war-ravaged area has been in progress for a very long time.[4]

The early Jewish community in Rome grew. Other congregations appeared all over Italy, often made up of freed slaves. In the high medieval period the Italian Jews developed a rich literary culture, not least through their contacts with Sephardic Jews in Spain. The translations of Jewish-Arab thinkers also had a great influence on Christian culture. One of the most important of these was Maimonides, usually regarded as the most significant Jewish philosopher in the medieval period. Maimonides sought to demonstrate that the philosophy of Aristotle could be reconciled with the Judaic faith. This greatly influenced the theologian Thomas Aquinas, who similarly tried to integrate the philosophical system of Aristotle with the Christian faith.[5]

At the same time, during the high medieval age, an increasingly repressive and anti-Semitic policy was taking form in the Catholic church. A leading role in this was played by Innocent III, one of the most powerful, influential popes, who proclaimed the Fourth Crusade and set in motion a ruthless persecution of "heretics" in Europe. In 1215 he convoked one of the most important synod meetings of the medieval era, the Fourth Lateran Council, where amendments were made to canonical law. In the meeting it was decided that Jews would be barred from holding public appointments, as their crime against Christ made it inappropriate for them to make decisions on behalf of Christians. Jews were also to wear clothes that clearly distinguished them from Christians. At a later meeting it was agreed that Jews should be made to wear a cloth badge on their breast of half a hand's-width. Innocent III's decree of 1215 was the origin of the yellow star that Jews were forced to wear under the Nazis, seven hundred years later.[6]

Innocent III's successors pursued the same line, including his cousin Pope Gregory IX, who in 1234 asserted with the doctrine *perpetua servitus iudaeorum* that Jews should be banned from all political life and live in political slavery until Judgment Day, which in principle removed any opportunity for Jews to exert social influence until the 1800s. Gregory IX formally established the Inquisition, primarily to clamp down on religious sects such as the Cathars—and also Jews.[7]

In the 1500s, thousands of Sephardic Jews from Spain and Portugal sought refuge in Italy and the Vatican state. They were initially welcomed, thanks to more tolerant popes. Many of the arrivals were translators, poets, and teachers—including the historian Samuel Usque, author of the book damaged by the bullet in Amsterdam. Pope Leo X gave the Italian Jews permission to print the Talmud. But the Jewish community in Rome only had a short time to catch its breath. By the mid-1500s, the Counter-Reformation had taken form within the Catholic church, and there was a drive to defend the true faith against heretical Protestantism. The spiritual defense gave rise to a more intolerant religious climate, which was also directed against Judaism.

The first attack was on Jewish literature, which had flourished in Italy at the beginning of the 1500s, with many Jewish book printers. On the day of the Jewish New Year, September 9, 1553, the pope ordered the confiscation and burning of all editions of the Talmud and related texts. In a papal bull, the Talmud was branded as blasphemous against the Christian faith. In the Campo de' Fiori in Rome, the Inquisition built a large pyre of books and writings confiscated from Jewish homes in the city. Book burnings also took place in Ferrara, Florence, and Venice, all centers of Jewish printing. Thousands of editions of the Talmud were consumed by the flames. In Rome, no books in Hebrew were printed for hundreds of years. [8]

Jewish literature was stymied by Inquisitional censorship, and traces of these events can be found in the cellar of the Centro Bibliografico. Gisèle Lèvy shows me a book in which the Inquisition has crossed out sections in the text. "If for instance it said in a book, 'Our God is the only God,' this would be erased. There could not be anything written down which might be regarded as critical of the Catholic church. The Inquisition examiners were not usually themselves able to read Hebrew, but they used rabbis who had been forced to convert to Catholicism. So it was often the case that 'Jews' censored other Jews. It's a very tragic story," Lèvy explains.

Other books in the library also bear the signs of persecution. Lèvy takes out a book bound in vellum. The outer edges of the pages have a faint nuance of red, but what I notice at once are two columns of text written in longhand on the white cover.

"There were very many pogroms in Italy, especially in the Middle Ages, when synagogues were plundered and burned. At this time parchment was very valuable, so Jewish writings on parchment were stolen and sold to the church, which reused the material for writing or bookbinding," Lèvy explains. The practice was particularly degrading, as they often used Torah scrolls. "The Torah is holy. One never throws it away; it is respectfully buried when it is worn out. Therefore, whenever Jews have been persecuted, it has always been important to save their Torah. It has almost been as important as saving human lives."

According to Lèvy, in old libraries in areas around Bologna, Parma, Ferrara, and Ravenna, it is possible to find books bound with parchment still bearing clear signs of Hebrew writing. "These books are of great value to us, because the pieces of reused parchment are preserved fragments of a lost culture. Sometimes you can find books which have been made from the same parchment source, and you can start assembling the parts to try to find out where it came from, and who wrote it." The text on the parchment before us is written in both Hebrew and Ladino, the Spanish-Jewish dialect spoken by the Sephardim. "It's very easy to see that a Sephardic Jew wrote this; the Hebrew text is very similar to Arabic in its style," says Lèvy, running her fingers over the lines.

Yet another catastrophe descended on Rome's Jews only two years after the book pyres in 1553. Pope Paul IV, in the papal bull known as *Cum nimis absurdum*, took away the rights of the Jewish community. According to Paul IV, it was "absurd" to let the Jews—who, as a consequence of the guilt that they had laid on their own heads, were sentenced to "perpetual slavery"—live among Christians and enjoy the same rights. Jews had to be made to see that they were "slaves as a result of their deeds."[9]

Jews lost the right to own property, and were forced to go into unskilled jobs such as rag-and-bone collection, pawnbroking, or dealing in fish. Jewish men were made to wear pointed yellow hats, while the women had to wear shawls of the same color. Jews were forbidden from sharing dinners, engaging in amusement, or in any other way fraternizing with Christians. And on the Sabbath, falling on a Saturday, they had to go to church to hear Catholic homilies, the purpose of which was to encourage them to convert.

*Cum nimis absurdum* established Rome's ghetto, which was placed between the Portico of Octavia and the bank of the Tiber, an area that was regularly affected by flooding. Sanitary problems and a lack of space meant that epidemics often raged in the ghetto. Almost a quarter of the inhabitants died in an outbreak of the plague in 1656.[10] Rome's ghetto, locked every night from the outside, was in actual fact a large prison.

The liberation of Italy's Jews only began with the coming of Napoleon. During the French Revolution, for the first time, Jews had been given equal rights as citizens. Napoleon rolled out this "radical policy" all over the Continent, banning ghettos, lifting all restrictions, and putting Judaism on an equal footing with the Christian religions. He even had the pope disavow all his worldly power.

But these freedoms came and went with Napoleon. As soon as Pius VII was reinstated, he locked up the city's Jews in the ghetto and resumed the Inquisition. However, time was not on the side of the church state as liberal, social, and democratic movements gained ground in the 1800s. The medieval system of ghettos, restrictions, and slavery were in dissolution all over Europe. In the revolutions of 1848, many European Jews regained their rights. Even in the Italian states the anti-Semitic restrictions were being removed and the ghetto rule ended. The church state resisted the development until the bitter end. Liberation came in 1870, when Italian troops marched into Rome and dissolved the church state. The ghetto in Rome was actually the last of its kind in Europe, before the Nazis reinstituted the ghetto system and reimposed medieval restrictions on the Jewish population.

In the late 1800s the walls surrounding the ghetto were demolished along with most of the run-down area nearby. Nonetheless a literary treasure trove was rescued out of the demolished ghetto, where it had somehow survived hundreds of years of the Inquisition's confiscations and book pyres.

A priceless collection of Jewish writings, manuscripts, and books was assembled from the synagogues, schools, and homes in the ghetto, which laid the foundations for the Biblioteca della Comunità Israelitica.[11] This unique library testified to the tragic history of the Jews in Rome. Not only were the Italian Jews the cultural heirs of the oldest Jewish community in Europe, in their isolation they had also developed a dialect of their own, which came close to being a language in its own right: Giudeo-Romanesco, or Ladino, with roots from the medieval era.[12]

A full catalog of the Biblioteca della Comunità Israelitica was never made, with the exception of a lesser compilation of its more valuable texts, which was made by the Jewish researcher Isaiah Sonne in 1934. But before the outbreak of the Second World War, the library contained some seven thousand volumes, including both manuscripts and books that could not be found anywhere else. There were incunabula and books from Italian printers of the 1500s, including a rare edition of the Talmud in twenty-one volumes by Soncino, the printer who had been banned by the papacy.[13] There were books from other famous Jewish printers such as Bomberg and Bragadin, as well as medieval manuscripts by the Jewish poet, rabbi, and medical doctor Moses Rieti, who had been the personal physician of Pope Pius II in the 1400s. And alongside manuscripts on medicine and astronomy from the 1300s, there were books brought by Sephardic Jews from Spain, including a Portuguese incunabulum from 1494.

The library was the literary remnant of two thousand years of Jewish presence in Rome, an inheritance that not only told the history of the Jews in the city, but also the beginnings of Christianity. As Robert Katz describes in his book *Black Sabbath*, "Among the known material were the only copies of books and manuscripts dating from before the birth of Christ, from the time of the Caesars, the emperors, and the early popes. There were engravings from the Middle Ages, books from the earliest printers, and papers and documents handed down through the ages."[14]

◆  ◆  ◆

Dario Tedeschi cups his hand behind his ear and gives me a questioning look. I try again, slowly articulating every syllable. He shakes his head resignedly. He wears a starched white shirt, the arms of which are rolled up to his elbows. Through the windows, one can make out Rome's university buildings. We are in his legal chambers—a large, bright, and sparsely furnished office. I am unsure whether Tedeschi, nearing his eighties, is unable to hear what I am saying or simply does not understand my English. Maybe a bit of both. In the end he just hands me a pen. It turns into a curious interview, in which I write down my questions on a slip of paper that he scrutinizes for several minutes before he attempts to answer them.

"In the Biblioteca della Comunità Israelitica there were incredibly important, rare books. We are assuming that this was the most important Jewish library in Italy, maybe even the whole world," says Tedeschi, placing a book on the table with the title *Rapporto Sull'Attività della Commissione per il Recupero del Patrimonio Bibliografico della Comunità Ebraica di Roma, Razziato Nel 1943*—the results of the investigations conducted by the Italian government on the subject of stolen Jewish property. Italy, like many other European nations at the end of the 1990s, set up a public committee to investigate the plundering of Italian Jewish property during the Second World War. Tedeschi, a member of this committee, was one of those urging that particular attention should be given to the disappearance of the Biblioteca della Comunità Israelitica. "I have a personal interest in this; I am a Roman Jew myself. My father's parents both died in the Holocaust. But this library is not only of interest to the Jewish congregation in Rome, but for the whole of Italy," says Tedeschi.

Until then almost nothing had been known about the library's disappearance. Some attempts, all fruitless, had been made after the war to find the library. As late as 2002, after pressure from the Jewish congregation, a special commission was put together to find the Biblioteca della Comunità Israelitica, which was considered to have "priceless value for the cultural inheritance of Italy as a whole."[15]

Dario Tedeschi, at that time the chairman of the Unione delle Comunità Ebraiche Italiane, was chosen to lead the investigation. The members of the investigating commission, which included historians, archivists, and civil servants, managed after several years of detective work to uncover some new details of the mysterious disappearance of the library.

"We found documents that confirmed that Einsatzstab Reichsleiter Rosenberg stole the library. But the mystery was obviously that they did not steal one but two libraries, they also took the Biblioteca del Collegio Rabbinico Italiano. Yet why did only one of the libraries come back? This was the question we wanted to answer," Tedeschi tells me.

The plundering, and the circumstances leading up to it, was yet another tragic chapter in the long history of the Roman Jews. When Mussolini and his National Fascist Party took power in 1922, there were no outward signs of the movement being anti-Semitic in its outlook. Quite the contrary, the regime had the support of many Italian Jews, and some of the highest-ranking leaders within the party were Jews—for instance, the finance minister, Guido Jung.[16] But there existed a race-ideological phalanx within the Fascist movement. Not until the late 1930s when the Axis powers were formed through the union between Hitler and Mussolini did the regime begin to show signs of open anti-Semitism. In 1938 the Fascists introduced racial legislation modeled on the Nuremberg Laws, among other things prohibiting Jews from holding positions of public office or entering into matrimony with "non-Jews."[17]

When Italy entered into the war in 1940, the persecution was stepped up. Nazi Germany started exerting pressure on Italy to solve "the Jewish question." It offered to take on the role of executioner—all the Italian Fascists had to do was put the country's Jews on trains and send them to the north.

Despite widespread anti-Semitism, many groups in the Italian general public, the army, and even the Fascist Party responded with distaste to German racial politics. Pressure from Germany notwithstanding, the Italian military refused to take part in genocide. Thousands of Jews between 1941 and 1943 had taken refuge in Italian-occupied parts of Yugoslavia, Greece, and southeastern France, where for the time being they were safer than on German territory. The Italian regime had also evacuated four thousand Jews to the south of Italy, where they remained in security throughout the war.

It was Benito Mussolini's fall in July 1943 that sealed the fate of Italy's Jews. When the Western Allies landed on Sicily in the same month, the Italians' confidence in their leader and their appetite for war were both utterly spent. After the country surrendered to the Allies in September, Nazi Germany, which had long had misgivings about Italy, attacked immediately. Mussolini was freed and returned to power, but he was little more than a puppet for the occupiers.[18] The invasion would dramatically change the situation for the 43,000 Jews who had ended up under the jurisdiction of the German occupiers.

At the end of September 1943, Herbert Kappler, the recently appointed head of the secret police in Rome, called in the city's Jewish leaders. He assured them that the twelve thousand Jews living in Rome would avoid deportation if they assembled a ransom of fifty kilos of gold within six hours. Thousands of people streamed into the synagogue to leave their earrings, wedding rings, necklaces, and other items of gold. The required gold was handed in at the SS headquarters on Via Tasso before the expiration of the deadline. But in fact the extortion was fraudulent, as the deportation order had already been sent in secret.[19]

The day after the ransom was paid, some twenty SS men raided the synagogue on Lungotevere de' Cenci and went through its property, confiscating its archive among other things, which included a register of the names and addresses of the city's Jews. A few days later the synagogue was visited by two men from the ERR, who had come to inspect the Biblioteca del Collegio Rabbinico Italiano and the Biblioteca della Comunità Israelitica.[20] The ERR had set up a special group for its Italian operation, known as Sonderkommando Italien. One of the visitors to the synagogue was Johannes Pohl from the Hebraic Department at the Institut zur Erforschung der Judenfrage in Frankfurt, the very same Pohl who, the year before, had assessed the libraries Ets Haim and Rosenthaliana in Amsterdam.[21] A few days later yet more ERR staff arrived to start evaluating the collection.

An eyewitness, the Jewish journalist and literary critic Giacomo Debenedetti, later described what took place during these days:

> A German officer examined the collection as if it were fine embroidery; he caressed the papyrus and incunabula, turned the pages of the manuscripts and the rare editions. The gradations of his care and attention to the volumes stood in direct proportion to their value. These works were to a very great extent written in obscure alphabets. But when he opened their pages, his eyes fixed on them and widened and shone like a reader who is familiar with a subject and knows how to find a desired passage or a couple of revealing lines. In his elegant hands these ancient books spoke as if being submitted to a bloodless torture.[22]

The secretary of the synagogue, Rosina Sorani, was another witness. After going through the two collections, the same officer who had earlier caressed the incunabula told Sorani that the libraries were going to be confiscated and taken away within the next few days. He also threatened her, as she testified in her diary, saying that "everything had to stay exactly as they left it, and if not—I would pay with my life."[23]

The congregation, in a desperate attempt to save the library, pleaded with the Italian Fascists. But it was useless. In the new Fascist regime, which wore a German overcoat, the party's anti-Semitic wing had been moved into leading positions.

In the morning of October 13, 1943, two large German railroad cars, which had been placed on the city's tram lines, were moved to the synagogue by the Tiber. Putting their lives in danger, Rosina Sorani and her coworkers quickly hid some of the most valuable items. Religious artifacts of gold and silver were hidden inside a wall, while several

A book from 1745 at the Centro Bibliografico in Rome, with annotations from several generations of a family of Sephardic Jews in Pisa.

particularly valuable manuscripts were smuggled across to the nearby library, Biblioteca Vallicelliana. Early the following morning, ERR staff arrived with a gang of laborers. It took a whole day to fill the two freight cars—which disappeared after that. A few months later, in December 1943, they came back to pick up what had been left, especially the greater part of the Biblioteca del Collegio Rabbinico Italiano.

Fortunately, the Germans did not find the hidden objects, but Rome's Jews had no time to rejoice at this or mourn the loss of their library. On the orders of SS-Obersturmbannführer Herbert Kappler, other railroad cars had already arrived. Just two days after the first load of books had been removed from the synagogue, early in the morning of the Sabbath on October 16, Kappler's men raided hundreds of Jewish homes in Rome. Over a thousand people were taken prisoner, mostly women and children. They were taken to the military college, Collegio Militare, only a few blocks from the Vatican and St. Peter's Basilica, and held there over the weekend. A pregnant woman was forced to give birth outside the school, in the courtyard, when the guards refused to take her to a hospital. On Monday, the prisoners were loaded onto a freight train and taken to Auschwitz-Birkenau. Only a handful would survive.[24]

Pope Pius XII chose not to intervene or make any official protest against the persecution. The pope's role in the occupation is still a controversial issue, but most likely he did not dare risk his relations with the Axis powers, as this might have upset the Vatican's neutrality.[25]

However, the Nazis met with more resistance from other parts of Italian society. Rome's police refused to take part in the search for Jews, and large numbers of ordinary Roman citizens opened their homes to the fugitives. Many Jews also found sanctuary in monasteries, churches, and other Catholic institutions, thanks to the individual contributions of priests and nuns. In spite of rewards being offered to those who revealed where Jews were being hidden, Kappler's forces were only able to seize another eight hundred Jews. Thousands managed to stay in hiding in Rome until the city was liberated in June 1944.

In March 1947, the Biblioteca del Collegio Rabbinico came back the same way as it had been removed, by train from Germany. And until the return of the mouse-nibbled Jewish Bible in 2005, it had been assumed that the whole library had been returned in 1947. This assumption was something that Dario Tedeschi and his commission had to reevaluate during the process of their work. "It came as a total surprise to us," Tedeschi tells me, "but it was proof that not everything had come back after the war. What we know is that Biblioteca del Collegio Rabbinico was taken to Frankfurt, and that was where it was found after the war. But somewhere on the way from Rome to Germany, the Biblioteca della Comunità Israelitica went somewhere else."

The Biblioteca del Collegio Rabbinico was brought to Johannes Pohl's department for Jewish literature at the Institut zur Erforschung der Judenfrage in Frankfurt. The question is, Why was the library of the Jewish congregation not delivered to the same place? Tedeschi's commission would spend seven years trying to come up with an answer, and even after extensive investigations in archives, libraries, and collections across several continents, the fate of the library remained enveloped in an impenetrable historical fog.

On the way, parts were found, pieces of what had been lost. Isaiah Sonne's catalog of the collection from 1934 was found in the National Library in Jerusalem. "I was in contact with a friend who was working at the National Library in Jerusalem. One day he sent a photo of a book he had found in the library. It looked like a journal, a collation of books in Italian. I recognized his handwriting. He sent more, and that was when I understood that it was the register of the books," says Gisèle Lèvy, who took part in the search for the library. Two manuscripts with stamps from the library were found at the Jewish Theological Seminary in New York. The school, which had bought the manuscripts in the 1960s, could not account for how it had acquired them. There were also rumors that the library stamp had been seen in other collections, but this could never be confirmed.

In 2009 the commission presented its final report, in which it drew the conclusion that the books taken from the synagogue in October and December 1943 very likely took different routes. While the December train arrived at the Frankfurt institute, the October train with the Biblioteca della Comunità Israelitica probably continued to Berlin. But these conclusions remained speculative. The correspondence relating to the ERR's Italian operations was destroyed when Berlin was bombed in November 1943. However, if Tedeschi's commission was correct, it would explain the disappearance of the library. The books sent to Frankfurt and the books sent to Berlin met two entirely different destinies.

# 10

# FRAGMENTS OF A PEOPLE

## *Thessaloniki*

A warm deluge of rain colors the brick a dark red. The ruins of the palace of the Roman emperor Galerius occupy an entire block in the Greek port city of Thessaloniki. Today the Roman ruins have been made into a tasteful outdoor museum. The palace from AD 300 lies ripped open, and I can see into the emperor's baths and pleasure gardens. In the enormous throne hall, which has a diameter of thirty yards, there are still the remains of a beautiful marble floor. The best-kept part of the palace complex is the almost completely intact rotunda, a circular brick building that, with its nineteen-foot-thick walls, has held out against two millennia of war, weather, and earthquakes.

From the beginning, the building was used as a pagan temple, but it was later converted by Constantine the Great into one of the first churches in the world. A thousand years later, the Ottomans turned the rotunda into a mosque, and the minaret raised in the 1500s is still standing. The rotunda testifies to Thessaloniki's long history of cultural and religious diversity: a port on the borderlands between Europe and Asia, bearing the hallmarks of its various rulers—Greeks, Romans, Byzantines, and Turks. All have put their mark on the city with their monuments and their ruins. Yet there is one culture that has left few traces, although it dominated the city from the 1500s for the next four hundred years.

The signs of this erased culture are not easy to find. They are not marked out with signposts or detailed in the guidebooks. But they are there if you know where to look. A short distance from Galerius's magnificent palace ruins is a building that does not attract any particular attention. In the corner of a square is a dirty, dejected-looking garage for mopeds, its walls and roof covered in graffiti. Immediately behind the garage is a knee-high wall made of black slate. But in one section, the slate is suddenly interrupted by a block of marble on which, in spite of erosion and the stain of pollution, one can make out patterned foliage in relief. A little farther to the side sits another block of marble, a little piece of what seems to have once been the bottom of a Corinthian column. I find a more telling piece of masonry where the wall reaches the street—an eight-inch-high marble tablet. It is possible to vaguely discern letters carved into the surface of the stone. They are not Latin but Hebrew. The tablet is a piece of a smashed Jewish headstone, a fragment of a community that until quite recently used to exist here. Possibly this stone was shattered on a cold day early in December 1942, not far from here, when five hundred Greek workers armed with mallets, iron-bar levers, and dynamite arrived at the old Jewish cemetery, which lay outside the city's east wall.[1]

Thessaloniki's Jewish cemetery is believed to have been Europe's largest, covering an area of eighty-six acres, with almost 500,000 graves, the oldest of which dated from the 1400s. The city's Greek politicians had been wanting to move the burial ground for a long time, as there was a feeling that it impeded Thessaloniki's expansion. There had been resistance from the Jewish community. When the German army occupied Thessaloniki in 1941, the Greek authorities and the Nazis took joint action. After a few weeks of systematic destruction, the "vast necropolis, scattered with fragments of stone and rubble, resembled a city that had been bombed, or destroyed by a volcanic eruption," wrote one contemporary witness.[2]

The American consul in Istanbul, Burton Berry, reported that "the work of destroying the cemetery was done in such haste that very few Jews succeeded in finding the remains of their families and relatives. Recently buried dead were thrown to the dogs."[3] According to another witness, the "sight of it was devastating. People were running between the tombs begging the destroyers to spare those of their relatives; with tears they collected the remains."[4]

The hundreds of thousands of broken headstones and sepulchral monuments were used as a marble quarry, from which building materials were sourced for years to come. The Nazis were the first to make use of this morbid exchange. They had a swimming pool built from the

A piece of a headstone from the destroyed Jewish cemetery in
Thessaloniki. The burial ground was leveled during the war and the
stones used as construction material, one of the few remaining
traces of the city's erased Jewish community.

headstones. But mostly the stones were used by the Greeks themselves, for the repair of houses, building of lavatories, paving of school yards, and even the construction of a sailing club in the harbor. The square in front of the city's theater was paved with Jewish headstones. Even the Greek Orthodox Church made use of the devastation: seventeen churches in and around Thessaloniki put in a request to the authorities for marble from the Jewish cemetery.[5]

Today, broken stones from the destroyed burial ground can be found all over Thessaloniki. In most cases their history has been weathered off, polished, or hacked away, but sometimes—as in the case of this slate wall, in an alley that stinks of urine behind a run-down moped garage—there has been no effort to remove their origins. The slate wall was not built during the war but in the 1960s, when there was still a supply of stone from the Jewish burial ground.

These scattered fragments are the remains of Sephardic Saloníki, the largest and richest Jewish community in the eastern Mediterranean for centuries. Saloníki, as the city was known for a long time, was a Jewish center of knowledge, famous for its rabbis, schools, newspapers, and printers. But the city was much more than that; it was, in fact, the only substantial urban settlement in the world where the Jewish population was not in the minority.

For the first time on this journey I do not visit a library, because there isn't one to visit. Thessaloniki is a place where plunder, destruction, and the Holocaust left very little for posterity. Of the fifty thousand or so Jews living here in 1942, only a few thousand would survive.[6]

Today, Thessaloniki is a wholly Greek city, but there is still a small Jewish congregation in existence, with its roots in Sephardic Saloníki. Only in later years has it tried to reclaim the city's largely forgotten Jewish history. In the early 2000s the Jewish Museum was founded in Thessaloniki to honor the memory of this lost culture. It is a rather small museum, situated in a beautiful turn-of-the-century house in one of the few restored streets in the old Jewish quarter. On the first floor, in a room whose windows face onto the orange trees in the street, sits the museum's curator, Erika Perahia Zemour. When I find her, she is agitated. She has just found out that the monument recently erected in memory of the Jewish cemetery bears an inaccurate inscription.

"I'm so furious! It took us over seventy years to get this monument put up, so people would know what was here before. And then it's not even accurate. It's incredible! On the plaque it says it was the Germans who destroyed the cemetery and used the stone as building material. That's completely wrong. It was the Greeks who smashed up the cemetery and used most of the stone. That's very typical of how people reason here," says Zemour, drilling me with her eyes and taking a puff on her bright red e-cigarette.

In the museum, there has been an attempt to collect some of what has been lost; there are some undamaged gravestones, photographs, ritual artifacts, and a number of books that survived the Holocaust. But it is not a large collection. Most of what was plundered in Saloníki would never come back.

"Saloníki was a center of Jewish learning and dissemination in the eastern Mediterranean. Some of the first printers in the Ottoman Empire were set up here, in Saloníki, by Sephardic Jews. Even the first newspaper printed in the Ottoman Empire was a newspaper from Saloníki," Zemour tells me. What set Saloníki apart from other large Jewish settlements was the unique level of freedom the Jews had in the management of their own affairs. "This was the only place in Europe where Sephardic Jews were really welcomed after they had fled Spain. Jews from other parts of Europe also came here, fleeing persecution. They were in the majority here, so they could feel safe. There was no ghetto and there were no restrictions. Saloníki's Jews could devote themselves to any profession they chose. This made the city unique," Zemour tells me.

Saloníki became known as *la madre de Israel* (Israel's mother). The expression was coined by the Marrano Jew Samuel Usque, who in the 1500s described Saloníki as a paradise for Jews, while the rest of Europe was "my Hell on earth."[7]

There was already a Jewish settlement here in antiquity; there is even a reference to it in Paul's First Epistle to the Thessalonians in the

New Testament, in which Paul tries to persuade the city's Jewish population to convert, thereby triggering a riot.

When Constantinople fell in 1453 to the Ottoman Turks, Saloníki's population was reduced significantly when Sultan Mehmet II had thousands of people forcibly moved to Istanbul, the new capital built on the ruins of Constantinople. According to Ottoman registers, in 1478 there was not a single Jew remaining in Saloníki.[8] But when the Sephardic Jews were expelled from Spain in 1492, they were welcomed by the sultan, who regarded these well-educated Sephardic Jews as an asset to the rapidly developing Ottoman Empire. Many Jewish translators, doctors, and bankers were offered employment at the court. The benefits of the Ottomans' tolerance were well recognized at the time. The French geographer Nicolas de Nicolay visited Istanbul in the 1550s and wrote:

> To the great detriment and damage of the Christianitie, [the Jews] have taught the Turkes divers inventions, craftes and engines of warre, as to make artillerie, harquebuses, gunne powder, shot and other munitions; they have also there set up printing, not before seen in those countries, by the which in faire characters they put in light divers bookes in divers languages as Greek, Latin, Italian, Spanish and the Hebrew tongue, being to them naturell.[9]

The first Sephardic Jews came to Saloníki from Majorca in 1492. They were soon followed by others, from the mainland, and thereafter also from Provence, Italy, and Portugal. By 1519 tens of thousands had arrived, and the Jewish population was already in a majority. By the early 1500s there were twenty-five synagogues in Saloníki.[10] The Sephardic influence was so pronounced that Saloníki could really only be regarded as a Spanish-Jewish colony on the Greek coast, in which both their language and culture had remained intact.

Yet even if the Jews were to enjoy greater freedoms in the Ottoman Empire than in Christian Europe, they were never on an equal footing with Muslims. The Ottoman state rarely involved itself in religious questions involving the empire's many minorities; like other religious groups, the Jews were allowed their own law courts. In Saloníki, a prominent and influential class of rabbis was in charge of the running of civil society. The rabbis, who passed sentence on everything from ownership of property to adultery, sought answers to legal and moral disputes on the basis of complex and extensive Judaic legal writings. Entire libraries were imported from Spain, and Saloníki's rabbis collected writings, manuscripts, and books from Jewish educational centers in Europe such as Amsterdam, Venice, Kraków, and Vilnius. The first printing press in Saloníki, established in 1513, produced texts in Ladino and Hebrew.[11] In the early 1500s an official school for Talmudic studies was established, the Talmud Torah Hagadol, which was soon well known all over the Jewish world. The school grew rapidly into an enormous educational institution, with two hundred teachers, thousands of pupils, an extensive library, and its own printing press.

In the intellectual hothouse into which Saloníki had developed, there was a meeting between Jewish philosophy, classical literature, Arabic science, and the humanism of the Italian Renaissance. Their high level of education made the rabbis of Saloníki sought-after all over Europe.

The prerequisite for this cultural flowering was the economic prosperity of the city, one of the most important harbors in the eastern Mediterranean. The city's golden age was in the 1500s, and then, in the following centuries, it went through a decline as a consequence of new trading routes, religious splits in the community, and the gradual disintegration of the Ottoman Empire. Yet the city remained a cultural melting pot, with Sephardic culture at its heart. For several centuries, Saloníki was the largest Jewish city in the world. In the 1800s it enjoyed a revival and was at the forefront of industrial development in the Ottoman Empire. However, at that time it was not so much its religious or cultural identity as its political identity that occupied the central ground. The strong sense of freedom, identity, and self-rule that had set Saloníki's Jewish community apart resulted in a dynamic political development at the turn of the last century, with strong trade unions and a proliferation of daily newspapers, political organizations, and associations. Many Jewish workers involved themselves in Socialist and syndicalist movements. Zionism also attracted many followers in Saloníki, and before the outbreak of the Second World War there were some twenty Zionist organizations in the city.

The young David Ben-Gurion, who went on to be a founding father of Israel, was one of the many who came to study in Saloníki. As an East European Jew, Ben-Gurion was stunned by what he saw in Saloníki: an entirely different kind of culture to the one in which he had been raised. In Saloníki there was no need for Jews to decide between assimilation or isolation; they were free to do whatever they pleased. In Saloníki, "Jews are capable of all sorts of professions," he wrote in a letter, and went on, "[It is] a Jewish city unlike any other in the world, not even in Eretz, Israel."[12] This was a decisive insight for Ben-Gurion. In Saloníki he saw what a free Jewish people was capable of. For him, Saloníki's Jews were the very emblematic image of "the new Jew" to which the Zionist movement wanted to give shape.

Erika Perahia Zemour spreads a trio of yellowed newspapers over her desk. One is in Hebrew, one in French, and a third in Ladino. All three are newspapers from Saloníki, testifying to the simmering political life of the city at the turn of the last century. Thessaloniki had more newspapers than any other city in the Ottoman Empire. The house that now encompasses the museum was once the head office of one of the newspapers on the desk, the French-language *L'Independent*.

"This newspaper," says Zemour, pointing at another of the newspapers, "is written in Spanish but in the Hebraic alphabet. Ladino was the language spoken here by most Jews right up to the Second World War." Zemour herself is part of the small minority of about two hundred people with Sephardic roots still living in Thessaloniki.

In 1900, Saloníki was a cultural and ethnic melting pot with an explosively growing population, thanks to the quick industrialization of the city. Eighty thousand Jews living in Saloníki made up around half of the city's population at the time, with the rest consisting of Turks, Bulgars, Armenians, and Serbs. The city was the most modern and industrialized area in the Balkans, but at the same time it was part of a politically unstable Ottoman Empire. When the Nazis marched into Thessaloniki in 1941, it marked the nadir of a long series of catastrophes that had devastated the city's Sephardic community and, for the first time in hundreds of years, made them a minority. Alfred Rosenberg's commando groups also discovered that many of the city's famous libraries had been destroyed.

◆ ◆ ◆

On the afternoon of August 18, 1917, a black plume of smoke rose over Saloníki's Turkish quarter. The fire had started with a spark from an open kitchen fire, which caught in a pile of straw.[13] In the densely populated districts of central Saloníki, the flames jumped from house to house. A British journalist, Harry Collinson Owen, described how the sea was dyed red by barrels of wine exploding in the heat, while the city's minarets rose out of the flames like "white needles." What he saw was "a fantastical and sorrowful scene, the wailing families, the crashing of disintegrating houses wherever the flames passed through, swept along by the wind; and, in the narrow lanes, a slow, moving mass of carts and mules carrying enormous loads."[14]

The old, dense streets of housing by the port were hit worst of all, and on them were Jewish newspaper offices, schools, and sixteen synagogues, several of which dated back to the early 1500s. Fifty thousand of Saloníki's Jews saw their homes, properties, and businesses disappear in the flames. Even the renowned Kadima library on Jewish history was destroyed.[15]

The political consequences of the fire were yet another catastrophe for the Sephardic community. In 1913, after the Balkan Wars, Saloníki had been ceded to Greece. According to the Greek prime minister Eleftherios Venizelos, the fire in 1917 came as "a gift of divine intervention." Greek politicians now took the opportunity to build a modern Greek city on the foundations of one that had been principally Ottoman and Jewish.[16] Torched blocks of houses were expropriated and the Jewish families that had lived there for hundreds of years were forbidden from coming back. Instead, tens of thousands of people were moved into the suburbs and shantytowns outside the city. Many of the city's Jews regarded their Thessaloniki as lost. Between 1912 and 1940 tens of thousands of Jews left the city and emigrated to France, the United States, and Palestine.[17]

Although much of the old Saloníki had been lost, the Nazis were particularly fascinated by this "Jewish city." Alfred Rosenberg still regarded Thessaloniki as "one of the most important Jewish centers" and a city of more "racial chaos, formed by cosmopolitanism and Jewish finance."[18] Something that particularly surprised the Nazi researchers was that they could find no documentation to suggest that there had ever been a Jewish ghetto in the city.

As soon as Greece had surrendered to the German army in 1941, Rosenberg sent a group from the ERR to Thessaloniki, led by the "Jewish expert" Johannes Pohl. By the middle of June 1941 the organization had established an office in the city, in what had previously been the American consulate. But the ERR's operation would not be restricted to Thessaloniki alone—it would cover the entire Balkan area, because there had been smaller Jewish settlements in this part of the Mediterranean for hundreds of years.[19]

Between May and November 1941, thirty or so academics and researchers from the ERR, supported by the SD and troops from the Wehrmacht, made a sweep of Greece's Jewish communities. In all, raids were carried out on about fifty synagogues, Jewish schools, newspapers, book dealers, banks, and other organizations where material was confiscated. The ERR had further identified about sixty "prominent Jews" whose homes were searched for books, manuscripts, and archive material.[20]

The plundering in Thessaloniki was more thorough in order to collect material for research on the Sephardic Jews. Above all, there was an interest in their economic networks and commercial prowess. The researcher Hermann Kellenbenz wrote a study on the economy of the Sephardic Jews, commissioned by Walter Frank's Institute for the Jewish Question, part of his National Institute for the History of New Germany, and a competitor of Rosenberg's Frankfurt institute.

It had been a status symbol since the 1500s among the city's most eminent Jewish families to own a library. Many libraries and private collections had been created over the centuries. The first library confiscated by the ERR belonged to Joseph Nehama—the historian and principal of the Alliance Israélite Universelle's school in the city—who owned a large collection of works on Jewish history. Nehama was one of the leaders of the congregation who had argued, before the war, that Jews ought to remain in Thessaloniki. Other plundered libraries included those of the chief rabbi, Zvi Kortezs, which contained a thousand valuable books on Arabic and Jewish philosophy, and the collection of the historian Michael Mohlo, which contained many rare Jewish books. One of Mohlo's most significant contributions was that during the 1930s he had begun to document epitaphs in the Jewish cemetery—a tremendously valuable project, considering the later destruction of the cemetery. Luckily, the fruits of his labor managed to avoid being plundered.

Two hundred and fifty priceless Torah scrolls were stolen from the city's synagogues along with large collections of religious literature, incunabula, and books printed in Saloníki during the 1500s. Some of these Torah scrolls went back to the Middle Ages and had come to Saloníki with the Sephardic Jews from the Iberian Peninsula. They were richly decorated in the Arab-Sephardic style, with crowns of silver and gold, manufactured by Jewish tradesmen and artists during the Renaissance. They had been the first texts to be saved from the fire in 1917. Even the rabbinical court, Beth Din Tzedek, was robbed of its library of 2,500 books.

The archive of Thessaloniki's largest bank, Union, was a particularly important target for the ERR—it held documents that the Nazis could use to chart the economic networks of the Sephardic Jews.

There is no existing figure for how much was plundered in Thessaloniki, but according to the historian Mark Mazower, it must have been tens of thousands of books, manuscripts, and incunabula.[21] One important library that was lost belonged to Rabbi Haham Haim Habib, a collection that had been built up by his family over several generations. Haim Habib was one of the city's foremost Orthodox rabbis, and he had become well known for having on one occasion refused to shake the hand of the queen of Greece for religious reasons. Haim Habib's library contained eight thousand volumes on religion, philosophy, history, and Jewish law.[22] But the plundering was so systematic that not even small libraries got away. For instance, a library belonging to Jewish schoolteachers was taken, although it consisted of only six hundred books, mainly on language teaching and modern literature.

Most but not all of the plundered collections were taken back to Germany by train. Of the 250 confiscated Torah scrolls, 150 went to Germany. However, 100 scrolls, which were probably considered less interesting from a research perspective, were burned in Thessaloniki. For unknown reasons the same fate awaited Haim Habib's library, which was burned in the internment camp that the Nazis had set up.[23]

The deportations to the extermination camps in occupied Poland had started in earnest in Europe in 1942. But in Greece the deportations were delayed by the refusal of the Italians to cooperate. The SS was determined to "solve the Jewish question" in Greece. Heinrich Himmler had already in 1941 warned Hitler that a large Jewish population such as the one in Thessaloniki was a threat to the Reich. SS-Obersturmbannführer Adolf Eichmann, in charge of the logistics of the deportations, lost patience and finally, in February 1943, dispatched Dieter Wisliceny and Alois Brunner to Thessaloniki. Wisliceny and Brunner were among the most hardened and brutal murderers in the SS. Brunner, whom Eichmann called "my best man," had earlier organized the deportations of tens of thousands of Jews in Vienna. He personally executed the well-known Austrian banker Siegmund Bosel, who was dragged out of a hospital in Vienna and shot while still wearing his hospital clothes. After the war, Brunner fled to Syria, where he is believed to have worked as an adviser to the regime. According to the Simon Wiesenthal Center, Brunner very likely died there in 2010, at age ninety-eight.

In Thessaloniki, Wisliceny and Brunner set up their headquarters in a villa just outside the city center, which they decorated with a black SS flag. Two days after their arrival in the city all Jews over the age of five were ordered to wear a yellow star.[24] Within a week Jews were forbidden to use telephones, ride on trams, or move about in public places. At the same time, Wisliceny started drawing up plans for something that had never existed in Thessaloniki: ghettos. One ghetto was created in the western part of the city, another in the eastern suburbs.

At the same time, the SS, with the help of Jewish forced labor, started building a transit camp by the train station, surrounded by barbed-wire fences. The transit camp was built in such a way that it surrounded an already existing Jewish quarter. Its population would be the first to be deported.

By March, when Wisliceny and Brunner had forced most of the city's Jews into ghettos, these were sealed off from the surrounding world. A few thousand of the city's Jews, mostly young men and women, managed to escape by getting across the Italian-occupied zone or fleeing into the Macedonian mountains and joining ELAS, the Greek Communist resistance movement.

A little more than a month after Wisliceny and Brunner's arrival, the first trains started leaving— eighty tightly packed freight cars, with 2,800 people inside. Before their departure, the SS had made them change their drachmas into Polish złotys. In fact, this was a bluff, as the money they received was counterfeit. In the place where they were going, there was no need for money. They had been told that they were going to Kraków, but the actual final destination was Auschwitz-Birkenau. Two days later the next train departed. Jewish working-class people were sent off first, which spread hopeful rumors among the richer ghetto dwellers that only "Communists" would be sent to Poland. By mid-July 1943 there were only two thousand Jews left in Thessaloniki. Wisliceny and Brunner had saved the "privileged" Jews for last: the rabbis, local leaders, rich businessmen, and collaborators such as the units of Jewish security guards that the SS had organized as additional manpower. It was a cynical and efficient strategy for breaking down and murdering a people. The ones saved until last were the leaders, people who in a variety of ways held the society together. For reasons of self-preservation, naïveté, or an inability to appreciate the danger of their situation, these leaders persuaded others to follow the increasingly absurd demands, which step by step moved them closer to the gas chambers.

Of course, not even those saved till last got away. When the leaders had no one left to lead, it was their turn. Many of the more well-heeled among them were tortured by the SS for information about any caches of gold or other valuables they might have hidden. After that, the "privileged" Jews were sent to Bergen-Belsen.[25]

Forty-four thousand of Thessaloniki's Jews were deported to Auschwitz-Birkenau.[26] Within a few hours of their arrival most of them were dead, if they even got there—many died in the tightly packed freight cars on the long train journey to Poland. The unusually high death rate among Thessaloniki's Jews has been explained by the fact that many of them were in such a bad state when they arrived that they were sent directly to the gas chambers.

In a matter of a few months in 1943, four-hundred-year-old Sephardic Thessaloniki ceased to exist. Wisliceny and Brunner were able to report to Eichmann after the summer that Thessaloniki was *Judenrein*—cleansed of Jews. This was not entirely true. There were still fifteen Jews in Thessaloniki who were married to Greeks, and for this reason had been permitted to stay. But even their positions were precarious. When one of them lost his wife in childbirth, he was immediately deported. The newborn child was allowed to stay for the time being.[27]

About thirteen thousand of Thessaloniki's Jews avoided the gas chambers in Auschwitz-Birkenau by being selected for slave work. Their fate was seldom enviable. Many women and children from Thessaloniki would be subjected to experiments by, among others, Josef Mengele, who had started working at the camp only a few months earlier. Women from Thessaloniki, some of them pregnant, had cancers implanted into their wombs, and men had their testicles removed. Others were used for experiments with contagious diseases. Three hundred young women from Thessaloniki between sixteen and twenty years old were selected for this purpose. All were dead by September 1943. Of all the medical experiments carried out in Auschwitz-Birkenau, a quarter are believed to have been conducted on Jews from Thessaloniki.[28]

Many of the men from Thessaloniki were chosen to work in units known as Sonderkommandos, charged with carrying out the dead from the gas chambers and burning the corpses. Those who came into

contact with Jews from Thessaloniki in the camps have testified about
the impression they made on them, including Primo Levi:

> Next to us there is a group of Greeks, those admirable and terri-
> ble Jews of Salonica, tenacious, thieving, wise, ferocious and
> united, so determined to live, such pitiless opponents in the
> struggle for life; those Greeks who have conquered in the kitch-
> ens and in the yards, and whom even the Germans respect and
> the Poles fear. They are in their third year of camp, and nobody
> knows better than them what the camp means. They now stand
> closely in a circle, shoulder to shoulder, and sing one of their in-
> terminable chants.[29]

Short of two thousand would survive and return to Thessaloniki
after the war. There was not much to come back to. Most of the survivors came back alone, having lost all their families and relatives in the
camps. Their houses, apartments, and companies in Thessaloniki had
been taken over by Greeks, who had bought them from the Germans.
Any attempts to recover their lost property were stopped by the new,
right-wing Greek government. One survivor spoke of how, in Thessaloniki, there was not even "a rabbi who could give us a blessing."[30]

Most chose to move on, as they could not bear living in a city "that
had been robbed of its soul," as Erika Perahia Zemour puts it. Nor
would the rich cultural and literary legacy of the Sephardic community
ever come back. The greater part of it was scattered and gone, apart
from single pages of Jewish writings and pieces of Torah scrolls that
showed up in Thessaloniki's markets after the war. The paper was used
as stuffing for shoes and the parchment to make shoe soles.[31]

# 11

# THE MASS GRAVE IS A PAPER MILL

## *Vilnius*

With a printed-out map in my hand I have found my way to the address, Vivulskio gatvé 18, in Vilnius, Lithuania. I don't know what I was expecting to see. Maybe it has always been the same thing that attracts people to places of historical importance. A meadow where once an important battle was fought, or a café where an important novel was allegedly written. The pull of such places is that they offer us a way of getting closer to historical events and the people who figured in them. In our imagination, at least, they seem to offer a way of bridging the gulf of time that separates us.

At Vivulskio gatvé 18, a newly built nine-story block of apartments rises up, modern and black with glass windows reaching from floor to ceiling. A symbol of the new, young Vilnius with its hipsters, minimalist fusion restaurants, and nightclubs. But to those who know about it, this address is associated with something quite different. It played an important part in the most traumatic chapter in Vilnius's history.

In those times, the street name was spelled differently—it was known as Wiwulskiego when Vilnius was a part of Poland. It was the location of the Yidisher Visnshaftlekher Institut (Scientific Institute of Yiddish), abbreviated as YIVO. The institute was in a stone house, and the first thing that met visitors in the spacious entrance vestibule was a world map, on which the institute and its branch organizations were marked. When the ERR took over the house in 1942, it had been a barrack for German soldiers. Hanging over the world map was a flag with the German eagle and the swastika.[1] In the rooms, the ERR found books and newspapers flattened into the floor. But in the cellar it found what it was really looking for: tens of thousands of books and periodicals that had been flung down there when the soldiers moved in.

Thrown into that cellar was one of the most important Jewish libraries in Eastern Europe, a library that was the product of an ambitious project to save the literary, cultural, and historical heritage of the Ashkenazi Jews. It was a project, or rather a movement, that had its origins in the late 1800s.

Unlike in Western Europe, where Jews were given citizen's rights in the 1800s, most Jews in Eastern Europe were still at the turn of the century living under conditions that had not changed significantly since medieval times. Of the many restrictions imposed on Jews, perhaps the most debilitating was their exclusion from higher education. At least that was how Simon Dubnov saw it.

He was born in 1860 in the small Russian community of Mszislau, in the Jewish Pale of Settlement. Like other Ashkenazi Jews, his mother tongue was Yiddish, the Germanic language first spoken by Jews in Germany during the medieval era, based on German as then spoken, with additional influences from Hebrew, Aramaic, and Slavic languages. Dubnov had gone to a state Jewish school, where he learned Russian, but his education was cut short by a new law at the end of the 1800s that took away this possibility from Jews. Dubnov continued studying history and linguistics independently, managed to escape from the Jewish settlement area and, with the help of forged papers, went to St. Petersburg.

Before long he was a leading journalist, activist, and self-taught historian, who wrote about the predicament of Russian Jews. Dubnov fought above all for the right to a modern education for Russian Jews, which, he felt, was the only way to achieve their liberation.

But he also spoke of the need for more awareness among Jews of their own history and culture. Dubnov described the Ashkenazi Jews as "immature children" who lacked knowledge of their eight-hundred-year-long history in Eastern Europe. What especially concerned Dubnov was that this history was about to be lost, and that old Jewish documents and books were being neglected and ruined: "They are lying in attics, in piles of trash, or in equally unpleasant and filthy rooms, among various broken household items and rags. These manuscripts are rotting away, they are being eaten by mice and are being used by ignorant servants and children who tear off page after page for all sorts of purposes. In one

word: year by year they are disappearing and being lost to history," wrote
Dubnov in a pamphlet in 1891. To preserve what was about to be lost, he
called for an "archaeological expedition" to collect, preserve, and catalog
these literary treasures, which were dispersed all over Eastern Europe. In
his pamphlet he spoke enthusiastically, exhorting Jews to take part in
this epic expedition: "Let us work, gather our dispersed from their places
of exile, arrange them, publish them, and build upon their foundation
the temple of our history. Come, let us search and inquire."[2]

Dubnov's clarion call was taken note of, even though it would take a
few more decades before this expedition was implemented on any significant scale. Other Eastern European Yiddish intellectuals had, just
like Dubnov, realized the need to save Yiddish culture.

This culture was not only under assault by cultural neglect but also
by two new contemporary movements. On the one hand there were the
Zionists, who sought to create a "new Jew," and on the other there was
assimilation, meaning that more and more Jews chose to abandon their
Jewish identity. The movement that would later lead to the formation of
the YIVO Institute tried to confront both of these currents. There was
a desire to save what seemed under threat as increasing numbers of Jews
decided to assimilate, while also opposing the Zionists' attempts to replace other Jewish languages and dialects such as Yiddish, Ladino, and
Dzhidi with modern Hebrew—the language spoken in Israel today.

A new generation of young Jewish historians, authors, ethnographers, and archivists began to take on the research mission that Dubnov had advocated. In the years preceding the outbreak of the First
World War, the Russian-Jewish writer and folklore researcher Shloyme
Zanvl Rappoport, better known by his pseudonym of S. Ansky, had
led an expedition into small villages in the Ukraine, where he had documented hundreds of hours of songs, proverbs, and stories in Yiddish.
It was an invaluable portrait of the time, as many of these communities
were later wiped out during the pogroms under the Symon Petljura
regime after the Russian Revolution.

YIVO began to take form after the First World War. In 1924, the
linguist and historian Nokhem Shtif sketched out an idea for a Yiddish
research institute, with departments focusing on history, philology,

pedagogy, and economics, as well as an archive and a library. The mission of the institute would be to add legitimacy to Yiddish as a language, but also to modernize the language to ensure its continued use.

The following year, in 1925, YIVO was founded in Berlin, where two other historians and linguists would be the driving forces: Elias Tcherikower and Max Weinreich. The institute's headquarters were located in Vilnius, the historical center of Yiddish culture in Eastern Europe.

Before the Second World War, the city boasted 105 synagogues and meetinghouses and six Jewish daily newspapers. Its Jewish population of about sixty thousand represented a third of the city's total. For hundreds of years, rabbis, Jewish authors, intellectuals, and artists had been drawn to the city. According to legend, when Napoleon stopped there on his way to Moscow in 1812, he called Vilnius "the Jerusalem of the North."[3]

Its most renowned citizen was the eighteenth-century rabbi Elijah ben Solomon Zalman, referred to as the Vilna Gaon (Genius of Vilnius). He was regarded in his time as one of the foremost interpreters of the Torah and the Talmud. Of equal importance was his opposition to orthodox Hasidism, which was spreading almost like a Jewish evangelical movement during the 1700s. He dismissed Hasidism's more emotional position in relation to faith, and its focus on miracles, and instead urged Jews to study secular sources and science.

Around the turn of the century, Vilnius had evolved into a center of cultural and political opposition to the pogroms and restrictions that had tormented Jews in the settlement areas. In 1897, the General Jewish Labor Bund in Lithuania, Poland, and Russia was formed, this being a secular socialist party working to improve Jewish rights. The party, often known as Der Bund, advocated the use of Yiddish as the first language of choice of Lithuanian, Polish, and Russian Jews.[4]

Vilnius was a city vibrating with activity, with new Jewish schools, libraries, theaters, publishers, and newspapers. The development was further augmented when, after the war, the city was amalgamated into the reincarnated Polish nation. In the interwar years, Vilnius became the home of a movement that sought to renew Yiddish in a literary sense. Yung Vilne (Young Vilnius) was a group of experimental Jewish poets and authors, including Chaim Grade and Abraham Sutzkever.

The city was the obvious nerve center for the mission that the researchers in YIVO would launch in the mid-1920s. The institute was built from nothing. There was no state sponsorship and in the early phase the headquarters were located in a room of Max Weinreich's Vilnius apartment.

But financial backing was soon in evidence from overseas, from donors in the United States, South America, and Germany—many of them Ashkenazi immigrants. Thanks to this support it was possible, in the early 1930s, to move into the house on Vivulskio gatvé 18, in order to have space for the fast-growing collection. Branches of the institute were also opened in Berlin, Warsaw, and New York. A small YIVO army of historians, ethnographers, philologists, literary experts, philosophers, writers, and other Jewish intellectuals set out to save the neglected cultural legacy of Eastern Europe's Jewry. One of their number was Simon Dubnov, who now got to see his thirty-year-old dream fulfilled.

The institute became the temple of a collectors' cult, in which enormous amounts of firsthand sources, books, documents, photographs, recordings, and other items associated with Yiddish culture were saved, gathered, and studied.

YIVO's work had much in common with the movement that had emerged in several European countries, when romanticism and a latent nationalism awoke a newfangled interest in folkloric culture. Early pioneers such as Elias Lönnrot traveled to Karelia to gather the fairy tales that he would eventually incorporate into the epic poem *Kalevala*. A hundred years later the methods were more scientific, even if the enthusiasm and nationalistic undertones were much the same. The institute's folkloric group was one of the most active, and already by 1929 it had collected over fifty thousand tales, sagas, and songs in Yiddish.[5]

But YIVO was more than an institution to preserve a cultural legacy; it also collected contemporary information on Yiddish culture and initiated a project of linguistic reform: to standardize spelling in Yiddish. Correspondents in all countries where the language was spoken were encouraged to study and document local customs, and then pass on their material to YIVO. According to Cecile E. Kuznitz, the historian, the institute was not so much a historical project as a project for the future:

> As the most prestigious institution in its cultural movement, YIVO went far beyond collecting historical documents or publishing academic monographs to play a central role in the redefinition of Jewish peoplehood in modern times. . . . By focusing on a future when their . . . vision of Jewish scholarship would be within reach, YIVO leaders were able to look beyond the current economic and political marginalization and preserve their faith in their vision of Jewish culture.[6]

By the end of the 1930s the collection had grown to the extent that the institute built a new wing to accommodate its material. In thirteen short years, YIVO had achieved miracles. Tied to the institute were over five hundred groups of collectors spread across the whole world. Before the war the archive was estimated to have included some 100,000 volumes and another 100,000 objects: manuscripts, photographs, letters, diaries, and other archive material.[7] The institute had also built up one of the largest collections in the world of cultural and ethnographic artifacts relating to the history of Eastern European Jewry. In addition, the institute had built up an impressive art collection of about a hundred works by Jewish artists such as Marc Chagall, who was one of the institute's more prominent patrons and collaborators, alongside figures like Sigmund Freud and Albert Einstein.[8,9]

◆ ◆ ◆

On September 19, 1939, two days after the Soviet Union's attack on Poland, the Red Army took Vilnius. Poland's fate had been decided in the last few days of August, when Nazi Germany and the Soviet Union signed the Molotov-Ribbentrop Pact. This was formally a nonaggression pact, but in a secret appendix, Hitler and Stalin had divided up Eastern Europe between themselves. By the time over half a million Red Army troops crossed the border, the Polish army was already largely defeated, after the German attack of a few weeks earlier.

After the invasion, Vilnius was assigned to Lithuania, which viewed the city as its historical capital. But this was a short-lived development, as in 1940 the Red Army also attacked Lithuania. In a series of brutal raids, the Soviet authorities clamped down on their enemies, real and imagined. Between 1939 and 1941, hundreds of thousands of Poles and Lithuanians, of which tens of thousands were Jewish, were deported to the east by the Soviet rulers.

The hammer fell hardest on Jewish employers and factory owners, who saw their property nationalized and were often the victims of deportation. Jews owned the majority of private companies and industries in Vilnius. The new regime also suffocated the expression of free Jewish culture in Vilnius. Education in Hebrew was made illegal, as well as religious institutions and organizations. All newspapers in Yiddish except one, *Vilner Emes*, were shut down. Jewish "nationalism," as well as all other expressions of national sentiment among minority groups, was systematically repressed. YIVO, which was nationalized, was renamed the Institute for Jewish Culture and absorbed into the Soviet academic system, formally by the Lithuanian Academy of Science in the newly formed Soviet Socialist Republic of Lithuania.

An order was issued to seize the journalist and Yiddish researcher Zalmen Reyzen, who was the editor of the institute's journal, *YIVO-bleter*. In 1941 the Soviet regime had him executed by firing squad.[10]

Max Weinreich, the founder and head of the institute, did however get away, as he was on his way to a conference in Copenhagen when the war broke out in 1939. Weinreich immediately left Europe to set up the new YIVO headquarters in New York. At that time, it was the only remaining branch of the institute. Its Berlin office had been dissolved after the Nazis took over, and in 1939 its activities in Warsaw had also ceased when the city fell to the Nazis.

YIVO in Vilnius may have been nationalized and robbed of its independence under the Soviet regime, yet something considerably worse lay in store. Premonitions of what this might be could already be discerned in those parts of Poland under Nazi occupation.

The plunder of Polish libraries and collections had begun within weeks of the country's surrender in 1939. But this time it was not the ERR that was responsible for the thieving, as this organization was only founded in the summer of 1940.

Instead, the operation was taken care of by a special unit known as Sonderkommando Paulsen, led by an SS officer and professor of archaeology by the name of Peter Paulsen. Paulsen's task was first and foremost to repatriate "Germanic" cultural treasures to the fatherland—as for instance the Veit Stoss Altar in the Church of the Virgin Mary in Kraków.

The commandos made a raid on the seminary in Pelplin to secure the Gutenberg Bible that was known to be there, yet it was found that it had already been smuggled out of the country by Father Antoni Liedtke. When the SS realized that the Bible had slipped out of its hands, it took its revenge by burning a part of the Pelplin library in the ovens of a nearby sugar factory.[11] The remaining books were transported to an old church in Poznań, which had been set up as a book depot. The church would eventually house over a million plundered Polish books.

Sonderkommando Paulsen soon directed its attention to Jewish and Polish institutions, museums, libraries, and synagogues. The plunder of Poland was of an entirely different kind from the selective thieving that had above all afflicted Jews and ideological enemies in occupied western and southern Europe. In Poland, the plundering operation targeted the entire population. The reason for this was the quite different kinds of warfare being applied on the western and eastern fronts. Danes, Norwegians, the Dutch, Belgians, Frenchmen, and the British were Aryans and thereby fraternal peoples in what would one day be National Socialist Europe. The Nazis viewed themselves as liberators who had rescued these people from the pernicious effect of global Jewry. The regime devoted significant resources to propaganda exercises in an attempt to try to win over the "fraternal populations" of the West to the justice of its ideological purpose.

The war in the East could not have been more different. The millions of Jews who lived in Eastern Europe were not the only enemies—also, by extension, all the Slavs were too. It was in the East that Germany's lebensraum would extend itself. In the future of Europe there was therefore neither space for Poland nor for the Polish people. The plunder was a direct consequence of this political line, and intended to rob the Poles of all forms of higher culture, learning, literature, and education. In this way its people would be intellectually reduced to subhumans.

The plunder was closely associated with Intelligenzaktion. This was an operation aiming to destroy Polish culture and education by exterminating those who embodied it. In a very literal sense the intention was to "cut off the head" of the Polish social structure by murdering that society's intellectual, religious, and political elite. Intelligenzaktion was put into effect immediately after the invasion in 1939, and worked in accordance with an already prepared list, *Sonderfahndungsbuch Polen* (Special Prosecution Book Poland), numbering some 61,000 names. The list included politicians, entrepreneurs, professors, teachers, journalists, writers, aristocrats, actors, judges, priests, and military officers—also a number of high-profile athletes who had participated in the Olympic Games in Berlin in 1936.[12]

The detention and murder of academics, teachers, writers, journalists, and priests went hand in hand with the plunder of libraries, universities, churches, and private collections. The scale of the plunder in Poland was enormous, with the theft of some two to three million books. The most valuable of these, including more than two thousand incunabula, were sent to Germany.[13]

Because the goal of all this was intellectual subjugation, books were also stolen that had no interest from the point of view of Nazi "research": schoolbooks, children's books, and literary works. These fell victim to a systematic and planned eradication. Therefore, the destruction of books in Poland exceeded the numbers that were plundered. According to one estimate, some 15 million Polish books were destroyed in this operation.[14] The stock of over 350 libraries was sent to paper mills for conversion into paper pulp.[15]

The war in Poland was so violent and brutal that even many of the historically most valuable collections were decimated. Warsaw's finest libraries were the hardest hit of all. During the Warsaw Uprising in 1944, German troops torched several collections, including the Biblioteka Załuskich, built in 1747, the oldest public library in Poland. Of the collection, which included some 400,000 volumes, maps, and manuscripts, only less than 10 percent survived. In October 1944 German troops set fire to the historical collection of the National Library. Eighty thousand early prints from the 1500s to the 1700s were destroyed. In addition, 100,000 drawings and engravings, 35,000 manuscripts, 2,500 incunabula, and 50,000 sheets of musical notes and plays were consumed in the flames.[16]

Even the Military Library in Warsaw, with a collection of 350,000 volumes, was set aflame. The main building housed the Rapperswil Library, a Polish émigré library that had been set up in Switzerland in the 1800s and brought back to Poland in the 1920s.

The extermination of Poland's literary heritage was frighteningly efficient. Researchers have estimated that 70 percent of all books in Poland were destroyed or lost through plunder. Over 90 percent of collections belonging to public libraries or schools were lost or destroyed.[17]

Only the Polish Jews and their culture were hit harder. Of a population of over 3 million before the war, only about 100,000 would still be alive in 1945. Much like the Polish collections, the Jewish libraries in Poland were not only plundered but also destroyed. One of the most valuable libraries that was lost was the great Talmudic library of the Jewish Theological Seminary in Lublin. One of the Nazis who took part in its destruction testified about the events:

> For us it was a matter of special pride to destroy the Talmudic Academy which has been known as the greatest in Poland. . . . We threw out of the building the great Talmudic Library and carted it to market. There we set fire to the books. The fire lasted for twenty hours. The Jews of Lublin were assembled around and cried bitterly. Their cries almost silenced us. Then we summoned the military band, and the joyful shouts of the soldiers silenced the sound of the Jewish cries.[18]

Even in Polish libraries, Jewish literature and books by Jewish writers were removed:

"The primary intention of outlawing works by Polish Jews was quite simply to eradicate all Jewish influence from what remained of Polish culture. The Nazis even regarded guidebooks about Jewish places as dangerous and hostile," writes the historian Marek Sroka, who has studied the destruction of Jewish libraries in Poland. Sroka suggests that "the plan to eliminate the Jewish cultural and literary contribution to Polish as well as European civilization became almost as important to the Germans as the physical extermination of the Jewish people."[19]

An explanation for the destruction of even the most important Jewish and Polish collections in Poland was that the plunder was less organized. The ERR had still not been involved in the operation. But the process could also be explained by the merciless nature of the war and the occupation. A great deal was destroyed by the sheer speed of it.

The scale of the plunder and destruction of Jewish libraries stood in immediate relation to the extermination of the Polish Jews. Not only synagogues, schools, and organizations were plundered, but every single Jewish home; anything from large private libraries to the few books owned by the very poorest families. When the Nazis started large-scale deportation of Jews to the death camps in 1942, the ghettos were shut down and any libraries still remaining were plundered, burned, or sent to paper mills. When the ghettos were cleared, some collections were also found that the inhabitants had made desperate attempts to save. For instance, 150 Torahs from Kraków's synagogues were found hidden in a specially constructed secret compartment in an attic above an undertaker's shop. Most of the scrolls were burned.[20]

In Warsaw, Sonderkommando Paulsen plundered thirty thousand books from the Great Synagogue, one of the largest in Europe. The synagogue was used after that as a warehouse for many of the city's more than fifty Jewish libraries.[21]

In April 1943 an uprising started among the remaining Jews in Warsaw's ghetto. By this point in time, only fifty thousand people were left of a population that one year earlier had stood at almost half a million. The uprising was an act of desperation without hope of success, but on the other hand the men and women who had instigated it were well aware of what was to come. Most of the people who had been deported from the ghetto were already dead.

The uprising was put down in an inferno, as the SS with the aid of flamethrowers and grenades torched the ghetto house by house. On May 16, the day the uprising was crushed, engineers from the SS, under the command of SS-Gruppenführer Jürgen Stroop, mined the Great Synagogue. In an interview with the Polish journalist Kazimierz Moczarski, who shared a prison cell with him after the war, Stroop described the event:

What a marvelous sight it was. A fantastic piece of theater. My staff and I stood at a distance. I held the electrical device which would detonate all of the charges simultaneously. Jesuiter called for silence. I glanced over at my brave officers and men, tired and dirty, silhouetted against the glow of the burning buildings. After prolonging the suspense for a moment, I shouted, "Heil Hitler," and pressed the button. With a thunderous, deafening bang and a rainbow burst of colors, the fiery explosion soared toward the clouds, an unforgettable tribute to our triumph over the Jews. The Warsaw ghetto was no more. The will of Adolf Hitler and Heinrich Himmler had been done.[22]

♦ ♦ ♦

Two years after the invasion of Poland, the same kind of merciless plundering and destruction would be repeated on a greater scale when on June 22, 1941, Nazi Germany began Operation Barbarossa, the code name for the attack on the Soviet Union. By this time, both Alfred Rosenberg and Heinrich Himmler had built up highly functional plundering organizations, and their "expertise" would now be targeting the eastern front. The ERR had grown into the most efficient plundering organization in the Third Reich. The ERR was also in a good position as a consequence of Alfred Rosenberg's rise in the Nazi power hierarchy. Adolf Hitler had for long considered the Baltic German the party's authoritative voice on questions relating to the East. Now that the invasion was in motion, Hitler finally gave Rosenberg a proper department to run: Reichsministerium für die besetzten Ostgebiete (Reich Ministry for the Occupied Eastern Territories). The function of the ministry was to establish and implement civil authority in the occupied areas of the Soviet Union.

The Reich Ministry would control the Reichskommissariats set up by the regime in the occupied territories to the east. Rosenberg had suggested that the Soviet Union should be subdivided into a number of smaller regions, in order to make the enormous area more manageable. Two of the intended six regions were established during the war. The Baltic region, White Russia, and parts of western Russia made up the Reichskommissariat Ostland, while Reichskommissariat Ukraine covered parts of what is now the country of Ukraine. Four other commissariats were planned for the regions around Moscow, the Caucasus, Central Asia, and the Volga basin.

On paper, his promotion gave Alfred Rosenberg enormous power, but in practice his influence would always be undercut by Hitler. Rosenberg and the Führer quickly fell out about how best to handle the people in the East.

Rosenberg regarded Slavs as Aryans, though admittedly on a lower level. He was convinced that Germany would never be able to control the enormous Russian territory without strategic alliances with the ethnic groups that had been forced into submission by Bolshevism. His plan, which he presented to Hitler, was that the Germans should portray themselves as liberators and then turn the strong anti-Communist and anti-Russian sentiment, which went back hundreds of years, against the rulers in the Kremlin. Especially the Ukrainians, Rosenberg felt, could be turned into allies against Bolshevism. For this reason, they should be given a measure of self-rule and be permitted to set up a vassal state under a Nazi leadership.

It was a pragmatic plan, in which Rosenberg for once seemed to be aware of realpolitik. Probably his plan was based on practical experience—he was well aware of the extraordinarily complex patch-work of people and cultures within the span of the Soviet Empire. Un-like other leading Nazis, he had actually seen the endless Russian and Ukrainian steppes. It was a plan that, had it been implemented, might have changed the course of the war.

But it never gained any traction among the Nazi leadership. As far as Adolf Hitler and Heinrich Himmler were concerned, it was quite unthinkable that slaves could be given self-rule—even less, that these "subhumans" could be made into real comrades in arms. In one of his conversations around the table, which was noted down on Martin Bor-mann's orders, Hitler expressed the view that the Slavic people were "born to be slaves."[23] Not only Hitler and Himmler opposed Rosenberg's eastern politics, but also Hermann Göring and Martin Bormann. Faced with such formidable opposition, Rosenberg did not stand a chance.

Leaders of the Reichskommissariats were directly appointed by and subordinated to Adolf Hitler, and this led to a dilution of Rosenberg's authority.

The brutish Nazi, Erich Koch, was chosen to lead the Reichskom-missariat Ukraine. "If I meet a Ukrainian worthy of sitting at my table I have to have him shot," he said, summarizing his view of his new subjects. According to Koch, "The lowest possible German worker is racially and biologically more valuable than the population here."[24]

Koch's summary policies had a detrimental effect on the initially posi-tive response to the Germans, as Rosenberg had predicted. A ferocious resistance was put up against the occupying power and its extermination policies once the population realized that repressive Bolsheviks were, in every sense, preferable to the Nazis.

Another reality that undercut Rosenberg's position of power was that he lacked military resources in the two Reichskommissariats that had been set up. The power vacuum that arose was filled by Himmler and the SS. Since the outbreak of war, the influence of the SS had been consolidated in almost every part of the regime. Hitler, with a certain amount of justification, had an almost paranoid mistrust of his gener-als in the Wehrmacht, and he successively transferred power to his loyal Praetorian Guard.

What had strengthened Himmler's position of power more than anything was the organization's military wing, Waffen-SS, which had consistently kept growing from 1939 into an army that by the end of the war comprised almost a million soldiers. In the merciless war being waged on the eastern front, the SS would take over many of the Wehrmacht's tasks. One of these was the fight against "partisans," an activity that in practice was used as a way of implementing extermination policies.

In spite of Alfred Rosenberg's failed attempts to influence policy toward the East, he found solace in the ERR's successful work in the Soviet zone. Adolf Hitler had given the ERR a thoroughgoing mandate to finecomb "libraries, archives, Masonic lodges, and other ideological and cultural institutions of all kinds, to identify useful material and confiscate it for the use of the NSDAP's ideological sphere and the research work of the Hohe Schule."

In principle, the ERR was mandated to use any means and methods considered necessary for the plundering. The Führer also ordered the Wehrmacht to assist the ERR in its work. What made things fundamentally different from routines on the western front was that the ERR now became *Wehrmachtsgefolge*—that is, it accompanied the army. In the West, the Wehrmacht had often distanced itself or even actively worked against the plundering, which many of the generals felt gave a bad name to the army.

But in the Soviet Union the moral stance of the Wehrmacht was considerably less elevated.

In the West, the plundering had been limited to clearly defined groups: Jews, Freemasons, and political enemies—while property belonging to "normal" Frenchmen, the Dutch, and Danes had largely been respected. In the East, the rules of play were quite different. Resisting all pragmatism, Rosenberg involved himself in the plundering with systematic ruthlessness—which at root related to his personal hatred of Bolshevism, as he testified at the Nuremberg trials after the war: "Because those whom we considered as our adversaries or opponents from the point of view of our conception of the world are different in the West from what they are in the East. In the West there were certain

Jewish organizations and Masonic lodges, and in the East there was nothing more than the Communist Party."[25]

As Rosenberg saw it, the property of the Communist Party had to be regarded as "Jewish," because the Bolshevik regime was a part of the Jewish world conspiracy.

Despite its strong position, the ERR did not lack for competitors in the Soviet Union. As the advance continued, a special task force known as Sonderkommando Künsberg, following the three army groups closely, had made raids on museums, libraries, and archives, with impounded materials sent back to Berlin. Formally, its units were under the command of Joachim von Ribbentrop's foreign affairs department, but they were led by an SS-Obersturmbannführer, the historian Baron Eberhard von Künsberg.

The three units formed a sort of advance party, with more thorough plundering routines following on behind. Sonderkommando Künsberg made raids on significant targets, and just as with the earlier mentioned Sonderkommando Paulsen in Poland, artifacts viewed as "Germanic" were at the top of the list. Among these were Andreas Schlüter's famous Amber Room in the Catherine Palace outside Leningrad. But tens of thousands of books were also taken from the tsar's palace and shipped to Germany in boxes labeled "Zarenbibliothek Quatchina." Some of Künsberg's seizures would later be handed to the ERR, including books from the tsar's palace and a large share of confiscated Jewish literature.[26]

The ERR had a more academic approach, based on inspections of institutions, libraries, archives, and museums. The sort of plundering it carried out was methodical, scrutinizing, and selective. Experts were dispatched to the Soviet Union in the summer and autumn of 1941 to make an initial inspection and compile lists of valuable collections. One of these experts, the Baltic German archivist Gottlieb Ney, would spend a whole year assessing libraries in the occupied areas of the Soviet Union. Ney, who worked for Hohe Schule der NSDAP's library, moved to Sweden after the war and worked as an archivist in Lund.

The ERR set up three separate groups: Hauptarbeitsgruppe Ostland (Baltic region), Hauptarbeitsgruppe Mitte (White Russia and

west Russia), and Hauptarbeitsgruppe Ukraine. Offices were established in Riga, Minsk, and Kiev to administer the plundering work
across the territories, which included the Jewish settlement areas where
most eastern Jews were still living.

To a certain extent Rosenberg was right when he claimed that in
the east there was "only" the Communist Party. The Soviet regime had
really cleared the way for the Nazi plunderers, because most of the collections had already been confiscated and nationalized, and Freemasons and similar organizations were banned. Much of the loot had
either been sold off to the West or integrated into the public collections. The Nazis therefore focused on plundering the public institutions, which had the richest collections.[27]

The process of nationalization had also been initiated in the Baltic
region and eastern Poland during the short period of Soviet rule, of
which the YIVO Institute was just one example. But the nationaliza-
tions had mainly been focused on public collections, institutions, and
religious groups, whereas state appropriation of private property had
not yet come so far.[28]

The ERR's plundering operation in the Soviet Union was as ambitious as it was extensive. According to one of the organization's own
reports, 2,265 institutions were searched. The work required far-
reaching cooperation with the Wehrmacht and the SD, but also with
archivists, librarians, and experts from other German institutions.

Within Hauptarbeitsgruppe Ukraine, for instance, there were 150
experts organizing the plunder of hundreds of libraries, public collections, universities, churches, palaces, and synagogues.[29] Religious institutions in the Soviet Union, which had already been assaulted by the
Bolsheviks, were hit extra hard. Thousands of priests had been murdered or sent to labor camps in Siberia by the Soviet regime. In all,
Nazi organizations are estimated to have plundered 1,670 Russian Orthodox churches, 532 synagogues, and 237 Catholic churches.

Particular interest, apart from Jewish collections, was focused on
archives and libraries belonging to the Communist Party. The RSHA
laid claim to anything of significance for intelligence, while much other
material went to Alfred Rosenberg's library project in the East, the

Ostbücherei, into which the émigré libraries from Paris were also incorporated. In addition, other German research institutes on eastern studies, such as the Wannsee Institute and the Institute for Eastern Europe in Breslau, claimed a share of the loot from the Soviet Union.

Several hundred libraries were looted in Minsk, of which the Lenin Library alone filled seventeen railroad cars.[30] In Kiev, the so-called revolutionary archive—an enormous collection of documents pertaining to the years of the Russian Revolution—was taken. This archive also included documentation from the Ukrainian National Republic led by Symon Petljura. The ERR further managed to acquire the Communist Party's complete archive for Smolensk Oblast—all fifteen hundred shelf-yards of it.[31]

This material was earmarked for the production of anti-Bolshevik propaganda, but it was also taken because "Germans have to know more about Bolshevism in order to be able to fight it," as a bulletin from the ERR explained. The Ostbücherei, on Gertraudenstrasse in Berlin, would become the principal hub of this research. Already in the first year after the invasion in 1941, the library absorbed half a million books. Two hundred thousand books were shipped in from the ERR's office in Riga, while up to three hundred thousand were plundered in Smolensk.[32] The library also collected large amounts of archive material, photographs, newspapers, journals, and maps.

Just as in Poland, destruction of materials in the Soviet Union exceeded the plunder by a very wide margin. One researcher has estimated that the Nazis may have destroyed upward of 100 million books in the war, of which the overwhelming share was in the Soviet Union.[33]

The war between Nazi Germany and Soviet Union between 1941 and 1945 was the single most brutal conflict in world history, with a human cost somewhere in the region of 30 million lives. It was a war that in a material and cultural sense caused unparalleled devastation. Some of this was attributable to the Red Army itself, when it used the traditional Russian scorched-earth tactic, leaving as little as possible of value for the enemy. The scorched earth would be scorched yet again when the Germans applied the same tactic during their own retreat.

But the Nazis waged war on Slavic culture for the purpose of its diminishment and extermination. Tens of millions of books that lacked relevance to Nazi research were destroyed. Because of the sheer scale of the booty, the selection process was also very stringent.

Important cultural and historical symbols, such as royal palaces, were systematically destroyed. Hitler's goal was to utterly level the large cities of the Soviet Union. The cultural city of Leningrad (St. Petersburg), which he regarded as the "foot-in-the-door of Europe" for Asiatic people, was going to be demolished and the population starved to death. The Baltic region would eventually be annexed by the Third Reich. Moscow, the center of Bolshevism, would be wiped off the surface of the earth by the creation of an artificial lake where the city stood—the Nazis planned to open the dam gates of the Volga Canal and flood the whole area.[34] Even Kiev would be leveled to the ground. According to Hitler's plan, Crimea and large areas of southern Ukraine would be emptied of their inhabitants, creating space for a Germanic colony.

Even areas like the Baku district, Galicia (western Ukraine), and the Volga colony, which had been an autonomous Soviet republic in the Soviet Union populated by a German minority that had settled in Russia in the 1700s, would be annexed by the Third Reich. This was how lebensraum would be carved out in the east for German people. As in Poland, the plan was for Russians, Ukrainians, Cossacks, and other peoples to be degraded into slavery under their new German overlords. However, in areas intended for immediate incorporation into the Third Reich, the existing population would be displaced or exterminated to make way for German settlers. In these places, everything that might remind one of the previous culture had to be utterly expunged.

Meanwhile, Nazi researchers were continuously seeking—often fruitlessly—traces of a historical Germanic presence in these regions that might legitimize the annexations. No other area was as devastated by destruction and plunder as Ukraine. According to one estimate, some 50 million books were destroyed there during the war.[35]

◆　◆　◆

On the stone wall above one of the windows in the street, the color has faded in the sunlight. Beneath, one can make out a few faint, but graceful, Hebrew letters. Vilnius's Jewish quarter hides itself under a thin layer of yellow paint—a few picturesque blocks of low-built stone houses and winding medieval streets. Many of the houses seem largely untouched since the war. Some of the houses have sunk into themselves, their roofs buckling, and they seem close to collapse. Today, vegetarian restaurants coexist with strip clubs and small book publishers along the blocks that were once the center of Jewish Vilnius.

I walk along the street that used to be known as Straszuna, but was renamed Žemaitijos gatvę after the war. The street originally derived its name from the rabbi, researcher, and businessman Mattityahu Strashun, one of Vilnius's prominent intellectual personalities of the 1800s. Among other things, Strashun contributed to the expansion of the city's Jewish education system. But his fame was built on the great library he founded. Strashun, who spoke German, French, Latin, and Russian, collected everything from medieval manuscripts in Hebrew to literary works, poetry, travel books, and scientific literature. On his death in 1885, he donated his library to the Jewish congregation in Vilnius, which, a few years later, opened the library to the public. After being further added to by donations, the library was soon regarded as one of the foremost Jewish libraries in Eastern Europe. The historical collection attracted researchers, historians, and rabbis from all over the world.

The library was a strong contributory factor in the establishment of Vilnius as the beating heart of Yiddish culture, suggested the writer Hirsz Abramowicz.[36] Abramowicz paid several visits himself to the library, and was particularly appreciative of Khaykl Lunski, Strashun's eccentric and somewhat legendary librarian. Lunski was a man who lived and breathed the library, and who kept himself to a side building of the large synagogue in the Jewish quarter. Lunski had a record of the whole collection in his head: "He knew every religious text, every secular text, and every journal." Every researcher and author who had a subject in mind had to meet the "inimitable" Khaykl Lunski.[37]

According to Abramowicz, Lunski always wore the same clothes and could live a whole day on "a bit of rye bread and a herring head." Approaching sixty, he was still working at the library when the Wehrmacht took Vilnius on June 24, 1941. Operation Barbarossa—Nazi

Germany's attack against the Soviet Union—had started two days earlier. The city was taken without any significant battles, as the Red
Army chose to withdraw before the advancing German forces.

In July 1941 Alfred Rosenberg sent a researcher named Hermann
Gotthardt to Vilnius. At first, Gotthardt adopted Vilnius almost as if
he were a culturally interested tourist or a researcher on a visit to pre-
pare for the writing of a thesis. He visited the city's museums, synagogues, and libraries to form his ideas about the existing Jewish
congregations. He interviewed employees and inquired about the city's
Jewish researchers. By the end of July, he had made an overall assessment and asked the Gestapo to detain three men: the linguist and journalist Noah Prilutski, who had been the head of the Institute for Jewish
Culture (YIVO) during the brief Soviet rule, and the Yiddish-language
journalist Elijah Jacob Goldschmidt, who was the chief curator for the
ethnographic S. Ansky Museum in Vilnius. The third man was Khaykl
Lunski, librarian at the Strashun Library. Every day in the coming
weeks the men were fetched from their cells at the Gestapo headquarters and taken to the Strashun Library, where they were forced to compile lists of the most valuable works in the city's collections.

At the same time, there was a massacre going on outside the library's
windows. In July, one of the SS murder units, the Einsatz group, had
arrived in Vilnius and arrested five thousand Jewish men. In groups of a
hundred at a time they were brought to the little holiday resort town of
Ponar, about six miles south of Vilnius. Before the war, the Red Army
had dug large pits in which to store fuel tanks adjoining a military airfield. The men were ordered to undress and were then taken ten or
twenty at a time to the edge of the pit, where they were shot. The bodies
in the pit were covered by a thin layer of sand before the next group was
forced to come forward for execution.[38] The Nazis also set up murder
units composed of Lithuanian volunteers, the Ypatingasis Būrys. Jews
were arrested in sudden mobilizations, often carried out on Jewish holy
days. Elderly people, the sick, and others considered as "unproductive"
were weeded out. Most of the victims were buried in the pits in Ponar,
where seven thousand Soviet prisoners of war and some twenty thousand
Poles were also murdered.

Before long women and children were also seized and taken to the pits in Ponar. By the time Goldschmidt, Prilutski, and Lunski had finished their work for Hermann Gotthardt in August, thousands of Vilnius's Jews had been murdered. Shortly after Gotthardt returned to Berlin with his list, Noah Prilutski and Elijah Jacob Goldschmidt were shot by the Gestapo. For unclear reasons, Khaykl Lunski was released.[39]

It was soon clear to Rosenberg's staff in Berlin that the plunder in the East required a quite different implementation than in the West. The sheer number of libraries, archives, and other collections were simply too large, as also demonstrated by Gotthardt's conclusions drawn in Vilnius. It was neither possible nor practical to confiscate such enormous amounts of material in a single raid, as had been the practice in Paris or Rome. Another problem was the lack of German researchers who spoke Hebrew and Yiddish, making it difficult to determine which books would be of value in future research. The solution to these problems was often sadistic, but this was also a defining characteristic of the Nazis—they delegated the work to the victims themselves.

In April 1942, Johannes Pohl, from the Institute for Research on the Jewish Question in Frankfurt, traveled with three other "experts on Jewry" to Vilnius.[40] By this time only a third of Vilnius's Jews were still alive. Forty thousand had been executed by the Einsatz group in the late summer and autumn of 1941. Just before Pohl's arrival the pace of mass executions had started slowing down. The Wehrmacht and Germany's armaments industry needed more slave workers at the same time as the SS had started changing its strategy for the mass murders, from firing squads to extermination camps. The twenty thousand Jews who were still alive had been forced into a cramped ghetto, which had been set up in the Jewish quarter.

The beginning of 1942 was marked by a treacherous sense of calm in the ghetto, where life as far as possible had returned to a sort of normality. A library had even been set up in the ghetto, under the guidance of a librarian, Herman Kruk. The library, a clear manifestation of the spiritual resistance of the residents of the ghetto, had been established right in the midst of the mass executions. The library was housed in a building on Straszuna 6, which is still there today. A beautiful red house with red pointing, it remains the most imposing building on the street despite its obvious dilapidation.

The ghetto dwellers had donated their books, archives, and artworks to the library. But the books had also been taken from abandoned apartments in which the residents had been murdered. The house on Straszuna 6 was more than a library, and became known as The Museum for Jewish Art and Culture. In addition to a library comprising 45,000 volumes, the building offered a bookshop, a museum, an archive, and a research department. Secretly, evidence of Nazi crimes was collected as they took place. Eyewitnesses wrote down their accounts, and German orders and other documents were stored. A group of writers started working on a history of the ghetto.

"In spite of all the pain, all the troubles, and in spite of the difficult circumstances of the ghetto, a heart of culture beats here," Kruk wrote in his diary. Thousands of Jews in the ghetto came to their library to borrow books. Reading gave both hope and consolation to the inhabitants, as a fifteen-year-old boy, Yitzhak Rudashevski, wrote in his diary on the same day that the library celebrated its hundred thousandth book loan: "'Hundreds of people read in the ghetto. Reading has become the ghetto's greatest pleasure. Books give one a feeling of freedom; books connect us to the world. The loan of the hundred thousandth copy is something the ghetto can be proud of.'"[41]

Herman Kruk would keep careful notes on the library's activities, who borrowed books and what was most popular. He found that one group of readers looked for analogies of their own situation in the ghetto. The history of the Jews during medieval times, the Crusades, and the Inquisition were such subjects, but most popular of all with these readers was Tolstoy's *War and Peace*. Another group sought the opposite; they wanted literature that "bore them away from reality and took them to far countries." In both groups the drive to read was strong: "A human being can endure hunger, poverty, and pain, but she cannot endure isolation. Then, more than ever, the need for books and reading is at its greatest," wrote Kruk.[42]

It was during this period of relative calm in the ghetto that the ERR began its work. A dozen learned Jews had been selected for the forced labor. Included in the group was Khaykl Lunski, who had also survived the extermination campaign of the autumn.

The designated leaders were Herman Kruk and an earlier colleague of his at YIVO, the philologist and historian Zelig Kalmanovitj. Large premises were set in order outside the ghetto as a sorting station, in a building belonging to Vilnius's university library.

The group's work consisted of the sorting and packing of literary treasures for transportation to Germany. The first consignment to arrive was forty thousand books from the Strashun Library. Kruk, Kalmanovitj, Lunski, and the others in the group were faced with a choice, either option being just as terrible.

They were forced to select and catalog the books of greatest "value" in the collection, and in so doing they would be contributing to research, which would fundamentally have the intention of justifying the Holocaust. The alternative was hardly any better, because books that were not selected were sent to a nearby paper mill, where they were pulped.

Either they helped the Nazis and "saved" the most valuable books or they refused and had to see these works being lost. "Kalmanovitj and I do not know if we are redeemers or gravediggers," Kruk wrote dejectedly in his diary.[43]

What gave strength to the group, which would later become known in the ghetto as Die Papier Brigade (The Paper Brigade), was in spite of it all the hope that they were saving this literary heritage. Soon, books started arriving from synagogues and also a valuable collection of books from Elijah ben Solomon Zalman's school.

The work was so successful that the ERR was soon expanding its operations. In the spring of 1942 a second sorting station was set up at the YIVO Institute on Vivulskio gatvé 18. The Paper Brigade grew until it numbered just over forty persons, including the thirty-year-old poet Abraham Sutzkever. With his intellectual prominence, his slanted black-rimmed glasses, and an almost religious belief in the power of language, he had become a figurehead for the younger generation of poets in Yiddish in the Yung Vilne group.

The ERR also sent both sorting stations the stock of Jewish libraries plundered in nearby towns and villages. The work was carefully checked by the ERR: "Just as in the Holocaust, minute records were kept of the destruction of Jewish books, with reports submitted every other week including statistics of how many books had been sent to Germany and how many to the paper mill, with the books subdivided by their language and year of publication," writes the historian David E. Fishman.[44]

The Paper Brigade could not save more books by letting less valuable books pass the selection procedure. The ERR had imposed specific quotas in advance, whereby some two-thirds of the books had to be destroyed. Kruk writes in his diary that the work is "heart-breaking" and that members of the group have tears in their eyes as they go about their compulsory tasks: "YIVO is dying; and its mass grave is a paper mill."[45] Sutzkever describes the work in Vivulskio gatvé 18 as "a Ponar for our Jewish culture." Watched over by their German guards, "we are digging the grave for our souls."[46]

But from the very beginning the members of the Paper Brigade tried to find opportunities to put up resistance. One such way was passivity: as soon as the Germans left the building, the members stopped working. Sutzkever, who worked in the YIVO building, used to give poetry readings in Yiddish to the others. Several of the members carried on writing poetry, theses, and journals throughout their time in the ghetto. It had been a question of survival, Sutzkever said afterward: "I thought that, just as an attentive Jew believes in the Messiah, as long as I kept writing, as long as I was a poet, I had a weapon against death."[47]

Before long the Paper Brigade started involving itself in more active forms of resistance, by smuggling out valuable works. At the end of their working day, before they were brought back to the ghetto, Sutzkever and others in the brigade hid manuscripts in their clothes. This was less risky on the days when their guards were from the Jewish ghetto police. Well aware of what was going on, these were also the guards that gave the group its nickname. The Paper Brigade were warriors of paper, who risked their own lives to smuggle one document after another into the ghetto. "Other Jews looked at us as if we were mad. They smuggled food into the ghetto, hidden in their clothes and boots, but we smuggled in books, scraps of paper, and sometimes a Torah," wrote one of the members of the group.[48]

Sutzkever, the group's most active smuggler, managed to bring out among other things a diary that had belonged to the father of Zionism, Theodor Herzl. He was also the one to come up with the idea of asking the Germans for permission to remove "spare paper." Sutzkever convinced the Germans that this would be burned in stoves in the ghetto. By means of this permission, various "rubbish" was saved, such as letters and manuscripts by Tolstoy, Gorky, and Elijah ben Solomon Zalman, and drawings by Chagall.

Despite this risky and courageous action, another dilemma remained: the brigade had merely smuggled books and manuscripts from one prison to another—where could they be moved to after that? Herman Kruk had some of the stash hidden away in the ghetto library, while Abraham Sutzkever divided up his material between a number of hiding places, including behind the wallpaper in his apartment. The most ingenious hiding place was a bunker that had been covertly constructed by an engineer by the name of Gerson Abramovitsj. The bunker, as deep as sixty feet underground, had both electricity and its own ventilation system. Abramovitsj had built the bunker to hide his handicapped mother from the Nazis. Soon she also had the company of manuscripts, letters, books, and works of art, which were buried under the floor.[49] The Paper Brigade managed to smuggle some of the material out of the ghetto, partly by the efforts of Ona Simaite, the Lithuanian librarian, who tricked her way into the ghetto by alleging that she wanted to reclaim books that Jewish students had not returned. When she left she brought out valuable books and manuscripts. She also hid a Jewish girl but was caught in 1944. Simaite was detained, tortured, and deported to Dachau, the concentration camp, but she managed to survive the war.[50]

Abraham Sutzkever smuggled not only books but also weapons. He was a member of the clandestine group Fareynikte Partizaner Organizatsye (Unified Partisan Organizations), a militant Jewish resistance group that had been formed in the ghetto and whose motto was "We will not let ourselves be taken like sheep to slaughter." Using

Lithuanian contacts, while working at the YIVO building Sutzkever received pistols and parts of submachine guns, which were smuggled in and assembled in the ghetto.

As time passed, the Paper Brigade members grew more daring and brought out large volumes of materials. As a final desperate measure, the brigade started hiding books in the actual YIVO building. Between the spring of 1943 and September 1944, the Paper Brigade succeeded in smuggling out thousands of books and manuscripts. But in the final analysis, what was saved was a small part of the hundreds of thousands of books and manuscripts that were either sent to the paper mill or to Germany.

◆  ◆  ◆

Late in the summer of 1943 the members of the Paper Brigade realized that their work would soon be over. No more libraries were being delivered for sorting, and the ERR started shutting down the operation.

Kalmanovitj makes one of his last journal entries at the end of August: "All week I have selected books, thousands of them, and thrown them into a rubbish pile with my own two hands. A pile of books in YIVO's reading room, a place of burial for books, a brother's grave, books that were afflicted by war like Gog and Magog, just as their owners. . . . Whatever we can save will survive with God's help! We will see them again when we come back here as human beings."[51]

It was not only the ERR's work that was being wound down, but the entire German eastern campaign. After its defeat at Stalingrad in the winter of 1943, the German army was in retreat. This meant that the German armaments industry in the east was disassembled and millions of slave workers became superfluous. Many were sent directly to the gas chambers.

The Jewish uprising in Warsaw in the spring of 1943 had also made Heinrich Himmler nervous. He suspected, justifiably so, that Jews in other ghettos were planning armed resistance. A few weeks after the revolt, Himmler issued an order about the discontinuation of the ghettos in Ostland (the Baltic region). The ghetto in Vilnius, regarded by the German intelligence service as a potential hive of resistance, had to be destroyed as soon as possible.[52]

The deportations of Vilnius's remaining Jews began early in August of 1943. Within two months the ghetto had been emptied. Those of working age were sent to labor camps to carry out tasks such as the digging of trenches. Those who were too old, too young, or too sick were murdered.

But before the liquidation of the ghetto, the 180 members of the Unified Partisan Organizations managed to flee and hide in the forests outside Vilnius. One of them was Abraham Sutzkever, who got away on September 12 with his wife and another poet from the Yung Vilne group, Shmerke Kaczerginski. Back in the ghetto, Sutzkever had already lost both his mother and his newborn son, who had been poisoned by the Nazis in the ghetto hospital.[53]

News of Abraham Sutzkever's flight soon reached Moscow. Early in 1944, Ilya Ehrenburg, the most renowned writer and journalist in the Soviet Union, helped Sutzkever and his wife flee to Moscow. A light Soviet aircraft managed to cross the front and land on a frozen lake in the forests outside Vilnius. Under heavy flak from the Germans, the plane succeeded in making it back to the Soviet side. Ehrenburg's article about Sutzkever in *Pravda*, the Communist Party newspaper, was the first to ever mention the mass murder of Jews in the Soviet Union.[54]

However, most of the people in the ghetto and the Paper Brigade did not manage to escape. In Ponar, the SS continued with the mass executions. One of those executed toward the end of this period was the fifteen-year-old diary writer, Yitzhak Rudashevski. At the same time the SS launched a wide-ranging campaign to cover up the mass murders. In the autumn of 1943 inmates of a nearby concentration camp, Stutthof, were forced to dig up tens of thousands of decomposing bodies in Ponar. The corpses were burned in enormous fires and the ashes mixed with sand and buried. It took several months for the slave workers to burn the remains of 100,000 victims.

YIVO's spiritual father, Simon Dubnov, had already been murdered in 1941. Dubnov, who was eighty years old when the war broke out, had settled in Riga in the 1930s to write his memoirs. Friends, who could see the approaching danger, had helped Dubnov get a Swedish visa in 1940, but he chose not to make use of it. When the Nazis occupied Riga in 1941, Dubnov was kicked out of his apartment and had to see his large library confiscated. With the rest of the city's Jewish population he was shut up in a ghetto. Early in 1941 the SS forced 24,000 Jews to leave the ghetto and go to the forest of Rumbula, outside Riga. Here Soviet prisoners of war had dug six large pits, where the Jews were executed. Simon Dubnov, who was too sick to walk several miles to the spot, was shot in the street by a Gestapo officer. According to witnesses, Dubnov to the very end exhorted the inhabitants of the ghetto, "Jews, write and keep a record."

How the librarian Khaykl Lunski died is unclear. According to one witness he was deported with his daughter to Treblinka, while another testimony suggests he was beaten to death in September 1943. Zelig Kalmanovitj, the head of the Paper Brigade, was transported to the concentration camp of Vaivara in Estonia, where he died in 1944. Herman Kruk was deported to a forced-labor camp in Lagedi, Estonia. He would continue keeping a journal to the very end. On September 17 he wrote a final note: "I am burying the manuscripts in Lagedi, in Herr Schulma's barrack opposite the guardhouse. Six people are present for the funeral."[55] Kruk had a sense of what awaited him. The next day he and two thousand other prisoners were forced to carry wooden logs to a forest in the vicinity. The logs were put down in long rows, whereupon the prisoners were forced to lie down on top of them. They had built their own funeral pyres. After the SS guards shot the prisoners in the head, another layer of logs and prisoners was added on top—and thereafter the bodies were burned. But when the Red Army reached the scene a few days later, unburned bodies still lay in piles. One of the witnesses of Kruk's "funeral" managed to flee and went back to dig up his diaries.

By then, Vilnius had been liberated by the Red Army. In the first week of July 1944 an offensive was launched against the city, and by July 13 the last of the Nazis had withdrawn. Among the liberators were Abraham Sutzkever and Shmerke Kaczerginski, who were fighting for the Jewish partisan group Nekome (the Avengers). Once the battle was over, they started to look for hidden manuscripts and books. With great sadness they found that the YIVO Institute at Vivulskio gatvé 18 was a burned-out, gutted ruin, after the house was hit by artillery fire. Kruk's hiding place in the ghetto library had been discovered and the books burned in the courtyard. On the other hand, the secret bunker had not been destroyed. From beneath the floor, Sutzkever and Kaczerginski dug out manuscripts, letters, diaries, and a bust of Tolstoy. As they continued digging, a hand suddenly appeared in the ground. One of the Jews who had hidden in the bunker died there, and someone buried him among the books.[56]

# 12

# THE TALMUD UNIT

## *Theresienstadt*

From the bridge I can see the light brown backs of the fish against the sandy bottom. From time to time one of them swivels, turning its scales toward the sun and projecting a silvery reflection. On the other side of the bridge I see families with children, lying on an exposed sand spit reaching into the river Ohře. It is high summer and the water level is low. The children throw themselves into the current and let themselves be pulled along to a calmer section. Farther down, where the trees along the riverbank stop, the ashes of 22,000 camp prisoners were dumped in the river.

Twelve or so miles south of the Zittau mountain chain, which forms the boundary between Germany and the Czech Republic, lies the old Hapsburg fortress and garrison town of Theresienstadt, or Terezín as it is known today. In the parking area where the bus stops, one can buy soft drinks, key rings, and postcards of concentration camp prisoners in tents. But today there are few customers, the thermometer is inching toward 104 degrees Fahrenheit, and the town streets are eerily deserted—apart from a few girls on bicycles with rolled-up towels on their parcel racks, on their way to the river. These days, only a couple of thousand people live inside the star-shaped fortress walls, in a town that has not changed significantly since the war, apart from a few apartment blocks that catch the eye because of their Soviet bleakness.

Inside these walls, during the war, the SS established what may have been the most curious concentration camp of all. Most of the German concentration camps were similar, arranged according to a model developed by SS-Oberführer Theodor Eicke, the commandant of Dachau, the very first concentration camp, which opened in 1933. Here Eicke refined the structure and culture that would function as a model for almost all future camps.

Theresienstadt was both a concentration camp and a ghetto, which served several different functions. It was a collection and transit camp. Most who were deported here were sent on after a while to extermination camps in occupied Poland. But Theresienstadt was also a model camp, featured in German propaganda.

The garrison town had been built by the Austrian emperor Joseph II at the end of the 1700s. In the smaller fortress adjoining the town, the most famous prisoner of the First World War had been kept—Gavrilo Princip—who in 1914 shot the heir to the Austro-Hungarian throne in Sarajevo, triggering the outbreak of the war.

In 1942, the SS instigated the compulsory eviction of seven thousand Czechs living in Theresienstadt in order to make space for a camp. The walls and moats that had once protected the town would now serve as the boundaries of an enormous prison. In the model camp the Jews would live in normal houses and wear everyday civilian clothes, which meant that Theresienstadt was very much like a ghetto. As in other ghettos, there was also a Judenrat, a Jewish council exerting self-governance under SS control.

Many of the people sent to Theresienstadt were "selected Jews" from Germany, and western and northern Europe, including Jews who had previously been high-ranking civil servants or war veterans from the First World War. But the most visible and important group—from a propaganda perspective—was made up of the many artists, actors, directors, musicians, authors, academics, and other intellectuals. One of these was Isaac Leo Seeligmann, the Bible scholar and book collector from Amsterdam, who was deported here with his family.

In German propaganda Theresienstadt was presented as "the city the Führer gave to the Jews." For the sake of propaganda once again, the Nazis had a bank and shops opened, and built playgrounds for the children. There was even a local "camp currency" known as Theresienstadt-crowns, established to create the image of an autonomous, internal economy.

A significant part of camp life were the many cultural activities, which were encouraged by the camp commandant and staff. In a two-story yellow stone house at the camp address L304, a library known as Ghettobücherei Theresienstadt was set up in November 1942—on the floor above it was the Freizeitgestaltung, the leisure department, which took care of various camp activities. The Freizeitgestaltung had theater performances, as well as concerts and lectures. There was no shortage of actors, musicians, and writers. Some of the most outstanding talent of the age was deported to the camp, such as the Austrian actor Jaro Fürth, the playwright Elsa Bernstein, and the pianist Alice Herz-Sommer. No fewer than five members of the Vienna Philharmonic Orchestra were sent to Theresienstadt, including its former concertmaster Julius Stwertka.[1] Even a Jewish jazz band, the Ghetto Swingers, was formed in the camp.

When the Ghettobücherei opened in 1942, it had four thousand books, which the Nazis had plundered from places including the rabbinical seminary in Berlin. Other deliveries of books to Theresienstadt went ahead, these having been plundered from synagogues, Jewish families, churches, and Masonic orders. Yet most of the books were brought by the prisoners themselves, for with every new influx of people came more books. Of the few possessions the Jews were allowed to bring when they were deported, many chose to pack one or two of their favorite books. These were confiscated on arrival and handed over to the Ghettobücherei. Within a year, the library collection had grown to 50,000 volumes and by 1944 it comprised 120,000 books.[2]

The cultural life of the camp was highlighted in Nazi propaganda. The climax of this Potemkin village was a carefully planned visit by the Red Cross in 1944. The year before, the SS had already begun preparations, implementing a "beautification process," which included renovations of barracks, repainting of houses, and the planting of trees and flowers. The prisoners were given more substantial rations so that they looked better fed. In May, 7,503 people had also been deported from Theresienstadt to Auschwitz, to make the camp seem less crowded.

The visit by the Red Cross came about as a result of pressure from Denmark and Sweden, and when the inspectors arrived in June 1944, Theresienstadt was an idyll of staged soccer games, concerts, and a choir of Jewish children singing for the visitors. From the square came the sound of jazz music played by the Ghetto Swingers, despite the fact that jazz had been banned in the Third Reich and was regarded as "degenerate music." The transformation was also linguistic, as the camp changed its name from Ghetto Theresienstadt to Jüdisches Siedlungsgebiet (Jewish Settlement Area).

In connection with the visit, work began on a propaganda film in which the camp was described as a "health resort for Jews." Cynically enough, camp prisoners were recruited to produce the film under the leadership of the SS. Jewish prisoners were responsible for the script, direction, and music, the latter also provided by the Ghetto Swingers.[3] The film, entitled *Der Führer schenkt den Juden eine Stadt* (The Führer Gives a City to the Jews), was directed by the German-Jewish actor and director Kurt Gerron, who had had his breakthrough in 1930 opposite Marlene Dietrich in *The Blue Angel*.

The library made an appearance in a surviving section of the film— the librarians eagerly working on cataloging books and the chief librarian, Emil Utitz, giving a talk. In the film the library had a new name: no longer Ghettobücherei Theresienstadt, it was called the more neutral Zentralbücherei.

However, the theatrical backdrops collapsed as soon as the inspectors from the Red Cross left the camp, and the deportations immediately resumed. Behind the image of the model ghetto there existed a concentration camp that hardly differed from any other, defined as it was by starvation, disease, slave labor, torture, and overcrowding. The Jewish film team was deported soon after wrapping in September. As for Kurt Gerron and the members of the Ghetto Swingers, they were put on the last train from Theresienstadt to Auschwitz at the end of 1944.[4]

Of the 144,000 Jews who were sent to Theresienstadt, just over 17,000 survived the war. About 33,000 died in the actual camp, while close to 90,000 were deported to Auschwitz. Many died in the typhoid epidemic that broke out in the camp at the end of the war. The library books helped spread the contagion from one reader to another, and tens of thousands of infected books from the Ghettobücherei eventually had to be burned. The library was also decimated by the frequent deportations toward the end: "Every train load robs us of 1,000 books, because every person brings two or three books . . . I did nothing about this," wrote Emil Utitz.[5] Although many knew, or at least had a sense of, what lay ahead, they wanted to bring a book with them for the journey.

But there was also a secret library in Theresienstadt, which did not appear in the propaganda film. Available only to a select group, it was a library of an altogether different kind, and of a completely different value.

◆ ◆ ◆

With the help of a wartime map I try to orient myself through the streets of Terezín. Traces of the camp are still discernible everywhere; on certain street corners one can make out the old "street names" painted in black letters using camp abbreviations: "Block C.V/Q2— 09-15." I walk past one of the most beautiful houses in the city, in which the camp's Danish Jews were once housed.

Just outside the south walls, not far from the crematorium, is a small stone house with the pointing missing along the gable. In the little garden surrounded by a rusty fence I see tomato plants, currant bushes, and vines climbing up the fortress walls. Here worked a group of people referred to by the SS as the Bücherfassungsgruppe.

In April 1943 the SS had ordered that a special group of Jewish scholars should be assembled, composed of rabbis, theologians, linguists, and historians. While other prisoners in the camp were working in a nearby mine, breaking coal, or manufacturing military uniforms, the Bücherfassungsgruppe busied itself with cataloging plundered books for the SS.[6] Like the ERR, the SS was short of researchers who could read, interpret, and catalog the mountains of confiscated Jewish literature. Theresienstadt with its many Jewish academics was a resource that the SS felt obliged to use. There was also another underlying reason, namely that in the spring of 1943 the SS had begun evacuating its book depots in Berlin, because of the many air raids against the capital. Theresienstadt was one of the places chosen as a safer location.

The Bücherfassungsgruppe was the SS equivalent of the ERR's Paper Brigade in Vilnius, and just as in Vilnius, the working group, in ghetto slang, would go under a quite different name: Talmudkommando (Talmud Unit). In all, some forty Jewish scholars were included in the group.

Some of the foremost Hebrew scholars in Europe were "recruited" into the Talmudkommando. The Czech Judaist and book collector Otto Muneles was selected as the head of the group. Previously, he had worked for the Jewish Museum in Prague and attended the same school as Franz Kafka. Other members of the group included Moses Woskin-Nahartabi, who had been the professor of Semitic languages at Leipzig University, as well as the historian and book collector from Amsterdam, Isaac Leo Seeligmann. His own and his father Sigmund Seeligmann's great book collection, confiscated in 1941, had been absorbed by the RSHA library in Berlin. In 1943 the RSHA moved a part of the section on Jewish literature to Theresienstadt and placed it with the Talmudkommando.[7]

Seeligmann found books from his own collection in this consignment of about sixty thousand volumes. Members of the group seem to have been plagued by the same moral dilemmas as the Paper Brigade in Vilnius. They looked for consolation in the fact that their work was preserving their Jewish heritage, although they were doing it on behalf of an organization that more than any other had to be considered responsible for the extermination of the Jewish people. The work was a balancing act between satisfying their "masters" and doing a meaningful job in its own right. They were also painfully aware that completion of the task would probably be synonymous with their own deaths. As a result, they intentionally slowed down their productivity.

Although the Talmudkommando enjoyed a certain amount of privilege from the camp administration, there was a constant threat of deportation. The Talmudkommando was generally exempt, but the SS consciously used the sense of threat to engender a feeling of insecurity.

In 1944 one of the foremost experts in the group, Moses Woskin-Nahartabi, was deported to Auschwitz along with his whole family.

For others the exception could be both an escape and a curse. Otto

Muneles, effectively the head of the Talmudkommando, had to witness the deportation of his entire family. As soon as Muneles learned of their fate, he volunteered to go with them, but this was denied. He continued to put his name on the list every time new deportations were announced, but his request was rejected every time.[8]

The work of the Talmudkommando would continue until the SS guards abandoned the camp early in April 1945, just a few days before the capitulation of Nazi Germany. By that time the group had cataloged close to thirty thousand books, the spines carefully labeled with yellow tickets and handwritten serial numbers. The camp was left in such a hurry that the SS did not even take the books that had been cataloged and already packed into more than 250 crates.

◆ ◆ ◆

At around midnight on May 31, 1942, the largest-ever hostile bomber fleet entered German airspace. It was part of a new strategy in which attacks would not only be directed at German armaments industries but also at those who worked in them—in other words, the civilian workforce. The intention was to bomb Germans in their own homes and break their appetite for continuing the war. In ninety minutes some fifteen hundred tons of bombs were dropped over medieval Cologne. Twenty-five hundred fires raged in the city, leaving fifty thousand people homeless. The operation created the model for raids during the coming years, with increasingly devastating bomb attacks on German cities. Encouraged by their success, the Western Allies started focusing their attention on Berlin, the political and administrative core of the Third Reich.

The millions of plundered books that had been collected in warehouses all over the city were an inferno waiting to happen. The Jewish section at the RSHA's library of the enemies of the state is estimated in 1943 to have held between 200,000 and 300,000 books, including Jewish literature from schools, synagogues, and seminaries all over Europe, as well as outstanding private collections such as those of Isaac Leo Seeligmann, the pianist Arthur Rubinstein, and the French-Jewish author André Maurois.[9]

The inflow of books had been so great that the SS had only had time to catalog a small proportion of the confiscated Jewish literature. There were not even enough shelves to accommodate the collection, most of which was piled in enormous stacks in the rooms of the seized Freemasons' lodge at Eisenacher Strasse in Berlin.

In 1943 both the RSHA and the ERR began to evacuate their collections from Berlin. Not only the depots were cleared and shipped out—entire plundering operations involving sorting, cataloging, and research were also moved. In August 1943, Section VII, RSHA's section for ideological research, relocated most of its books to various castles that the SS had at its disposal, primarily in Silesia close to the borders between Germany, Poland, and Czechoslovakia. A part of the uncataloged collection at the Jewish department in Section VII was sent to Theresienstadt, while the rest was shipped to a castle outside Reichenberg in Bavaria. Parts of the RSHA's section for Freemasonry literature, including the organization's occult library, was moved to Heinrich Himmler's favorite castle, Schlawa (today known as Sława), while archive material was moved to Wölfelsdorf (today known as Wilkanów), where the material filled a castle and a brewery.[10] One of the collections evacuated to Silesia was the so-called Schwedenkiste, the archive of the Illuminati. The new headquarters were transferred to Schloss Niemes, about nine miles east of Česká Lípa. In all, the plundered collections were housed in about ten castles and fortresses in Central Europe.

The Talmudkommando was not the first time that the RSHA had made use of intellectual slave labor. By the time the libraries began to be moved out of Berlin in 1943 there was already a Jewish group at work in Section VII, where it had spent several years cataloging the collections. As early as 1941 the SS had kidnapped eight Jewish intellectuals, who had been forced to work at Section VII's depot on Eisenacher Strasse, one of them being Ernst Grumach, previously the professor of philology at the university in Königsberg.

In the spring of 1943 yet another working group was set up, consisting of nineteen Jewish academics. Although they were working in central Berlin, their conditions were not much better than in a concentration camp. The Jewish workers were carefully monitored by the SD, which kept them locked up in special rooms for up to sixteen hours a day. Forbidden to talk to other Germans, they were even allocated their own "Jewish toilet." Death threats and physical abuse were part of the daily routine, and "none among the Jewish forced labor knew when he walked into the building, which was surrounded by a high fence, whether he would come out alive," Grumach testified. [11]

Initially, Ernst Grumach's group busied themselves with cataloging and sorting the books that came to Eisenacher Strasse from all over the occupied territories of Europe. But when the evacuations began, the work shifted to the packing and loading of books, preparing them for transport—a heavy task for which the often elderly academics were ill suited.

In November 1943, the RAF began its bombing raids on Berlin. The most devastating of all was on the night of November 23, when Tiergarten, Charlottenburg, Schöneberg, and Spandau were bombed. The firestorms that followed made 175,000 people homeless. That night, the Kaiser Wilhelm Memorial Church on Kurfürstendamm was hit, and today its broken steeple is one of the most famous monuments in Berlin.

The RSHA's depot in Eisenacher Strasse, about half a mile from there, was also hit by bombs, and a large number of books that had not yet been evacuated caught fire. According to Grumach, most of the Jewish collections in the building were destroyed, including the libraries of the Jewish congregations of Vienna and Warsaw. The RSHA's other book depot, a Masonic lodge on Emser Strasse, was hit by bombs.

It was the lot of the Jewish slave laborers to save whatever remained. According to Grumach, this took place while the buildings were still on fire, and Jews were "sent into burning rooms and made to carry out heavy furniture through rooms where the ceilings were buckling and on the verge of collapsing at any moment." [12]

In spite of the fires, there were still large numbers of books in various depots, bunkers, and cellars in Berlin. The packing and removal of books would continue "right up until the Russians were drawing close to Berlin." [13] By this time the most important collections had already been evacuated, but there were still upward of half a million books in the RSHA depots when the war ended, of which many were collected by the Bergungsstelle für wissenschaftliche Bibliotheken and distributed among Berlin's libraries. Some ended up at the Zentral- und Landesbibliothek, where seventy years later Sebastian Finsterwalder and Detlef Bockenkamm would raise them from their obscurity.

◆ ◆ ◆

In the summer of 1943, Alfred Rosenberg also began to empty his depots in both Berlin and Frankfurt. Amt Rosenberg's headquarters lay west of Potsdamer Platz in Berlin. Rosenberg's organization had swelled and bifurcated like a tree trunk; every branch had thrown out new buds, in the form of new projects, operations, and organizations. By 1943, millions of plundered books had been collected for Rosenberg's various library projects, the most ambitious being the Jewish library of the Frankfurt institute, Zentralbibliothek der Hohen Schule, and the Ostbücherei, the library specializing in questions relating to the East.

The Frankfurt institute had built up "the finest Jewish library on the Continent," as the American historian Patricia Kennedy Grimsted puts it.[14] In 1941, the first operational year of the institute, 2,136 crates of plundered books arrived. As with the other library projects, there was a constant discrepancy between the incoming flow of books and what the staff had time to process. The bounty was so extensive that it would probably have taken the Nazi librarians and archivists decades to catalog everything. Of the aforementioned 2,136 book crates, the institute only had time to unpack 700 and to catalog some 25,000 books. Only about a tenth of the collection would ever be cataloged.

By the spring of 1943 the institute had built up a collection of over half a million books—in no small part because of the work of Johannes Pohl.[15] In his earlier life as a Catholic priest, Pohl had personally visited and secured many of the most important Jewish libraries in Europe. In Amsterdam, the Jewish libraries Ets Haim and Rosenthaliana had been seized. In Paris, he had overseen the taking of Alliance Israélite Universelle's library, and in Rome, the ERR had confiscated Biblioteca del Collegio Rabbinico Italiano. Over ten thousand books had been plundered from the Jewish community in Thessaloniki. On his visit to Thessaloniki early in 1943, Pohl had personally brought some of the congregation's archives back to Frankfurt.

And from the Soviet Union and Eastern Europe, train after train pulled in with plundered Jewish archives and libraries, in many cases from communities that by 1943 had already been extinguished. Books came from Kiev, Minsk, Riga, and hundreds of smaller communities in between. Above all, they came from Vilnius.

In the latter half of 1943 the evacuation from Frankfurt began. Because of its western position and its important armaments factories it was particularly targeted by Allied bombing raids. About twenty bombing raids during the war reduced Frankfurt's renowned medieval city core, the largest in Germany, to gravel and lumber. There were no great distances involved; the institute was established in Hungen, a town about thirty-one miles north of Frankfurt where the collections were kept in eight different storage depots. During the last two years of the institute's existence, the collections grew further when libraries from both the east and the west were moved as the Germans retreated. In 1945, it is calculated, there were about a million books in Hungen, in addition to the large number of archive materials and Jewish religious artifacts.[16]

The libraries and archives that had been plundered by the ERR had been divided up between the institute in Frankfurt, which received many of the most important Jewish collections, and the various departments in Berlin. The ERR had set up a so-called Buchleitstelle in Berlin, a kind of sorting center that checked through the inventories and decided where they should be sent. One tragic consequence of this work was that many of the collections were fragmented. As far as the ERR was concerned, there was no inherent value in keeping a plundered collection together. After all, the operative point was to build entirely new collections. Particularly affected by this were the smaller, more specialized collections, in which books with a "Jewish" theme could be set aside for the Frankfurt institute, while others were sent to the Ostbücherei or the Zentralbibliothek der Hohen Schule (ZBHS).[17] The

ERR voluntarily shared or was made to share what it had in the way of books and archive material with other organizations, institutes, universities, and libraries. However, the materials were also divided between different projects within Amt Rosenberg. The result of this fragmentation was that many collections, for instance those from Vilnius and Thessaloniki, ended up in a number of places. This fragmentation was a kind of destruction in its own right, a fate that led to many libraries never again being reassembled.

Apart from the institute in Frankfurt, the ZBHS was the most important recipient of books. The library was one of the first of Rosenberg's collections to be evacuated from Berlin, beginning in October 1942. Initially the library moved into the Grand Hotel Annenheim, near Lake Ossiach in southern Austria, but it was soon moved again to the large Renaissance castle of Tanzenberg, just outside the town of Sankt Veit an der Glan.

As the crown jewel of Rosenberg's library projects, the ZBHS would be awarded some of the finest collections. But the foundation of the library had been a couple of collections acquired from German academics, including the Orientalist and racist Hugo Grothe, who in the early 1900s had advocated genocide as a way for Germans to gain lebensraum in the colonies. There was also a library belonging to the church historian Ulrich Stutz and the Napoleon researcher Friedrich Max Kircheisen. Alfred Rosenberg had added his own private library to the collection. However, these collections would only form a small part of what the ZBHS amassed during the war. In all, between 500,000 and 700,000 books were brought to Zentralbibliothek der Hohe Schule in Tanzenberg.[18]

The collection could be regarded as a cross section of the ERR's plundering during the war. There were books from almost every country in which the ERR had operated: France, the Netherlands, the Soviet Union, but also Belgium, Greece, Italy, Poland, and Yugoslavia. There were even books that had been taken from the British Channel Islands, which Germany had occupied in 1940.[19]

The Frankfurt institute did not get all of the Jewish literature; a good deal also went to the ZBHS, including a number of valuable private collections such as libraries that had belonged to members of the French Rothschild family. The ZBHS received almost nine hundred crates of material from the IISG in Amsterdam, including most of the institute's collection of newspapers and journals.[20] Further, the library absorbed valuable libraries and archives from the Soviet Union, for instance, 35,000 books that had been stolen from the libraries in imperial palaces outside Leningrad. Even rare and very early prints that had been seized in Novgorod and Kiev were sent to Tanzenberg, including books from Kiev Pechersk Lavra, better known as the Kiev Monastery of the Caves, founded in the 1000s.

The ERR's main depot would be in neither Austria nor Hungen. Instead, it was in the small town of Ratibor, today known as Racibórz, in southwest Poland. Ratibor was the main market town of Upper Silesia and had traditions going back to the early Middle Ages. Like so many places in these borderlands, it had a mixed population of Czechs, Poles, and Germans. An important reason for the choice seems to have been the town's strategic position between Berlin, Kraków, and Vienna. The possibility of waterborne transport was just as important—the Oder flowed through the town on its way to the Baltic. ERR personnel arrived in Ratibor in May 1943 to make preparations, and a few months later an initial delivery of ten railroad cars of books and archives arrived from Berlin.[21] A lot more would arrive by the river route, with over six thousand crates of material transported via barges on the Oder.

The new head office of the organization was established in a Franciscan monastery by the river, while the Ostbücherei was installed in what had previously been a bathhouse. A bank, the town library, a synagogue, and a number of warehouses were also occupied. The ERR's departments for press, music, popular culture, and science all followed suit and moved to Ratibor. The lack of available space soon meant that they had to leave the town and seek premises in the countryside; among other places a cigar factory was requisitioned along with several nearby castles. Trains loaded with furnishings plundered from Jewish apartments in the M-Aktion provided the various departments with what they required. The dispersal of the activities was an attempt to keep the operation as covert as possible. For instance, the owners of the castles were allowed to remain as residents in order to preserve an outer semblance of normality.

The sorting operation, Buchleitstelle, also moved to Ratibor, and this seems to suggest that all the plundered archives and libraries had been taken to Ratibor for sorting. The Allied landings in Normandy and the advances of the Red Army on the eastern front meant that large numbers of books arrived in the last years of the war. A list of collections checked through by Buchleitstelle in the summer of 1944 included many that had belonged to eminent French Jews, including the former director of the French National Library, Julien Cain, and the general secretary of French PEN, Benjamin Crémieux—both men had been deported to Buchenwald.[22] Furthermore, the archives of the French-Jewish politician Léon Blum and the author André Gide ended up in Ratibor.

A significant part of the activities in Ratibor was centered on the Ostbücherei, which had expanded enormously as a consequence of the plundering in the Soviet Union. The Ostbücherei's collections were stored in the synagogue and a half-dozen other buildings. The large Lenin Library, which arrived in seventeen railroad cars from Minsk, was transferred to the cigar factory outside Ratibor. Hundreds of thousands of other books and journals were stored in a medieval castle, Schloss Pless, not far from Ratibor. The Turgenev and Petljura libraries, along with a few other émigré libraries found by the ERR in the west, filled several rooms in the synagogue. Plans for a western equivalent of the library on eastern lands, which would be known as the Westbücherei, never materialized.[23] Books continued arriving in Ratibor right up to the closing moments of the war. Not even the Germans seem to have known how many books the Ostbücherei had amassed in Ratibor. According to some estimates, the figure may have been at least two million volumes, and quite possibly even more.

# 13

# "JEWISH STUDIES WITHOUT JEWS"

## *Ratibor–Frankfurt*

When the Institut zur Erforschung der Judenfrage opened in Frankfurt in 1941, there was a sense that this was taking place not only in a city with a certain amount of symbolism attached to it but also in a unique building. The institute moved into one of the Rothschild family's palaces at Bockenheimer Landstrasse 68.[1] That Europe's leading anti-Semitic institute opened in Frankfurt rather than elsewhere, according to Alfred Rosenberg, was a symbolic ending of the power of the Rothschilds over the city.[2]

It was in Frankfurt that the family's ancestor Mayer Amschel Rothschild had laid down the foundations of its banking dynasty at the end of the 1700s. From here, he had sent out his sons across Europe to establish a new, powerful banking dynasty with a network of family ties.[3] As the Nazis saw it, Frankfurt was the birthplace of a globally reaching evil—and as far as they were concerned, no other family had ever embodied the destructive avarice of Jewish finance as much as the Rothschilds. In placing Institut zur Erforschung der Judenfrage in the heart of this "evil," there was the desire to both symbolically and literally separate the Jewish world conspiracy from one of its most important roots.

The city's Nazi mayor, Friedrich Krebs, had used the Rothschildsche Bibliothek as an enticement to bring Rosenberg to Frankfurt. In a letter, Krebs wrote: "The collection was built up during a time when Frankfurt's political and cultural life was under Jewish influence, but in our time this library offers a unique opportunity to research Judaism and the Jewish Question."[4] This was one Jewish library that the Nazis did not need to steal. Instead, the Frankfurt institute housed its own collection there until the evacuations began in 1943. Much like the RSHA's Section VII and other departments of Amt Rosenberg, the Frankfurt institute devoted considerably more time and effort during the war years to the transportation, storage, sorting, and cataloging of books than to any actual research. Sustained research efforts were seen as something that would follow after the war, when the rich material stolen from the regime's ideological enemies could be properly studied and evaluated.[5]

Like the high school near Chiemsee, the many research institutes that were being planned under the umbrella of the Hohe Schule would open in the future, after Germany had won its victory. However, several of these institutes were in a preparatory phase during the war, taking in literature, archives, and other plundered materials, even though they had not yet officially opened.

The most important wartime task was the actual plundering, which supplied the institutes with extensive materials to use in their eventual research. Materials were distributed to, among others, the Institute of Biology and Racial Studies in Stuttgart, the Institute of Indo-European Intellectual History in Munich, and the Institute of Ideological Colonial Research in Hamburg. Yet another new institute was being planned in 1944 as a consequence of the great haul of books and archives belonging to the Communist Party in the Soviet Union: Institut zur Erforschung des Bolsjewismus (Institute for Research on Bolshevism).[6]

But, in the end, the Institut zur Erforschung der Judenfrage was the only one of Hohe Schule's institutes to be fully up and running during the war. While research on Germanic people, Celts, and religion could wait until after the war, the Jewish question was too important to be postponed. In a broader sense it was no coincidence that the institute opened at the same time as the plans for the Holocaust were about to be set in motion.

Although the collection of material had the highest priority, there was nonetheless a certain amount of research going on. After the evacuation of 1943, the institute's research division moved into the medieval castle in Hungen, which looked like a sort of fusion between a hunting lodge and a fairy-tale castle, with its redbrick details and winding turrets. The organization allowed the owners of the castle, the Solms-Braunfel family, to stay on as a cover for the operation. Throughout the war, the institute remained in close contact with political developments concerning Jews and anti-Semitic legislation in German-occupied territories, and regularly received secret reports from the foreign ministry and its consulates.[7] Meanwhile, the institute's "Jewish experts" contributed their knowledge of the various Jewish cultures with which the Germans were coming into contact.

From the very beginning, the Frankfurt institute would also busy itself with the production of studies, articles, and books, based on the rich material that had been plundered from all over the Continent. By building up Europe's and probably also the world's foremost Jewish collection, the institute's researchers had the power to form the future of Jewish studies. The perspective of these studies was made abundantly clear in an article about the institute in the party newspaper, the *Völkischer Beobachter*, in 1942: "For the first time in history: Jewish studies without Jews."

The most important outlet for this research was the institute's own journal, *Der Weltkampf* (The Battle for the World), which was issued monthly and described itself as a "monthly journal on world politics, folk culture, and the Jewish Question in all countries." For the first issue, six thousand copies were printed. Most of its subscribers were teachers and researchers.[8] The journal would also produce special themed issues. Number 2/1943 focused on the Jewish question in France, with contributions from French anti-Semitic correspondents. The issue was also published in French. The special feature was a consequence of the rich pickings that the institute had received from France.

Among other pieces, the issue contained an "analysis" of a letter sent by Heinrich Heine, the German-Jewish poet of the 1800s, to Baron James de Rothschild in Paris, to ask for some money. Another article analyzes letters in which Albert Einstein had directed criticism at the Hebrew University in Jerusalem, founded in 1925. Einstein was himself on the board of the university. Both articles referenced materials that the ERR had found in Paris.[9] Although the documents hardly revealed any conspiracy worth mentioning, they were used in an insinuating way to uncover the hidden economic, political, and social networks of the Jews. Any evidence of a conspiracy was never presented, nor was it necessary. This was research carried out by believers for the delectation of other believers. Every little connection was regarded as a thread in a global conspiracy. The research was characterized by the same sort of philosophical approach that Goebbels had taken to *The Protocols of the Elders of Zion*—namely that it was the inherent rather than the factual truth that was decisive.

Also in the institute's journal were articles based on newly discovered material and "study visits" that the researchers had made. Johannes Pohl, the head of the Hebrew collection, wrote about his findings in Vilnius on "Yiddish literature in the Soviet Union." Pohl would also publish shorter studies on Jewish culture in Greece and the Ukraine. Other researchers at the institute devoted themselves to subjects such as the Jewish-Bolshevik conspiracy or Jewish ritual murders.

In addition to *Der Weltkampf*, the institute issued books, writings, and anthologies. Particular emphasis was given to handbooks, as typified by *Lexikon der Juden in der Musik*. A *Lexikon der Juden auf dem Theater* was also being planned and the author was going to be the literature scholar Elisabeth Frenzel, who in 1943 had published *Der Jude im Theater*. Frenzel was highly influenced by the star of German racial research, the "Race Pope" Hans F. K. Günther—her book on Jewish theater has been described by the German literature expert Jochen Hörisch as one of the "worst anti-Semitic publications" of the Third Reich. The purpose of the handbooks was to identify "Jewish" influences in theater and music, in order to separate these from Germanic culture. The handbooks addressed themselves to professionals working in these fields—such as theater directors and music teachers—just in case they accidentally performed a composition or work of a "Jewish" nature.

Ambitious works were also being planned on the history of the ghettos and anti-Judaism. For the former, the institute asked local administrators in Eastern Europe to contribute with maps of various ghettos. It is also likely that a relatively unknown branch of the Frankfurt institute that had opened in Lodz at the end of 1942, called the Institut zur Erforschung der Ostjudenfrage, was participating in the project. This institute, which was headed by a professor of theology named Adolf Frank, was a special department whose function was to "conduct research" into the Lodz ghetto while it was still in existence. The institute, which had three employees, also collected material for anti-Jewish exhibitions. For instance, the institute placed classified ads in local newspapers, offering to pay for "*judenkündlichem Material* [Jewish materials]."[10]

While no exhibition was ever held in Frankfurt, greater success was had in Ratibor. By 1943, Amt Rosenberg's departments of research and propaganda in Berlin had been evacuated along with the collections. Even the ERR's local branches in the Soviet Union had been forced to retreat with the German army. Not only books and archives but also local academics and specialists were evacuated—including ten Ukrainian professors who, with their families, were moved from Kiev to Ratibor.[11]

Research activity in Ratibor was focused on the countries to the east and related directly to the large amounts of material that had been collected for the Ostbücherei. Studies were made of subjects including the Soviet system, or there were polemical anti-Bolshevik propaganda pieces with titles such as "The Battle Against Bolshevism" and "The True Face of Bolshevism." Above all, the purpose of the research was to demonstrate the true goals of Bolshevism, and that a Jewish conspiracy lay hidden behind this ideology. The research efforts were led by the librarian and historian Gerd Wunder, who had earlier been stationed in Paris and Riga, where he had been responsible for the confiscation of libraries. Wunder's research department, known as Hauptabteilung IV, had established itself at Schloss Pless, outside Ratibor, where the greater part of the Ostbücherei's collections had also been moved.[12] Wunder also busied himself with the writing of "personal files" based on confiscated archive material of leading Jews such as members of the Rothschild family, Walter Rathenau, and Albert Einstein. His output included a family tree of the Rothschilds with their "connections."

The most startling project that took form in Wunder's research unit was the large, secret exhibition that was put on for Nazi officials in May 1944, covering the full range of materials seized by the ERR during the war. It was also a combination of the work of the ERR with that of Hauptabteilung IV. The exhibition featured various sections in which material was shown from France, the Netherlands, and the Soviet Union, the latter of these taking the dominant role. There were also special displays relating to the Jews of Thessaloniki, the Rothschild family, and Freemasons. Some of the exhibition materials, posters, photographs, and illustrations have survived. They represent the ideas and conceptions that had been cultivated in the organization and were effectively a direct reflection of the worldview of their leader. Photographs show a relatively traditional exhibition with posters and tables of selected materials from archives and libraries.[13]

Among the Freemasonry material, some of the items shown related to Franklin D. Roosevelt and Winston Churchill—both Freemasons since the early 1900s. Among other exhibits, there was a printed speech that Roosevelt had given at a Freemasonry convention, and a letter on Freemasonry sent by Churchill to the French-Jewish politician Léon Blum—who at this time was imprisoned at Buchenwald.

The most telling of the surviving exhibition material is an illustration of a spiderweb, an attempt to visualize the world conspiracy, in which the Star of David—the Masonic symbol—and the hammer and sickle are equated with people such as Walter Rathenau, Cecil Rhodes, Kurt Eisner, Leon Trotsky, Vladimir Lenin, and the Rothschild family. These were Rosenberg's demons, linked in a network that encircled the whole world in its evil conspiracy.[14] As seen here, they were a pictorial representation of the conspiracy theory that Alfred Rosenberg had been constructing for almost thirty years. It was a holistic conspiracy; everything was connected. Enemies such as Socialists, Bolsheviks, Freemasons, Catholics, and capitalists—along with British, American, and French politicians—were all caught up in a single and all-encompassing net that had been spun by the Jews.

For anti-Semites, the spiderweb was one of the most powerful metaphors. The Jew had often been likened to a spider, a parasite sucking blood from the people, culture, and nation. The spider metaphor functioned on several different levels; it worked as a simile for the economic extortion of the Jews, for the racial mixing and besmirching of Aryan blood, and the ancient blood libel—the ritual sacrifice of children.

Another poster in the exhibition mapped the genealogy of the Rothschild family back to their ancestor James Mayer de Rothschild.[15]

The Rothschilds' economic "world dominion," going back to the 1700s, was the hub of this Jewish plot in the West by means of control of the global economy, while in the East it was Bolshevism that formed the center of the attack. The Third Reich, squeezed between these mighty enemies, struggled indefatigably for the freedom of Germans and the Germanic race.

According to the National Socialist view of the world, it was never the Nazi regime that had waged offensive war; all it had done was pursue a defensive action against, on the one hand, "Jewish finance" in the West and, on the other, "Jewish Bolshevism" in the East. Before the war, in January 1939, Adolf Hitler had already said in a speech to the Reichstag: "International finance Jewry in Europe and beyond should succeed once more in plunging the peoples into a world war, then the result will be not the Bolshevization of the earth and thus the victory of Jewry, but the annihilation of the Jewish race in Europe."[16]

At this time what he meant by "extirpation" was not one and the same as Auschwitz—this "solution" to the Jewish question would only take form at a later stage. In the beginning the Jewish question was not about genocide but the exclusion of Jews from all areas of German society and culture—and later from Europe. In the 1930s the solution was legal, social, cultural, and economic segregation, with the goal of forcing Jews to emigrate. Plans were also made to move the Jewish population in Europe to a "reservation." Central Asia, Palestine, and Madagascar were some of the suggested areas on the table. The Holocaust—mass murder—was a solution that emerged from mid-1941.

Research under the leadership of Alfred Rosenberg toed this sort of line—in the fight against Jewry the researchers were considered to be "intellectual" warriors fetching their ammunition from the stolen libraries and archives—thus demolishing the Jewish conspiracy from within. By plundering and collecting the Jewish people's historical, literary, and cultural legacy around Europe, Rosenberg and ultimately the Institut zur Erforschung der Judenfrage were building the foundations on which, in the future, they would be able to defend and justify the extinction of the Jewish people. The completed studies were mere pseudoscience, designed to knit together the web of myths, misconceptions, and historical fabrications on which National Socialist ideology was based into a respectable scientific discipline.

It was "research" with a clearly articulated goal. In his inaugural speech, when the institute was opened in 1941, its director Wilhelm Grau described his vision of a Europe free of Jews.[17] In the following year came a new edition of Grau's published work from 1937, *Die Judenfrage in der deutschen Geschichte* (The Jewish Question in German History). Just like Adolf Hitler, he blamed the Jews for the war. According to Grau, it was a war that could only end once the "Jewish question" had come to a point of solution.

The "intellectual" justification for the Holocaust was never made as clear as when the Propaganda Ministry in 1944 commissioned Grau's successor, Dr. Klaus Schickert, to write a follow-up to his book and doctoral thesis from 1937 about the Jewish question in Hungary, *Die Judenfrage in Ungarn. Jüdische Assimilation und antisemitische Bewegung im 19. und 20. Jahrhundert* (The Jewish Question in Hungary. Jewish Assimilation and Anti-Semitic Movements in the Nineteenth and Twentieth Centuries). The work on the second book took place while the Hungarian Jews were being deported to Auschwitz.[18] Schickert had earlier helped establish an anti-Semitic institute in Budapest, which, after the German occupation of Hungary in March 1944, was made into a state institution. The members of the institute were given leading positions in the new regime, with authority to quickly implement anti-Jewish policies.

Rosenberg's ambition was to present the "true history" of the Jews in Germany and Europe. But to understand why "the Jew" was the enemy before any other, one must take into consideration that for Nazi Germany's ideologues, the history of the Jews was also that of Germans. "It cannot be overemphasized that modern and contemporary German and European history must be written while taking the Jewish question into account," wrote Wilhelm Grau, who argued that the Jewish problem hailed back to the medieval era.[19] German history could only be understood on the basis of this thousand-year battle between Jews and Germans. By "studying the hard and finally victorious struggle between our German nation and the racially alien Judaism, we can come to a better understanding of the German character. And through this we not only improve our knowledge, we also strengthen our commitment to our national life," wrote Volkmar Eichstät, librarian at Nazi historian Walter Frank's National Institute for the History of New Germany.

Goebbels's Propaganda Ministry put it even more clearly in 1944: "The Jewish Question is the key to world history."[20] The fundamental force driving history was, as Gobineau, Chamberlain, and Rosenberg had asserted, the struggle between the races—this being a sort of race-ideological equivalent of the class war of Marxism. At the center of this struggle stood the Aryans and the Jews, supreme antagonists to each other. In the National Socialist world, the Jews were an incarnation of historical evil, the root of all corruption, interbreeding between races, degeneration, fragmentation, and the suffering of the German people.

In order for a new Germany to rise, the thousand-year-old adversary had to be defeated, not only in a physical sense but also symbolically. "The Nazis persecuted the Jews because they were a key element that came from within their own German and European-Christian civilization," writes the historian Alon Confino. "Jews gave the overall meaning to the Nazi fight between good and evil: the Messianic struggle to create a Nazi civilization that depended on the extermination of the Jews. Creation and extermination were inextricably linked, giving meaning to each other."[21]

But it was not solely a war of physical extermination, it was also a battle for memory and history. And in this Alfred Rosenberg's project played a leading role. The plundering of libraries and archives went to the very core of this battle for control of memory. This was also what set the book thefts apart from other kinds of looting, such as that of art. Art was also ideological, but only in a symbolic sense. Works of art were trophies that glorified leaders and the nation. Art would also reflect and legitimize the National Socialist ideals and the new human being. But the actual ideology would be underpinned by books and archives. The future would be built by a control of memory and history, on the basis of the written word.

The Nazis strove to exterminate the Jewish people, but not their memory. "The Jew" would be preserved as a historical and symbolic enemy. That this was one of the goals of the Frankfurt institute was something that Alfred Rosenberg had already highlighted in his inaugural speech in 1941.[22] In the speech, he predicted that there might one day come a generation, even in a National Socialist future, that judged his own. For this reason, the history of the Jews, their significance and their crimes, had to be preserved, and the merciless war into which the German people had been "forced" had to be possible to justify. For these reasons, the important expressions of Jewish culture, the libraries and the archives, were plundered but not destroyed. They were necessary in order to be able to write the history of the thousand-year battle and the final victory. Given that this was the battle that gave the movement its very meaning, the memory of the Jews had to be kept alive as a symbolic evil long after they had gone. In his book *A World Without Jews*, Alon Confino writes:

> Remembering the Jews after the victorious war would have been important precisely because total liquidation of the Jew could not have been achieved through physical annihilation alone; it required as well the overcoming of Jewish memory and history. A win in the war would have extinguished the alleged power of world Jewry in the White House and the Kremlin and eliminated the Jewish racial menace from German society, but the Nazi struggle against the Jews was never principally about political and economic influence. It was over identity and was waged by means of Nazi appropriation of Jewish history, memory, and books.[23]

It was therefore both meaningful and significant that the ability to remember became an act of resistance in its own right. When Herman Kruk, the librarian at the ghetto library in Vilnius, buried his diaries in the forced-labor camp in Estonia just before his death in 1944, it was in a sense an attempt to defeat the perpetrators of the violence against him by preserving his memories. Despite the ambivalence that was a defining mark of the work done by the Paper Brigade in Vilnius, and the Talmudkommando in Theresienstadt, both groups found a source of hope in the thought that, ultimately, they were saving their own history.

There was also another closely related aspect in this struggle for memory, words, and books. After all, it was being fought between possibly two of the world's most highly literary and intellectual people—between two of the "people of the book." It was a similarity noted in the 1939 diary of Chaim Kaplan, a Jewish teacher in Warsaw:

> We are dealing with a nation of high culture, with "a people of the book." Germany has become a madhouse—mad for books. Say what you will, I fear such people! Where plunder is based on an ideology, on a world outlook which in essence is spiritual, it cannot be equalled in strength and durability. . . . The Nazi has robbed us not only of material possessions, but also of our good name as "the people of the Book." The Nazi has both book and sword, and this is his strength and might.[24]

Maybe it was symbolic that Chaim Kaplan's diary, which had been left behind, became one of the most important testaments of Jewish life in Warsaw before and after the invasion. In 1942, when he realized that he was about to be arrested, the diary was smuggled out. His last entry reads, "13,000 people have been seized and sent off, among them 5,000 who came to the transfer of their own free will. They had had their fill of the ghetto life, which is a life of hunger and fear of death. They escaped from the trap. Would that I could allow myself to do as they did! If my life ends—what will become of my diary?"[25]

✦   ✦   ✦

At Section VII of the Reich Security Office some other research projects were destined to go on until the end of the war. However, the research that had taken form within the RSHA was different and, in many ways, more fanciful. Just as Alfred Rosenberg's version of reality had permeated his activities, the RSHA research had aspects that clearly reflected Himmler's special interests in Freemasonry and occultism.

The collections and research projects at the RSHA had been evacuated to various castles in Central Europe. At Schloss Niemes, Section VII had begun compiling a registry of occult science—*Geheimwissenschaftlichen*. The result was a catalog running to more than four hundred pages, with seven thousand books and eighteen thousand journals on subjects such as astrology, spiritualism, mysticism, prophecy, hypnosis, alchemy, hedonism, and dream interpretation. One of the most curious RSHA research projects went under the name of Leo and was headed by SS-Obersturmbannführer Werner Göttsch, one of the most trusted men of the chief of the RSHA, Ernst Kaltenbrunner. Kaltenbrunner had replaced Reinhard Heydrich after his assassination in Czechoslovakia in 1942.

Göttsch had worked earlier at the foreign department of the SD, but his military career had slowed after he contracted tuberculosis. Instead, he was set the special task of studying Section VII's section on Masonic literature with particular emphasis on occult material. Assisting him was SS-Sturmbannführer Hans Richter, who was the RSHA's expert on Freemasons and who had also been responsible for compiling the section on witchcraft and magic. Richter drafted reading lists for Göttsch on subjects such as magic, telepathy, and spiritualism, and even on books from the pornography collection. After the evacuation from Berlin, several rooms of the fifteenth-century castle Neufalkenburg (known today as Nový Falkenburk) in Czechoslovakia were given over to Göttsch's top secret project, and a small occult library was built up. Richter, with responsibility for this part of the operation, put out calls for important works, which were located in other confiscated collections and brought to the castle. Even secret reports from the SD, which in the 1930s had hounded various anthroposophical groups in Germany, were a part of the collection.[26]

Paul Dittel, the last head of Section VII, claimed under interrogation after the war that the purpose of Leo was to create "some kind of Masonic order or esoteric sect" connected to the SS.

Dittel stated that Kaltenbrunner was striving to build up a fraternal Nazi order whose members would be free to devote themselves to whatever they wished, while remaining loyal to the regime and functioning as "observers and informers."[27] According to Dittel, Göttsch's research was about creating the required underpinnings of such an organization—most likely by studying how the Freemasons, through rites and secrecy, had built up loyal brotherhoods. The project was given the very highest priority by the top leaders of the SS, at a time when it was increasingly clear that Germany was about to lose the war. This seems to suggest that the "order" could have functioned as a way of preparing underground activities in a post-Nazi Germany.

Another project that had been in progress for considerably longer was Heinrich Himmler's Hexenkartothek, which had already been set in motion in the mid-1930s. The research into witchcraft, which went under the name of Hexen-Sonderauftrag, was an investigation into witches and their persecution. Himmler had given orders that this subject should be submitted to a "scientific investigation." One of the reasons for the SS leader's interest was supposedly that one of his ancestors, Margareth Himbler, was burned at the stake in 1632, in Bad Mergentheim, after being found guilty of witchcraft.[28]

A dozen full-time SS researchers had spent almost a decade working on Hexen-Sonderauftrag, sifting through 260 libraries and archives in pursuit of material on witches, trial protocols, witness descriptions, and confessions. The material was compiled in a card index, the Hexenkartothek, in which every "witch" was given her own section including her history, family ties, and fate. It took the form of victim documentation, which was also precisely what it was.

Himmler viewed the witch trials as an expression of the millennial battle between the northern and southern European cultures. This persecution, according to Himmler, had been a way for the Catholic church to fight the original spiritual beliefs of the northern peoples— an attack on, and destruction of, ancient Germanic customs. The witches thus represented Nordic "popular culture," which, according to this view, had been opposed by a southern, Mediterranean-based Christianity with its roots in the Judaic world.

There was a certain amount of truth in this—many of these women had indeed been burned because they had been accused of practicing magic and pagan, pre-Christian rites. Not altogether unexpectedly, however, Himmler suspected that the persecution was a part of a Jewish conspiracy to destroy genuinely Germanic culture. In the SS universe, the witches were Aryan martyrs, Nordic Amazons who had stood up to the "Semitic priesthood."[29]

To a certain degree, the Hexen-Sonderauftrag research was made use of during the Third Reich. Joseph Goebbels had recognized the propaganda value of the witch hunts, in order to justify attacks on the Catholic church. Even in Nazi parades and propaganda performances the witches were elevated into German heroines.

A writer named Friedrich Soukup was employed to write light fiction, either books for young adults or historical novels on the witch hunts, with an edge of blame directed at the church. Soukup allegedly planned an ambitious trilogy based on the research, a project, however, that was never realized. Hexen-Sonderauftrag's documentation on the persecution of witches was the most detailed research on the subject that had ever been carried out in Europe. During the nine years of the project, the card index grew until it covered the lives of 3,600 witches. Further, an archive and library of some 150,000 documents and books was built up. After the war, Himmler's Hexenkartothek disappeared and was forgotten—until its rediscovery in Poland in the 1980s by the German historian Gerhard Schormann.

According to Schormann, the project served dual aims. It was a source of propaganda as well as an attempt to recover and preserve aspects of Germanic beliefs that had been lost.[30] Oddly enough, Himmler's research into witchcraft, despite its many academic shortcomings, gained a certain amount of importance in modern research into the witch hunts because of the extensive amount of historical source material that had been amassed. "As Europe's first and only 'pro-witch' government, the Nazi regime has also exerted some lasting influence on popular understanding of witchcraft and on some forms of popular magical practices," writes the American historian Michael David Bailey.[31] Gerhard Schormann himself would end up using Himmler's Hexenkartothek as the basis of his research into the witch trials in Germany.

Jewish literature was also sent to Schloss Niemes, but this seems only to have been placed in storage, while the occult literature was very much prioritized. Grimsted feels that this interest in occultism at a time when the regime was preoccupied by the idea of "total war" cannot be dismissed as "insignificant sensationalism"—but rather, that it was regarded as highly significant by the SS elite at the end of the war: "Perhaps RSHA leaders, such as Himmler and Kaltenbrunner, both of whom as we now know were secretly initiating peace feelers at that time, were themselves also not ready to abandon the pursuit of spiritual or even pagan sources for survival or renewal of their mission, while the world around them was destroying the Nazi regime and its ideology for which they were assigned to provide security."[32]

In the end, the total war also reached the SS castles. In April 1945, Section VII personnel were called to the front to take part in the final battle for the Third Reich.

◆　◆　◆

Within Amt Rosenberg there were no plans to give up the fight against world Jewry, despite the fact that Germany was retreating on all fronts. If anything, the work was intensified. In the closing stages of the war, Alfred Rosenberg started drawing up plans for a last, grandiose project that was as unworldly as it was futile: an international anti-Jewish congress in 1944 on the theme of "Jewry in Global Politics in Our Time." To lend an air of legitimacy to the project, he had even initiated a collaboration with his rivals within the RSHA, the Propaganda Ministry, and the Foreign Ministry. The head of the Frankfurt institute, Klaus Schickert, had been assigned as the editor of a work entitled *A Yearbook of Jewish World Politics*, which was very likely intended to be launched at the congress. The book, an anthology, would show how Jews were controlling political developments and must therefore be held accountable for the war.[33]

The plans for the congress were described in a classified document from June 15, 1944, a week after the Western Allies made their landings in Normandy.[34] The document was written by Hans Hagemeyer, one of Alfred Rosenberg's most trusted men, who had been tasked with organizing the congress. According to the document, Hitler had personally approved the plans and decided that the conference would be held in Kraków. Hagemeyer went on to describe the congress in detail.

In addition to a series of "Jewish experts" there would be speeches from three German ministers. The Berlin Philharmonic would put on a performance under chief conductor Wilhelm Furtwängler.

"Prominent Europeans" would be invited to the congress, as well as state representatives from countries both in and outside Europe. Some of their names were given, including several of Europe's leading anti-Semites, Fascists, and Nazis. From Italy would come the minister Fernando Mezzasoma, a man who had been something of a correlative in his country of Joseph Goebbels. From the Netherlands, Anton Mussert, the leader and founder of the Nazi Party there, Nationaal-Socialistische Beweging in Nederland. From France would come the poet and minister of education in the Vichy regime, Abel Bonnard. Hagemeyer also mentioned that Alfred Rosenberg had gone to Norway, "so that he can personally extend an invitation to the ministerial president, Quisling." The Arab world would be represented by the Grand Mufti of Jerusalem, Haj Amin al-Husseini, who in 1941 had fled to Nazi Germany and tried to persuade Hitler to expand the reach of the Holocaust to the Middle East. Undertakings to send delegates had, according to Hagemeyer, been received from Sweden, Romania, Switzerland, Spain, and Portugal—but no names were given. According to Hagemeyer, preparations for the congress were in progress with the utmost secrecy.[35]

Since its inauguration, the Institut zur Erforschung der Judenfrage in Frankfurt had been actively building up international contacts, as evidenced by the guest list at the opening ceremony, which included representatives from Denmark, Hungary, Romania, the Netherlands, Belgium, and Norway. The institute created a continental network of anti-Semitic organizations and authorities to help disseminate anti-Semitic information to the general public.[36] Nazi Germany regularly made use of local anti-Semites, racists, and organizations, which were often given German funding. At times this also occurred under a local facade, such as the French Institut d'Etudes des Questions Juives (Institute for Studies on the Jewish Question), which was headed by a Frenchman, Paul Sézille, but overseen by the SS and financed by the German embassy.[37] The institute, which marketed a German model of anti-Jewish politics, arranged events such as the anti-Semitic exhibition *Le Juif et la France* (The Jew and France) in Paris in 1941, which set out to show how Jews had infiltrated society and corrupted French culture as well as national customs and traditions.

The Institut d'Etudes des Questions Juives collaborated closely with the Frankfurt institute. Its overseer, SS-Hauptsturmführer Theodor Dannecker, had suggested that it should become a branch of Rosenberg's Hohe Schule—something that never came about. However, the Frankfurt institute provided assistance for its French colleagues in the creation of a journal, *La question juive en France et dans le monde*, modeled on *Der Weltkampf*.

Hans Hagemeyer's document revealed that in actual fact, the planned 1944 congress in Kraków had an entirely different purpose than merely being an anti-Semitic research conference. Hagemeyer wrote that while the whole event had the semblance of a "historical and scientific congress," its actual purpose was to "create an international organization that will examine and fight Jewry." In other words, a sort of anti-Semitic United Nations.[38] Heinrich Himmler, Joachim von Ribbentrop, Joseph Goebbels, and Hans Frank would be made honorary members of this international organization, along with a number of the more prominent participants such as Mezzasoma, Mussert, Bonnard, and the Grand Mufti of Jerusalem. The organization would counteract "pro-Jewish propaganda" and uncover how the Allies were actually fighting for "Jewish world domination."[39]

The problem was that the Europe that Rosenberg wanted to unite in this anti-Jewish fellowship was rapidly disintegrating in 1944. Before the end of the year, Nazi Germany stood alone among the intended participants. Adolf Hitler, realizing the political impossibility of Rosenberg's plans, canceled the congress.

Early in 1944 the Red Army liberated Leningrad after a siege lasting 872 days. The Soviet Union was freed in the summer, and by August the Red Army was at the gates of Warsaw, which was where Stalin stopped the offensive. For almost half a year the eastern front was still, while the Red Army amassed enormous resources in preparation for a last attack. Six million soldiers were moved to the front, almost twice the manpower that Hitler had had at his disposal when he attacked the Soviet Union in 1941.

In Ratibor there seems to have been an awareness of the impending attack, and at the end of 1944 plans were once again drawn up to evacuate the collections to Bavaria. However, by this time it was no longer realistic that millions of books stockpiled in Ratibor could be quickly moved. After one and a half years of activity, there had not even been enough time to complete the evacuation of books from Berlin. How many books the ERR evacuated in those last few months is still uncertain. The work continued right up to the first week of February 1945, when the Red Army reached the town. It is really quite remarkable that both the SS and the ERR carried on working on the libraries at a time when there could no longer be the slightest doubt, even for the most fanatical of Nazis, that the Third Reich was lost. The answer probably has both an ideological and a very human explanation.

These organizations were the intellectual guardians of the movement, and had long functioned as a sort of concentration of true believers. Based on and built up from the central core of National Socialism, there was a morass of myths, historical falsifications, and conspiracy theories, which these "intellectual guardians" were intent on proving and establishing on firm foundations through their "research." In these circles fatalism was a mortal sin, even in a literal sense. At the same time they probably also had very human reasons to continue their work. After all, for as long as this could be justified, it would keep them away from frontline duty. Being sent to the eastern front was regarded, quite rightly, as a death sentence.

In January 1945 the collections began to be evacuated from Schloss Pless. But in the middle of the month, the Soviet offensive began, and two million Red Army soldiers pressed their way into Poland. Thousands of books were left at the train station in Pless, when the ERR staff was forced to flee from the advancing Russians.[40] In early February, personnel in Ratibor also had to escape when the town was subjected to artillery bombardment. When the Red Army took Ratibor, there were still barges on the Oder, loaded with books. There had been plans to burn certain portions of the collections, and a plentiful supply of gasoline had been stockpiled for this purpose, but for some reason a decision was made to simply abandon the books.[41]

Rosenberg's activities on the other front, in Hungen, also continued until the very last moment, and the Frankfurt institute continued lending books to researchers, universities, and other research institutions—documentation of outgoing loans indicates that this activity went on until February 1945, by which time the Red Army was outside Berlin and the western front was a mere 124 miles from Frankfurt.[42] The institute continued making purchases of books for another month.

Early in April 1945, American forces from the Fifth Infantry Division reached Hungen and took possession of the castle. Before long the huge book depots were found. The unit that made the discovery was led by a thirty-two-year-old lawyer and lieutenant named Robert Schoenfeld, a Polish-born Jew who had fled the Nazis in 1939 and made his way to the United States.[43] This was probably the moment when a soldier from Schoenfeld's unit, armed with a British-made automatic rifle, made his way into one of the dark book depots, firing a warning shot that hit a crate and penetrated a book from the Bibliotheca Rosenthaliana: Samuel Usque's *Consolation for the Tribulations of Israel*.

# 14

# A WAGON OF SHOES

*Prague*

In a little square in central Prague, where the two streets Dušní and Vězeňská meet, Franz Kafka rides a headless figure. The black bronze sculpture is inspired by one of the author's short stories, "Description of a Struggle," in which the narrator defeats an apparently invincible opponent by leaping onto his shoulders and riding him like a horse.

The statue has become an attraction. A group of Russian tourists take turns photographing each other in front of the emblematic national writer. The place is loaded with symbolism: the Kafka family lived on Dušní Street, and this is the heart of Prague's old Jewish quarter—only a few yards from the Spanish Synagogue. In front of the synagogue, built in Middle Eastern architectural style, lies a considerably more modern building: Prague's Jewish Museum, constructed in a gray-yellow functional style. In a room on the second floor sits the librarian and researcher Michal Bušek, a man in his thirties with a shaved head, a well-trimmed beard, and gray checkered shorts. Beside his desk stands a library cart, fully loaded with old, shabby books. All have the same sodium-bleached label, glued onto the lower part of their spines—with a handwritten "Jc" or "Jb," followed by a number. These are the books marked by the Talmudkommando in Theresienstadt, *J* being an abbreviation of "Judaica."

"The Nazis knew how important books were to the Jews. Reading makes you into a human being. When someone takes it away from you they also steal your thoughts. They wanted to destroy the Jews by robbing them of what was most important to them," says Bušek, and looks at the cart. He is in the midst of an extensive process of checking the large collection of books that ended up at the Jewish Museum after the war, including some from Theresienstadt. "I look for signs of the owner of a book, ex libris, stamps, notes, and I enter these into a database that we are building."

The work is much like what is being done at the libraries in Germany. A horribly time-consuming process, each book having to be examined for signs of its previous owner. Sometimes it is easy, for instance if a book has an eye-catching ex libris with a full name. Sometimes there is a signature, a dedication, or a few lines written by someone who has once read the book. But this is an exception. Many of the books lack any kind of indication of previous owners. In some cases, names have been crossed out and bookplates scraped off.

"The first step is entering any name and the number of the book. Next, you put in all the details about the book in the database, its title, publication year, and even photographs of the book. Eventually every book in the collection will have a detailed description," Bušek tells me. He estimates that the first step will take about a year, while the second will take considerably longer. Hebrew text is also entered into the database, which has required a special software system, he explains, but a necessary one in view of the fact that many of the books, not least those from the Talmudkommando, are written in Hebrew. In this collection there are more owners' marks, as several of the books come from important collections.

That this work is only now being done, seventy years after the books were "liberated," speaks volumes about the state of book restitution as a whole but also about the tragic fate that befell so many of the collections by the end of the war, stranded behind Soviet lines. The Jewish Museum in Prague is in fact one of the very few institutions behind what was once the Iron Curtain that is actively engaged in the project.

After the war, in 1945, most of the collections from Theresienstadt were moved to the Jewish Museum in Prague. The museum, founded in 1906, had been taken over in 1939 by the Nazis, but was to some extent permitted to continue with some of its activities. During the war, the museum became a collection and sorting station for books and religious artifacts taken from deported Jewish communities. "Boxes of plundered objects from synagogues were sent here; they were cataloged and sorted by a group of Jewish researchers. The Jews and the Nazis did not have the same agenda. The Jews wanted to save these artifacts because they hoped the war would soon be over. The Nazis, on the other hand, wanted to create a Jewish museum where they could exhibit how odd and different the Jews were," says Bušek.

For a few years, the museum became a center of an extensive rescue operation of Jewish culture. The reward for the degrading work that had been done under the Nazis was that thousands of books and historical and religious objects had been saved for posterity. Many came from Jewish communities that no longer existed. The Jewish population, estimated at over 300,000 before the war, had been reduced to just a sixth of what it once was. Most died in the Holocaust; many others would never come back.[1]

Czechoslovakia was the only country behind Soviet lines that had been permitted to form an independent republic after the war, even though it was short-lived. This meant that the collections that had ended up here were subjected to the restitution philosophy that was common practice in the West but also to the diametrically opposed approach in Eastern Europe. It ended up being a sort of semi-restitution.

In 1945 the collections left in Theresienstadt were brought to the museum in Prague, as was one of the survivors of the Talmudkommando, Otto Muneles, who was made chief librarian for the museum's collection. Plundered books also arrived from other sources. In the SS castles on the Czech side of the border, including Schloss Neufalkenburg and Schloss Niemes, hundreds of thousands of books had been found, evacuated by the RSHA.[2]

Today, only a small part of the collections brought here after the war still remain. Bušek has tried to unravel what happened to the books. "It's very difficult to know. There's not a lot of documentation left from that time. We only have one small ledger from between 1945 and 1949," he says. From Theresienstadt and other Nazi depots, some 190,000 books came to the museum. "Some books were handed back after the war, but it was not proper restitution, as we see it today. No one looked into who these books had belonged to or where they came from. There was neither staff to do it nor anywhere to put them. There were only two or three employees in the entire museum."

According to Bušek, the books were scattered in many directions; some were distributed among Jewish congregations in Czechoslovakia while others were sent to Israel. "There's nothing to suggest that the books were checked. Most of the books were still in the crates the Nazis had packed them into. I believe they just picked a crate and gave it away without checking so very carefully what was inside. People came to the museum and asked, 'Can we have fifty books?' and then they got what they wanted." Many were also taken over by Jewish organizations such as the Jewish Cultural Reconstruction (JCR), which had been set up to share out plundered Jewish property in Jewish communities. The greater part of what remained of the Ghettobücherei in Theresienstadt was distributed in this way.[3]

One of the more significant projects, which would later become part of Israel's National Library, was first conceived by the Hebrew University in Jerusalem. It was a politically Zionist "rescue project" that, in the prevailing mood during the immediate aftermath of the Holocaust, attempted to bring as much as possible of Europe's Jewish cultural legacy to Israel, where hundreds of thousands of survivors immigrated.[4] At the end of 1946, the chief librarian at the Hebrew University, Hugo Bergmann, paid a visit with Otto Muneles to the RSHA's depot in Niemes. They estimated that there were 650,000 books at the castle.

"Some of them are Jewish; others are books of all different kinds. I saw Catholic books from monasteries, theosophist books, socialist books, etc. . . . In the attic of the castle I found a Dutch archive that I could not identify, flung on the floor. There were also newspapers in Yiddish, bound or packed into cardboard boxes. They were from YIVO, Vilnius," wrote Bergmann in his report.[5] He brought between forty thousand and seventy thousand Jewish books from Czechoslovakia back to Israel. The figure is uncertain, as many boxes were also smuggled out by Bergmann, who had covertly hidden valuable manuscripts inside.[6]

That so many books left Czechoslovakia in the first few years after the war was attributable to the support of the museum and the Jewish

Books at the Jewish Museum in Prague that still bear the
markings of the Talmudkommando in Theresienstadt

congregation. The Czech government, on the other hand, had taken a significantly more restrictive approach to the idea of returning plundered goods: "The Czech government generally has a negative attitude towards the question of restitution and [has] in certain instances labeled the desire of persons or organizations for the return of their property as 'Fascist,' 'bourgeois,' or whatever is the appropriate term at that particular time," wrote one American observer.[7] Private individuals had a more difficult time than anyone else in reclaiming their books. There is only one documented case of books in postwar Czechoslovakia being returned to a family.[8]

One collection that would largely remain in Prague were the sixty thousand books from RSHA Section VII's Hebrew section, on which the Talmudkommando had been working. Michal Bušek does not yet know how many books from this collection are still in the Jewish Museum library. "It may be about thirty thousand books, but we don't know for sure. We're in the process of cataloging them now. It does seem that Otto Muneles, after the war, separated these books from the others in the collection so they could remain in Prague." But Bušek and his colleagues have also found books in the collection that were plundered from all over Europe. "Mostly they come from Jewish congregations in Berlin, Budapest, Warsaw, Amsterdam, and other cities. We have found over 3,800 books that can be traced back to Vienna, both from congregations and private individuals," Bušek tells me as he picks out a couple of books from his cart and shows me a stamp from Israelitische Kultusgemeinde, with an ex libris indicating that the book was donated by Salo Cohn, who led Vienna's Jewish congregation until the early 1900s.

Bušek then shows me into the library's reading room. The valuable historical collection is kept in a glassed-in, locked annex to the side. Thick volumes bound in leather and gray vellum are handled with white cotton gloves. Bušek fetches one of the books that I have asked for—a book from Amsterdam. He places the slim volume on the white reading table, its cover so heavily marbled that it brings to mind one of August Strindberg's expressionistic motifs of the sea. The title of the book is *Der Mediciner Maimonides im Kampfe mit dem Theologen*—a study of the medieval philosopher Maimonides and his advocacy of secular research.

On the inside of the cover is an ex libris. It looks as if someone could have glued it in yesterday, although it must be close to a hundred years old. It shows an illustration against a white background, a stag and a lion rearing up on either side of a Star of David. Beneath, a name is written: Sigmund Seeligmann. The symbol is very likely a reference to a line from the Mishnah, the Jewish redaction of oral traditions: "Be swift as a gazelle and strong as a lion to do the will of God in Heaven."[9]

On the spine is a glued-on label marked "Jb 812," placed there by the Talmudkommando. Maybe it was even glued on by Isaac Leo Seeligmann himself, thus labeling one of his father's books. Bušek shows me a biography of the Sephardic religious philosopher Uriel da Costa, who fled the persecutions in Portugal in 1617 and settled in the Netherlands. The book has a personal dedication to Sigmund Seeligmann from its author, the Portuguese historian Artur de Magalhães Basto. Sigmund's own signature is written inside a third book, a German translation of the Koran.

The Seeligmann collection, plundered in Amsterdam by the ERR, was divided up among several of the RSHA's depots. Apart from the books in Theresienstadt, other parts of the collection were found at various castles, including Schloss Niemes. Hugo Bergmann took about two thousand books from Seeligmann's collection to Israel, while a smaller proportion remained at the Jewish Museum in Prague. Bušek has been able to identify about sixty of Seeligmann's books here. But the whereabouts of the greater part of the collection, which, before the war, was estimated at between 20,000 and 25,000 books, have never been established. Perhaps the collection was scattered in depots all over the Nazi German Reich, or books may have been discarded during the war, or destroyed in bombing raids in Berlin.

Isaac Leo Seeligmann survived Theresienstadt and returned to Amsterdam in 1945. If he ever made any attempt to recover his books from Czechoslovakia, this would quickly have been ruled out by the establishment of the Iron Curtain. Especially as Czechoslovakia played a central part in the events that followed.

Edvard Beneš, the president, had tried to position his nation as a bridge between East and West—Czechoslovakia being a free republic. It was a political project that soon collapsed. The young republic was troubled by political instability, actively encouraged by the Soviet-backed Communist Party, which had a parliamentary majority. In 1947, Czechoslovakia accepted Marshall Plan assistance from the United States—financial support for reconstruction. However, pressure from the Kremlin forced the leadership to reverse this decision. Six months later, in early 1948, the Communists seized power in a coup backed by Moscow. Not long afterward, the Jewish Museum and its collections were nationalized.

"After that, basically all restitution was stopped," explains Bušek. The Communists could not entirely shut down the Jewish Museum, because it was so well known, but both research and exhibitions were limited to an absolute minimum. The museum placed a great deal of focus on Theresienstadt. But in the Communist narrative, this was a prisoner-of-war camp, not a camp for Jews. The Communists also chose to dispose of parts of the Jewish collections, including valuable Torah scrolls that were sold to the West. "These collections did not mean anything to them. The government needed money, they needed dollars, so they decided to sell them." The Jewish library was transformed into what was effectively a wholly isolated institution, whose activities were carefully monitored by the regime. Both visitors and loans were registered. "Very few people came here. Researchers were afraid of visiting the library," explains Bušek.

In spite of the dismal circumstances, Otto Muneles, who had lost his entire family in the Holocaust, continued his work as head of the library until his death in the 1960s. He would spend almost twenty years trying to bring some order to the Jewish collection. Those who knew him have spoken of how he was absolutely absorbed in this work, as if these scattered, plundered books had the capacity to console him in some way: "It was like seeing a ghost wandering through these rooms filled with books, without anyone to read or study them . . . and still

*An ex libris from one of the books in the collection of Sigmund Seeligmann of Amsterdam. During the war, the book was moved to Theresienstadt and later ended up at the Jewish Museum in Prague, where it remains today.*

Dr. Muneles cherished a dream of an enormous library that would serve as a monument to the Jews who were once here, yet now no more."[10]

◆ ◆ ◆

After the war, when the Czech authorities inspected the plundered collections at the SS castles in Czechoslovakia, a good deal of material had already disappeared, including the large archive taken from the French secret service, hidden by the Gestapo in Schloss Oberliebich, near Česká Lípa. In fact, the depot had already been found by the Red Army intelligence organ SMERSH as early as May 1945. Lavrenty Beria, the head of the Soviet security service NKVD, had secretly sent archivists from Moscow to confiscate the archive, and in the summer twenty-eight railroad cars filled with archive materials were dispatched to Moscow, where they would form the foundation of a new, secret archive: Tsentral'nyi Gosudarstvennyi Osobyi Arkhiv (TsGOA). This, Stalin's special archive for trophy documents, was filled with enormous amounts of documentation confiscated from a variety of Nazi depots in Germany and Eastern Europe.[11]

In February 1945, when the Red Army marched into Germany, Joseph Stalin had signed a top secret order that led to the establishment of the Special Committee for War Reparations. Admittedly Stalin had already in 1943 signed an agreement with the Western Allies that prohibited the plunder of cultural objects—this agreement, however, was not honored.

This new committee, despite the seeming innocence of its name, kicked off a plundering operation that in its scope rivaled that of the Nazis. Stalin's approach was that Germany must pay *in kind* for the enormous destruction in the Soviet Union, by a corresponding amount of thieving by the Soviets. To avoid disrupting relations with the Western Allies, the operation was kept secret.

The units carrying out the plundering, known as trophy brigades, were essentially not unlike their German counterparts. The units consisted of Soviet archivists, librarians, scientists, and other experts. Cultural artifacts, such as works of art, archives, and books, were only a small portion of what was stolen. The dedicated government department that organized the plundering calculated that in 1945 alone, some 400,000 railroad cars of plundered goods were sent to the Soviet Union. Some of this was also reclaimed Soviet property. A list of goods sent from Germany to the Ukraine in 1945 testifies to the diversity of the cargo: 11 railroad cars of laboratory instruments, 123 vehicles, 2.5 tons of scientific books, 75 paintings from Dresden's art museum, 12 tons of plates from the porcelain manufacturer August Wellner & Söhne; 46 railroad cars loaded with two disassembled printing presses; and 27 cars filled with the parts of a factory to manufacture photographic paper.[12]

There was also widespread plundering—to some extent officially sanctioned—by soldiers, officers, and generals in the Red Army. Soldiers had the opportunity of repeatedly sending home packages of stolen goods. The busiest robbers tended to be the high-ranking officers and generals. Stalin's top general, Georgy Zhukov, filled several trains with his war loot. This made Stalin's war hero immensely rich, which Stalin later used against him to get rid of him.

However, it was the trophy brigades that accounted for the more organized plundering, and units were sent to the castles of Central Europe to hunt for trophies. The castles were emptied of furniture, art, statues, pianos, porcelain, and any other furnishings that could be transported. There were also books. When it came to book confiscation there were special library units within the trophy brigades, which visited hundreds of libraries in Germany and Poland and also the book depots that the ERR and the RSHA had established when evacuating their book holdings to the east. The book plundering, organized by a group of representatives from larger libraries in the Soviet Union, was led by Margarita Rudomino, superintendent of the Library for Foreign Literature in Moscow.

In the spring of 1946, Rudomino mentions in a report that between four thousand and five thousand crates of books had been placed in storage in Mysłowice, Poland. This was probably the main book holdings of the ERR from Ratibor, which lay only thirty-seven miles east of there. Whether these books had been evacuated by the ERR at the closing stages of the war or by the Red Army in the spring of 1945 is not specified.[13]

In Pless, where the ERR's employees escaped enemy fire from the front, a unit of the Fourth Ukrainian Front had seized about ten railroad cars loaded with books, journals, and archives. Some 150,000 books and 100,000 documents were found inside. The renowned library of Schloss Pless, with 100,000 volumes, was also packed up and removed while they were at it.

A large part of the ERR's collections found by the trophy brigades had originally come from Minsk, Smolensk, Kiev, and other places in the Soviet Union. But there were also collections from the West, including the émigré libraries in Paris that had been integrated into the Ostbücherei. In July 1945 the Red Army had already stated in a report that the Turgenev Library from Paris had been found in Mysłowice. There was "an estimated 1,200,000 volumes in Russian and foreign languages" there.[14] The Turgenev Library was not classed as a trophy library, because it was "Russian" and thereby regarded as Soviet property.

There seems not to have been any particular order in the Mysłowice depot either—thousands of crates had been stored haphazardly. According to one member of the trophy brigades, a part of the collection was plundered by soldiers. Sometimes "people took what they wanted," wrote Rudomino in a report. This was how many older, valuable books and manuscripts went missing.[15]

In some locations where depots had been opened up, the collections had been destroyed by soldiers before the trophy brigades could get to them: "The manor house had been occupied by Polish frontline troops and the crates opened. Many of the books lay in the courtyard, wet with rain; there were no guards; many of the books were ruined, damaged, burned."[16]

A more organized form of dispersal of these collections would follow once the books had been shipped eastward. In the autumn of 1945, forty-five railroad cars moved around one million books from Mysłowice to Minsk. In addition to Mysłowice, the trophy brigades had tracked down other collection points in Poland, from which around three million books were sent to the Soviet Union. In addition, thousands of shelf-yards of archive material was sent to Stalin's archive in Moscow, including some from the International Institute of Social History in Amsterdam, and the various archives of the Rothschild family.[17]

The trophy brigades would also confiscate many of the finest German collections that ended up behind Soviet lines, including libraries such as Preussische Staatsbibliothek, Berliner Stadtbibliothek, Breslau's university library, and Kaiser Wilhelm II's court library. From Berlin, Dresden, and Breslau more than a hundred railroad cars of books were removed. Several hundred German libraries were emptied.[18]

The Lenin Library in Moscow ended up as the largest single recipient of trophy books, almost two million all told. The most valuable books that had been confiscated in Germany—medieval manuscripts, incunabula, and a Gutenberg Bible—were sent by air in a number of special deliveries to Moscow.

After the war, the book units of the trophy brigades are estimated to have sent back between 10 million and 11 million books. But this would not cover all the books that were taken, as books were also plundered by other trophy units more focused on seizing, for instance, scientific equipment—which also included libraries and archives from schools, laboratories, universities, institutes, and other research organs. Trophy brigades that were stealing art also took museum libraries. In addition, there were large numbers of books stolen by Red Army soldiers.

The historian Patricia Kennedy Grimsted writes that the Soviet trophy brigades usually made no distinction between books plundered from German libraries and those that were being plundered a second time and had earlier been stolen by various Nazi organizations from occupied territories.

Unfortunately, the books were affected by problems similar to those that had plagued other areas of the Soviet trophy operation. Many of the factories, machines, instruments, tools, and scientific apparatus that had been taken to the Soviet Union would end up never being used. The lack of skilled personnel, an inability to understand instruction manuals or a lack of the same, incompatible standards, and other logistical, technical, and practical problems often made the equipment unusable. And the lack of suitable storage meant that millions of trophy books were left in depositories in the Soviet Union. Cities such as Kiev, Minsk, and Leningrad had suffered large-scale destruction. In central Minsk only a few buildings were still standing, but almost half a million books were taken to this city of ruins. In Moscow, several million German books were stored and left untouched in an abandoned church in Uzkoye, southwest of the city.[19] In other cases the books were in such poor condition that they were not very useful. For instance, the science academy in Tbilisi received about 100,000 rain-damaged German trophy books.

Hundreds of trophy libraries were split up, and single copies of books were distributed to libraries all over the Soviet Union. Even this distribution was fraught with problems, as the libraries tended to receive books on haphazardly chosen subjects and in languages that the readers often did not understand. A Soviet postwar report describes how a workers' library at a chemical factory received books on ancient Greek literature, while another took delivery of confiscated French fashion magazines. Once or twice portraits of Adolf Hitler were even sent to workplaces.[20] The distribution was so chaotic that even Soviet librarians at this time began to question the purpose of the whole process. How many of these often damaged books were removed and discarded during the postwar years, no one knows. Books also had to be subjected to a political assessment, and "politically dangerous," "decadent," or "bourgeois" literature was removed.

The fate of the Turgenev Library from Paris was not entirely atypical. Like many other collections, the library was scattered. Some of the books ended up in Moscow, but the greater part of the collection was sent to Minsk. Half of the collection, about sixty thousand books, was sent to one of the Red Army officers clubs in Legnica, south of Mysłowice—the headquarters of the army in Silesia.[21] It seems to have been a mistake, a result of the chaos that characterized the whole operation.

When the mistake was discovered, the finer parts of the collection, such as manuscripts, first editions, and books with signatures and dedications by famous authors, were fetched and taken to the Lenin Library in Moscow. Especially, books with references to Lenin and Bunin were separated. But most of the collection remained in Legnica. After the fall of the Soviet Union in 1991, a Russian officer, Vladimir Sashonko, who was stationed there in the mid-1950s, revealed what had happened to the books.

According to Sashonko there were many books in the library that carried the stamp "Bibliothèque Russe Tourguéniev—Rue du Val-de-Grâce 9." One day a lieutenant who was in charge of the library explained that they "had received orders from Moscow to burn the books in the fireplace." Sashonko saved one book from the collection, which he took home with him as a souvenir, but the rest of the books were destroyed: "Slowly, the Turgenev Library was reduced to smoke and ashes, which settled over Legnica . . . sharing the tragic fate of the millions of unfortunates who went under in the concentration camps of the Fascists, and were burned in the crematoria."[22]

◆　◆　◆

Early in May 1945, Alfred Rosenberg wandered along the edge of Flensburg Fjord, on the border with Denmark. The fjord, which defines the most westerly point of the Baltic Sea, is a very beautiful place in May, and popular with boaters. The war seemed remote, almost. Rosenberg had left Berlin, bombed to smithereens, at the very last moment. He had checked into a hotel room in Flensburg, one of the few cities in Germany that was more or less undamaged by the war. Flensburg was the place where Nazi Germany's last government had established itself under Hitler's successor, Grand Admiral Karl Dönitz. On May 7, 1945, Dönitz had finally put his name to the capitulation of the Third Reich. Rosenberg, as he walked there at the water's edge, was considering how he should meet his own fate. Suicide would certainly have been in his thoughts, as it was for so many other leading Nazis. In his pocket he carried ampoules of cyanide.

Over the course of that last year, Rosenberg had watched his empire crumbling. After the Red Army reconquered the Soviet territories, Rosenberg's National Ministry for the Occupied East was nothing more than a semantic device. His once enormous kingdom in the east, and the dreams tied to this, had bit by bit been reduced to nothing, first by Hitler and then by Stalin. The enemy he feared more than any other, the regime he had made it his mission to fight, which had stolen his Estonia, was now also engulfing the German fatherland.

In February 1944, Rosenberg had visited his Ostland for the last time, in his private train, *Gotenland*. But he had not even reached Reval before Hitler called him back. During his absence, his headquarters in Berlin had been destroyed in a bombing raid. After that time, Rosenberg had to hold court in his train, parked in a Berlin suburb. He continued working in the spring on his plans for the congress in Kraków, but even this was snatched away from him in the summer when Hitler canceled all further planning for the event.[23] Repeatedly he tried to get a meeting with the Führer, whom he had not seen one-to-one since November 1943. However, access to Hitler was absolutely controlled by another of his enemies—Martin Bormann. Rosenberg's constant complaints about the regime's policy toward the East had created a rift with the Führer and the rest of the leadership. Hitler had appointed Erich Koch, earlier the Reich commissioner in the Ukraine, to apply similarly brutal methods in the exploitation and plundering of the Baltic region. Rosenberg was under strict orders not to interfere with Koch's work.

Rosenberg's attempts to get to his Führer failed, even when he tried to get past Bormann by going directly to Hitler's female secretary. In October he decided to give it all up, and he wrote an embittered letter in which he resigned from his post as Reich Minister for the Occupied East. Hitler never replied. During the last months of the war, Rosenberg lived in the cellar of his family's house, from which the roof had been blown off in a bombing raid. Rosenberg spent his time digging in his vegetable patch, planting various greens, which, as he must have known, he was highly unlikely ever to harvest.

Hitler saw Rosenberg one last time during a meeting with the leaders in February 1945, when the Führer spoke of a "secret weapon" that would earn their victory. It was the final straw, to which fanatical National Socialists clung as the downfall came closer. The two men did not speak, and Rosenberg had no faith in Hitler's miracle weapon.

In March, Rosenberg was visited by the leader of the Hitler Youth, Artur Axmann, who was planning to dig in and conduct guerrilla war in the Alps. He tried to win over Rosenberg, but the chief ideologue had already given up. Axmann asked Rosenberg what had really gone wrong, was it the National Socialist idea itself or its interpretation? Rosenberg chose to blame it on his party comrades: "I told him it was a great idea that had been abused by small men. Himmler was the evil symbol of all that," he wrote in his posthumously published settlement of accounts with Hitler, *Grossdeutschland, Traum und Tragödie*.[24] On a personal level, Rosenberg had resigned in the face of the constant rejection he had had to endure from Hitler. But in his private thoughts, Rosenberg seems to have retained his ideology without the slightest doubt.

On April 20, Rosenberg had been ordered to leave Berlin, even though he had declared that he was willing to stay on until the end—but, like an abandoned dog, faced with the last command he was ever given by the Führer, he set off. During his walk along the beautiful shore close to Flensburg, a few weeks later, Rosenberg finally took his cyanide ampoules out of his pocket and threw them into the sea. He had decided to meet with his vanquishers.[25]

Heinrich Himmler had no such plans. He had shaved off his mustache, put on an eye patch, changed his uniform, and taken the name of Heinrich Hitzinger—but he was quickly arrested on suspicion by British troops and confessed his identity shortly thereafter. By means of a hidden ampoule in his mouth he committed suicide on May 23 in a camp outside Lüneburg, south of Hamburg.

Alfred Rosenberg returned to his hotel and wrote a letter of surrender to the commander of the British forces, Field Marshal Bernard Montgomery.

Rosenberg was placed under arrest and taken to Kiel to be interrogated. Both Stalin and Churchill had advocated summary execution of the Nazi leadership. Furthermore, during the Allied conference in Tehran in 1943, Stalin had suggested that between 50,000 and 100,000 German officers should be shot—a suggestion that Roosevelt tried to make light of. In the spring of 1945, as the Allied victory grew imminent, there was increasing support for the idea of an international trial of the German war criminals. After negotiations between the Allies, these trials opened on November 19, 1945, in Nuremberg, the town where the National Socialists had once held their annual rallies.

Alfred Rosenberg was one of twenty-three high-ranking Nazis in the dock. Four of the most serious charges were leveled by the prosecution at the former chief of ideology: planning of offensive war, disturbance of the peace, war crimes, and crimes against humanity. Rosenberg proclaimed himself innocent on all four counts.

While the Nuremberg trials were under way, the Western Allies had already begun the work of trying to impose some order on the chaos created by Rosenberg's plundering operations. Placed in trust of this task was the Monuments, Fine Arts and Archives (MFAA) program, better known as the Monuments Men—a special unit of the Western Allied army, whose brief was to protect the European cultural legacy. The war was being fought on two fronts. After the Allied invasion of Italy in 1943 and France in 1944, the unit would spend most of its time saving monuments and cultural treasures from its own troops, who often did not even know what they were firing at. After the invasion of Germany, it turned more to the processing of enormous quantities of plundered art, antiquities, and books, which were found in warehouses, mines, barns, castles, and caves.

The Monuments Men set up a number of depots for the sorting and identification of recovered treasure. Stolen art, antiquities, and other artifacts were collected in the Nazi Party buildings in Munich. The Rothschild Library in Frankfurt was an early collection point, but the sheer quantity of books soon meant that the unit had to start looking for bigger premises. They found a suitable space in Offenbach am Main, a suburb of Frankfurt where the German industrial giant IG Farben had its head office. The conglomerate's headquarters, the largest office complex in Europe, was made into a new central depot for stolen books and archives: the Offenbach Archival Depot. The task of running the operation was given to a gifted archivist from the National Archives in Washington, Seymour J. Pomrenze, who arrived in Frankfurt in February 1946 while the city was being battered by a blizzard.[26]

Pomrenze was of Jewish origin, and his family had fled the Ukraine in the early 1920s. He was faced with an enormous task in Offenbach:

> My first impressions of the Offenbach Collecting Point were overwhelming and amazing at once. As I stood before a seemingly endless sea of crates and books, I thought what a horrible mess! What could I do with all these materials? How could I carry out my assignment successfully? Beyond the mess, however, was an even larger mission. Indeed, the only action possible was to return the items to their owners as quickly as possible.[27]

Pomrenze had been recruited by another MFAA participant, the librarian Leslie I. Poste, who was the brains behind the Offenbach Archival Depot. Ever since the arrival of the unit in Europe in 1943, the Monuments Men had focused their efforts on saving art, monuments, and historically important buildings. Libraries had not been given any great attention until Poste was hired in 1945. Prior to Pomrenze's arrival, Poste had spent almost half a year driving tens of thousands of miles, criss-crossing Europe through the ruins of the Third Reich, looking for plundered libraries and archives.

Pomrenze organized a workforce of two hundred archivists, librarians, and workers at the Offenbach Archival Depot, who started plowing their way through the "endless sea" of books. Security was tight, and everyone was frisked before leaving at the end of the day, although Pomrenze conceded that thefts did take place, especially smaller books that were easy to hide. The Monuments Men developed a sort of conveyor-belt system of identifying books, with ex librises and other owners' marks photographed. A less qualified group of the workforce kept photographs of the more common ex librises while they were sifting through the books. More unusual marks were sent on to be examined by experts. In this way, enormous piles of books could quickly be divided up into piles of identified and unidentified volumes. In the case of the former, they were immediately packed and sent off to officers in charge of restitution in the relevant country.[28]

Thousands of photographs of ex libris marks, the result of this work, are still kept in the National Archives in Washington. Already by March 1946, Pomrenze's group at the Offenbach Archival Depot had sorted some 1.8 million objects. And that same month some of the collections began to be sent back. However, the restitution process was not complete. The Western Allied armies, wanting the question out of their hair as quickly as possible, advocated a simple restitution model of returning each collection to the government of the country in which it was stolen. The model worked fairly well in cases of large, fairly integrated collections that belonged to established institutions.

Two libraries that were returned already by the spring of 1946 were Bibliotheca Rosenthaliana and Ets Haims from Amsterdam. Both had been found in Hungen still in the crates in which the ERR had packed them. Because these libraries had not been moved to Germany until 1943 and 1944, the Frankfurt institute had never had the time to check through the collections, and they were probably taken directly to storage in Hungen. By March the first consignment was sent to Amsterdam, but it was a return overshadowed by sorrow, as it had emerged that Rosenthaliana's previous curator, Louis Hirschel, had died in Poland with his entire family. Not many were left alive of the Jewish intellectual circle of scholarly librarians and biblical researchers who had once been such a fixture of the library. The choice for Hirschel's successor fell on a survivor of Theresienstadt's Talmudkommando: Isaac Leo Seeligmann.

For Seeligmann, who had lost his own collection, and for Amsterdam, which had lost a large proportion of its Jewish population, the appointment was a sort of consolation, even if rather a small one. Yet, with the return of the library to Amsterdam, a portion of the city's Jewish cultural identity was also revived.[29] Without these collections, a significant part of four hundred years of Jewish religious, intellectual, and economic history in "Jeruzalem van het Westen" would have been lost.

A more notable return were the collections that had belonged to the International Institute of Social History in Amsterdam. Because of the internal tug-of-war, the IISG's library and archive had left the Netherlands relatively late, in 1943 and 1944, which meant that a fair share of it was still packed in crates. Some of the material had been evacuated so late that it was found loaded on ferries in northern Germany. Hundreds of boxes were found in Hungen and at Tanzenberg Castle in Austria, where ZBHS had moved its collections. The latter were handed back by the British army, which had set up a similar restitution operation as the one in Offenbach.

However, some IISG material ended up in Stalin's special archive in Moscow.[30] The institute's archive, with its focus on the workers' movement, trade unions, and Socialist leaders, was of particular interest to the Soviet Union. At the Amsterdam institute there was for a long time a belief that the missing archives and books had been destroyed during the war. It took almost fifty years before it emerged that this was not the case. When I met him at the IISG, Huub Sanders recounted, "The miraculous part is that most of the archive came back after the war. The loss, in the end, was fairly small, just around 5 percent. What was lost was taken to the Soviet Union, which is also where the Trotsky papers are that were taken by the Soviet secret service in the 1930s."

Another Dutch library that would come back almost intact was Klossiana, the collection of the Masonic order of Grootoosten der Nederlanden in The Hague. The collection was returned to the Offenbach Archival Depot in 1946. But some of the archives of the order disappeared, and long afterward it was shown that they had been absorbed by the Stalin archive.

If the Netherlands libraries were lucky, the same could not be said of the French. In addition to the Turgenev Library, the Symon Petljura Library was lost and seems to have met a similar end by dispersal. The archives ended up both in Kiev and Stalin's trophy archive, where the material was kept in the section reserved for "Ukrainian nationalists."[31]

The exception was the Polish émigré library, Bibliothèque Polonaise de Paris. There is still a lack of clarity about where this library was on the cessation of hostilities—in East Germany or Poland. Either way, the collection fell into Polish hands and, in 1945, was brought to the National Library in Warsaw. Most likely the library was saved from the attentions of the trophy brigades because it was mistaken for "Polish property." After long-drawn-out negotiations and diplomatic pressure, the Polish exiles in Paris managed to take back a part of the collection in 1947. But it was not a complete library that was sent back. Of the 136,000 volumes that originally made up the collection, only 42,592 books, 878 manuscripts, 85 drawings, and 1,229 journals came back. The rest disappeared.[32]

When the coworkers at Alliance Israélite Universelle went back to the headquarters of the organization at 45 rue la Bruyère in Paris, the building was far from empty. The shelves in the library were still full of books; however, these were not the Alliance's own books but plundered collections left by the ERR. Instead, parts of the library of the Alliance Israélite Universelle were found at Offenbach Archival Depot and in Tanzenberg.

"We don't know how much never came back, because even lists, inventories, registers, and catalogs from the prewar years disappeared. The librarian, after the war, estimated that about 50 percent of the books were returned; the rest had been removed and were never found," said Jean-Claude Kuperminc at the Alliance.

Even parts of the archive disappeared. A half century later, documents with the organization's stamp appeared in Minsk, Moscow, and Lithuania. In all, Seymour J. Pomrenze and his colleagues would hand back about two and a half million books from the Offenbach Archival Depot. Another half million books were returned by the British army from Tanzenberg.[33]

Despite the extensive amount of work that had been done, only a small proportion of what had been plundered was ever sent back. From Offenbach, 323,836 books were sent to France, which was far off the estimate of 1.7 million books that had been plundered, not counting those taken when 29,000 apartments in Paris were cleared of their contents in the ERR's M-Aktion. Belgium, where hundreds of thousands of books had been plundered, only took return delivery of 198 crates of materials.[34] The Netherlands, relative to its size, got the most books back: 329,000. The Western Allies also returned books to Italy, Germany, Czechoslovakia, Hungary, Poland, Yugoslavia, and Greece.

Of all the libraries and archives that were plundered in Thessaloniki, only some ten thousand books were handed back to Greece, but not even these came back to their proper homes. When I met with Erika

Perahia Zemour in Thessaloniki, she commented, "I don't think any books came back to Thessaloniki, ever. The books that were repatriated were stored in Athens. Then they disappeared. No one knows what happened to them after the war. We have tried to look for them, but we haven't found anything. Most likely they were taken by the Jewish congregation in Athens."

On the other hand, the Western Allies found a larger amount of Jewish archival material from Greece. "A total of 17 tons of archive material was shipped to Athens, of which seven tons came to Thessaloniki. Unfortunately, someone sent most of this to Jerusalem after the war. The Americans also mistakenly sent material from Thessaloniki to YIVO in New York. But a lot of it also ended up in Moscow. We have a little left here, but most of it was scattered all over the world," Zemour told me.

In the end it was private collectors who were hardest hit by the plundering. Books in private collections were more difficult to identify because they had rarely been cataloged. If the books lacked owners' marks they were in practice absolutely impossible to trace back.

The Western Allies model, which worked in such a way that the final restitution had to be handled by national governments, proved ineffectual when it came to returning books to private individuals. While organizations and institutions were better placed to pressure authorities and gain compensation, individuals tended to relocate and many had also changed their nationalities, which hardly made the recovery process easier.

But the national restitution authorities were guilty of a significant share of the blame. For instance, the Belgian restitution authority, the Office de Récupération Economique, did very little to return private collections even when their owners had been identified at Offenbach and Tanzenberg.[35] One possible explanation for this was that after the war, the Office de Récupération Economique, like so many restitution authorities in other European countries, focused on financial compensation for, and restitution of, goods that were more valuable than books—such as art, gemstones, and gold.

Private owners who demanded restitution of their libraries, after the war, were mostly unsuccessful. If they recovered any books, this would usually be a case of a few copies from large collections. For instance, one Belgian citizen, Valérie Marie, had sixty-one books returned from a library that had amounted to two thousand volumes. In another case, Salvatore Van Wien got eight books out of six hundred.

The Office de Récupération Economique did not actively seek the owners, even when the origins of a particular library had been established. This was a passive approach to restitution, which would also characterize the process in many other countries.[36] By the end of the 1940s, the Office de Récupération Economique began selling off books that had not been claimed.

The Western Allies ended up returning a relatively large number of collections to the Soviet Union, primarily books that had been stolen from the Communist Party and other state institutions. Almost a quarter of a million books were dispatched from Offenbach to the Soviet Union in August 1946. Several railroad-car loads were also sent from Tanzenberg. Unfortunately, there was a paucity of traffic in the other direction.[37]

But the Western Allies were not entirely innocent themselves. Almost a million books were sent to the Library of Congress in Washington. Several large American libraries sent delegations to Europe to top up their collections. Some books were purchased, but many German libraries were also confiscated—sometimes on rather unclear grounds. Books that were seized from Nazi individuals, organizations, or public institutions were regarded as "enemy literature" and "propaganda." For instance, the "working library" of Institut zur Erforschung der Judenfrage, about twenty thousand books, was sent to Washington. According to regulations, no "Nazi plundered" books were allowed to be taken out of Germany. But in many cases this was impossible to establish, in cases where the books lacked owners' marks. Long afterward it would emerge that plundered books had also been taken to the United States.[38]

Nor is there any doubt that large numbers of books, just as had happened on the eastern front, were plundered by American, French, and British soldiers. Sargent Burrage Child, an archive specialist with the Monuments Men who came to Europe in 1945, made the claim in a letter that American soldiers all over Germany were "liberating books." "I have now gained a better understanding of the old stories of northerners plundering in the South. Their grandchildren, and also the grandchildren of the Yankees, are now following the same pattern." [39]

When the first round of sifting had been completed at Offenbach and Tanzenberg, hundreds of thousands of books remained whose origins or owners could not be established. Seymour Pomrenze and his colleagues often felt compelled to ask themselves whether there would even be anyone left to give these books to. Many of these books, as Pomrenze's successor, Isaac Bencowitz, stated, were the leavings of communities and people that no longer existed:

> In the sorting room, I would come upon a box of books which the sorters had brought together, like scattered sheep into one fold—books from a library which once had been in some distant town in Poland, or an extinct Yeshiva. There was something sad and mournful about these volumes . . . as if they were whispering a tale of yearning and hope since obliterated. . . . I would find myself straightening out these books and arranging them in the boxes with a personal sense of tenderness as if they had belonged to someone dear to me, someone recently deceased. [40]

Officers at the Offenbach Archival Depot faced a difficult dilemma. Europe, after the Second World War, was no longer the same. Communities had been wiped out, entire populations had been ejected, and the geographical map had been redrawn. While the restitution process was in motion, one of the biggest refugee crises in European history was under way, with about 30 million people fleeing or being moved in Central and Eastern Europe. [41] Thousands of Jewish communities all over Europe, but especially in the East, had disappeared. In many cases the survivors did not go back to their homes, especially not if these were in Eastern Europe, where the war in many cases had not impacted on a deep-rooted anti-Semitism. Already in 1946 a pogrom had broken out in the town of Kielce in Poland, after rumors that Jews had kidnapped and ritually murdered a Polish boy—the medieval myth resuscitated only a year after the liberation of the concentration camps. Forty-two Jews were shot or beaten to death in the pogrom. The perpetrators were both civilian Poles and Communist security officials. Hundreds of thousands of Holocaust survivors were in flight, most of them heading for Palestine, South America, or the United States to start new lives or reunite with relatives.

The hundreds of thousands of Jewish books at Offenbach that were regarded as "ownerless" required a special solution, and this came about with the help of an organization called Jewish Cultural Reconstruction (JCR), set up in 1947 and financed by various Jewish groups. The organization was led by the eminent historian Salo Baron, and the philosopher Hannah Arendt also sat on the executive committee.

In 1949, when most of the identifiable collections had been returned, about half a million books were handed to JCR to help rebuild Jewish communities and congregations. These books would follow the streams of Jewish refugees and immigrants in the years following the war. The largest proportion, almost 200,000 books, were sent to Israel, while almost 160,000 were taken to the United States.[42] Books were also sent to Great Britain, Canada, South Africa, and a number of countries in South America: Argentina, 5,053 books; Bolivia, 1,218 books; and Ecuador, 225 books. The books went mainly to congregations, but in certain cases also to schools. The Hebrew University in Jerusalem received a large number of valuable books and manuscripts. The recipients were barred from selling the books, and in many countries the books were marked with a special ex libris. Each of the 2,031 books shared out among congregations in Canada carried the following text inside: "This book was once owned by a Jew, a victim of the great massacre in Europe."[43]

✦  ✦  ✦

In February 1947 a young American historian by the name of Lucy S. Dawidowicz came to the Offenbach Archival Depot. Her task was to select less valuable "ownerless" books for dispatch to refugee camps for Holocaust survivors, where there was a great demand for books. How-

ever, when Dawidowicz started going through the collections, she discovered books and archive materials that she recognized.

Dawidowicz, a child of Polish-Jewish immigrants, had specialized in
European Jewish history while a student at Columbia University in the
1930s. Determined to learn Yiddish, she went to Vilnius in 1938 to work
at the YIVO Institute. Later she described how she had traveled to Vilnius "with the romantic conviction that the city would turn into a world
center for independent Yiddish culture."[44] She described the scenes that
met her at the famous Strashun Library: "In a single day you might see, at
the two long tables of the reading room, venerable elderly men in beards
and hats, absorbed in Talmudic texts, sitting beside young bareheaded
men and even women with bare shoulders on warm days. Sometimes you
heard the old men muttering and complaining about the state of the
world. And the young people tittering."[45] Dawidowicz left Vilnius in August 1939, just a few weeks before the outbreak of war and the beginning
of the catastrophe that would exterminate Jewish Vilnius.

One of YIVO's founders, Max Weinreich, who was in Copenhagen
when the war broke out in 1939, made his way to New York and set up
the institute's new headquarters there. Dawidowicz, who had gotten
close to Weinreich and the other YIVO researchers, started working
for the institute. In YIVO's new headquarters there were fears that
priceless collections, which had been built up over decades, had been
lost forever. YIVO's original mission, to strengthen and highlight Yiddish culture, had now changed in a most tragic way. It was no longer a
case of highlighting a living culture, rather of saving something from a
lost civilization. The great, living body of Yiddish culture went under
in the Holocaust. In Israel, Hebrew would dominate, while Yiddish
was resisted when the new nation had to create a strong linguistic and
cultural identity.

In 1947, when Lucy Dawidowicz started sifting through the piles of
books in Offenbach, she found documents and books that she had seen
before in Vilnius.[46] "A feeling came over me that was almost holy, as if I was
touching something spiritual.... Every surviving book from that world has
become a historical document, a cultural artifact, and a testament to a

murdered civilization," wrote Dawidowicz in her memoirs. At the same time as she felt reverence as she went through the collections, she also had an awareness of "a stench of death emanating from these hundreds of thousands of books and religious objects, which had lost their parents, and were the mute remnants of their murdered owners."[47]

Dawidowicz found journals, books, and archive materials of historical and ethnographic documentation, collected by YIVO's researchers in communities in Russia, the Ukraine, Poland, and Lithuania that were no longer in existence. There were poems, letters, photographs, audio recordings, and compositions of Yiddish songs. Among these enormous mounds of material, she also found the remains of the Strashun Library, with its valuable religious books and manuscripts.

After negotiations, it was decided that the collections would not be returned to Lithuania, where the institute had been nationalized by the Bolsheviks even before the German invasion in 1941, but rather to the new headquarters of the institute in New York. YIVO also managed to appropriate the right to the remains of the Strashun Library, as the collection was regarded as "ownerless." Of the sixty thousand or so Jews that had lived in Vilnius at the outbreak of the war, few remained alive. In July 1949, the fragments of this "civilization" were loaded into 420 crates and left Europe on the American ship SS *Pioneer Cove*.

That the Jewish culture in Vilnius had completely disappeared was not quite true, but there were other compelling reasons for not sending the collections back there. For at the same time, in Vilnius, another rescue operation was under way in YIVO's name, of the books that had been smuggled out of sight and hidden by the Jewish sorters in the Paper Brigade. And material that the poets and partisans, Abraham Sutzkever and Shmerke Kaczerginski, had dug out from under the floor of the bunker in the ghetto. Just two weeks after the liberation of Vilnius in July 1944 they founded the Museum for Jewish Art and Culture. The museum was established in the one building of the former ghetto that had not been nationalized by the Communists, namely the house at Straszuna 6 where once the ghetto library had been.

In the coming months, Sutzkever, who became the curator of the museum, and a small group of volunteers, managed to save more hidden treasures. One of the most important finds was made at a local paper mill, where twenty tons of paper from YIVO and other Jewish collections had not yet had time to be pulped. Another thirty tons were found with the government authority that was in charge of clearing ruined buildings. The citizens of Vilnius who had secretly helped hide material handed in potato sacks filled with books and manuscripts. Impressively, they managed to collect 25,000 books in Yiddish and Hebrew, 10,000 in other European languages, and 600 sacks of archive material.[48]

All the work in saving these valuable books and documents was done only with the help of volunteers. Sutzkever's pleas to the Soviet authorities for practical and financial support went unanswered. Instead, these efforts to rebuild a Jewish cultural identity in Vilnius were met with suspicion and later with animosity. In the Soviet system there was no room for alternative identities.

Sutzkever was the first to understand that these treasures, which had been saved from the Nazis with such enormous effort, now had to be saved once more. In September 1944 he had already gone to Moscow, smuggling out with him selections from the collection. Among other things he brought the diaries of the murdered Herman Kruk. With the help of a foreign correspondent he managed to send off a parcel to YIVO in New York.

Shmerke Kaczerginski, who was more sympathetic to the new regime, replaced Sutzkever as the curator of the museum. But before long Kaczerginski was also forced to recognize what was happening, when the KGB became regulars at the museum. They started by forbidding the library from issuing any book loans unless they had first been approved by the regime censors. Unfortunately, none of the books that Kaczerginski sent off for inspection ever came back.

Kaczerginski found out that the thirty tons of books and archive material that had been found were being loaded on a train bound for a paper mill. He hurried off to the platform and managed to save a few works from YIVO and the Strashun Library from the open railroad cars. But while he was contacting the authorities and trying to have the transport stopped, the train moved off and the cargo was destroyed.[49]

"That is when we, the group of museum activists, had a bizarre realization—we must save our treasures *again*, and get them out of here. Otherwise, they will perish. In the best of cases, they will survive but will never see the light of day in the Jewish world," wrote Kaczerginski.[50]

In secret, Sutzkever and some Jewish activists began smuggling out the most valuable parts of the collection, while Kaczerginski maintained the facade of a loyal Soviet citizen, planning for the museum's future. One by one the activists fled to the West, bringing by subterfuge as much material as they could carry. By mid-1946, both Kaczerginski and Sutzkever had left Vilnius with their bags packed full. To their great sorrow they had to leave most of the collection behind, and once again watch as it fell into the hands of a totalitarian regime. Not long after their flight, the KGB raided the museum, which was confiscated. The collection was loaded onto trucks and driven to an old church in the city, where it was dumped in the cellars.

Shmerke Kaczerginski and Abraham Sutzkever made their way to Paris, and from there they sent what they had been able to save to New York. And then the two friends, who together had survived the Nazi occupation, the partisan war in the forests, and the Soviet regime, took their leave of each other. Kaczerginski emigrated to Argentina and Sutzkever went to Palestine. But before Sutzkever left Europe he gave a widely publicized testimony against those who had destroyed his culture for all time. On February 27, 1946, he stepped onto the witness stand at the Nuremberg trials. He wanted to give his testimony in his mother tongue, Yiddish, something that he had been denied from the very beginning by the tribunal. He was made to speak in Russian. In protest about this decision, like the other witnesses, he refused to sit despite being told to do so several times. He wanted to remain standing, as if he were reciting from the sacred scriptures. "For two nights before this testimony I have not been able to sleep at all. I saw before me how my mother ran, naked, across a snow-covered field; the warm blood running down her injured body started dripping from the walls of my room, and it engulfed me. It is difficult to compare feelings. Which is the strongest, the suffering or the longing for revenge?"[51]

In his testimony, Sutzkever speaks of the extermination of Jewish

Vilnius, and how he remained in the ghetto from the first to the last days. He talked about his mother. How one day she disappeared. How he looked for her in her apartment but only found an open prayer book on the table and an undrunk cup of tea.

Later he found out what had happened to her, when the Nazis in December 1941 had given a "gift" to the Jews. Carts filled with old shoes were rolled into the ghetto.[52] Not long after, Sutzkever wrote a poem entitled "A Vogn Shikh" (A Wagon of Shoes):

> The wheels are turning, turning—
> What are they bringing there?
> They are bringing me a cartload
> Of quivering footwear.
>
> A cartload like a wedding
> In the evening glow,
> The shoes—in heaps, dancing,
> Like people at a ball.
>
> Is it a wedding, a holiday
> Or have I been misled?
> I know these shoes at a glance,
> And look at them with dread.
>
> The heels are tapping
> "Where to, where to, what in?"
> "From the old Vilna streets
> They ship us to Berlin."
>
> I need not ask whose,
> But my heart is rent:
> Oh tell me shoes the truth
> Where were the feet sent?
>
> The feet of those boots
> With buttons like dew.
> The child of those slippers
> The woman of that shoe

And children's shoes everywhere—
Why don't I see a child?
Why are the bridal shoes there
Not worn by the bride?

Among the children's worn-out boots
My mother's shoes so fair!
Sabbath was the only day
She donned this footwear.

And the heels are tapping
"Where to, where to, what in?"
"From the old Vilna streets
They ship us to Berlin."

◆ ◆ ◆

In the dock sat Alfred Rosenberg. A decade earlier, here in Nuremberg, he had received the Deutscher Nationalpreis für Kunst und Wissenschaft, the Nazi equivalent of the Nobel Prize. The dedication had been as follows: "Because he helped establish and stabilize the National Socialist world picture both scientifically and intuitively." Time spent in a cell at Nuremberg Prison had not brought about any conversion or outbursts of remorse, but it had given him the possibility of reflecting on what had gone wrong, as he saw it. Apart from the ideological corruption of the leadership around Adolf Hitler, Rosenberg felt that the so-called Führer cult had caused the downfall of the Third Reich. The National Socialist movement had rested too squarely on one man's shoulders. These were thoughts he had entertained before, but they were dangerous if articulated.[53] To Rosenberg, National Socialism had always been bigger than Adolf Hitler, and his vision for Hohe Schule had been about laying down intellectual and ideological foundations that could stabilize the movement for the future. Rosenberg's analysis was probably true to a certain degree, but also naive and idealistic—without the "Führer cult" the regime would most likely have imploded on itself. Many more people followed Hitler than the dogmas.

Rosenberg "has always lived in a world of unreal philosophy. He is completely unable to organise his present very real situation and constantly seeks to escape in aimless speech," stated D. M. Kelly, one of the psychologists who examined Rosenberg during his time in prison.[54]

Rosenberg's lawyer, Ralph Thomas, who tried to get him to admit his guilt and reject his own ideological ideas during the trial, never had any chance. Rosenberg was no Albert Speer, but he did not fall to pieces either as Ribbentrop or Kaltenbrunner had done. Instead, he behaved coldly. Unlike his codefendants, he was not considered likely to attempt suicide: "No evidence of depression or suicidal preoccupation. Mood was entirely appropriate," wrote William Harold Dunn, who conducted a medical and psychological evaluation of Rosenberg.[55] "He gave the impression of clinging to his own theories in a fanatical and unyielding fashion and to have been little influenced by the unfolding during the trial of the cruelties and crimes of the party."[56]

When a film from the concentration camps was shown during the trial, Rosenberg looked away and refused to watch. He spent his time in the cell working on his memoirs, where he fixed on the idea that Germany was the victim of a Jewish conspiracy—which had now won. His own struggle had only been a defense against this world conspiracy. Rosenberg did not admit to any guilt. He did not feel that loyalty to his ideology could be a crime: "National Socialism was a European answer to the question of our century. It was the noblest idea to which a German could devote his powers," he wrote in his cell.[57]

Although Rosenberg had not in the same way as Himmler, Göring, Heydrich, and other Nazi leaders been directly involved in the planning of the war or the Holocaust, he was too entangled in his own role as chief ideologue to escape the inevitable verdict. The anti-Semitic conspiracy theories and the racial ideology that Rosenberg had been preaching for decades had contributed to events. But what chiefly led to his conviction was his position as Reichsminister für die besetzten Ostgebiete. While it was conceded that Rosenberg had protested about heavy-handed action, at the same time he had not done anything to stop it, and he stayed at his post until the end, which was mentioned in the summation during the final proceedings on October 1, 1946.

"Rosenberg's real crime was not that he acted as a weak man, but that he had written and spoken like a strong man," stated one historian.[58] Rosenberg was found guilty on all four counts. He was sentenced to death.

His henchmen got away with considerably more leniency—the Nazi researchers who plundered the world around them and helped build Rosenberg's ideological cathedral. Most were able to go back to academic life or other careers. Wilhelm Grau, who had led the Frankfurt institute in the first years, would end up working in the publishing business, and in the 1950s became the director of a printing company. His successor, Klaus Schickert, became the managing director of a company in Cologne. Gerd Wunder, who led the research at Ratibor, rebranded himself after the war as a "social historian." Instead of titles like *Racial Questions and Jewry* he went on to publish books such as *South America and Europe's Historical Relations*.

Some of the researchers became more high-profile than others, such as the historian Hermann Kellenbenz. After the war he was active for a time at Harvard University in the United States and later became an internationally respected economic historian. He continued publishing studies on the economic affairs of the Sephardic Jews, except with the ideology washed off.

Johannes Pohl, the "Jewish expert" of the Frankfurt institute and a leading looter, worked after the war at Franz Steiner Verlag, a respectable German scientific publisher, and judging by his writings in Catholic journals, he seems to have reverted to his earlier faith. Pohl's detailed reports from the various plundering fronts, where he listed what had been "secured," were used as evidence against Alfred Rosenberg in the Nuremberg trials. But Pohl himself was never prosecuted.[59]

Two weeks after being sentenced, in the early hours of October 16, 1946, Rosenberg was led from his cell into the inner courtyard of the prison. The ten war criminals were taken out one after another to the place of execution. The only one to avoid punishment was Hermann Göring, who, just two hours before his execution, bit into a cyanide capsule that had been smuggled in. After the foreign minister Joachim von Ribbentrop, the RSHA leader Ernst Kaltenbrunner, and the general field marshal Wilhelm Keitel, the chief ideologue's turn came.

"Rosenberg was dull and sunken-cheeked as he looked around the court. His complexion was pasty-brown, but he did not appear nervous and walked with a steady step to and up the gallows. Apart from giving his name and replying 'no' to a question as to whether he had anything to say, he did not utter a word. Despite his avowed atheism he was accompanied by a Protestant chaplain who followed him to the gallows and stood beside him praying. Rosenberg looked at the chaplain once, expressionless. Ninety seconds after, he was swinging from the end of a hangman's rope. His was the swiftest execution of the ten," wrote the American journalist Howard K. Smith, who covered the executions.[60]

With the others, Alfred Rosenberg's body was taken to Munich, where they were all cremated in Ostfriedhof cemetery. That same night, under cover of darkness, the ashes of the executed men were emptied into the river Isar.

# 15

# A BOOK FINDS ITS WAY HOME

*Berlin–Cannock*

Few cities are as gray as Berlin in March. The last time I was on Breite Strasse, a green alley of trees obscured the fact that this was the ugly side of Museumsinsel. The southern part of the island does not even go by the same name, it is simply called Spreeinsel. Sebastian Finsterwalder stubs out his cigarette outside the door of Berlin's Zentral- und Landesbibliothek.

More than six months have gone by since I started my journey here. A few weeks ago I received an e-mail from Finsterwalder. Something had turned up.

On the way up to his office, Finsterwalder tells me that other things are happening in the library, which is undergoing great change. Not only are the books being digitized, now also some of the librarians are going to be replaced by robots. The cataloging will be taken over by an external company that uses machines to do the job. It's cheaper. But many members of staff have to be laid off, says Finsterwalder, who is active in the union.

The restitution project at the Zentral- und Landesbibliothek will go on. But no one knows for how long. Years of work lie ahead before Finsterwalder and his colleagues can identify the plundered books in the collection.

"We don't know how long we've got. Our boss still talks about this as a project that will one day come to an end. Usually, restitution investigations in Germany only carry on for a limited period of two or three years. But this is not something that can be completed in the short run. It's a work over generations. And everyone knows it."

The office is unchanged, except that his colleague Detlef Bockenkamm is not there. He's in the hospital. "He broke his hip in an accident," Finsterwalder tells me. For his own part, he is still struggling on, is in the process of writing a new study, and has built a Web page to publish material that he and his colleagues have dug up from the archives. Among other things, how the library in 1943 made a bid to get its hands on some forty thousand books plundered from homes belonging to Berlin's deported Jews.

"It says here quite clearly that the money paid for the books would go toward the 'Solution for the Jewish Question.' The library was well aware of what the money would be used for," Finsterwalder says, and shows me the letter.

On the shelf along the wall, where volumes with bookplates from a variety of collections have been arranged, a few new names and piles of books have been added. My attention is immediately caught by a book with the signature "R. Wallenberg." Finsterwalder does not know how the book has ended up in the library, nor who "R. Wallenberg" might be, but he does know that the book is stolen. After comparing the signature with that of the missing Swedish diplomat, Raoul Wallenberg, we are able to confirm that this is another Wallenberg.

From a white paper box on his desk Finsterwalder picks up another find in the collection that he is currently investigating. Carefully he opens the book, and I see that the pages have been written in longhand—large, beautiful, intricate letters in ink on thick brown paper. Its origins are revealed by a stamped mark of three French lilies. "This is a parish register from the little congregation of Verpel. It's recorded here who was married, or baptized, between 1751 and 1771. It came to the library as a gift in 1945 but we don't really know how. It clearly doesn't belong here. It was stolen by someone during the war," he explains. Verpel lies in Champagne-Ardenne in northeast France, near the Belgian border. In 2010, there were eighty-five people living there.

It is very likely that the Zentral- und Landesbibliothek owns more plundered books drawn from scattered origins than any other library in Germany—and possibly in the whole of Europe. Apart from the library having bought whole batches of books from the Nazis, stolen from thousands of Jewish homes, after the war it took custody of books that were collected at 130 different places in Berlin—from individual Nazi officials, institutes, public authorities, and several Nazi libraries including Section VII's book depot on Eisenacher Strasse, where Jewish slave workers had sorted and packed the books. How many books still remained in the bombed ruins of what was previously the Freemasons' lodge is not known by anyone. All that can be said is that some of them did end up here. Then there were many plundered books after the war that were acquired in bulk from booksellers or as "gifts." Some of the book depots to which the library evacuated its collections would also remain untouched for decades. Finsterwalder explains that tens of thousands of the library's books were taken to a barn outside Berlin, where they stayed for forty years.

It was from these plundered, scattered collections that the library's predecessor, Berliner Stadtbibliothek, rebuilt its collection after the war—partly to fill the gaps caused by bombing raids, but also because the trophy brigades sent a large part of the original collection to the Soviet Union. Finsterwalder regards this part of the collection as irretrievably lost. He believes it is more important for the library to face up to its own history. Finding the owners of approximately a quarter of a million plundered books that are found in this building is a detective's task, which, as yet, no cataloging robot in the world could accomplish.

What this is about is finding the books that were once a part of libraries repeatedly divided up, scattered, sorted, and weeded. Even collections that were blown up, in a literal sense. "We have many books with traces of artillery shrapnel in them," says Finsterwalder.

It is about libraries fragmented to their smallest possible parts. There are books here from thousands of libraries, but often just a single book or a few copies from each collection. These fragments of what was once an integral library turn my thoughts to the destroyed Jewish cemetery in Thessaloniki. The way in which the broken gravestones were used as masonry in the walls of the town, and became a part of it. In the same way, the Zentral- und Landesbibliothek has been built using shards and ruins. The foundations are mainly unseen, but like a low slate wall behind a dirty moped garage, or a forgotten ex libris on a flyleaf, they offer a narrative about how these parts were once part of something or someone.

Boxes of archive material from the International Institute of Social History in Amsterdam, repatriated from what was once Stalin's secret archive in Moscow. The existence of enormous numbers of books and archives in Russia was revealed after the collapse of the Soviet Union.

The plunder was followed by destruction, both of a deliberate kind and as a consequence of war. Books disappeared into the grinders of paper mills, and they were blown up and torched. Others simply rotted away in forgotten depots, barns, and flooded cellars. But a greater, immeasurable destruction took place as a consequence of dispersal. Even if some scattered books still exist on the shelves of other libraries here and there, they have lost their context. They were a part of libraries that had a value in their own right—collections in which the parts became a greater whole.

Dispersal was a conscious strategy of the plunderers. Only by destroying these collections could they build up new ones. Many of these libraries were the results of decades, sometimes centuries, of careful collecting. There had been generations of learned collectors and readers. The books also said something about the people who owned and treasured them: what they read and what they thought and what they dreamed. Sometimes they left traces in the form of underlined passages, notations, notes in the margins, or short comments. The beautiful and personally designed ex librises that many readers had made for their books demonstrate the care and pride they took in their libraries. Each collection in its own right took form in a unique culture, a depiction of its creator's world, which was lost when the library was broken up. The books are fragments of a library, of a world that once existed.

But they are also fragments of individuals. The last time I came here, the librarian Detlef Bockenkamm, who was the one that uncovered the truth about this library, told me something that I could never quite let go of during my travels. The names he found in these forgotten books always gave the same answer: "Every time the trail led to Auschwitz." It is a disturbing insight into how this is not just a library, but also a place of remembrance of those who were rarely given a grave. In some cases, the books are the only things these people have left behind.

Most of the books are mute; they do not say a great deal about their owners. At best, a fragment, a note, possibly a name. Sometimes the name is too common and the victims too many. All Finsterwalder and his colleagues can do is enter the details into the database and wait.

Thousands of books wait there, all searchable, like a net waiting for someone, somewhere, to be caught. From time to time an e-mail comes and a book is opened.

A book whose trail went cold in Auschwitz long ago lies on the table in front of me. A small olive-green book faintly embossed in gold: a scythe in front of a wheat sheaf. It was already on the shelf behind Finsterwalder's desk when I was last here. The title of the book is *Recht, Staat und Gesellschaft* (Law, State and Society). It was written by the conservative politician Georg von Hertling, who was the chancellor of Bavaria in the turbulent period at the end of the First World War. Inside the cover, on a flyleaf, is a simply fashioned ex libris, creating a frame around a name: Richard Kobrak. In the top-right corner of the title page, someone—most likely Kobrak himself—has written the name in pencil. As with many other books here at the Zentral- und Landesbibliothek, it is difficult to say where this book came from.

"It's fairly complicated. We found it a few years ago; it came to the library in about 1950," says Finsterwalder, getting out a catalog in which about a thousand books have been cataloged. All come from the same source, a person by the name of Dombrowski. "It's a curious collection of books. There are many plundered books here, but others that could not have been plundered, because they were printed after the war. We don't have any certainty about the point of origin. Dombrowski sounds Polish, but it wasn't a wholly unusual name in Germany. There was a Dombrowski with Gestapo connections; it may have been him."

The library started entering the books into the catalog in 1958. "That's how we found most of these books. But it's also curious that they gave this collection a catalog of its own. That was not how it was usually done," Finsterwalder says, and turns the pages until he gets to book number 766—Richard Kobrak's book. "These numbers are still in use today, so with the help of this catalog I could make my way through the shelves and find the books. Most of them were still here. I began looking through them, searching for owners' marks. They came from many different collections that had been fragmented before and during the war. Then I photographed the books and put them in our public database. Kobrak's book was one of them."

Some of the books that have been found in the Zentral- und Landesbibliothek come from well-known individuals and libraries. On the shelf are a few books belonging to the world-famous pianist Arthur Rubinstein, including a collection of sonnets with a personal dedication by the Brazilian poet Ronald de Carvalho. But most of the books here were the property of ordinary people.

A search in various archives for Richard Kobrak's name does not give away much information. In a genealogy register I find a few brief lines: "Dr. Richard Kobrak was born in 1890. During the war he was deported on Transport I/90 from Berlin to Theresienstadt 18/03/1943. Then deported on Transport Er from Theresienstadt to Auschwitz 16/10/1944. Dr. Kobrak lost his life in the Shoah."[1] Thanks to the hideous, dry scrupulousness of Nazi bureaucracy, we know more about the transportation numbers of the trains used to deport him than about Kobrak as a person. Mere numbers to designate a person among millions being transported to their deaths. Many times there is nothing else.

The sheer number of plundered books in the collection make it impossible for Finsterwalder and his colleagues to go much deeper into it. "Sometimes we actively search for owners, but usually we just put them in the database and hope that someone will find them, if there are any descendants," he says. But a month or so after my first visit to the library in June 2014, it suddenly received an e-mail. Someone had found book number 766, entered by Finsterwalder into the database. The message had been sent from the other side of the world, by a female scientist studying dengue fever in Hawaii. She was not a descendant herself, but she believed she knew who the book belonged to. She had married into another branch of the Kobrak family, that of a brother of Richard Kobrak who had emigrated from Nazi Germany in the 1930s. At the end of the year, Finsterwalder told me, another e-mail came from England from a woman by the name of Christine Ellse who described herself as a grandchild of Richard Kobrak.

In a German database I find out a little more about Kobrak, namely

Richard Kobrak managed to get his three children out of Germany in 1939, including Christine Ellse's father, Helmut Kobrak. However, once he got to England, he was deported to Australia as an "enemy alien."

that until 1933 he was a lawyer and civil servant at the city office in Berlin. He was married to Charlotte Kobrak, three years younger than he was. The couple had three children. Neither Richard nor Charlotte have a specific day on which they died. All we know is that they were on one of the last transports from Theresienstadt to Auschwitz on October 16, 1944.

It is likely that, much like hundreds of thousands of others in the autumn of 1944, they were taken at once to the gas chambers. But I can see that the couple's three children, who were only teenagers when the war broke out, survived. But how?

Finsterwalder slides the olive-green book into a brown padded envelope, with two copies of a contract. It is two pages long, and in it the Zentral- und Landesbibliothek transfers the book to the ownership of "the descendants of Dr. Richard Kobrak."

Recently the left-wing political party Die Linke and the environmental party Die Grünen proposed in the Bundestag that there should be better possibilities in Germany for the victims of Nazism to recover lost property, but Finsterwalder does not believe this will ever become a reality. "In Germany the attitude is that we have already paid our debt. Unfortunately, there is no political interest in tackling this question in a meaningful way." In this regard, Sebastian Finsterwalder and Detlef Bockenkamm have an air of restitution activism about them. Despite limited resources and bureaucratic resistance, they continue digging up and exposing this graveyard of books.

The question of restitution, and the media attention it has had since its reemergence in the 1990s, has primarily focused on spectacular cases of plundered art and the legal conflicts and return of works of art worth millions of dollars—for instance, the successful legal battle of Maria Altmann, a Holocaust survivor, to reclaim some of the artist Gustav Klimt's greatest masterpieces from the Austrian state. In 2006, five paintings handed over in the same year were sold for $325 million. These cases have often involved dirty games between museums, governments, and profiteering lawyers at the expense of the legitimate demands of survivors and descendants. Above all, these cases, and the fantastic sums involved from time to time, have thrown a veil over the moral basis of the question of restitution. This has provided ammunition for the opponents of restitution, who have tried to lend credence to the suggestion that the entire process is actually fueled by greed. It has not been unusual for the voices calling for an end or "deadline" for restitution to be one and the same as those who carry some moral blame in these cases: art dealers, museums, and governments.

In Sebastian Finsterwalder's spartan office at the Zentral- und Landesbibliothek we are far from these spectacular restitution cases, but much closer to the core of the whole issue of restitution. Here the return of property—several hundred cases since the process began a few years ago—proceeds largely without any attention at all. There are no headlines, no scandals, and no interest from well-remunerated law firms. In most cases the cost of the postage exceeds the value of the actual books being returned. It is a restitution process entirely liberated from the capital-driven art market. The value of these books resides in something else, which cannot be computed in monetary terms. As far as Finsterwalder and his colleagues are concerned, there is a moral obligation underlying their work, namely the return of something that was lost—book by book.

"I've been asked by people in Israel why we go on with this small-scale, time-consuming work. Why don't we just donate the books of Jewish families to the National Library in Israel? But if there is still a possibility of finding descendants or survivors, which there often is, I think we should hand the books back to them. I'm convinced this is the right way. After that, they can donate the books if they choose to, but that's a decision I can't make, and not some library in Israel either."

I pack the brown envelope with the olive-green notebook into my rucksack. I am overwhelmed by a sense of responsibility, which soon transforms itself into something else. A few days later when I board a plane in Berlin bound for Birmingham, England, the book is still stowed in my rucksack. I have hardly touched it. But several times these last few days I have opened the rucksack and peered into the brown envelope, to reassure myself that it is still there. Where it could possibly go I don't know. Nor who would want to steal it. But the thought of its disappearance has left me unsettled. Admittedly the little olive-green book is not a treasure—if it was, it might in some ways have made things easier. Maybe then it could have been replaced if it was lost, but this book is irreplaceable.

But books were not only rotting away in barns outside Berlin. In October 1990, a Russian cultural journal, *Literaturnaia gazeta*, revealed that two and a half million German trophy books had been dumped and forgotten in a church in Uzkoye, outside Moscow. Several decades of damp, vermin, and a growing blanket of pigeon droppings had transformed the books into rotting pulp.[2] The article caused a great deal of attention, not only in the Soviet Union but also in Germany. It was the first time that the extensive plunder of German collections had come into the public domain, largely as a consequence of glasnost, the policy of transparency and openness that Mikhail Gorbachev had launched in an attempt to modernize the Soviet system.

Gorbachev's reforms, glasnost (openness) and perestroika (innovation), ended up accelerating the collapse of the empire. Not least, glasnost contributed to the exposure of failings in the system and thereby undercut its legitimacy. This was also the first time that information had come to light of trophy plundering during the war, which until then had been classified. The postwar period had seen some of the collections returned, but only as a rule in the Eastern bloc. There had never been a question of restitution, especially not to the West and not of any materials that had ended up in Stalin's secret archive.

The successive opening up of the Soviet archives not only provided new insights into the Nazi plundering by means of millions of confiscated German documents, it also emerged that millions of books and thousands of shelf-yards of archive material, which for years had been assumed as lost in the war, were in actual fact still there on different sets of shelves in the Soviet Union.

Even the tragic fate of the trophy books was revealed. Trophy books had been worn out, rotted away, or discarded. They had been subjected to extensive clean-outs by archivists, censors, and librarians—not entirely unlike the clean-outs of "degenerate literature" conducted in Nazi Germany in the 1930s. Often, the same books had been selected by both sides, either bourgeois or decadent literature.[3]

In the years that followed the collapse of the Soviet Union, the question of restitution of these trophy hoards was raised. A step toward this process was taken in 1992, when a conference was arranged for Russian and German libraries. Among the Russian delegates were some from the biggest recipients of foreign trophy books, including the Vserossiyskaya Gosudarstvennaya Biblioteka Inostrannoy Literatury im. M. I. Rudomino (VGBIL). In other words, the Margarita Rudomino All-Russia State Library for Foreign Literature. Rudomino, its superintendent during the war, had been in charge of the plunder of books in Germany. In the spirit of glasnost, the library made public a catalog of valuable books from the 1500s, which had been confiscated.[4]

The conference led to the creation of a commission to investigate the return of old, valuable books. Other countries, such as the Netherlands, Belgium, Hungary, Norway, Poland, Austria, and France, also opened negotiations with the new Russian Federation in an attempt to recover lost book and archive collections. Similar negotiations were set in motion with the now independent Ukraine and Belorussia, which had both received millions of trophy books.

Several libraries, such as the VGBIL in Moscow, took a voluntary initiative, and before the 1992 conference, 604 books plundered by the Nazis had already been returned to the University of Amsterdam.[5] The Netherlands, Belgium, and France took part in a collaborative process to identify and retake possession of lost archive material, which was assumed to be somewhere in Russia. The scale of the Russian archive plunder was revealed when a deal was struck with France for the return of 7,000 shelf-yards of material from Stalin's secret archive in Moscow. Among other things, the material included archives of the French secret police and French Freemasons orders, but also private archives belonging to Léon Blum, Marc Bloch, and the French branch of the Rothschild family. The exchange came at a price. In addition to a cash sum of 3.5 million francs, Russian-related archives were also handed over by France.[6]

Priceless historical documents from secret Russian archives also started surfacing. A messenger from President Boris Yeltsin handed over secret documents to Poland about the Katyn massacre during the war, when 22,000 Poles, including thousands of Polish officers, were executed by the Soviet security service, the NKVD.

However, the optimism and high hopes, which for a few years in the early 1990s defined relations between East and West, would soon fall to the wayside. Although Russia's President Yeltsin had entered into agreements on restitution with a number of affected countries, criticism of the president's open-handed policies grew in the Duma.

The resistance came principally from right-wing nationalists and Communists, both of whom actively rejected each and every instance of restitution. Before long the opponents held a majority in the Duma and the ongoing return of French archives was frozen in 1994. By this time some three-quarters of the haul had already been handed back to France, but several of the trucks that had been dispatched to Moscow had to come back empty. The large sum of money that France had paid, which was supposedly going to be used to microfilm the documents, was never received by the archive and must have disappeared en route.[7] It was not the last time such things occurred.

The opponents of restitution claimed that the treasures brought back to Russia by the trophy brigades had not been plundered but "liberated by the Soviet Army" and were therefore quite legally brought into the Soviet Union. The prevailing attitude was that there was no obligation for Russia to hand back anything. But this resistance was far from unanimous, and many academics, librarians, and above all the Yeltsin administration believed that some sort of restitution was needed in order to rebuild relations with the West. Yet Russian nationalists and the Communist Party firmly rejected such arguments and ran fierce campaigns against the restitution process. In *Pravda*, the Communist Party newspaper, there were headlines such as "Will the Russian People Be Robbed One More Time?"[8]

In other countries in the former Soviet Union, the approach to restitution of scattered trophy treasure seesawed between animosity, indifference, and a spirit of cooperation. Countries like Belorussia and Ukraine took a similar approach to that of Russia, while Georgia, in 1996, returned 96,000 trophy books to Germany, and Armenia followed, returning books to Germany as well.[9]

A general thaw seemed imminent when Russia joined the Council of Europe in 1996. One of the requirements of membership was that Russia must begin negotiations on restitution with other European countries. But the high expectations were soon dashed. Already in July of that same year, the Duma tried to push through a piece of legislation that would "nationalize" all trophy treasures and thereby make them impossible to hand back. Yeltsin, declaring that Russia's international reputation was at stake, vetoed the attempt. However, the proposal was reintroduced in the Duma. One parliamentary representative declared that returning these treasures would be like "spitting on the graves of the 27 million Soviet citizens killed in the war."[10] Another ultranationalist representative complained about Yeltsin's compliance toward the Germans, who were "Fascist villains then as now."[11] While the Soviet Union had folded, feelings about the Great Patriotic War were undiminished. Yeltsin's veto was overturned in 1997, but the president refused for a whole year to sign the proposal into law. In 1998, the Russian Constitutional Court finally made Yeltsin sign off on the legislation. The new law not only stopped the restitution of art treasures to Western Europe, it also halted the restitution of large amounts of artifacts stolen from republics in the former Soviet bloc.

Another aggravating circumstance was that Soviet archives were once again being closed off to researchers from the West, which made it almost impossible to trace the stolen treasures. Glasnost, the short era of openness, went back to a culture of secrecy that was much like the "old Soviet way."

While the Russian anti-restitution law effectively put a stop to an extensive return of trophy treasures, it was still possible to reclaim minor collections, even if this often proved both complicated and costly. It would also take diplomatic approaches, legal loopholes, and in some cases bribes pure and simple, with the requirement that one altogether avoided that politically sensitive word *restitution*. One early case of the sort of "return" that the Duma was willing to accept concerned the Liechtenstein archive. An agreement was reached in 1996 as a result of negotiations on the part of the princely family of Liechtenstein, whose archive was in Moscow. However, this was not a case of restitution, as the Duma saw it, but an exchange. The royal family, acting on a Russian prompt, had bought a valuable collection of documents on the subject of the Bolsheviks' murder of the tsar and his family in 1918. The documents, which had remained hidden in a bank vault in Paris for seventy years, had recently surfaced at the auction house Sotheby's. They went under the hammer for half a million dollars.

The case was the beginning of a new phase in which "restitution" was substituted for "exchange." Soon there would be more of such cases of bartering for archives and libraries. But it cannot be said that this sort of exchange was new; it was more of a reversion to the old Soviet system, where the regime exchanged materials such as letters or books in order to take possession of items it wanted—especially if these related to Lenin and Marx, for which almost any price would be paid. For instance, there is a case where the regime offered a painting by Wassily Kandinsky for an autograph by Lenin.

In the new Russia, where nationalism had replaced Leninism, the imperial legacy had taken on central importance. The Russian position was that trophy treasures had not been plundered but liberated by the Red Army, and for this reason there should be compensation for anything returned. The director of the Hermitage in St. Petersburg commented to a British newspaper: "If these paintings had remained in Germany after 1945 they would have been hit by inheritance tax two or three times by now. It is obvious to me that Russia, as the custodian of these works, is more entitled to the treasures than Germany." [12]

In 1999, Great Britain acquired documentation on British prisoners of war in German concentration camps by offering in exchange some classified documents on the murder of Tsar Nicholas II. France, by avoiding any mention of the sensitive concept of "restitution," managed to successfully negotiate the repossession of remaining parts of the archive that had earlier been blocked. In 2000, several truckloads of materials were handed back, including some belonging to Alliance Israélite Universelle in Paris, which received more than 34,000 documents.

The Netherlands and Belgium, after long-drawn-out negotiations, also took back some archives. The Belgians were made to pay $130,000, a retroactive rental fee to the Russians for "preserving and storing" these archives for fifty years.

The Netherlands had reached an agreement with Yeltsin as early as 1992, but this was stopped by the Duma. The solution, after years of fruitless and time-consuming negotiations, had been to send over Queen Beatrix in 2001 to sign an agreement with Vladimir Putin. The chief archivist for the Netherlands State Archive had heard from an Israeli ambassador that the Russian regime was keen on royal glamour. Later that same year, the first boxes of archive materials started arriving in the Netherlands. It was rich material, over three thousand files, containing hundreds of thousands of documents. Most belonged to a series of Jewish organizations and institutions, including the International Institute of Social History in Amsterdam and the Grootoosten der Nederlanden in The Hague. However, the material was not given freely. The Netherlands had to pay over $100,000 in archive rent, administrative costs, and microfilming of the material for Russian archives.[13]

For private individuals it proved almost impossible to reclaim material, with one spectacular exception: the Rothschilds. As early as 1993, a researcher looking for documents relating to Auschwitz in Stalin's special archive came across documents touching upon branches of the famous family in both Austria and France. There was just about enough time for the French papers to be sent back to France in 1994, including the archives of the Paris-based family bank, de Rothschild Frères. On the very day that the archives came to Paris, an aggressive debate began in the Duma that led to the blocking of all restitution. The documents were taken to the Rothschild Archive in London, which has collected and housed a large part of the famous family's archive since 1978.

However, the papers from Austria were still in Moscow, and these were considered to be priceless historical material about one of the world's most powerful industrial and banking families in the 1800s. It also emerged that the archive contained some of the earliest of all Rothschild documents, harking back to Frankfurt and the first steps in the career of the family's ancestor, Mayer Amschel, who established himself as a banker in the 1760s.[14] The Rothschild documents were not only of significance for the family itself, but in a much broader sense had importance for the writing of history from the end of the 1700s and up to the First World War.

Any prospects of relying on a legal restitution process to regain these documents from the Russian archives—which were increasingly being shut off from the outside world—seemed absolutely unlikely. But there was another possibility, namely offering the Russian authorities something they could not refuse, which, in the end, proved to be a collection of Russian love letters. In the summer of 1999, a large number of rare letters that Tsar Alexander II of Russia had written to his second wife, Princess Ekaterina Mikhailovna Dolgorukova, turned up at Christie's auction house. The Rothschilds bought the five thousand letters for 180,000 pounds. It had been indicated to them that the Russian state archive was interested in the letters but did not have the funds to acquire them.[15] The bait worked, and almost at once the negotiations came unstuck.

As with several other exchanges, the government had a good excuse for returning the archives, namely that they had been seized in Poland and not in Germany. It was more than anything the idea of restitution to the old "Fascists" (Germany and Austria) that was politically impossible in Russia. But in the anti-restitution legislation there was a clause stating that "exceptions" could be made for victims of Nazism. After the government found that the Rothschild papers were not trophy documents, the archives were returned in 2001. The tsar's love letters were offset against Russian "costs" incurred in preserving the archive.

But although some documents have been returned, much remains in Russian, Belorussian, and Ukrainian archives, including documents stolen from the Jews in Thessaloniki. A great deal has still not been recovered, and the political situation in Russia has made further investigation almost impossible. Even if some of the plundered archives found their way home after the fall of the Soviet Union, considerably fewer of the millions of trophy books ever did. The return of 604 books to the Netherlands in 1992 remains the only "restitution," in accordance with rules and regulations, of books from Russia.

Already before 1991, information had surfaced about many of the more valuable libraries, or rather parts of them, which were still in existence in the former Soviet Union. One of these was the Turgenev Library of Paris. However, it was soon learned that the relevant books had been hopelessly dispersed all over Russia, Belorussia, and the Ukraine. In the 1980s, books bearing the stamp of the Turgenev Library had turned up in secondhand bookshops in Moscow.[16] Later, fifteen books were found in the university library, Voronezh, in central Russia, while another book was found at the university in Luhansk in the Ukraine. Odd copies were found as far east as a library on the Russian island of Sakhalin, north of Japan.[17] Some of the books had found their way out into the world, probably by exchanges or Russian emigration. For instance, two books from the Turgenev Library were found at Stanford University in California.

When the Turgenev Library celebrated its 125th anniversary in 2001, only a single book of the 100,000 that were plundered had found its way back to Paris. Among the 600 books returned to the Netherlands in the early 1990s, there was a Bible with the library's stamp inside. Most likely the book had been sent to Amsterdam by accident, as it was printed in Dutch. In the early 2000s it was confirmed that between 8,000 and 10,000 books from the Turgenev Library were still in Russian state collections, primarily in the former Lenin Library in Moscow.[18] Finally, a few years later, 118 books were sent back, which can be seen today in the library in Paris. The reason for their being handed back was a legal loophole, which meant that these particular books were not subject to the anti-restitution laws passed by the Duma. The books had been found earlier in Poland, and in the 1980s they were given as a gift by Poland to the Communist Party in the Soviet Union. They were therefore not regarded as "trophy books" protected by law. They were handed to the French embassy in Moscow toward the end of 2002.

A possibly even more tragic case was that of the Biblioteca della Comunità Israelitica, the missing library of the Jewish congregation in Rome. The commission set up by the Italian government in 2002, after due pressure by the congregation, had concluded that it was "not inconceivable" that the books had been taken to the Soviet Union.[19] Its sister

library, Biblioteca del Collegio Rabbinico, which had also been housed
in the synagogue on Lungotevere de' Cenci in Rome, had been found in
Hungen and handed over to Offenbach Archival Depot. But the Biblioteca della Comunità Israelitica was never found, and the fate of the library has remained a mystery. It was not likely that such a remarkable
library would have been missed at the sorting stage in Offenbach or
Tanzenberg—as the library's books were clearly stamped.

The conclusion of the commission was that the libraries were dispatched in two stages in 1943; while Biblioteca del Collegio Rabbinico
ended up in Frankfurt, the train transporting the Biblioteca della Comunità Israelitica had taken another route. The most likely hypothesis
was that this library was moved either to the ERR or the RSHA in
Berlin, and from there was evacuated east, to Poland, Sudetenland, or
Silesia. Yet there was no supporting evidence for this, as documents
relating to the activities of the ERR and the SS in Italy had largely been
destroyed.[20] The commission's further investigation into relative archives had not yielded any clues as to the whereabouts of the library, yet
indications seemed to suggest that the library had been taken to the
Soviet Union, most likely to Moscow.

For this reason, in 2005 the commission started investigating the
possibilities of looking for the books in Russian collections, something
that required negotiation at the very highest political level. The commission's own researchers were not given independent access to the
Russian archives—the investigations had to be handled by a Russian
"party." In 2007 an agreement was reached in which the commission,
with the backing of a bank, paid 30,000 euros to Moscow's Library for
Foreign Literature to look for the books. The library presented three
reports, which the commission dismissed as insufficient, because they
were largely based on references to already known sources, archives, and
collections. When the commission presented its final report in 2009, not
a single book had been recovered. Although it was not possible to prove
that the books were to be found somewhere in the former Soviet Union,
the commission declared with some resignation that further
investigations would only be possible "after an end to the limitations
to consultation in Russian archives encountered by the commission

After a long wait, Christine Ellse from Cannock outside Birmingham
finally holds her grandfather's book. It is the only thing belonging
to Richard Kobrak that has ever been returned.

during its activity."[21] In the present climate there is no political will to make Russian archives more accessible, nor to go back to restitution. The political situation does not seem likely to change in the foreseeable future. Until such a time, millions of trophy books—although no one can say how many there are—will remain as "prisoners of war," which is how the historian Patricia Kennedy Grimsted chooses to see it: "To-day, in Russia, there is no willingness to return books to the countries or families that were plundered. But we still have to know what books are still represented there from Europe's cultural inheritance, a monu-ment to the libraries that were destroyed and scattered as a conse-quence of the most terrible war in human history."[22]

◆ ◆ ◆

Christine Ellse is holding up a sheet of A4 paper on which she has writ-ten my name in large capital letters in green felt-tip pen. It is not really necessary, because we are alone in the little station in Cannock. Even calling it a station is a bit of an exaggeration, because it is more of a breather for the diesel train that has brought me here from Birming-ham. Cannock in Staffordshire, in central England, is an old mining community of terraced brick houses built back when coal mining was the lifeblood of the town. But after the Thatcher era there is not much left of it.

"They say we have the highest teenage pregnancy rate in England, but I don't know if that's true," says Ellse as she drives me the short distance to the family house in Cannock's "only good street," as she puts it with a laugh. Ellse, a lanky woman of about fifty with a delivery that one would describe in England as "witty," works as a music teacher at a nearby school.

Moments later Christine Ellse sits on a beige leather sofa, taking a deep breath. Outside lies the big garden, rustically unkempt. She holds the little olive-green book in both her hands—looks at it for a long time and then at me.

"Today I wrote on Facebook that I was waiting for this book. I tried to do some other things today, but it didn't go so very well. I've been waiting and waiting for this book to come back. And I've asked myself why, I mean I can't even read it; it's in German. I really just wanted it, I suppose. Although I'm a Christian I have always felt very Jewish. I've never been able to talk about the Holocaust without crying. I feel so connected to all this," says Ellse, opening the book and turning the pages for a while before she goes on.

"I'm very grateful for this book, because . . . I knew my English grandparents on my mother's side. They lived and then they died. It was normal, not having any grandparents on your father's side. Many people didn't, but there was something abnormal about this. I didn't even have a photograph of them. There was a hole there, an emotional vacuum, if you see what I mean. There was always something hanging midair, something unexpressed," Ellse says, squeezing the book.

"You know, my father never spoke about this. About the past, the war. But my aunt talked about it endlessly, all the time. She was the eldest of the siblings, so she was also the most 'German' of them. She coped with it by talking; my father coped with it by staying silent about it. I knew already when I was small that something horrible had happened. I knew my grandparents had died in the war. Then I found out they'd been gassed, but when you're a child you don't know what that means. It's just a story—you don't understand it. Then I learned they'd died at Auschwitz. Only after I grew up did I begin to understand and get a grip on it. It was very difficult when I found out they'd been murdered just ten days before the gas chambers were shut down. It was agonizing. I imagined myself sitting on that train, experiencing the cold and the hunger. And then straight into the gas chambers. I've never been able to get over it."

Christine Ellse stands up and goes to a table, where she's spread out folders and files on her family history. Most of this she has been given by the German historian Tomas Unglaube, who has done research on the Kobrak family. From one of the folders she gets out a family portrait, taken just before the Second World War. Richard Kobrak sits on the right—an elderly man with a round face, a small, neat mustache, his hands clasped together. His wife, Charlotte Kobrak, sits in the middle of the group, smiling at the camera, a beautiful woman with graying temples. Around them stand the three children of the couple, their daughters

Käthe Kobrak and Eva-Maria Kobrak. And then Christine Ellse's father, Helmut Kobrak, his hand resting on his father's shoulder. He was in his late teens when the photograph was taken.

The family had moved from Breslau to Berlin in 1927 when Richard Kobrak got a job in Berlin's city hall. The family was Christian and did not identify itself as Jewish. Fifty years after the war, the elder sister, Käthe Kobrak, wrote down her memories in a book, which Ellse shows me:

> The Sunday after Hitler had been made Chancellor our parents informed us about our Jewish background. None of them had been practising Jews. They had married in a church, had never observed any Jewish traditions, and taught us children Christian prayers. But their grandparents had been Jews, and so according to Hitler's definition they were also Jews, and for the same reason we were too.[23]

By 1933, Richard Kobrak had already been demoted to a less important position, but he was allowed to keep his job because he had been a frontline soldier in the German army during the First World War. He had been awarded the Iron Cross. But in 1936, once the Nuremberg Laws were introduced, Kobrak was forced into "retirement" at the age of forty-five. Käthe describes her family life in the 1930s, and how she grew increasingly isolated:

"I was popular at school but I was worried that if my friends found out they wouldn't want to socialize with me anymore. For that reason, I kept away from real friendships and I stopped visiting or inviting home my old friends. It could have been dangerous for them or their parents to socialize with Jews.[24]

"It's so tragic. The children didn't know they were Jewish until their parents told them. But I don't understand how they could have stayed. Why they didn't emigrate. My grandfather was an intelligent man, how could he make such a mistake? He was a high-ranking civil servant. Couldn't he see what was coming?"

In her recorded memories, Christine Ellse's aunt answers this very question, and her answer could to some extent be applicable to many of those who chose to stay in Nazi Germany:

"The reason was my father's fixedness: We are Germans, we belong here and Hitler (that Austrian demagogue!) is not going to drive us out. He and his deranged ideas will not last forever. It was a fatal error of judgement by my usually so wise and politically well-informed father."[25]

One can see for oneself in Käthe Kobrak's journal how the noose slowly tightens. Her father loses his job, friends are taken away by the Gestapo, and one by one the siblings lose any possibility of an education. As the children of a war veteran they have been allowed to keep attending classes, when other Jewish children have been kicked out. After Kristallnacht in November 1938 even Richard Kobrak had to admit that there was no future. By then it was almost too late. Just a few months before the outbreak of war, the family managed to get the children out. Their youngest daughter, Eva-Maria, was sent out on the Kindertransport, while Helmut and Käthe got out on work and student visas. Käthe, the last to depart, left in early August, one month before the declaration of war.

"By the time they realized what was about to happen it was too late. My grandparents invested everything they had to get the children out, but unfortunately they did not manage to leave themselves. They didn't have enough money for that."

After the war began, contact with their parents in Germany was sporadic. From time to time they managed to send a letter in which the children were given "piecemeal information." They learned that their parents had been evicted from their apartment and allotted a small room in an apartment in Charlottenburg, how their father's mother had disappeared, most likely deported to the "East," and how they had very little food. Käthe got one last postcard from Theresienstadt, where the parents were deported in 1943. After that there was silence. The little olive-green book, *Recht, Staat und Gesellschaft*, was most likely plundered from the family apartment in Berlin when the homes of deported Jews were being cleared. The path of the book from there to the Berliner Stadtbibliothek is unclear, but certainly it was just one of hundreds of thousands of books to be confiscated, sorted, and sold.

In England the sisters were placed with various foster families and continued their studies. But Christine Ellse's father, Helmut, who was nineteen years old, was detained by the authorities.

"When the war broke out he was arrested by the British. As far as they were concerned he was a 'German boy' and therefore an enemy. First he was deported to the Isle of Man, then he was put on a ship with other Germans who were going to be interned in Australia."

In the summer of 1940 he was secretly deported with 2,542 "enemy aliens" on the notorious ship *Dunera*, bound for Australia. Some two thousand of these "aliens" were Jewish refugees, men between twenty-six and sixty who had fled the Nazis in Europe. The fifty-seven-day journey on the ship was marked by the most terrible conditions:

> The ship was an over-populated hell-hole, the hammocks bumped into each other, and many of the men were forced to sleep on tables or the floor. Twenty men had to share a single bar of soap, ten men had one towel between them. . . . The latrines overflowed and dysentery spread on the ship. Physical abuse and beatings with rifle butts were daily occurrences. One refugee tried to go to the latrine at night, which was forbidden. He got a bayonet in the stomach.[26]

Helmut Kobrak, later released, tried to make his way back to Europe, but the ship he boarded was commandeered by the British.

"They threw him off in Bombay. He was twenty years old. He had no job, no money, and no home. He told me that he spent three nights walking the streets. Finally, he managed to find a job in a cotton factory, but he did not make it back to England until 1949. He never spoke about the voyage on the *Dunera* either; he was probably quite traumatized by it. I only found out about it when I started looking into it myself," says Ellse.

She tells me that the hardest thing for her father was never getting an education.

"I don't think he ever recovered from that. He was very gifted at school, but he had to walk away from it. He always dreamed of being a doctor. He was social, but he still had those Prussian ideals of justice and duty. I really could have imagined him as a doctor, but in the end he worked in the jewelry trade in London. He got his stimulation from reading. He was an absolute bookworm. Whenever we went anywhere on holiday he always brought a whole suitcase of books."

Christine Ellse's father, Helmut, died in 1994, and only then did she start looking into her family history. Over the last ten years, with the help of Tomas Unglaube, she has been trying to form a picture of her father and her grandparents' lives. The piles of files, folders, and loose scraps of paper from archives, all spread over her desk, are only part of the material she has managed to put together.

"This year, Tomas has sent parcel after parcel with materials: photocopies, studies, and documents. And then we have tried to put everything together, like pieces of a puzzle. I only knew some aspects of what happened to my father because there was so much he was unwilling to talk about. Only once did he open up. It was one Christmas when I was having problems. I was very upset and I was keeping myself to myself. Then he came to me and told me about Kristallnacht. He'd only been fourteen at the time and he went on the run to avoid being arrested. He spent all night walking around between one hiding place and another."

Dusk is falling and, after a few hours of talking, we have decided to resume the conversation tomorrow. Her husband, Mark Ellse, keeps us company in the wintry garden and later opens a bottle of Bordeaux. He's a talkative, retired principal shuffling about in his slippers and robe.

"Let's have the best wine. We have to celebrate."

Christine offers us venison casserole with roast potatoes and brussels sprouts. Before I retire to one of the guest rooms, she wants to show me her aunt Eva-Maria's paintings, which are hanging all over the house—expressionistic landscape paintings in bright colors, many with motifs from the South of France.

"She was the youngest, so she became very English. She was extremely anti-German. She never spent a single night in her life on German soil. She never wanted anything to do with Germany again."

Christine Ellse stands in the kitchen, immersed in a book with a wine-red binding, its pages covered from top to bottom in tiny, neat blue handwriting. It is her aunt Käthe's war diary.

"She kept writing it throughout the war. It starts on August 3, 1939, when she goes to England, and ends in March 1945," says Ellse, wiping her eyes with a napkin. She says she can never read it without crying, although it has become a little easier over the years. She has put her grandfather's olive-green book next to her, and I ask her why she wanted it.

"Because I don't have a single thing of his. I have my aunt's pictures. And I have a Persian rug with a hole in it, which I inherited. I have things from my father, but I have nothing from my grandparents. And I feel very emotionally attached to them. I don't know what I'll do with the book. I just want to look at it. Hold it. It was important to me," says Ellse.

She wants to read a passage from her aunt's diary, and she opens it on the page of the last entry, on March 31, 1945. After that she never wrote anything else, because she found out "the truth," Ellse explains, and then starts reading:

The Russians are occupying the whole of Eastern Prussia and almost all of Silesia. They are on Austrian territory and deep inside Czechoslovakia. This really looks like the end—but can it really be so? Do we dare hope? Can this really be true? And where will this leave you? A few days ago we heard a description of life in Theresienstadt—which by and large was consoling. We heard that thousands of people from the camp had been released into Switzerland—were even more released later? Will you be found to be among them? So many questions, so much anxiety—and the only answer is "wait and see." As Louis Palmer says at school: "Keep believing." Tomorrow is Easter, and that is all we can do—carry on hoping.[27]

# Acknowledgments

I have never had more people to thank. So many individuals have generously contributed both their knowledge and time. For this reason, I would humbly like to offer my thanks to all those who have made this book possible, particularly the librarians, archivists, and researchers who have received me, opened up their collections and archives, and generously shared their research, opinions, and contacts.

I want to thank the librarians and researchers who took me in during my visits to Germany, not least Sebastian Finsterwalder and Detlef Bockenkamm at the Zentral- und Landesbibliothek in Berlin, whose devoted and tireless work to return the library's hundreds of thousands of plundered books I greatly admire. I also want to thank the art historian Uwe Hartmann from the Arbeitsstelle für Provenienzforschung in Berlin; as well as Michael Knoche, Rüdiger Haufe, and Heike Krokowski at the Herzogin Anna Amalia Bibliothek in Weimar, and Stephan Kellner at the Bayerische Staatsbibliothek in Munich.

In the Netherlands, I want to give particular thanks to Frits J. Hoogewoud, previously the librarian of Bibliotheca Rosenthaliana, whose investigations into the plunder of Amsterdam's Jewish libraries have been invaluable—and who has also offered many important viewpoints on my work. Further, I wish to thank Wout Visser at the Bibliotheca Rosenthaliana, Heide Warncke at Ets Haim, and Huub Sanders at the Internationaal Instituut voor Sociale. Great thanks are also due to Jac Piepenbrock and Theo Walter at the Cultureel Masonniek Centrum, who initiated me into the secrets of the Freemasons and the exciting history of Bibliotheca Klossiana.

In Paris, I would like to thank the chief curator and archivist of Alliance Israélite Universelle's library, Jean-Claude Kuperminc, who offered me the opportunity to return for several visits. A warm thanks also goes out to the custodian and librarian of Bibliothèque Russe Tourguéniev, Hélène Kaplan, who generously provided me with an unforgettable meeting and shared the tragic fate of her library. My sincere thanks also goes to Witold Zahorski at the Bibliothèque Polonaise de Paris and Marek Sroka, historian and librarian at the University of Illinois, who contributed with supporting material on the Polish libraries.

For assistance during my work in Rome, I wish to thank Dario Tedeschi, who led the Italian governmental commission to recover the lost Biblioteca Comunità Israelitica, and Gisèle Lèvy at the Centro Bibliografico, who deepened my understanding of the thrilling and rich literary history of the Italian Jews.

In Thessaloniki, I want to thank Erika Perahia Zemour at the Jewish Museum, also the independent researcher Paul Isaac Hagouel, who generously allowed me to partake of his unparalleled research material on the city's Jewish history. And, in Vilnius, I would like to extend special thanks to Faina Kuklainsky, the chief of Lithuania's Jewish congregation, who received me with open arms.

In the Czech Republic, I owe a great deal to the librarian Michal Bušek, who welcomed me to the Jewish Museum in Prague and whose investigations into the library units in Theresienstadt were exceptionally valuable. Thanks also to Tomáš Fedorovič at Terezín's historical section and Renata Košťálová at the Documentation Centre, who added insights into the plundering operation in Czechoslovakia during the Second World War.

I would like to thank those whose stories, for various reasons, never found a place in the book. Particular thanks must go to Dr. Christine Sauer at the Stadtbibliothek im Bildungscampus in Nuremburg, Christina Köstner-Pemsel at the Fachbereichsbibliothek Zeitgeschichte Universität in Vienna, and Margot Werner at the Österreichische Nationalbibliothek.

I would like to extend warm thanks to Christine Ellse, grandchild of Richard Kobrak, who welcomed me into her home in Cannock outside Birmingham and allowed me to share in her family history.

An enormous debt is owed to Patricia Grimsted Kennedy, research associate at the Ukrainian Research Institute at Harvard University and an honorary Fellow of the International Institute of Social History (Amsterdam). No one has done more to illuminate and detail the libraries and archives that were dispersed during the Second World War. The essays, articles, and contacts she contributed were of huge importance to me. Of equal importance were her many books on the subject, which are required reading for anyone wishing to go more deeply into this complicated question. I would especially recommend *Trophies of War and Empire: The Archival Heritage of Ukraine, World War II, and the International Politics of Restitution* (2001), and *Returned from Russia: Nazi Archival Plunder in Western Europe and Recent Restitution Issues* (2013).

I also wish to thank those who have worked to ensure that the process has resulted in a book: My publisher Norstedts, and particularly my publisher Stefan Skog, who believed in the book from our very first meeting. Also my two excellent editors, Ingemar Karlsson and Malin Tynderfeldt.

Last but not least, I would like to thank those who have in a variety of ways assisted with views and fact-checking. Thanks to the writer Artur Szulcs for wide-ranging remarks on the book. Thanks to Andreas Önnerfors, university reader at the Department of Literature and the History of Ideas at Gothenburg University, for his valuable insights into the history of the Freemasons. And thanks to Anders Burman, lecturer in the History of Ideas at Södertörns högskola; Er Tängerstad, teacher at the Department of History and Contempor Studies at Södertörns högskola; and Staffan Lundgren, publisher at Axl Books and editor of SITE, who all offered important insights into Weimar Classicism, German Idealism, and Goethe.

For grants and support that in various ways have made this project possible, I wish to thank Författarfonden, Natur & Kultur, and the San Michele Foundation.

*Anders Rydell, June 2015*

# Notes

## 1: A Fire That Consumes the World: Berlin

1. Todd Kontje, *The Cambridge Introduction to Thomas Mann*, Cambridge University Press, 2011, pp. 73–74.
2. E. Leonidas Hill, "The Nazi Attack on 'Un-German' Literature, 1933–1945," p. 12, in *The Holocaust and the Book* (ed. Jonathan Rose), Amherst: University of Massachusetts Press, 2001.
3. *Völkischer Beobachter*, April 14, 1933.
4. Hill, "The Nazi Attack on 'Un-German' Literature, 1933–1945," p. 14.
5. Rebecca Knuth, *Libricide: The Regime-Sponsored Destruction of Books and Libraries in the Twentieth Century*, Westport, CT: Praeger, 2003, p. 97.
6. Hill, "The Nazi Attack on 'Un-German' Literature, 1933–1945," p. 14.
7. Jan-Pieter Barbian, *The Politics of Literature in Nazi Germany: Books in the Media Dictatorship*, New York: Bloomsbury Academic, 2013, p. 169.
8. Jay Worthington, "Mein Royalties," *Cabinet* issue 10, 2003. http://www.cabinet magazine.org/issues/10/mein_royalties.php.
9. Hill, "The Nazi Attack on 'Un-German' Literature, 1933–1945," p. 16.
10. Joseph Goebbels, *Völkischer Beobachter*, May 12, 1933.
11. Stefan Zweig, *Varlden av i gar*, trans. Hugo Hultenberg, Stockholm: Ersatz, 2011, p. 395.
12. Guy Stern, "The Burning of the Books in Nazi Germany, 1933: The American Response," *Simon Wiesenthal Annual*, vol. 2, ch. 5.
13. *Holocaust Encyclopedia*, "Immediate American Responses to the Nazi Book Burnings," https://www.ushmm.org/wlc/en/article.php?ModuleId=10007169, United States Holocaust Memorial Museum, 2014.
14. Christoph Daxelmüller, "Nazi Concept of Culture and the Erasure of Jewish Folklore," p. 79, *The Nazification of an Academic Discipline: Folklore in the Third Reich*, Bloomington: University of Indiana Press, 1994.

## 2: Ghosts at Berliner Stadtbibliothek: Berlin

1. Rudi Joelsohn, memorial book. https://www.bundesarchiv.de/gedenkbuch /intro.html.en.
2. Akt nummer 512–515 och 515/1. Inventarienummer C Rep. 120. Landesarchiv, Berlin.

3. Sebastian Finsterwalder and Peter Prölls, "Tracing the Rightful Owners: Nazi-Looted Books in the Central and Regional Library of Berlin," in 'The West' Versus 'The East' or The United Europe?, Proceedings of an international academic conference held in Poděbrady on October 8–9, 2013, ed. Mečislav Borák. https://socialhistory.org/sites/default/files/docs/grimsted-podebradyessay13 .pdf. Documentation Centre for Property Transfers of Cultural Assets of WWII Victims, Prague, 2014. pp. 92–102.

4. Melonie Magruder, "A Holocaust Survivor's Childhood Book Comes Home," *Malibu Times*, July 22, 2009.

5. Michael Sontheimer, "Retracing the Nazi Book Theft: German Libraries Hold Thousands of Looted Volumes," *Der Spiegel*, October 24, 2008. http:// www.spiegel.de/international/germany/retracing-the-nazi-book-theft -german-libraries-hold-thousands-of-looted-volumes-a-586379-2.html.

6. Heike Pudler and Michaela Scheibe, "Provenienzforschung/-erschließung an der Staatsbibliothek zu Berlin," *Bibliothek Forschung und Praxis*, vol. 34, April 2010, pp. 51–56.

7. Cornelia Briel, *Beschlagnahmt, erpresst, erbeutet. NS-Raubgut, Reichstauschstelle und Preusische Staatsbibliothek zwischen 1933 und 1945*, Berlin: Akademie Verlag, 2013.

8. Rebecca Knuth, *Libricide: The Regime-Sponsored Destruction of Books and Libraries in the Twentieth Century*, Westport, CT: Praeger, 2003, p. 99.

9. Briel, *Beschlagnahmt, erpresst, erbeutet*.

10. Sontheimer, "Retracing the Nazi Book Theft."

11. Regine Dehnel, "Perpetrators, Victims, and Art: The National Socialists' Campaign of Pillage," *Eurozine*, September 26, 2007. http://www.eurozine .com/articles/2007-09-26-dehnel-en.html.

12. Knuth, *Libricide*, p. 99.

13. Ibid.

14. Michael Dobbs, "Epilogue to a Story of Nazi-Looted Books; Library of Congress Trove of War Propaganda Included Many Stolen Jewish Works," *Washington Post*, January 5, 2000.

15. Sontheimer, "Retracing the Nazi Book Theft."

## 3: Goethe's Oak: Weimar

1. White House, Office of the Press Secretary, "Remarks by President Obama, German Chancellor Merkel, and Elie Wiesel at Buchenwald Concentration Camp," June 5, 2009. https://www.whitehouse.gov/the-press-office/remarks -president-obama-german-chancellor-merkel-and-elie-wiesel-buchenwald -concent.

2. David A. Hackett (ed.), *Der Buchenwald-Report: Bericht uber das Konzentrationslager Buchenwald bei Weimar*, Munich: C. H. Beck, 2010, p. 188.

3. Klaus Neumann, *Shifting Memories: The Nazi Past in the New Germany*, Ann Arbor: University of Michigan Press, 2000, p. 179.

4. Ernst Wiechert, *I dodens skog*, trans. Irma Nordvang, pp. 119–120. Stockholm: Wahlström & Widstrand, 1946.

5. Prisøner no. 4935, "Über die Goethe-Eiche im Lager Buchenwald." *Neue Zürcher Zeitung*, November 4, 2006. http://www.nzz.ch/articleEMAWX-1.73138.

6. Johann Gottlieb Fichte, *Fichte: Addresses to the German Nation*, Cambridge University Press, 2009, p. 10.

7. Paul Zanker, *The Mask of Socrates: The Image of the Intellectual in Antiquity*, Berkeley: University of California Press, 1996, p. 4.

8. Wolf Lepenies, *The Seduction of Culture in German History*, Princeton University Press, 2006, p. 157.

9. Peter Gay, *Weimarkulturen 1918–1933*, trans. Per Lennart Mansson, Nova, Sweden: Nya Doxa, 2003, pp. 22–23.

10. Ibid., p. 24.

11. Ingemar Karlsson and Arne Ruth, *Samhället som teater*, Stockholm: Liber, 1983, p. 56.

12. Karl-Heinz Schoeps, *Literature and Film in the Third Reich*, Rochester, NY: Camden House, 2003, pp. 3–6.

13. Manfred Görtemaker, *Thomas Mann und die Politik*, Frankfurt: Fischer Verlag, 2005, p. 51.

14. E. Alan Steinweis, "Weimar Culture and the Rise of National Socialism," *Central European History*, vol. 24, no. 4, Cambridge University Press, 1991, pp. 402–14.

15. W. Daniel Wilson, "Goethe and the Nazis," *Times Literary Supplement*, March 14, 2014.

16. Ibid.

17. Inez Hedges, *Framing Faust: Twentieth-Century Cultural Struggles*, Carbondale: Southern Illinois University Press, 2009, p. 73.

18. Wilson, "Goethe and the Nazis."

19. Jürgen Weber, ". . . because Herr Goldschmidt is a Jew of course." *Arsprototo*, issue 1 (2013). http://www.kulturstiftung.de/category/arsprototo/jahrgang-2013/ausgabe-12013/].

20. Ibid.

21. Ibid.

22. The Anna Amalia Library's predecessor before the war was the Central Library of German Classical Literature.

## 4: Himmler's Library: Munich

1. Hermann Kurzke, *Thomas Mann: Life as a Work of Art: A Biography*, Princeton University Press, 2001, p. 364.

2. Chris McNab, *The SS, 1923–1945: The Essential Facts and Figures for Himmler's Stormtroopers*, London: Amber Books, 2009, p. 18.

3. Roderick Stackelberg, *Hitler's Germany: Origins, Interpretations, Legacies*, London; New York: Routledge, 1999, p. 116.

4. Werner Schroeder, "Bücherraub. Strukturen des Bücherraubs: Die Bibliotheken des Reichssicherheitshauptamtes (RSHA), ihr Aufbau und ihr Verbleib," *Zeitschrift für Bibliothekswesen und Bibliographie* vol. 51, 2004, pp. 316–324.

5. Ibid. p. 316.

6. Jan-Pieter Barbian, *The Politics of Literature in Nazi Germany: Books in the Media Dictatorship*, New York: Bloomsbury Academic, 2013, p. 112.

7. Schroeder, "Bücherraub," pp. 316–324.

8. Michael Berenbaum, *The World Must Know*, Baltimore: Johns Hopkins University Press, 2009, p. 49.

9. Alan Confino, *A World Without Jews: The Nazi Imagination from Persecution to Genocide*, New Haven, CT: Yale University Press, 2014, pp. 115–117.

10. Patricia Kennedy Grimsted, "Restitution of Confiscated Art Works: Wish or Reality?" Proceedings of the International Academic Conference held in Liberec on October 24–26, 2007, Tilia, 2008, p. 131.

11. Schroeder, "Bücherraub," pp. 316–324.

12. Grimsted, "Restitution of Confiscated Art Works: Wish or Reality?" p. 128.

13. Ibid., p. 132.

14. Ibid., p. 144.

## 5: A Warrior Against Jerusalem: Chiemsee

1. "Models for a Nazi party school on the Chiemsee and for buildings on the Adolf Hitler-Platz in Weimar," c. 1939, Prints and Photographs Division, LOT 8613 (G) [P&P], Library of Congress, Washington, DC. https://www.loc.gov/item/2005683331/.

2. Nuremberg Trial Proceedings, vol. 7, February 6, 1946. The Avalon Project.

3. Ingemar Karlsson and Arne Ruth, *Samhallet som teater*, Stockholm: Liber, 1983, p. 82.

4. Jan-Pieter Barbian, *The Politics of Literature in Nazi Germany: Books in the Media Dictatorship*, Bloomsbury Academic, 2013, p. 117.

5. Joachim Fest, *The Face of the Third Reich*, New York: Pantheon Books, 1970, p. 163.

6. Alfred Rosenberg, *Pest in Russland*, Munich: Franz Eher, 1938, p. 16.

7. Robert Cecil, *The Myth of the Master Race*, London: B. T. Batsford, 1972, p. 17.

8. Alfred Rosenberg, *The Myth of the Twentieth Century*, CreateSpace Independent Publishing Platform, 2011, p. 65.

9. Karlsson and Ruth, *Samhallet som teater*, p. 90.

10. Ibid., p. 93.

11. Cecil, *The Myth of the Master Race*, p. 17.

12. Ibid., pp. 20–24.

13. Alfred Rosenberg, *Dietrich Eckart: Ein Vermaechtnis*, Munich: Franz Eher, 1928, p. 45.

14. Albert Speer, *Inside the Third Reich*, London: Orion Books, 1970, p. 96.
15. Ernst Piper, *Alfred Rosenberg: Hitlers Chefideologe*, Munich: Karl Blessing Verlag, 2005.
16. Volker Ullrich, *Adolf Hitler: Die Jahres des Aufstiegs*, Frankfurt: Fischer Verlag, 2013.
17. Adolf Hitler, *Mein Kampf D. 1, En uppgorelse*, trans. Anders Qviding, Stockholm: Hägglunds förlag, 2010, p. 322.
18. *Holocaust Encyclopedia*, "Protocols of the Elders of Zion," United States Holocaust Memorial Museum, 2014, www.ushmm.org/wlc/en/article.php?ModuleId-10007058.
19. Rosenberg, *The Myth of the Twentieth Century*, p. 66.
20. Ibid., p. 201.
21. Ibid., p. 15.
22. Ibid., p. 381.
23. Alfred Rosenberg, *Gestaltung der Idee*, Munich: Zentralverlag der NSDAP, 1943, p. 53.
24. Rosenberg, *The Myth of the Twentieth Century*, p. 4.
25. Kristie Macrakis, *Surviving the Swastika: Scientific Research in Nazi Germany*, Oxford University Press, 1993, p. 79.
26. Philipp Lenard, "Great Men of Science," p. 105, *Physics and National Socialism: An Anthology of Primary Sources*, Basel: Birkhäuser, 1996.
27. Macrakis, *Surviving the Swastika*, p. 75.
28. Cecil, *The Myth of the Master Race*, p. 128.
29. Ibid., p. 154.
30. Franz Albert Heinen, *The Ordensburg Vogelsang*, Berlin: Christoph Links Verlag, 2014, p. 17.
31. Frank H. W. Edler, "Alfred Baeumler on Hölderlin and the Greeks: Reflections on the Heidegger-Baeumler Relationship," *Janushead*, vol. 1, no. 3, 1999, part 1.
32. Ibid., vol. 2, no. 2, 1999, part 12.
33. Simon Gerd, *Chronologie Hohe Schule der NSDAP*, Universität Tübingen, 2008.

## 6: Consolation for the Tribulations of Israel: Amsterdam

1. Jonathan Israel, *Conflicts of Empires: Spain, the Low Countries and the Struggle for World Supremacy*, New York: Bloomsbury Academic, 2003, p. 324.
2. Brian Pearce and A. D. Lublinskaya, *French Absolutism: The Crucial Phase, 1620–1629*, Cambridge University Press, 2008, p. 118.
3. Harm Den Boer, "Amsterdam as Locus of Iberian Printing in the Seventeenth and Eighteenth Centuries," p. 87, in *The Dutch Intersection: The Jews and the Netherlands in Modern History* (ed. Yosef Kaplan), Leiden; Boston: Brill, 2008.
4. K. Adri Offenberg (ed.), *Bibliotheca Rosenthaliana: Treasures of Jewish Booklore*, Amsterdam University Press, 2009, pp 4–20.

5. J. Frits Hoogewoud, "An Introduction to H. de la Fontaine Verwey's Bibliotheca Rosenthaliana During the German Occupation," *Omnia in Eo: Studies on Jewish Books and Libraries in Honor of Adri Offenberg Celebrating the 125th Anniversary of the Bibliotheca Rosenthaliana in Amsterdam*, Leuven, Belgium: Peeters, 2006, p. 55.

6. Jaap Kloosterman and Jan Lucassen, "Working for Labour: Three Quarters of a Century of Collecting at the IISH," in *Rebels with a Cause: Five Centuries of Social History Collected by International Institute of Social History*, Amsterdam: Aksant, 2010, p. 17.

7. Simon Gerd, *Chronologie Hohe Schule der NSDAP*, Universität Tübingen, 2008.

8. Ibid.

9. Michael Curtis, *Verdict on Vichy: Power and Prejudice in the Vichy France Regime*, New York: Arcade, 2003, p. 149.

10. Patricia Kennedy Grimsted, "Reconstructing the Record of Nazi Cultural Plunder," Amsterdam: IISH, 2011, p. 30.

11. Kloosterman and Lucassen, *Working for Labour: Three Quarters of a Century of Collecting at the IISH*, p. 14.

12. Matthew Battles, *Library: An Unquiet History*, New York; London: Norton, 2003, p. 64.

13. Meyuhas Alisa Ginio, *Jews, Christians, and Muslims in the Mediterranean World After 1492*, London; New York: Routledge, 1992, p. 8.

14. Frits J. Hoogewoud, "The Looting of a Private and a Public Library of Judaica and Hebraica in Amsterdam During World War II. The Cases of Ets Haim/Livraria Montezinos and Bibliotheca Rosenthaliana," in *Jewish Studies in a New Europe*, Copenhagen: C.A. Reitel A/S International Publishers, 1998, pp. 379–390.

15. Ibid.

16. Ibid.

17. Alan E. Steinweis, *Studying the Jew: Scholarly Antisemitism in Nazi Germany*, Cambridge, MA: Harvard University Press, 2009, pp. 115–116.

18. Frits J. Hoogewoud, *Dutch Jewish Ex Libris Found Among Looted Books in the Offenbach Archival Depot* (1946). Leiden; Boston: Brill, 1998.

19. Grimsted, "Reconstructing the Record of Nazi Cultural Plunder," p. 253.

20. E. Leonidas Hill: "The Nazi Attack on 'Un-German' Literature, 1933–1945," p. 30, in *The Holocaust and the Book*, Amherst: University of Massachusetts Press, 2001.

21. Frits J. Hoogewoud, "Omnia in Eo: Studies on Jewish Books and Libraries in Honour of Adri Offenberg Celebrating the 125th Anniversary of the Bibliotheca Rosenthaliana in Amsterdam," pp. 50–51.

22. *Holocaust Encyclopedia*, "Westerbork," United States Holocaust Memorial Museum, 2014, www.ushmm.org/wlc/en/article.php?ModuleId-10005217.

23. Hoogewoud, "Omnia in Eo," p. 56.

24. Levie Jehuda (Louis) Hirschel: www.dutchjewry.org.

## 7: The Hunt for the Secrets of the Freemasons: The Hague

1. Christopher Campbell Thomas, "Compass, Square and Swastika: Freemasonry in the Third Reich," thesis, Texas A&M, 2011, p. 55.

2. Paul M. Bessel, "Bigotry and the Murder of Freemasonry," www.bessel.org/naziartI.htm.

3. *Holocaust Encyclopedia*, "Freemasonry Under the Nazi Regime," United States Holocaust Memorial Museum, 2014, www.ushmm.org/wlc/en/article/php?ModuleId-10007187.

4. Wendy Lower, *Hitler's Furies: German Women in the Nazi Killing Fields*, Boston: Houghton Mifflin Harcourt, 2013, p. 34.

5. Jimmy Koppen, "The Conspiracy of Freemasons, Jews and Communists: An Analysis of the French and German Nationalist Discourse (1918–1940)," thesis, Free University, Brussels, 2009.

6. Jimmy Koppen, "The Anti-Masonic Writings of General Erich Ludendorff," thesis, Free University, Brussels, 2010.

7. Ibid.

8. Ibid.

9. Ibid.

10. Leo XIII, "The Letter 'Humanum Genus' of the Pope, Leo XIII, against Free-Masonry and the Spirit of the Age, April 20, 1884." Trans. Albert Pike. Charleston: Grand Orient of Charleston, 1884.

11. *Holocaust Encyclopedia*, "Freemasonry," United States Holocaust Memorial Museum, 2014, www.ushmm.org/wlc/en/article.php?ModuleId-10007186.

12. Koppen, *The Conspiracy of Freemasons, Jews and Communists*.

13. Alfred Rosenberg, *The Myth of the Twentieth Century*, CreateSpace Independent Publishing Platform, 2011, p. 116.

14. Thomas, *Compass, Square and Swastika*, p. 134.

15. Bessel, "Bigotry and the Murder of Freemasonry."

16. Thomas, *Compass, Square and Swastika*, p. 134.

17. István Fodor, et al. (eds.), *Spoils of War*, No. 3. Bremeb: Koordinierungsstelle der Länder für die Rückführung von Kulturgütern beim Senator für Bildung, Wissenschaft, Kunst und Sport, No. 3, 1996.

18. Patricia Kennedy Grimsted, "Reconstructing the Record of Nazi Cultural Plunder," p. 27.

19. Fodor et al., *Spoils of War*, p. 18.

20. Cultural Masonic Centre Prins Fredrik: Archives, Library and Museum of the Grand East of the Netherlands, p. 6.

21. Irvine Wiest, "Freemasonry and the Nuremberg Trials. A Study in Nazi Persecution." Paper presented at at the Fifteenth Annual Consistory of the Society of Blue Friars, Washington, DC, February 1959.

22. Ibid.

23. Ibid.

## 8: Lenin Worked Here: Paris

1. Jean-Marc Dreyfus and Sarah Gensburger, *Nazi Labour Camps in Paris: Auster-litz, Levitan, Bassano, July 1943–August 1944*, New York: Berghahn Books, 2011, pp. 9–11.
2. Ibid.
3. Sem C. Sutter, "The Lost Jewish Libraries of Vilna and the Frankfurt Institut zur Erforschung der Judenfrage," p. 221, in *Lost Libraries* (ed. James Raven). New York: Palgrave Macmillan, 2004.
4. Patricia Kennedy Grimsted, "The Road to Minsk for Western 'Trophy' Books: Twice Plundered but Not Yet Home from the War," *Libraries & Culture*, vol. 39, no. 4, 2004.
5. Gilles Rozier, "The Bibliothèque Medem: Eighty Years Serving Yiddish Culture," *Judaica Librarianship*, 2004, pp. 4–15.
6. E. Leonidas Hill, "The Nazi Attack on 'Un-German' Literature, 1933–1945," p. 31, *The Holocaust and the Book* (ed. Jonathan Rose), Amherst: University of Massachusetts Press, 2001.
7. Michael Curtis, *Verdict on Vichy: Power and Prejudice in the Vichy France Regime*, New York: Arcade, 2003, pp. 148–149.
8. James Cowan, "Sebald's Austerlitz and the Great Library," in *W. G. Sebald: Schreiben ex patria* (ed. Gerhard Fischer), Amsterdam: Rodopi, 2009.
9. Rebecca Knuth, *Libricide: The Regime-Sponsored Destruction of Books and Libraries in the Twentieth Century*, Westport, CT: Praeger, 2003, pp. 92–93.
10. Sutter, "The Lost Jewish Libraries of Vilna and the Frankfurt Institut zur Erforschung der Judenfrage," p. 222.
11. Patricia Kennedy Grimsted, "Reconstructing the Record of Nazi Cultural Plunder," Amsterdam: IISH, 2011, p. 30.
12. John Glad, *Conversations in Exile: Russian Writers Abroad*, Durham, NC: Duke University Press Books, 1992, pp. 271–273.
13. Robert Service, *Lenin: A Biography*, London: Pan, 2010, p. 189.
14. Patricia Kennedy Grimsted, "The Odyssey of the Turgenev Library from Paris, 1940–2002. Books as Victims and Trophies of War," Amsterdam: IISH, 2003, p. 24.
15. Avraham Greenbaum, "Bibliographical Essay," p. 381, in *Pogroms: Anti-Jewish Violence in Modern Russian History*. Cambridge University Press, 2004.
16. Patricia Kennedy Grimsted, "The Odyssey of the Petliura Library and the Records of the Ukrainian National Republic During World War II." Text from *Cultures and Nations of Central and Eastern Europe in Honor of Roman Szporluk* (ed. Zvi Gitelman), Cambridge, MA: Harvard Ukrainian Research Institute, 2000, pp. 181–208.
17. Nina Berberova, "The Disappearance of the Turgenev Library," trans. Patsy Southgate, *Grand Street*, no. 41, 1992, pp. 94–101.

18. Ibid.
19. Grimsted, "The Odyssey of the Turgenev Library from Paris, 1940–2002," pp. 36–37.
20. Hanna Laskarzewska, *La Bibliothèque Polonaise de Paris: Les Peregrinations de Collections dans les Annees 1940–1992*, Paris: Bibliothèque Polonaise, 2004.
21. Sem C. Sutter, "Polish Books in Exile: Cultural Booty Across Two Continents, Through Two Wars," pp. 144–145, *The Holocaust and the Book* (ed. Jonathan Rose), Amherst: University of Massachusetts Press, 2001.
22. Ibid., pp.144–147.
23. Ibid., p. 148
24. Laskarzewska, *La Bibliotheque Polonaise de Paris*.
25. Ibid.
26. Astrid Eckert, *The Struggle for the Files: The Western Allies and the Return of German Archives After the Second World War*, Cambridge University Press, pp. 99–100.
27. Grimsted, "The Odyssey of the Petliura Library and the Records of the Ukrainian National Republic During World War II," pp. 181–208.
28. Grimsted, "The Odyssey of the Turgenev Library from Paris, 1940–2002," pp. 38–34.

## 9: The Lost Library: Rome

1. Wayne A .Wiegand and Donald G. Davis Jr., *Encyclopedia of Library History*, New York: Routledge, 2015, p. 323.
2. Male circumcision.
3. Stanislao G. Pugliese, "The Book of the Roman Ghetto under the Nazi Occupation," p. 52, *The Holocaust and the Book* (ed. Jonathan Rose), Amherst: University of Massachusetts Press, 2001.
4. Zvi Ben-Dor Benite, *The Ten Lost Tribes: A World History*, Oxford University Press, 2009, pp. 17–18.
5. Salah Asher, "A Matter of Quotation," pp. 170–78, *The Italia Judaica Jubilee Conference* (eds. Shlomo Simonsohn, et al.), Leiden; Boston: Brill, 2012.
6. Jacob D'Ancona, *The City of Light*, New York: Citadel, 2003, pp. 23–24.
7. Matthew Fishburn, *Burning Books*, New York: Palgrave Macmillan, 2008, p. 4.
8. Kenneth R. Stow, "The Burning of the Talmud in 1553, in the Light of Sixteenth Century Catholic Attitudes Toward the Talmud," *Bibliothèque d'Humanisme et Renaissance* 34, 1972, pp. 435–439.
9. David Berger, "Cum Nimis Absurdum and the Conversion of the Jews," *Jewish Quarterly Review*, pp. 41–49. New Series 70, 1979.
10. Kenneth R. Stow, *Popes, Church, and Jews in the Middle Ages: Confrontation and Response*, Aldershot, England: Ashgate, 2007, p. 51.
11. Pugliese, "The Book of the Roman Ghetto Under the Nazi Occupation," p. 51.

12. Seth Jerchower, "Judeo-Italian." The Jewish Language Research Website, Bar-Ilan University. http://www.jewish-languages.org/judes-italian.html.

13. Pugliese, "The Book of the Roman Ghetto Under the Nazi Occupation," p. 52.

14. Robert Katz, *Black Sabbath: A Journey Through a Crime Against Humanity*, London: Arthur Barker, 1969, p. 120.

15. Commission for recovery of the bibliographic patrimony of the Jewish Community of Rome stolen in 1943, *Report on the Activities of the Commission for Recovery of the Bibliographic Patrimony of the Jewish Community of Rome Stolen in 1943*. Translated by Lenore Rosenberg. Governo Italiano, 2009. p. 15. http://presidenza.governo.it/USRI/confessioni/doc/rapporto_finale _eng.pdf.

16. Pugliese, "The Book of the Roman Ghetto Under the Nazi Occupation," p. 48.

17. Susan Zuccotti, *The Italians and the Holocaust: Persecution, Rescue, and Survival*, Lincoln: University of Nebraska Press, 1987, p. 33.

18. Michele Sarfatti and Anne C. Tedeschi, *The Jews in Mussolini's Italy: From Equality to Persecution*, Madison: University of Wisconsin Press, 2006, p. 179.

19. Ibid., pp. 186–187.

20. Pugliese, "The Book of the Roman Ghetto Under the Nazi Occupation," p. 52.

21. *Report on the Activities of the Commission for Recovery of the Bibliographic Patrimony of the Jewish Community of Rome Stolen in 1943*, p. 30.

22. Pugliese, "The Book of the Roman Ghetto Under the Nazi Occupation," p. 52.

23. Ibid., p. 52.

24. Robert G. Weisbord and Wallace P. Sillanpoa, *The Chief Rabbi, the Pope, and the Holocaust: An Era in Vatican-Jewish Relations*, New Brunswick, NJ: Transaction, 2011, pp. 61–66.

25. Joshua D. Zimmerman, *Jews in Italy Under Fascist and Nazi Rule, 1922–1945*, Cambridge University Press, 2005, p. 231.

## 10: Fragments of a People: Thessaloniki

1. Mark Mazower, *Salonica, City of Ghosts: Christians, Muslims and Jews 1430–1950*, New York: Vintage Books, 2006, p. 398.

2. Leon Saltiel, "Dehumanizing the Dead: The Destruction of Thessaloniki's Jewish Cemetery in the Light of New Sources," *Yad Vashem Studies*, vol. 42, no. 1, 2014, pp. 11–46.

3. Ibid.

4. Mazower, *Salonica, City of Ghosts*, p. 398.

5. Saltiel, "Dehumanizing the Dead," pp. 11–46.

6. Mazower, *Salonica, City of Ghosts*, p. 398.

7. Ibid., p. 50.

8. Gilles Veinstein, *Salonique 1850–1918: La "ville des Juifs" et le reveil des Balkans*, Paris: Editions Autrement, 1992, pp. 42–45.

9. Mazower, *Salonica, City of Ghosts*, p. 48.

10. Ibid., 36–54.

11. Yitzchak Kerem, "The Confiscation of Jewish Books in Salonika in the Holocaust," p. 60, *The Holocaust and the Book* (ed. Jonathan Rose), Amherst: University of Massachusetts Press, 2001.

12. Leah Aini, "No Other Jews Like Them," *Haaretz*, August 12, 2010.

13. Mazower, *Salonica, City of Ghosts*, p. 298.

14. Ibid., pp. 298–301.

15. Kerem, "The Confiscation of Jewish Books in Salonika in the Holocaust," p. 300.

16. Mazower, *Salonica, City of Ghosts*, p. 60.

17. Vilma Hastaoglou-Martinidis and Rena Molho, *Jewish Sites in Thessaloniki: Brief History and Guide*, Athens: Lacabettus Press, 2009, p. 18.

18. Kerem, "The Confiscation of Jewish Books in Salonika in the Holocaust," p. 59.

19. Aini, "No Other Jews Like Them," *Haaretz*, August 12, 2010.

20. Kerem, "The Confiscation of Jewish Books in Salonika in the Holocaust," p. 60.

21. Mazower, *Salonica, City of Ghosts*, p. 394.

22. Kerem, "The Confiscation of Jewish Books in Salonika in the Holocaust," p. 62.

23. Ibid.

24. Mazower, *Salonica, City of Ghosts*, p. 400.

25. Steven Bowman (ed.), *The Holocaust in Salonika: Eyewitness Accounts*, New York: Bloch, 2002 p. 160.

26. Paul Isaac Hagouel, *History of the Jews of Thessaloniki and the Holocaust*, West Chester: University of Pennsylvania Press, 2006, p. 17.

27. Bowman, *The Holocaust in Salonika*, p. 166.

28. Steven Bowman, *The Agony of Greek Jews, 1940–1945*, Stanford University Press, 2009, pp. 104–108.

29. Primo Levi, *If This Is a Man*, New York: The Orion Press, 1959, p. 80.

30. Braha Rivlin, "Retorno del Inferno," *Aki Yerushalayim*, no. 49–50, 1995.

31. Kerem, "The Confiscation of Jewish Books in Salonika in the Holocaust," p. 63.

## 11: The Mass Grave Is a Paper Mill: Vilnius

1. David E. Fishman, "Embers Plucked from the Fire: The Rescue of Jewish Cultural Treasures from Vilna," p. 69, *The Holocaust and the Book* (ed. Jonathan Rose), Amherst: University of Massachusetts Press, 2001.

2. Ibid., pp. 66–67.

3. Shivaun Woolfson, *Holocaust Legacy in Post-Soviet Lithuania: People, Places and Objects*, London: Bloomsbury, 2014, p. 34.

4. Susanne Marten-Finnis, *Vilna as a Centre of the Modern Jewish Press, 1840–1928: Aspirations, Challenges, and Progress*, Oxford; New York: Peter Lang, 2014, pp. 59–60.

5. Cecile Esther Kuznitz, "YIVO," *The YIVO Encyclopedia of Jews in Eastern Europe*, YIVO Institute for Jewish Research. http://www.yivoencyclopedia .org/article.aspx/YIVO.

6. Cecile Esther Kuznitz, *The Origins of Yiddish Scholarship and the YIVO Institute for Jewish Research*, Ph.D. diss., Stanford University, 2000, quoted in Marek Web, "Operating on Faith: YIVO's Eighty Years." *Yedies*, no. 199, 2005.

7. "Special Masters for Holocaust Victims Assets Litigation," YIVO, 2005.

8. Carl J. Rheins, "Recovering YIVO's Stolen Art Collection," *YIVO News*, no. 191, 2000–2001.

9. Albert Einstein, "Letter of support for the YIVO Institute by Albert Einstein," April 8, 1929, YIVO digital archive, Document no: RG 82/ yarg82f2243d002.

10. Avraham Novershtern, "Reyzen, Zalmen," *The YIVO Encyclopedia of Jews in Eastern Europe*, YIVO Institute for Jewish Research. http://www.yivoencyclope dia.org/article.aspx/Reyzen-Zalmen.

11. Sem C. Sutter, "Polish Books in Exile: Cultural Booty Across Two Continents, Through Two Wars," p. 149, *The Holocaust and the Book* (ed. Jonathan Rose), Amherst: University of Massachusetts Press, 2001.

12. Maria Wardzyńska, *Był rok 1939. Operacja niemieckiej policji bezpieczeństwa w Polsce.Intelligenzaktion*, Institute of National Remembrance, 2009.

13. Sutter, "Polish Books in Exile," p. 149.

14. Hans van der Hoeven and Joan van Albada, "Memory of the World: Lost Memory: Libraries and Archives Destroyed in the Twentieth Century," UNESCO, 1996.

15. Sutter, "Polish Books in Exile," p. 149.

16. Joanna Pasztaleniec-Jarzyńska and Halina Tchórzewska-Kabata, *The National Library in Warsaw: Tradition and the Present Day*, Warsaw: Biblioteka Narodowa, 2000, p. 9.

17. Marek Sroka, "The Destruction of Jewish Libraries and Archives in Cracow During World War II," *Libraries and Cultures*, vol. 38, no. 2, 2003.

18. Rebecca Knuth, *Libricide: The Regime-Sponsored Destruction of Books and Libraries in the Twentieth Century*, Leiden; Boston: Praeger, 2003, p. 84.

19. Sroka, "The Destruction of Jewish Libraries and Archives in Cracow During World War II."

20. Ibid.

21. Knuth, *Libricide*, p. 84.

22. Kazimierz Moczarski, *Conversations with an Executioner*, Englewood Cliffs, NJ: Prentice-Hall, 1984, p. 164.

23. Hugh Trevor-Roper and Gerhard L. Weinberg (eds.), *Hitler's Table Talk 1941–1944: Secret Conversations*, New York: Enigma Books, 2013, p. 27.

24. Norman Davies, *Europe at War 1939–1945: No Simple Victory*, London: Pan Macmillan, 2008, p. 306.
25. Patricia Kennedy Grimsted, "Reconstructing the Record of Nazi Cultural Plunder," Amsterdam: IISH, 2011, p. 33.
26. Patricia Kennedy Grimsted, "Roads to Ratibor: Library and Archival Plunder by the Einsatzstab Reichsleiter Rosenberg," *Holocaust Genocide Studies*, no. 19, 2005.
27. Grimsted, "Reconstructing the Record of Nazi Cultural Plunder," p. 23.
28. Yitzhak Arad, *The Holocaust in the Soviet Union*, Lincoln: University of Nebraska Press, 2009, pp. 413–414.
29. Leonidas E. Hill, "The Nazi Attack on 'Un-German' Literature, 1933–1945," p. 31, *The Holocaust and the Book* (ed. Jonathan Rose), Amherst: University of Massachusetts Press, 2001.
30. Patricia Kennedy Grimsted, "Roads to Ratibor."
31. Ibid.
32. Grimsted, "Reconstructing the Record of Nazi Cultural Plunder," p. 23.
33. Hill, "The Nazi Attack on 'Un-German' Literature, 1933–1945," p. 32.
34. Jörg Ganzenmüller, "Blockade Leningrads: Hunger als Waffe," Zeit Online, July 18, 2011. http:www.zeit.de/zeit-geschichte/2011/02/Kriegsziele-Generalplan-Ost.
35. Hill, "The Nazi Attack on 'Un-German' Literature, 1933–1945," p. 31.
36. Hirsz Abramowicz, "Khaykl Lunski," pp. 260–264, *Profiles of a Lost World: Memoirs of East European Jewish Life Before World War II*, Detroit: Wayne State University Press, 1999.
37. Ibid.
38. Joseph H. Prouser, *Noble Soul: The Life and Legend of the Vilna Ger Tzedek Count Walenty Potocki*, Piscataway, NJ: Gorgias Press LLC, 2005, pp. 1–3.
39. Fishman, "Embers Plucked from the Fire," p. 68.
40. Ibid.
41. Yitskhok Rudashevski, *Diary of the Vilna Ghetto*, Washington, DC: United States Holocaust Memorial Council, 1991, pp. 77–78.
42. Herman Kruk, "The Ghetto and the Readers," pp. 192–197, *The Holocaust and the Book* (ed. Jonathan Rose), Amherst: University of Massachusetts Press, 2001.
43. Fishman, "Embers Plucked from the Fire," p. 69.
44. Ibid.
45. Ibid.
46. Web, "Operating on Faith: YIVO's Eighty Years."
47. Joseph Berger, "Yiddish Poet Celebrates Life with his Language," *New York Times*, March 17, 1985.
48. Fishman, "Embers Plucked from the Fire," p. 71.
49. Ibid.
50. "Ona Simaite," Shoah Resource Center, the International School for Holocaust Studies, www.yadvashem.org/odot_pdf/Microsoft%20Word%20-%206025.pdf.

51. Web, "Operating on Faith: YIVO's Eighty Years."
52. Yitzhak Arad, *In the Shadow of the Red Banner: Soviet Jews in the War Against Nazi Germany*, Jerusalem; New York: Gefen, 2010, p. 205.
53. Joseph Berger, "Abraham Sutzkever, 96, Jewish Poet and Partisan, Dies," *New York Times*, January 23, 2010.
54. Ruth Wisse, "Abraham Sutzkever," *Holocaust Literature: Lerner to Zychlinsky*, London; New York: Routledge, 2003, pp. 1234–1237.
55. Saul Friedländer, *The Years of Extermination: Nazi Germany and the Jews, 1939–1945*, New York: Harper Perennial, 2008, p 633.
56. Fishman, "Embers Plucked from the Fire," p. 73.

## 12: The Talmud Unit: Theresienstadt

1. Luke Harding and Louise Osborne, "Vienna Philharmonic and the Jewish Musicians Who Perished Under Hitler," *Guardian*, March 11, 2013.
2. Michal Bušek et al., *Hope Is on the Next Page: 100 Years of the Jewish Library in Prague*, Prague: Jewish Museum, 2007, p. 37.
3. "Nazi propaganda film about Theresienstadt/Terezín," Steven Spielberg Film and Video Archive, US Holocaust Memorial Museum, Film ID: 140.
4. Robert Skloot, "Staying Ungooselike: The Holocaust and the Theatre of Choice," p. 248, *Jewish Theatre: A Global View* (ed. Edna Nahshon), Leiden; Boston: Brill, 2009.
5. Bušek et al., *Hope Is on the Next Page*, p. 44.
6. Ibid., pp. 38–39.
7. Ibid., p. 41.
8. Ibid., p. 63.
9. Dov Schidorsky, "Confiscation of Libraries and Assignments to Forced Labor: Two Documents of the Holocaust," *Libraries and Culture*, vol. 33, 1998, pp. 347–388.
10. Patricia Kennedy Grimsted, "Restitution of Confiscated Art Works: Wish or Reality?" Proceedings of the International Academic Conference held in Liberec on October 24–26, 2007, Prague: Tilia, 2008, pp. 144-145.
11. Schidorsky, "Confiscation of Libraries and Assignments to Forced Labor."
12. Ibid.
13. Ibid.
14. Patricia Kennedy Grimsted, "Roads to Ratibor: Library and Archival Plunder by the Einsatzstab Reichsleiter Rosenberg," *Holocaust Genocide Studies*, vol. 19, no. 3, Winter 2005, pp. 390–458.
15. Ibid.
16. Anne Rothfeld, "Returning Looted European Library Collections: An Historical Analysis of the Offenbach Archival Depot, 1945–1948," *RBM: A Journal of Rare Books, Manuscripts, and Cultural Heritage*, vol. 6, no. 1, 2005.
17. Grimsted, "Roads to Ratibor."

18. Evelyn Adunka, "The Nazi Looting of Books in Austria and Their Partial Restitution," www.lootedart.com/MFVALY48822.
19. Ibid.
20. Grimsted, "Roads to Ratibor."
21. Adunka, "The Nazi Looting of Books in Austria and Their Partial Restitution."
22. Alan Riding, *And the Show Went On: Cultural Life in Nazi-Occupied Paris*, New York: Alfred A. Knopf, 2010.
23. Grimsted, "Roads to Ratibor."

## 13: "Jewish Studies Without Jews": Ratibor–Frankfurt

1. Patricia Kennedy Grimsted, "Roads to Ratibor: Library and Archival Plunder by the Einsatzstab Reichsleiter Rosenberg," *Holocaust Genocide Studies*, no.19, 2005, pp. 390–458.
2. Ernst Piper, "Die Theorie des mörderischen Wahns," *Frankfurter Rundschau*, October 12, 2005.
3. Steven Topik and Kenneth Pomeranz, *The World That Trade Created: Society, Culture and the World Economy, 1400 to the Present*, London; New York: Routledge, 2014, p. 208.
4. Sem C. Sutter, "The Lost Jewish Libraries of Vilna and the Frankfurt Institut zur Erforschung der Judenfrage," p. 222, *Lost Libraries* (ed. James Raven), New York: Palgrave Macmillan, 2004.
5. Patricia Kennedy Grimsted, "The Odyssey of the Turgenev Library from Paris, 1940–2002. Books as Victims and Trophies of War," Amsterdam: IISH, 2003, p. 38.
6. Grimsted, "Roads to Ratibor."
7. Patricia von Papen-Bodek, "Anti-Jewish Research of the Institut zur Erforschung der Judenfrage in Frankfurt am Main between 1939 and 1945," pp. 155–173, *Lessons and Legacies VI: New Currents in Holocaust Research*, Evanston, IL: Northwestern University Press, 2004.
8. Ibid.
9. Sutter, "The Lost Jewish Libraries of Vilna and the Frankfurt Institut zur Erforschung der Judenfrage," p. 220.
10. Jan Björn Potthast, *Das judische Zentralmuseum der SS in Prag: Gegnerforschung und Volkermord im Nationalsozialismus*, Frankfurt: Campus Verlag 2002, p. 180.
11. Grimsted, "Roads to Ratibor."
12. Ibid.
13. Ardelia Hall Collections, Records Concerning the Central Collecting Points, Offenbach Archival Depot, 1946–1957, National Archives and Records Administration, M1942, Section 1, photos 15–17.
14. Ibid., photo 12.

15. Ibid., photo 13.
16. Alon Confino, *A World Without Jews. The Nazi Imagination from Persecution to Genocide*, New Haven, CT: Yale University Press, 2014, p. 151.
17. von Papen-Bodek, "Anti-Jewish Research of the Institut zur Erforschung der Judenfrage in Frankfurt am Main between 1939 and 1945," pp. 155–173.
18. Ibid.
19. Wilhelm Grau, "Die Geschichte des Judenfrage und ihr Erforschung," *Blatter fur deutsche Landesgeschichte* 83, no. 3, 1937, p. 167, quoted in A. Confino, *A World Without Jews*, p. 110.
20. Ibid., p. 194.
21. Ibid., p. 196.
22. Ibid., p. 177.
23. Ibid., p. 241.
24. Chaim Kaplan, *Scroll of Agony: The Warsaw Ghetto Diary of Chaim A. Kaplan*, Trans. Abraham Katsh, New York: Macmillan, 1965, pp. 90–91.
25. Ibid., pp. 399–400.
26. Patricia Kennedy Grimsted, "Sudeten Crossroads for Europe's Displaced Books: The Mysterious Twilight of the RSHA Amt VII Library and the Fate of a Million Victims of War," *Restitution of Confiscated Art Works: Wish or Reality?*, ed. Mecislav Borak, Prague: Tilia, 2008, pp. 160–161.
27. Ibid., p. 142.
28. Katarzyna Leszczyńska, *Hexen und Germanen: Das Interesse des Nationalsozialismus an der Geschichte der Hexenverfolgung*, Bielefeld: Transcript Verlag, 2009, p. 52.
29. Michael David Bailey, *Magic and Superstition in Europe: A Concise History from Antiquity to the Present*, Lanham, MD: Rowman & Littlefield, 2007, pp. 235–237.
30. Leszczyńska, *Hexen und Germanen*, pp. 18–20.
31. Bailey, *Magic and Superstition in Europe*, pp. 235–240.
32. Grimsted, "Sudeten Crossroads for Europe's Displaced Books," pp. 162–163.
33. von Papen-Bodek, "Anti-Jewish Research of the Institut zur Erforschung der Judenfrage in Frankfurt am Main between 1939 and 1945," p. 170.
34. Hans Hagemeyer, "Preparations already made for the International Congress." Nazi Conspiracy and Aggression Vol. IV, Document No. 1752-PS. Avalon Project. Letter dated June 15, 1944. http://avalon.law.yale.edu/imt/1752-ps.asp.
35. Ibid.
36. von Papen-Bodek, "Anti-Jewish Research of the Institut zur Erforschung der Judenfrage in Frankfurt am Main between 1939 and 1945," p. 163.
37. Ibid.
38. Hagemeyer, "Preparations already made for the International Congress."
39. Ibid.
40. Grimsted, "Roads to Ratibor."
41. Ibid., "The Odyssey of the Turgenev Library from Paris, 1940–2002," p. 45.

42. Patricia Kennedy Grimsted, "Reconstructing the Record of Nazi Cultural Plunder," IISH Research Paper 47, 2011, p. 427.

43. Violet Brown and Walter Crosby, "Jew Finds Hebrew Collection Nazis Stole in Lie Drive," *Brooklyn Daily Eagle*, April 9, 1945.

## 14: A Wagon of Shoes: Prague

1. Tomas Sniegon, *Vanished History: The Holocaust in Czech and Slovak Historical Culture*, New York: Berghahn Books, 2014, p. 214.

2. Andrea Jelinkova, "Books in the Terezín Ghetto and their Post-War Fate," *Judaica Bohemiae*, 2012, pp. 85–107.

3. Ibid.

4. Patricia Kennedy Grimsted, "Sudeten Crossroads for Europe's Displaced Books: The Mysterious Twilight of the RSHA Amt VII Library and the Fate of a Million Victims of War," p. 165, *Restitution of Confiscated Art Works: Wish or Reality?*, ed. Mecislav Borak, Prague: Tilia, 2008.

5. Ibid., p. 165.

6. Ibid., pp. 172–174.

7. Lucy Schildkret to Joseph A. Horne, "Subject: Restitutable books in Czechoslovakia," April 19, 1947. Records Concerning the Central Collecting Points ("Ardelia Hall Collection"): Offenbach Archival Depot, 1946–1951. M1942, Roll 006, p. 101. https://www.fold3.com/image/232161141/.

8. Grimsted, "Sudeten Crossroads for Europe's Displaced Books," p. 175.

9. Frits J. Hoogewoud, "Dutch Jewish Ex Libris Found Among Looted Books in the Offenbach Archival Depot," *Dutch Jews as Perceived by Themselves and by Others: Proceedings of the Eighth International Symposium on the History of the Jews in the Netherlands*, Leiden; Boston: Brill, 2001, p. 254.

10. Michal Bušek et al., *Hope Is on the Next Page: 100 Years of the Jewish Library in Prague*, Jewish Museum, Prague, 2007, p. 63.

11. Grimsted, "Sudeten Crossroads for Europe's Displaced Books," p. 180.

12. Patricia Kennedy Grimsted, *Trophies of War and Empire: The Archival Heritage of Ukraine, World War II, and the International Politics of Restitution*, Cambridge, MA: Harvard University Press, 2001, p. 251.

13. Patricia Kennedy Grimsted, "The Odyssey of the Turgenev Library from Paris, 1940–2002: Books as Victims and Trophies of War," Amsterdam: IISH, 2003, p. 48.

14. Ibid., pp. 50–51.

15. Ibid., pp. 52–53.

16. Ibid., p. 59

17. Patricia Kennedy Grimsted, "The Road to Minsk for Western 'Trophy' Books: Twice Plundered but Not Yet Home from the War," *Libraries & Culture*, vol. 39, no. 4, 2004.

18. Patricia Kennedy Grimsted, "Tracing Trophy Books in Russia," *Solanus* 19, 2005, pp. 131–145.

19. Ibid.
20. Grimsted, *Trophies of War and Empire*, pp. 259–260.
21. Grimsted, "The Odyssey of the Turgenev Library from Paris, 1940–2002," p. 56.
22. Ibid., p.65.
23. Robert Cecil, *The Myth of the Master Race*, London: B. T. Batsford, 1972, p. 214.
24. Alfred Rosenberg, *Grossdeutschland, Traum und Tragödie*, Selbstverlag H. Härtle, 1970, p. 180.
25. Cecil, *The Myth of the Master Race*, pp. 216–217.
26. Seymour J. Pomrenze, "Personal Reminiscences of the Offenbach Archival Depot, 1946–1949: Fulfilling International and Moral Obligations," *Washington Conference on Holocaust Era Assets*, ed. J. D. Bindenagel, Washington, DC: Dept. of State, 1999, pp. 523–528.
27. Ibid.
28. Ibid.
29. Herman de la Fontaine Verwey, "Bibliotheca Rosenthaliana During the German Occupation," in *Omnia in Eo: Studies on Jewish Books and Libraries in Honor of Adri Offenberg, Celebrating the 125th Anniversary of the Bibliotheca Rosenthaliana in Amsterdam*, Leuven: Peeters, 2006, pp. 70–71.
30. Jaap Kloosterman and Jan Lucassen, "Working for Labour: Three Quarters of a Century of Collecting at the IISH," p. 14, in *Rebels with a Cause*, Amsterdam: Askant, 2010.
31. Patricia Kennedy Grimsted, "The Odyssey of the Petliura Library and the Records of the Ukrainian National Republic During World War II," pp. 181–208, *Cultures and Nations of Central and Eastern Europe in Honor of Roman Szporluk* (ed. Zvi Gitelman), Cambridge, MA: Harvard Ukrainian Research Institute, 2000.
32. Hanna Laskarzewska, *La Bibliotheque Polonaise de Paris: Les Peregrinations de Collections Dans les Annees 1940–1992*, Paris: Bibliothèque Polonaise, 2004.
33. Patricia Kennedy Grimsted, *Returned from Russia: Nazi Archival Plunder in Western Europe and Recent Restitution Issues*, Builth Wells, Wales: Institute of Art and Law, 2013, p. 207.
34. Ibid., p. 206.
35. Ibid.
36. Ibid., p. 209.
37. Grimsted, "The Road to Minsk for Western 'Trophy' Books."
38. Michael Dobbs, "Epilogue to a Story of Nazi-Looted Books," *Washington Post*, January 5, 2000.
39. Ibid.
40. Sem C. Sutter, "The Lost Jewish Libraries of Vilna and the Frankfurt Institut zur Erforschung der Judenfrage," p. 231, *Lost Libraries* (ed. James Raven), New York: Palgrave Macmillan, 2004.
41. Paul Robert Magocsi, *Historical Atlas of East Central Europe*, Seattle; London: University of Washington Press, 1993, pp. 164–168.
42. Ibid.

43. Ibid.

44. W. Gelles, "Interview with Historian, and the Author of 'The War Against the Jews' and 'From That Place and Time.'" *Publishers Weekly*, December 5, 1989.

45. Lucy S. Dawidowicz, *From That Place and Time: A Memoir, 1938–1947*, New York: W. W. Norton, 1989, p. 119.

46. Walter Ings Farmer, *The Safekeepers: A Memoir of the Arts at the End of World War II*, Berlin; New York: Walter de Gruyter, 2000, p. 101.

47. Dawidowicz, *From That Place and Time*, p. 316.

48. David E. Fishman, "Embers Plucked from the Fire: The Rescue of Jewish Cultural Treasures from Vilna," pp. 73–74, *The Holocaust and the Book* (ed. Jonathan Rose), Amherst: University of Massachusetts Press, 2001.

49. Ibid.

50. Ibid.

51. Abraham Sutzkever, "Mon témoignage au procès de Nuremberg," *Les Ecrivains et la Guerre*, Paris: Messidor, 1995.

52. Christian Delage, "The Place of the Filmed Witness: From Nuremberg to the Khmer Rouge Trial," *Cardozo Law Review*, vol. 31, 2010.

53. Robert Cecil, *The Myth of the Master Race*, p. 221.

54. Burton C. Andrus, *The Infamous of Nuremberg*, London: Leslie Frewin, 1969, p. 172.

55. Cecil, *The Myth of the Master Race*, p. 219.

56. Ibid.

57. Ibid., p. 228.

58. Ibid., p. 229.

59. Alan E. Steinweis, *Studying the Jew: Scholarly Antisemitism in Nazi Germany*, Cambridge, MA: Harvard University Press, 2009, pp. 115–116.

60. Howard K. Smith, "The Execution of Nazi War Criminals," International News Service, October 16, 1946.

## 15: A Book Finds Its Way Home: Berlin–Cannock

1. Richard Kobrak, ID: 123546. Ancestry.com.

2. Patricia Kennedy Grimsted, *Trophies of War and Empire: The Archival Heritage of Ukraine, World War II, and the International Politics of Restitution*, Cambridge, MA: Harvard University Press, 2001, p. 257.

3. Ibid.

4. Ibid., p. 258.

5. Ibid.

6. Ibid., p. 394.

7. Ibid., p. 396.

8. Ibid., p. 400.

9. Patricia Kennedy Grimsted, "The Road to Minsk for Western 'Trophy' Books: Twice Plundered but Not Yet Home from the War," *Libraries & Culture*, vol. 39, no. 4, 2004.

10. Patricia Kennedy Grimsted, *Returned from Russia: Nazi Archival Plunder in Western Europe and Recent Restitution Issues*, Builth Wells, Wales: Institute of Art and Law, 2013, p. 291.

11. Grimsted, *Trophies of War and Empire*, p. 403.

12. Tanya Chebotarev and Jared S. Ingersoll (eds.), "Russian and East European Books and Manuscripts in the United States," pp. 114–119, *Proceedings of a Conference in Honor of the Fiftieth Anniversary of the Bakhmeteff Archive of Russia*. New York: Routledge, 2014.

13. Grimsted, *Returned from Russia*, p. 245.

14. Ibid., p. 289.

15. Chebotarev and Ingersoll, "Russian and East European Books and Manuscripts in the United States," pp. 117–119.

16. Patricia Kennedy Grimsted, "The Odyssey of the Turgenev Library from Paris, 1940–2002. Books as Victims and Trophies of War," Amsterdam: IISH, 2003, p. 14.

17. Ibid., p. 90.

18. Ibid., p. 96.

19. Commission for recovery of the bibliographic patrimony of the Jewish Community of Rome stolen in 1943, *Report on the Activities of the Commission for Recovery of the Bibliographic Patrimony of the Jewish Community of Rome Stolen in 1943*. Translated by Lenore Rosenberg, Governo Italiano, 2009, p. 6.

20. Ibid., p. 26.

21. Ibid., p. 43.

22. Grimsted, "The Road to Minsk for Western 'Trophy' Books."

23. Käthe Kobrak: Diary, August 10–15, 1995, private collection.

24. Ibid.

25. Ibid.

26. Alan Parkinson, *From Marple to Hay and Back*. Marple Local History Society, 2002. http://www.marple-uk.com/misc/dunera.pdf.

27. Käthe Kobrak: Diary, August 3, 1939–March 31, 1945, private collection.

# Index

Note: Page numbers in *italics* refer to illustrations.